014568560 Liverpool Univ

KT-148-335

 Organizational Change

University of Liverpool

Withdrawn from stock

Organizational Change

Perspectives on Theory and Practice

Piers Myers, Sally Hulks,
and Liz Wiggins

OXFORD
UNIVERSITY PRESS

OXFORD
UNIVERSITY PRESS

Great Clarendon Street, Oxford OX2 6DP,
United Kingdom

Oxford University Press is a department of the University of Oxford.
It furthers the University's objective of excellence in research, scholarship,
and education by publishing worldwide. Oxford is a registered trade mark of Oxford
University Press in the UK and in certain other countries

© Oxford University Press, 2012

The moral rights of the authors have been asserted

All rights reserved. No part of this publication may be reproduced,
stored in a retrieval system, or transmitted, in any form or by any means,
without the prior permission in writing of Oxford University Press,
or as expressly permitted by law, by licence or under terms agreed with the appropriate
reprographics rights organization. Enquiries concerning reproduction
outside the scope of the above should be sent to the Rights Department,
Oxford University Press, at the address above

You must not circulate this work in any other form
and you must impose the same condition on any acquirer

Contains public sector information licensed under the Open Government Licence v1.0
(http://www.nationalarchives.gov.uk/doc/open-government-licence/open-government-licence.htm)

Crown Copyright material reproduced with the permission of the Controller,
HMSO (under the terms of the Click Use licence.)

British Library Cataloguing in Publication Data

Data available

Library of Congress Cataloging in Publication Data

Data available

ISBN 978-0-19-957378-3

Printed in Great Britain
on acid-free paper by
Ashford Colour Press Ltd, Gosport, Hampshire

10 9 8 7 6 5

Acknowledgements

Piers would like to thank all the students, colleagues, and clients from whom he has learned over the years: without you, there would have been nothing to write. He would also like to thank Liz and Sally, his wonderful co-authors: without you, nothing would have been written. Thanks to Andrew Summers, Belinda Kent-Lemon, Bruce Lloyd, Nick Briggs, and Penny Davis, who generously reviewed the manuscript at various stages. Many thanks also to Angela Adams for encouragement and advice in the early stages of this project, and to Fran Griffin, Jo Hardern, and the rest of the Oxford University Press team who took up the baton, and who have been both patient and appreciative by turns. Above all, thank you to Jocelyn and Verity for all of your support, inspiration, and loving kindness—no one could wish for more.

Sally would like to thank all her friends and family for their endless tolerance as she spent two years' worth of weekends writing in the library. Liz would like to thank Clive for his initial encouragement that she could—and should—embark on 'the book', and to thank Esther and Josh for their forbearance, generally speaking, when Mummy was writing rather than playing with them. Sally and Liz would also like to extend their thanks to Dave Bond and Margaret de Lattre for reading the manuscript, and giving helpful and insightful feedback, to Sally Pugh for help with our diagrams, and to all those in the Ashridge library for their practical help, interest, and support, so thank you to: Norman Allen, Sue Bainbridge, Anna Bosch, Barbara Egglesfield, Lorraine Oliver, Rachel Piper, Lynn Swann, and Celia Tucker.

Contents

Detailed Contents

List of Change in Practice Boxes

List of Integrative Case Studies

How to Use This Book

 Introduction

The purpose of this chapter is to explore the question: 'Why do organizations change?' Human beings are inherently curious about why things happen: small children can endlessly pester adults, wanting to know why glue is sticky or why oranges are orange; as adults, making sense of other people's behaviour often involves pondering why they chose to move home or take a particular job.

Introduction

Each chapter opens with an introduction and a bulleted list of key topics, which provide a route map through the material and summarize the main subjects covered.

external environment is important to its viability, and may affect its potential need to change, can be understood using a biological metaphor.

task environment, defined by the organization's direct interactions, for example with customers, competitors, suppliers, trade unions, local government,

contextual environment (Morgan, 1986). For each individual organization, there will be opportunities, threats, and constraints related to both. The type of infrastructure available, the ease of raising capital,

Key terms and concepts

Key terms are highlighted in purple and are defined in the glossary at the end of the book.

 Change in Practice 2.2

The evolution of a consulting firm

CommCo was a Manchester-based consultancy firm specializing in internal communication, established in 1989 by Bill O'Leary and Marie MacNeil. In the early days, there was an almost missionary zeal about the place. Bill, the ideas man, was very entrepreneurial, slightly maverick, with huge energy and passion.

'Change in Practice' boxes

Within each chapter, a selection of thought-provoking case studies place the theory in a practical context. The sources for these boxes are listed at the end of each chapter.

 Exercise 2.4

Ask someone who has worked in an organization for a while to tell you how it has grown. Explore with the changes in size, leadership, reward policies, and structure. Alternatively, reflect on your own experience of change in an organization.

Exercises

These enable you to relate your learning to your own experiences and to reflect on what you can draw from this.

Section 1 Summary

In this section, we have:
● examined two key scales of change, incremental and discontinuous, and considered how change processes can be local or span the organization;
● explored the implications of anticipatory and reactive timing for organizational change;
● considered the depth of change—first-order and second-order organizational change.

Section summaries

Each section of the chapter is briefly summarized, allowing you to consolidate your learning.

 Integrative Case Study

Nike: Emergent and planned change

The athletic footwear industry has experienced explosive growth in the last two decades. The branded shoe segment is dominated by a few large companies, including Nike, Reebok, and Adidas. The story of the Nike organization is often said to symbolize the benefits and risks inherent in globalization.

Integrative Case Study

A longer case study at the end of each chapter, with questions, provides an opportunity to explore issues in greater depth. The sources for all the case studies are listed at the end of each chapter.

Further reading

Beer, M. and Nohria, N. (2000) *Breaking the Code of Change*, Boston, MA: Harvard Business School Press. Particularly chs 10–12, which further explore planned and emergent change.
Stacey, R. (2011) *Strategic Management and Organisational Dynamics*, 6th edn, Harlow: FT Prentice Hall. A comprehensive review of approaches to change.

Further reading

An annotated list of suggested reading is provided at the end of each chapter to offer you ways in which to extend your learning.

References

Chapter 1

Balogun, J. and Johnson, G. (2005) 'From intended strategies to unintended outcomes: The impact of change recipient sensemaking', *Organization Studies*, **26**(11): 1573–601.
Bridges, W. (2003) *Managing Transitions: Making the Most of Change*, 2nd edn, London: Nicholas Brealey Publishing.

References

A chapter-specific list of references is supplied at the end of the book.

How to Use the Online Resource Centre

http://www.oxfordtextbooks.co.uk/orc/myers/

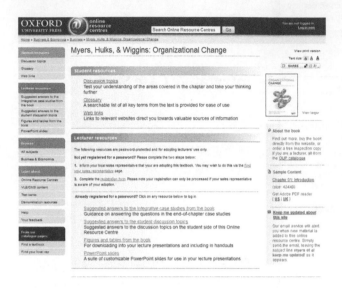

FOR REGISTERED ADOPTERS OF THE TEXT

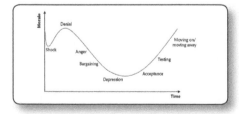

PowerPoint slides

A suite of PowerPoint slides has been designed by the authors for use in your lecture presentations. These highlight the main points from each chapter and can easily be customized to match your own lecture style.

Figures and tables from the book

The images from the textbook have been uploaded to the Online Resource Centre (ORC) and can be added to your lecture materials or Virtual Learning Environment.

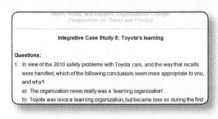

Indicative answers for the Integrative Case Study questions in the book

Guidance is provided on potential directions that answers to the end-of-chapter case studies may take.

Possible lines of argument for the discussion topics on the student side of the ORC

Suggested answers to the student discussion topics succinctly highlight the main points that students might cover.

FOR STUDENTS

Annotated web links

Links to relevant websites direct you towards valuable sources of information. Where appropriate, the authors have included links to online video and audio clips that illustrate key issues.

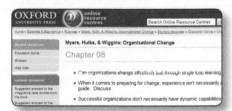

Discussion topics

Test your understanding of the areas covered in the chapter and take your thinking further.

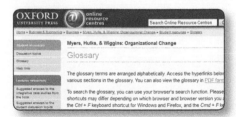

Online version of the glossary

A searchable list of all key terms from the text is provided.

Introduction

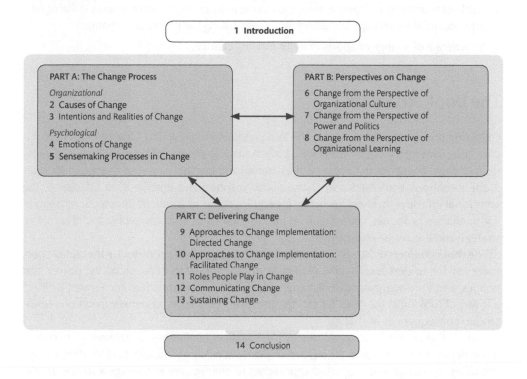

1 Introduction

PART A: The Change Process

Organizational
2 Causes of Change
3 Intentions and Realities of Change

Psychological
4 Emotions of Change
5 Sensemaking Processes in Change

PART B: Perspectives on Change

6 Change from the Perspective of Organizational Culture
7 Change from the Perspective of Power and Politics
8 Change from the Perspective of Organizational Learning

PART C: Delivering Change

9 Approaches to Change Implementation: Directed Change
10 Approaches to Change Implementation: Facilitated Change
11 Roles People Play in Change
12 Communicating Change
13 Sustaining Change

14 Conclusion

Welcome to *Organizational Change: Perspectives on Theory and Practice*. Change management is a core responsibility for many employees, managers, and executives. The leadership, implementation, and analysis of organizational change are, therefore, central topics for professional development and for undergraduate and postgraduate courses in business to address. As well as authoring this book, we have been involved for many years in the arena of organizational change as academics, consultants, and managers. We find in our teaching a need for a text that is accessible, well structured, and focused, but theoretically rigorous and grounded in both workplace realities and academic research. So, in this book, we combine explanation of theory with practical insights from those who are 'in the thick of it', managing change. The book aims to offer both breadth and depth, helping you to navigate the landscape of change and, in doing so, to look at organizational change from different perspectives rather than being firmly wedded to just one.

This book addresses why change happens, what changes, and how change is achieved, within a framework that we hope you will find interesting, coherent, logical, and challenging, helping you to appreciate and question both theory and practice. The book encompasses the emotional and psychological dimensions of change, deals with culture, politics, and learning in changing organizations, and reviews a range of current change methods. It will help you to develop:

- an in-depth understanding of organizational change, including its emotional, psychological, planned, and emergent dimensions;
- a robust foundation of theory, as well as the capacity to apply this to analysing the need and potential for change, and planning and evaluating the progress of change;
- knowledge of a range of approaches for tackling change.

The book structure

Following this introductory chapter, the four chapters in Part A: The Change Process, elucidate complementary organizational and psychological aspects of how and why organizations change. These are: in Chapter 2, the external and internal causes of change; in Chapter 3, the intentions and realities of change, both planned and emergent; in Chapter 4, the emotional journeys involved in change for employees at all levels; in Chapter 5, sensemaking in change processes, including how interpretations of changes evolve and the role of strategy and employee engagement.

The three chapters in Part B: Perspectives on Change, provide contrasting theoretical perspectives for understanding change: firstly, organizational culture; secondly, power and politics; and thirdly, organizational learning. Each of these perspectives encourages a different way of looking at the need for change, the levers of change, and the impacts and unintended consequences of change.

Part C: Delivering Change, addresses the practical challenges of achieving change in more depth. Chapters 9 and 10 explore different methods of implementation: directed approaches to change and facilitated approaches to change. We encourage a stance of critical appreciation, in order to assess the strengths and weaknesses of techniques. Chapter 11 considers the roles required to carry through successful transitions, including leadership, change agency, and consultancy. Chapter 12 deals with communication modes and methods, their application, and their impact on change trajectories. Chapter 13 explores how change can be sustained and evaluated, and starts to draw the threads of the book together.

Finally, Chapter 14, a conclusion, critically considers current views of organizational change and the challenges it presents.

A distinctive characteristic of the book is the clear structure we provide for navigating through the topics. This is visually represented in Figure 1.1. It allows for different approaches to traversing the material (for example, Part B might be read prior to Part A). At the beginning of each chapter, a version of this diagram provides you with a signpost indicating where you are in the structure. On the other hand, throughout the text, there are cross-references between the chapters, as a reminder that each is not covering a discrete sub-topic, but rather interrelated elements.

Theory, practice, and you

We believe that theory and practice should inform each other. We have endeavoured to make this book as practical as possible while, at the same time, aiming to build a rigorous foundation of theory. Kurt Lewin is reputed to have said: 'There's nothing as practical as a good theory.' Was he right? In which way can theory be practical? Brief and Dukerich (1991) point out that people can aspire to employ theory in at least two ways. The first hope for theory is that it might make useful predictions about what will happen: if we intervene in such-and-such a way, the organization will change like this or like that. People, however, tend to be unpredictable. You can make informed decisions within a theoretical framework about strategies with the best chance of success, but certainty is likely to elude you. The second hope for theory that Brief and Dukerich point to is that it may open up new insights. Often, this is a more realistic aspiration. Theory and theoretical concepts may allow you to 're-view' workplace situations—that is, to reflect on change, opportunities for change, approaches to change, and constraints on change, in a new light. In this book, taking a fresh look at organizational change from different perspectives is the central focus of Part B, where we explicitly take three alternative perspectives for viewing the what, why, and how

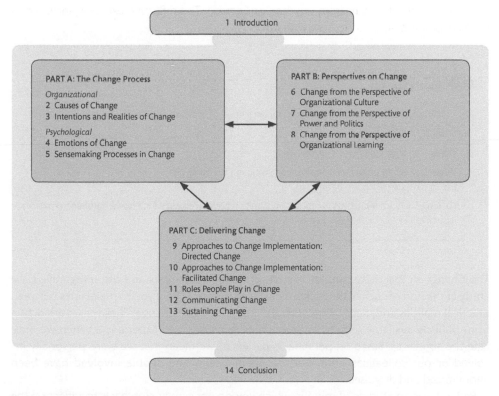

Figure 1.1 Structure of the book

of change. But we hope that the book as a whole will provide you with many fresh insights as you engage with organizational change, in addition to aiding you in more informed decision-making. Our intention is that new thinking, conversations, and practice will be provoked, and that you will be better able to translate your beliefs, abilities, experience, and ethics into the accomplishment of change.

We encourage you to bring two key qualities to your reading of this book and your development as a change practitioner: reflectiveness and reflexivity. Reflexivity is discussed below, but, first, reflectiveness. *Reflectiveness* involves engaging with the links between theory, concepts, and frameworks for change introduced here and your own knowledge of change. We think that leading, managing, implementing, or consulting on organizational change is not something that can, or should, be taught as if the authors are the experts and you are simply learners. Rather, we would like to see this book as a collaborative endeavour. We will share with you some of our experiences and the frameworks, concepts, and ideas from which we have learnt. We believe you will get the most value from the book if you engage with the links between your own experience and ours. We suggest you do not take anything you read here (or in other books, articles, etc.) as necessarily correct or helpful, but, instead, question what you read: does this stack up against my experience? How does this relate to what I am reading elsewhere? How can I use it to better understand my work or to improve my skills?

In our experience, the more you commit yourself in this way, the more potential for learning and development from any book or course. The reflective exercises included in each chapter are designed to help with this.

 Exercise 1.1

Recall an organizational change with which you are familiar (it could be at work, in your university, or in a voluntary setting).

- Was the change intended, or unintended?
- What do you see as the challenges faced by you and the other people involved? What would you like to have been handled better?
- Looking back, what puzzles you about this situation and the way in which it was handled? What would you like to understand better?

The Change in Practice examples in each of the main chapters and the Integrative Case Study at the end of each of these chapters are also there to help you to make links between practical realities and theory, concepts, and frameworks for change. These cases are drawn from publicly available sources or, sometimes, from our own experience. When we indicate the source as 'Based on personal experience', we mean that we were personally involved or our colleagues were, but the organizations and people involved have been anonymized and disguised.

Reflexivity is an attitude of mind in which you do not simply 'step back' to reflect on the dynamics around you, but recognize that you are part of those dynamics. A great deal of what happens during organizational change, and its causes and consequences, are hidden from everyday view. In Chapter 6, we use the metaphor of the bulk of an iceberg below the waterline for these hidden dynamics. This makes you, yourself, an invaluable resource for learning and teaching about organizational change. You know most about what *you* think, feel, and do during organizational change. So thinking about the whole dynamics of change around you, including your part in them, will give you extra insight into how the ideas in this book apply to the realities of organizational change that you face, and more of a chance to test those ideas against experience. We would recommend that you find a small group of people whom you trust and with whom you can candidly discuss your experiences of change and of learning about change, whether or not you are reading the book with the support of a taught course.

Often, people realize that even if a theory, concept, or framework for change is new to them, they are already familiar with the gist of it. For example, the causes of change flagged up in Chapter 2 may be familiar to you. You may recognize, as you read Chapter 3, how change can be viewed as the result of deliberate planning or as an emergent process. You may already be aware of the tumult of emotions that change can evoke, and how people can endeavour to hide what they are feeling (Chapter 4), or the way in which 'strategy' is sometimes made up after the event (Chapter 5). You, yourself, may have experienced how organizational culture can obstruct or enable change efforts (Chapter 6), how politicking can be a hidden face of change (Chapter 7), or how productive some interactions can be for learning how to progress change and how unproductive other interactions can be (Chapter 8). And you may also be familiar with some of the methods and techniques to take change forward that we discuss in Part C of the book. In these cases, discussing the ideas presented here may allow you to refine and hone what you already know, or to compare and contrast it with other standpoints, and to reflect on the impact that the views, frameworks, and models you are familiar with have had on your own work with organizational change.

We hope you will pursue some of the further reading that is listed at the end of each chapter. Whenever a particular point interests you, you will also find it helpful to check out some of the references we flag up. Often, the books or articles referenced discuss issues in more depth or they argue for different points of view. In this arena, as in so many others, disagreement matters as much, or more, than unity.

Change and transition

What makes navigating change so challenging? If an organization changes from one state A to another state B, then we can think of the shift from A to B as the change itself or, to use Pettigrew's (1999) terminology, as the **content** of the change. As shown in Figure 1.2, change also has a **context**, including causes, constraints, and opportunities—an **inner context** inside the organization and an **outer context** in the organization's environment. If this were all there was to change, it might be rather straightforward. What is usually most interesting *and* most challenging is the **process** of change (Pettigrew, 1999), which William Bridges (2003) calls the **transition**—that is, how the people involved, in practice, accomplish the shift from A to B. However, process, content, and context are not as separable as

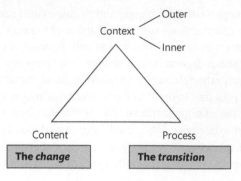

Figure 1.2 Aspects of organizational change
Source: Pettigrew (1999)

Figure 1.2 might suggest. In practice, the process of change usually develops and alters the content, as unintended consequences and new directions arise (see Chapter 3). Conversely, perceptions of content and context, and people's emotional response to them, are part of the process of change (see Chapters 4 and 5).

 Exercise 1.2

Consider again the example of organizational change you focused on in Exercise 1.1 or another organizational change with which you are familiar.

- Identify the content, outer and inner context, and process aspects of the change.
- How did the process affect how the content of the change worked out in practice and the way in which the outer and inner contexts were perceived?

Earlier in this introduction, we stated that people are unpredictable. This unpredictability is magnified in the case of organizational transitions. Transitions lead to unintended consequences. When Apple moved into MP3 players and music retailing in 2001–03, there was an unintended, albeit very beneficial, consequence that the portable electronics market—iPods, and the iPhone and iPad that followed—overtook its desktop computer business. So much so that, in 2007, Apple Computers Inc. changed its name to Apple Inc. Moreover transitions are also impacted by an outer context that includes unpredictable change in other organizations. As we discuss in Chapter 2, Nokia—originally a Wellington boot manufacturer—had become a dominant player in the mobile phone market, before struggling as it faced competition in the smartphone market following the release of the iPhone. Twitter, by 2011 a multibillion-dollar microblogging site, was developed as a project by the staff of an ailing podcasting start-up called Odeo that was facing competition from Apple's iTunes Store, which had entered the podcasting market. Emergent, unpredictable processes also lead to the failure of many change initiatives (Harris and Ogbonna, 2002) and the adaptation of most others (Balogun and Johnson, 2005).

See Chapter 2 for more on change at Nokia: p. 13

See Chapter 8 for more on change at Apple and Twitter: pp. 169–71, 181

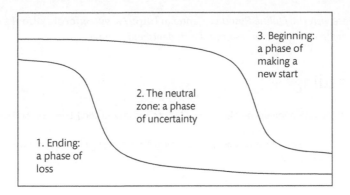

Figure 1.3 Phases of transition
Source: Bridges (2003)

For the people in a changing organization, much may be gained, but, as Bridges (2003) points out, all transitions also involve loss: loss, for example, of familiar ways of working, familiar working relationships, familiar workplaces, familiar certainties or roles, and so on. This applies even in the case of change that is positive for employees. For instance, promotion can involve losing the camaraderie of peers. This often leads to the fundamental challenge of engaging people in transitions that can disrupt their working lives and careers. Bridges' central insight is the suggestion that, paradoxically, all transitions begin with a phase of ending and end with a phase of beginning. In between these is a phase of uncertainty, which Bridges calls 'the neutral zone'. These phases are not rigid. As Figure 1.3 indicates, right from the start of a change process, new possibilities may be opening up for people about which they may be excited and enthusiastic. At the start, and still at the end, of a change process there are likely to be uncertainties. And a sense of loss, perhaps nostalgia, may continue even after people are well established in new ways of working. This psychological transition may last, for the people concerned, hours, weeks, years or, occasionally, even decades. Chapters 4 and 5 focus on the thinking and emotions that accompany, and may drive, the change process.

Organizational change can be both messy and fascinating, both disturbing and exciting. We hope you will find this book helpful as you get involved, whether you are an experienced change agent or just entering the fray.

> **? Exercise 1.3**
>
> ● What are the top three things that you would like to gain from reading and working with this book?
>
>   1. _____
>   2. _____
>   3. _____
>
> ● How can *you* help to ensure that you achieve those aspirations?

Please visit the Online Resource Centre at **http://www.oxfordtextbooks.co.uk/orc/ myers** *to access further resources for students and lecturers.*

Further reading

Bridges, W. (2003) *Managing Transitions: Making the Most of Change* (2nd edn.), London: Nicholas Brealey Publishing.
William Bridges' book is a good introduction to the challenges of managing change and includes some thought-provoking examples.

Part A

The Change Process

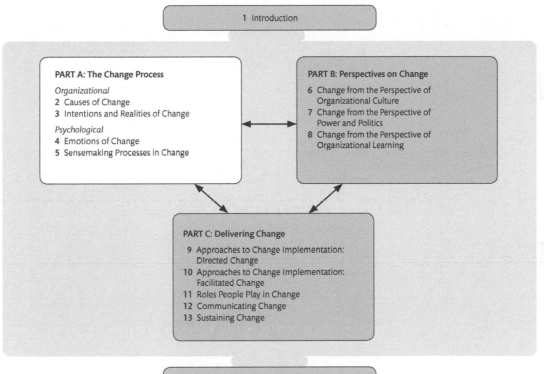

1 Introduction

PART A: The Change Process

Organizational
2 Causes of Change
3 Intentions and Realities of Change

Psychological
4 Emotions of Change
5 Sensemaking Processes in Change

PART B: Perspectives on Change

6 Change from the Perspective of
   Organizational Culture
7 Change from the Perspective of
   Power and Politics
8 Change from the Perspective of
   Organizational Learning

PART C: Delivering Change

 9 Approaches to Change Implementation:
   Directed Change
10 Approaches to Change Implementation:
   Facilitated Change
11 Roles People Play in Change
12 Communicating Change
13 Sustaining Change

14 Conclusion

Causes of Change

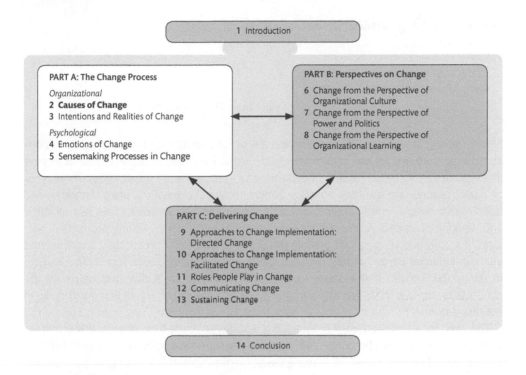

1 Introduction

PART A: The Change Process

Organizational
2 Causes of Change
3 Intentions and Realities of Change

Psychological
4 Emotions of Change
5 Sensemaking Processes in Change

PART B: Perspectives on Change

6 Change from the Perspective of
   Organizational Culture
7 Change from the Perspective of
   Power and Politics
8 Change from the Perspective of
   Organizational Learning

PART C: Delivering Change

 9 Approaches to Change Implementation:
   Directed Change
10 Approaches to Change Implementation:
   Facilitated Change
11 Roles People Play in Change
12 Communicating Change
13 Sustaining Change

14 Conclusion

Introduction

The purpose of this chapter is to explore the question: 'Why do organizations change?' Human beings are inherently curious about why things happen: small children can endlessly pester adults, wanting to know why glue is sticky or why oranges are orange; as adults, making sense of other people's behaviour often involves pondering why they chose to move home or take a particular job. Members of organizations, as well as those who study them, are interested in why things are the way they are, as well as why they may be changing. Understanding why change happens also matters to the many people in organizations charged with leading or managing change. If we can understand the potential causes of change, we can perhaps be better equipped to seize and seek opportunities, and to mitigate threats and challenges.

This chapter will show that there can be many different reasons why organizations change. Factors in both the external and internal environments may be triggers to actively initiate organizational change or they may be part of the general context in which change occurs.

Main topics to be covered in this chapter

- Organizational survival as the overarching reason for change
- The external environment, including different ways of conceptualizing trends
- Internal factors that may contribute to, or trigger, organizational change

Section 1: **Organizational survival**

There's nothing constant in the world,
All ebb and flow, and every shape that's born
Bears in its womb the seeds of change

(Ovid, 43BC–AD 17, *Metamorphoses*)

Before looking at why organizations change, it is worth considering a few basic assumptions about organizations. An essential characteristic is that they seek to achieve their objectives through converting resources into goods and services (Boxall and Purcell, 2008). Three types of basic resource are available to organizations: physical (inventory, plant, factories, and buildings); monetary (credit and money); and human (skills, knowledge, client relationships, and working practices). A return is received on these resources by selling products or services, if a commercial organization. If in the public or voluntary sector, they are converted into services in return for funding. An organization will remain viable if it is profitable enough to satisfy stakeholders that it is able to operate within the budget allocated, delivering the products or services it has promised, or at least convincing stakeholders that it will do so in the near future.

The need for viability is clear: 'The pursuit of viability is . . . the fundamental driver that we observe in management behaviour: without securing economic viability . . . firms fail' (Boxall and Purcell, 2008: 16). However, in many cases, mere survival is not enough if an organization is to be deemed successful by its employees and external stakeholders. Organizations aspire to thrive and to develop some form of sustained competitive advantage that improves the likelihood of them remaining viable in the long term. Viability does not necessarily imply the need to grow. Sometimes, leaders deliberately want to keep their organizations small in order to maintain the social climate that they believe is an essential element of their success (Palmer et al., 2006).

Continuing viability would be relatively easy for organizations to achieve were it not for the fact that organizations are operating in a dynamic environment, both externally and internally. Resources can be depleted; raw material costs can go up; the need for a particular service or product can go down; factories or machinery can become obsolete; buildings need repair; executives or highly qualified staff may retire or move elsewhere; and trading terms with a key country may suddenly become less favourable for political or economic reasons.

In addition, new providers or competitors can appear. To survive, or indeed to thrive, the response may be to collaborate. For instance, the iPhone, with its innovative touch screen, was the result of collaboration between Apple and AT&T Mobility; Ben and Jerry's, a maker of ice cream, collaborated with a distribution company to penetrate the American market. Charities often collaborate in response to natural disasters such as the 2010 earthquake in

Haiti. In other cases, organizations may choose, or be forced to, compete. Government departments compete for share of the overall tax income or to be subject to fewer budget cuts. Private companies now run services that used to be provided by the public sector, such as some prisons and GP surgeries in Germany, Sweden, and the UK. The concept of competition is also just as valid for non-governmental organizations (NGOs, such as Greenpeace) and charities. They compete with each other for media coverage, donor attention, and funding. Recent forms of not-for-profit organizations, such as the Bill and Melissa Gates Foundation, have emerged. Funded by extremely wealthy individuals, they often have far more money, and greater freedom to spend it, than more traditional charities such as Oxfam, Plan, and Christian Aid.

So, whatever the type of organization, a fundamental question is how to continue to be viable when changes are taking place around and within the organization. A second question is how to take advantage of those changes in order to thrive, not just survive.

This opening section concludes with the story of an organization that has changed significantly and flourished, despite many threats to its survival. 'Land of midnight mobiles: A former toilet paper maker from Finland has become the world's largest manufacturer of mobile phones' is the title of an article in the *Financial Times* (Burt et al., 1998). The story of Nokia demonstrates how radically an organization can change. It also highlights a range of different causes of organizational change and will therefore be a reference point throughout the rest of the chapter.

 Change in Practice 2.1

Nokia: A history of radical change

Nokia was founded in Finland in 1865, manufacturing paper products in a country with one major natural resource: its vast forests. In the 1960s, the board of Nokia realized that if the business were to do more than stagnate, it needed to expand beyond Finland. However, the Finnish government wanted Nokia to merge with two underperforming Finnish companies. When the amalgamation was complete, Nokia found itself involved in several new industries, including electronics, tyres, and Wellington boots, but still selling primarily in Finland.

Like many Finnish companies at the time, Nokia's major foreign market was the Communist Soviet Union, taking advantage of favourable trade deals offered in return for Finnish political neutrality in World War II. Nokia exchanged paper products for Soviet oil, but the price rose dramatically during the global oil crisis of 1973 and, therefore, in real terms, the purchasing power of Finnish companies such as Nokia was reduced significantly. The oil crisis thus forced Nokia to start reassessing its reliance on Soviet trade.

Under Kari Kairamo, who was appointed CEO in 1975, Nokia embarked on an acquisition plan to become a leader in electronics and to try again to take the company beyond Finland. During the 1980s, the company acquired nearly twenty electronics companies throughout Scandinavia. Revenue from electronics grew from 10 per cent of annual sales in 1980 to 60 per cent by the end of the decade.

Meanwhile, in 1986, Nokia reorganized its management structure from eleven divisions to four industry segments. Telecommunications was Nokia's best-performing area and, in 1986, the company chose the mobile telephone as the first product to be marketed internationally under the brand name Nokia. Although the company was thriving in terms of sales, finance was an issue. Nokia's growth had come largely through acquisition, an expensive strategy, and few Finnish investors, other than institutions, were willing to invest in the company. The company therefore negotiated a deal with the Finnish government that allowed it to seek more foreign investment, arguing that this was critical for its continued survival. Nokia gained a listing on the London Stock Exchange in 1987 and that year more than half of the new shares issued went to foreign investors.

In 1988, revenues soared, but profits dropped under pressure from severe price competition in the consumer electronics market, particularly in Asia. Arguably, the company was also just too diverse. Chairman Kari Kairamo committed suicide in December of that year, apparently because of stress. In the late 1980s and early 1990s, Finland underwent a severe economic depression, which also affected Nokia. The company was in a period of stagnation. Questions were asked about the company's viability.

An important strategic change was made in 1992 when the new CEO, Ollila, who had run Nokia's mobile phone business, decided to concentrate solely on telecommunications. He sold off all other businesses. At the same time, a British company, Technophone, was acquired, which enabled Nokia to sell digital phones in 1993, far ahead of its rivals, and gave it sustained competitive advantage. Sales more than doubled from 1991 to 1995 and a FMK723 million loss in 1992 became a profit of FMK2.2 billion in 1995.

The company was thriving, but the worldwide demand for mobile phones, which was beyond Nokia's most optimistic predictions, caused a logistics crisis in the mid-1990s. The company overhauled its logistics operations, which then became one of its greatest competitive advantages. By 1998, it had surpassed its arch-rival Motorola, which was slow to convert to digital technology, saddled with a large number of analogue phones. So, by 2000, Nokia had become number one in cellular phones worldwide. Half of the company's employees were Finnish, but only 2.4 per cent of its revenues came from Finland.

Nokia is still the world's largest manufacturer of mobile telephones. Its annual accounts for 2010 show a 31 per cent market share and Nokia was voted one of the five most valuable global brands in the Interbrand/Business Week Best Global Brands list of 2008. Environmentalists are challenging the throwaway culture associated with mobiles. In an effort to reduce its environmental impact, Nokia released a new phone concept, Remade, in 2008, constructed solely of recyclable materials. Ironically, given Nokia's early history, the outer part is made partly from used car tyres. However, the company is now facing severe competition from Apple's iPhone.[1-3]

This story illustrates the 'ebb and flow' in one organization's fortunes. It shows how some changes were related to features within Nokia's geographical context: the company's origins in paper manufacture, using Finland's greatest natural resource, but, equally, the limitations posed by the lack of other local natural resources on which to draw; the highly interventionist role the Finnish government played in Nokia's merger with two Finnish companies; the opportunity to take advantage, for a while, of the lucrative Finnish–Soviet trade deal; and the challenge posed by the tightly controlled Finnish banking system and limited number of Finnish institutional investors. Change prompted by internal factors is in evidence too: the ambition to expand beyond Finland, the strategy of acquisition initiated by one CEO, and the focus on telecommunications from another. The sudden death of Kairamo is an example of how an internal change can also lead to a period of inertia and stagnation. Other changes, and in particular the speed of change over the last twenty years, derive from the industry context: telecommunications has been one of the fastest-growing industries in the world. Global events such as the oil crisis of 1973 and the Asian market price collapse in the late 1980s also triggered changes within Nokia.

The rest of the chapter offers some frameworks for looking at why organizations in general change. In section 2, factors within the external environment are explored. Internal factors that may contribute to, or trigger, organizational change are covered in section 3.

 Section 1 Summary

In this section, we have:

- highlighted the need for organizations to remain viable as a fundamental cause of organizational change;
- explored how organizations take advantage of changing circumstances in order to thrive, not just survive.

Section 2: **External environment**

The idea that an organization's **external environment** is important to its viability, and may affect its potential need to change, can be understood using a biological metaphor. It 'builds on the principle that organizations, like organisms, are "open" to their environment and must achieve an appropriate relation with that environment if they are to survive' (Morgan, 1986: 45). The notion that there is a distinct boundary between an organization and its environment can be criticized as an oversimplification (Grey, 2002; Starbuck, 1976), however it provides a useful conceptual framework.

A distinction can be made between the immediate **task environment**, defined by the organization's direct interactions, for example with customers, competitors, suppliers, trade unions, local government, and the broader general, or **contextual environment** (Morgan, 1986). For each individual organization, there will be opportunities, threats, and constraints related to both. The type of infrastructure available, the ease of raising capital, the presence of an educated workforce, and the existence, or not, of economic and political stability all have an impact on an organization's ability to survive and thrive. The absence of some of these factors is one of the reasons why organizational growth and poverty alleviation in developing countries is often hard to achieve (Paavola and Adger, 2005). Yet there are differences too between countries in the developed world. For instance, the more liberal employment systems in the US and UK are quite different from the more regulated economies of Germany, France, and the Netherlands, where trade unions and works councils have a prominent role within organizations (Paauwe and Boselie, 2007, cited in Boxall and Purcell, 2008).

Sources of change within the environment

Dawson (1992) suggests that there are three sources of change within an organization's external environment.

1. The *constituent parts in the environment are not static*. As different organizations change, grow, and decline, the interests and intentions of others in the environment may alter.

A policy of acquisition and diversification may make a company less dependent on a particular customer; a change of government may make a particular service no longer economic; and the bankruptcy of a competitor can open up new opportunities.

2. There can be *changes in the patterns of interactions* between the constituent parts in the environment, as communication, cooperation, and competition between organizations ebb and flow. So competitors may band together to challenge trade unions or to lobby the government; conversely, a new market entrant may prompt more competitive behaviour.

3. There can be changes to constituent parts of the environment as a result of the power and *influence of the organization on the environment*, as well as vice versa. For instance, Nokia changed an element of its environment by successfully lobbying the Finnish government to allow it to seek foreign investment. Equally, the reorganization of its logistics division has given Nokia competitive advantage over other manufacturers in its task environment.

The implication of these three dynamic factors is that 'the environment is to some extent always a source of uncertainty . . . This explains why many of the activities and decisions which link . . . [an] organization to its environment are concerned with two things: a) generating and collecting information about relevant environmental segments; b) attempts to influence and control aspects of the environment' (Dawson, 1992: 80). Much organizational change can thus be seen as an attempt to ensure the organization's ongoing viability in response to, or in anticipation of, changes in the task environment and contextual environment.

The scope of external trends

Changes in the environment are characterized as trends when significant new patterns of behaviour or interactions emerge. Drawing on research into epidemics, Gladwell (2000) introduces the notion of **tipping points**. A tipping point is the critical moment in an evolving situation at which, after relative stability, the new pattern is far more apparent and the trend or growth is contagious and exponential: 'Ideas and products and messages and behaviours spread just like viruses do' (ibid: 7). To continue growing, or to remain viable, organizations must successfully resolve the challenges presented by trends and tipping points (Phelps et al., 2007).

One approach to categorizing trends is to look at the scope of their impact.

1. Taking a 'big picture' approach means looking at general *global trends* that affect the majority of organizations. Examples would be population growth, urbanization, growth of 'mega cities' (Vian, 2005). In the Nokia example, a trend that affected all companies, including Nokia, was the rise in oil prices following the oil crisis of 1973. A current trend affecting all industries in all countries is the continuing constraints on credit, triggered by the financial crisis that hit the headlines in September 2008 with the collapse of the investment bank Lehman Brothers and the subsequent government bailout of banks in the US and Europe.

2. There are also *geographic trends* that affect only one particular region of the world—in the case of Nokia, Finland's historical trading relationship with the Soviet Union had encouraged a significant degree of dependency on its powerful neighbour. Climate

change is already affecting the pattern of the seasons and rainfall in parts of the world, such as Africa, more than others. This in turn impacts raw material supplies, as well as the livelihoods of growers. Other geographic trends can be opportunities: in Northern Europe, the increase in mothers entering the workforce has created opportunities for the providers of nurseries and the manufacturers of ready meals, as well as increasing demand for online shopping.

3. Trends can be examined from an *industry* point of view. Depletion of a particular raw material, such as the overfishing of cod, can affect a whole industry and all of the different firms that serve and support that industry. In 2009, the economic downturn saw a significant decrease in consumer demand for new cars, with General Motors filing temporarily for bankruptcy and the German government bailout of Volvo. Parts manufacturers, haulage firms, dealers, and car finance companies were all affected by such a consumer-driven trend.

In summary, trends, whether potential or actual causes of change, can be categorized by the scope of their impact. There are global, macroscopic trends; others are industry-specific and some geography-specific. In addition, there may be trends that are local and affect only a few organizations, or even just a part of an organization.

The content of external trends

A framework frequently used to examine the content of trends is known by the acronym PEST (political, economic, social, and technological). Sometimes, two additional dimensions are added—legal and environmental—to create the longer acronym **PESTLE** (see Figure 2.1). In this section, several examples are given to illustrate the types of external trend that may impact some, if not all, organizations at the beginning of the twenty-first century. Some potential consequences for organizations are offered, but you may imagine many others.

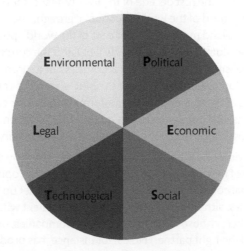

Figure 2.1 Types of external trend

Political

- A prominent political trend across Europe is the increasing **blurring of public and private sector** in service delivery. In the UK, the trend to privatize many public services began in the 1980s, under the Prime Minister, Margaret Thatcher, with the high-profile sales of British Gas, British Telecom, and the utilities companies. The White Paper of July 2010, *Reforming the UK National Health Service*, talks of demand being met by 'any willing provider', acknowledging the opportunity for the private sector. In emerging markets such as Eastern Europe, Russia, and China, some scholars argue that the blurring of boundaries between the public and private sectors is what has made wealth creation through entrepreneurial activity possible (Francis, 2001; Peng and Shrekshina, 2001).

- **A decline in the importance of the nation state**   For the last 200 years, the nation state has been seen as the primary source of both political power and identity. Increasing levels of mobility and fierce ethnic conflicts in Africa and the Balkans have led to questions about the nature and relevance of the concept of nationhood. Both the UK and the Netherlands have large immigrant populations, with increasing evidence of xenophobia and far-right extremism. There are open debates about what it now means to be British or Dutch. Globally, almost as many people believe they have at least a 'fair amount in common' with someone who shares their religion (31 per cent) or ethnicity (34 per cent) as they do with someone who shares their nationality (39 per cent). Yet 66 per cent of people globally claim they also worry that traditional aspects of their culture are being lost in the convergence towards a single global culture (The Futures Company Global Monitor, 2008). This may impact the appeal of global, as opposed to local, brands, suggesting further growth opportunities for multinationals; it may suggest that labour, a key resource for organizations, is far more mobile than before, making expansion into new markets easier.

- **The rise of the BRIC countries**   Brazil, Russia, India, and China, collectively known as the **BRIC** countries, are becoming increasingly powerful economically and politically. The acronym BRIC was coined in 2001 by Goldman Sachs economist Jim O'Neill. According to the investment bank, in the first decade of the twenty-first century, the four BRIC countries contributed one third of the world's economic growth. They already account for a quarter of the world's land mass and 40 per cent of the world's population. The prediction is that, by 2050, their combined economies will outstrip the current richest countries (Goldman Sachs website). With this data, it is perhaps not a surprise that Mercedes' recent car launch was in Moscow. In May 2009, at the BRIC summit at Yekaterinberg in Russia, there was evidence of the four countries transforming their economic power into greater geopolitical clout, as BRIC foreign ministers adopted very different positions on a number of themes from those espoused by the G8, International Monetary Fund, and World Bank.

  From the point of view of organizational change, these fast-growth economies can be seen as the source of new competitors or as attractive market opportunities for established, multinational companies. Some organizations have set up their own subsidiaries in the BRIC countries, although recruiting enough local talent who also speak English can be challenging. Others choose to partner with local companies, but here, again, it can be challenging to find the right partner. Nokia, for instance, has production units in China and India, as well as in Finland and Germany.

Economic

- The UK has continued to move towards **a service/knowledge-based economy** rather than one based on manufacturing. From 1986 to 2006, the proportion of jobs in manufacturing halved, from 20 per cent to 10 per cent, whilst the number of jobs in services has increased by 39 per cent (Brinkley et al., 2009). Examples would be the creative industries and those providing services for the elderly.

- **Rise in the parallel economy**   The UK counterfeit and pirate goods market is estimated to have a value of US $21.6 billion and even though it is hard to estimate, there are indications that the volume and scale are increasing. In pharmaceuticals alone, the National Audit Office report in 2009 estimates that the volume of counterfeits increased by 13 per cent in real terms over three years to £145 million by 2006–07. The music, film, and software industries are also significantly impacted by pirating.

Social

- **The growth in ubiquitous information**   The widespread availability of rapidly accessible information is changing the way information is retrieved, regarded, and used. Some examples of the volume of data at time of writing include: as of September 2010, there are over 5 billion images on Flickr; the English-language Wikipedia doubled in size in one year, in 2005; and there are over 196 million results for 'tax advice' on Google, as of April 2011. Such statistics have led the chief executive of one of Britain's biggest examination boards to suggest that, to be an effective citizen and employee, it is now more important to be able to process information than to have a good memory and that this is what exams should now be testing. A recent study (Rawsthorn 2008) has found that online behaviour is changing reading habits. New forms of reading include horizontal reading (dipping in and out between multiple texts), navigating (hunting for specific information), and squirrelling (storing information for later). This trend has implications for all organizations in the information and knowledge business, whether book publishers, libraries, universities, software producers, research firms, or policymakers. It may also prompt changes in the way organizations communicate internally if the younger generation are developing these new reading habits.

- **Growing importance of corporate social responsibility (CSR)**   There are growing expectations that companies need to earn the 'licence to operate' by demonstrating that they are committed to sustainable development of the communities in which they operate (Porter and Kramer, 2006). Indeed, 93 per cent of CEOs claim that sustainability issues are important to the future success of their businesses (EABIS, 2010). Influential stakeholders include NGOs, single-issue activist groups, governments, suppliers, retailers, and long-term investors. The end consumer also plays a key role, with the growing popularity of products certified through independent bodies such as The Rain Forest Alliance (Costa coffee, Lipton's tea, and PG Tips) and Fairtrade (Green and Black's chocolate, Ben and Jerry's vanilla ice cream). There is also growing evidence that a commitment to CSR is a key decision criterion amongst **Generation Y** when deciding which employer to join (PriceWaterhouseCoopers, 2007).

Technological

- **Development of mass customization**   Tailoring products and services to meet individuals' needs and wants is becoming a more dominant trend. Examples of adding an original or personal touch include the customizable colour schemes of Mini Cooper, Nike ID, which allows names to be added to football shirts and boots, and the Dutch postal service, TNT, which allows customers to create their own stamps using a photo or picture of their own choice. There are now also personalized public health offerings such as the 'choose and book' system for patients in the UK, allowing them to decide when and where they would like to go for tests or treatment.

- **The rise of GRIN technologies**   GRIN technologies are a shorthand term for a grouping of technologies that many scientists believe are most likely to radically transform society, and are thus likely to have a major impact on organizational change. The acronym stands for genetics, robotics, information technology, and nanotechnology. Examples of these potentially disruptive technologies include: biogerontology, which is a technology that dramatically reduces the aging process; robotics that could assist or replace humans in caring for the elderly; and 'the Internet of things' in which everything is Internet-enabled, from shoes to car keys, to allow remote control and monitoring of virtually everything. In addition, advances in nanotechnology and the artificial biological generation of materials, so called 'white biotech', could revolutionize production in areas such as construction and food processing, giving gains in efficiency and expanding the range of possible materials.

- **The rise in social networking and innovative devices**   The Internet has made it much easier for people to form new networks quickly, to share information, or to carry out economic transactions. Of UK consumers, 45 per cent always seek the opinion of other customers or look at customer reviews before buying a new product or service. 'Team buying' can allow individuals to get better purchasing deals. Online social networking platforms such as Facebook and LinkedIn make it easier for people to form new networks around shared interests, regardless of where they live or their existing social network. Facebook was started in February 2004 and, as of January 2011, has over 600 million active users (Business Insider, 2011). The falling cost of technology is enabling the fast adoption of new and advanced devices. BlackBerry devices are now in over forty countries with 28 million users. In some countries, such as China, mobile telephone use far outstrips landlines.

Legal

- **Increased corporate transparency**   Lack of trust in big business grew following the high-profile collapse of companies such as Enron and Worldcom in the 1990s. In the US, the Sarbanes-Oxley Act rules and procedures were introduced to curb what was seen as unethical corporate behaviour. More recently, the financial crisis has meant that the banking sector is now the least trusted industry sector (Edleman Trust Barometer, 2010). In terms of organizational change, what might governments, regulatory authorities such as the Financial Services Authority, or individual banks need to do, or be forced to do, to provide greater transparency on, say, bonus structures? Transparency International's

2008 Bribe Payer's Index ranks twenty-two of the world's wealthiest and most economically influential countries according to the likelihood of their employees to accept bribes abroad. UK ranks fifth best alongside Japan and Germany. What changes in working practices might the publication of such tables have on companies headquartered in different countries and on the places with whom they choose to do business? If an organization decides not to deal with a particular country, further changes may be necessary to find alternative raw material sources or to make up lost sales.

- **Increased anti-discrimination legislation**   Over the last fifteen years, there has been an increasing amount of legislation in Europe covering discrimination in the workplace. There is legislation against discrimination on the basis of religion, race, sexual orientation, gender, or age. This may require organizations to make changes in HR policies, as well as changes to behaviour. In 2011, lawyers in Strasbourg ruled that it was illegal to charge young male drivers more than young females for car insurance, an example of the way in which legislation can change the economics and policies in an industry.

Environmental

- **Climate change**   Climate change and concerns about global warming have sparked the development of a new industry (carbon trading) and a new use of agriculture (biofuels). For others, climate change may pose a threat to their very existence, particularly in developing countries, which are differentially worse affected and generally less able to respond (Paavola and Adger, 2005). In March 2007, European Union leaders at a climate change summit agreed to reduce carbon dioxide emissions by 20 per cent from the 1990 level by the year 2020. Car manufacturers, airlines, and energy companies are all under significant pressure to reduce their environmental impact and to rethink their business models. Other industries already impacted by climate change also include insurers, which bear the financial costs suffered by individuals and businesses following extreme weather events. Floods in the UK in 2007 saw 180,000 customers turning to the industry for assistance in rebuilding homes and businesses, with insurers paying out £3 billion. Nokia's development of the Remade phone is one example of a corporate response to the need to recycle; another is the drive to reduce the use of plastic bags in supermarkets.

 Exercise 2.1

Thinking about any organization that you know reasonably well, whether as an employee or as a user.

- Consider how the organization has already been impacted by the trends discussed here.
- Which of these trends might affect it in the future, and how?
- Create your own PESTLE analysis for the organization.
- Which trends would you label as global, affecting most organizations, and which might be industry- or geography-specific?

See Chapter 8 for more on scenario planning: p. 180

In summary, the PESTLE framework offers a useful way of categorizing current trends, be they global, industry, or geographic. In Chapter 8, we discuss scenario planning, which is based on the assumption that even when future trends cannot be predicted, futures based on *possible* political, economic, social, technological, legal, and environmental trends can be imagined and their implications discussed.

The historical view

So far, we have looked at current trends, in terms of both scope and content. However, in seeking to understand why organizations change, a historical view offers an alternative perspective on the cause of organizational change (Lawrence, 2006). It can also be a useful way of diagnosing the reasons why a particular organization has come to be the way it is. Exploring an organization's history, and its responses to changes in its external environment, shows that, in fact, the seeds to such success can be traced in the past (Steinbeck, 2001).

There were thirty years of unprecedented growth in the West after World War II. As most industries were doing well, it made sense to be involved in multiple activities to spread risk, and so many companies diversified. Nokia's acquisition in the 1960s of its fellow Finnish companies specializing in rubber and electronics is an example of this global trend.

The 1973 Yom Kippur War between Israel and some of its neighbours ended the boom period. Arab oil producers raised the price of crude oil significantly, angered by what they saw as Western support and sympathy for Israel. This geographic trend resulted in a global energy crisis, which triggered significant price rises and inflation, which in turn restricted growth and sparked high unemployment in many parts of the world. Nokia's trading relationship with the oil-producing Soviet Union was no longer as viable. There was a growing recognition generally that organizations needed to make choices, set priorities, and make trade-offs if they were to survive in this harsher economic climate. Strategy took centre stage on the board agenda and in its wake came a need to cut costs, to dispose of businesses, and a range of corporate solutions the names of which are very familiar, such as downsizing, delayering, outsourcing. Nokia divested all of its non-telecommunications business to focus solely on mobile telephony.

See Chapter 3 for more on large-scale change: p. 45

By the 1990s, there was a new challenge: industrial overcapacity globally—at least in terms of people and countries able to pay for goods and services generated by the global economies. This was partly the result of improved productivity from cost-cutting measures, but also the increase in manufacture in low-wage economies such as Hong Kong, Taiwan, Singapore, and Korea. In response to such overcapacity, there was a frenzy of mergers and acquisitions leading to the concentration of industries as diverse as cars, airlines, publishing, brewing, and pharmaceuticals. However, this particular global trend did not affect telecommunications, which, driven by technological advances and consumer demand, continued to show an industry trend of strong growth.

Then, in 2008, the financial crisis called into question the sustainability of continued growth and increasing financial risk, and the viability of global banking systems. As part of the fallout, many organizations have gone bankrupt rather than change and survive: Lehman Brothers, several Icelandic banks, and Woolworths are just a few high-profile examples.

This historical analysis illustrates the way in which changes in the economy and political landscape can lead to different types of organizational change, of growth and contraction, over the years. However, when asking the question 'why do organizations change?', how far back do you cast your glance? The Nokia story started in 1865, but how relevant is what happened then for understanding change and Nokia as an organization today? Go too far back and it can feel like economic history, but equally the culture of an organization is often created over many years. Culture and an organization's history can help to inform current and recent choices; the stories told about the past can also be carriers of organizational values and shape what possibilities are seen for the future.

See Chapter 6 for more on culture: p. 112

 Exercise 2.2

Find two or three different people who have worked in the same place for a while. It could be in any workplace: a shop, a company, or your college. If you can find people who are at different levels in the organization or have been there for different lengths of time, it will add extra interest to this exercise. Ask each of them the following questions.

- Looking back over the last five to ten years, what have been the main changes in your industry or sector?
- What do you think caused or triggered the changes in your own organization?
- How much is this a reflection of global, industry sector, or geographic trends?
- To what extent are the changes rooted in the organization's immediate task environment or history? Or might it be random, luck, or coincidence?

How much agreement did you find between the people you asked? Did people identify 'big picture', macroscopic reasons for their organization changing or did they tend to identify changes in the immediate task environment as the trigger for organizational change? How difficult was it for them to identify a single cause or did they tend to identify multiple, interconnected causes?

In our consulting work with organizations, we find an exercise such as this very informative for members of organizations because perceptions of cause often vary significantly as people attempt to make sense of what happened when and why. People often remember different things, because the events had a particular affect on them, but not others; even when people agree on a particular cause, they may differ as to how important it was, relative to other causes. Exploring how an organization got to where it is today is often a first important step in deciding what steps it could or should take next.

So, a historical perspective is a reminder of the interconnectedness of causes and the difficulty, if not impossibility, of identifying single triggers for organizational change. It can provide an initial platform for an individual organization to diagnose the origins of its survival and the source of its ambition to thrive in the future.

Management fashions

Since the 1990s, another trigger or stimulus of organizational change has become more evident: management ideas (Fincham and Clark, 2002). Visit the Google website or visit any bookshop, particularly those at airports, and look at the vast range of management books proclaiming the answer to almost any organizational challenge, frequently with evangelical fervour. Academics use the term 'management ideas' to describe a fairly stable body of knowledge about what managers ought to do to change and improve company or individual performance. These are generally popularized using powerful and highly effective marketing techniques, such as books, videos, and inspiring seminars (Sorge and van Witteloostuijn, 2004; Huczynski, 1993). The phrase 'fairly stable' is critical because a key feature of such ideas is that they have clearly identifiable life cycles. Indeed Abrahamson (1996) uses the term **management fashions**, which he defines as 'transitory collective beliefs that certain management techniques are at the forefront of management progress' (ibid: 254). In the 1980s, 'total quality management' was in vogue; in the 1990s, business process re-engineering and culture change were popular; currently 'Lean' and 'Six Sigma' are attracting attention, especially in the public sector.

See Chapter 10 for more on Lean and Six Sigma: pp. 203, 207

There are many reasons put forward to try to explain the appeal of management ideas to leaders. The challenges of ever-stronger competition, the complexity of change, and the enormity of the tasks facing them can make leaders and managers feel anxious and overwhelmed. The encouraging rhetoric of management ideas can thus be hugely appealing and reassuring (Sturdy, 1997). The stories of well-known companies successfully embracing a particular management fashion also legitimizes others to follow suit, reassured that other organizations have embarked on a similar change journey.

There is rarely independent research to corroborate the claims made in management books. Instead, great use is made of powerful case studies and compelling rhetoric (Clark, 1995; Guest, 1992). This is partly why academics tend to view management fashions sceptically. There are also concerns that 'the bewildering array of fads poses serious diversions and distractions from the complex task of running a company. Too many modern managers are like compulsive dieters, trying the latest craze for a few days, then moving relentlessly on' (Bryne, 1986: 61). The very word 'fad', rather than fashion, emphasizes negativity. Indeed, in her book of the same name, Shapiro defines fad-surfing as 'the practice of riding the crest of the latest management panacea and then paddling out again just in time to ride the next one; always absorbing for managers and lucrative for consultants; frequently disastrous for organizations' (Shapiro, 1998: xiii).

 Exercise 2.3

Go into a bookshop or search online for management books.

- Scan the titles to identify some of the current fashions and buzz words. Which of these buzz phrases have you heard of or experienced in your own organization?

- If you have time, buy a management book or borrow one from the library. Look at the rhetoric used, such as dramatic turnaround case studies or a confident affirmative tone, and see what convinces you.

- Talk to someone who has worked in a large organization for more than a decade and ask them what management fashions or trends they experienced and how they feel when a leader announces a new one.

Management fashions can thus be an external stimulus to inspire leaders to embark on change. The evangelical fervour with which they are expressed in conference speeches by 'gurus', and the conviction and persuasive case studies in books and videos, can create a confidence in the rightness of their prescriptions and labels for change. The very fashionability of such ideas can encourage leaders to believe that if others are adopting such an approach, so should they—although, ironically, if every company follows the same approach, there may be an increase in profitability or a reduction in costs, but there will be no competitive advantage because everyone else's profitably/costs will have changed too. Once adopted by a particular leader, or leadership group, and brought into the organization, such ideas then can become an internal trigger for change, the subject of section 3 in this chapter.

 Section 2 Summary

In this section, we have:

- examined the concept of the environment as a source of uncertainty;
- introduced ways of conceptualizing trends according to their scope;
- looked at the content focus of some current external trends using a PESTLE analysis;
- examined how an historical perspective is a reminder of the complexity and interconnectedness of causes of change;
- explained the way in which management ideas are themselves subject to trends and fashions, and provide an external stimulation that can contribute to organizational change.

Section 3: **Internal causes of change**

External trends potentially impact all organizations in a particular industry. However, organizations will not all respond in the same way. This suggests that organizational change is not determined only by external factors. Three different sources of change from within the organization itself are explored in this section: the role played by new leaders; an organization's growth as a driver of change; and the resources of the organization as a source of change.

New leaders

The presence of a new and charismatic leader is often seen as the reason why some organizations embark on change (Kotter and Cohen, 2002; Romanelli and Tushman, 1994). The Nokia story, at the start of this chapter, emphasizes the role of Kairamo, credited with expanding Nokia beyond Finland, and Ollila, seen as driving the transformation of Nokia into the world leader in mobile telephony. Here, we examine briefly the way in which the presence of new leaders can be an important trigger for change. It can also help to illuminate why some organizations embark on change and others stay as they are.

See Chapter 11 for more on leadership: p. 244

One perspective on leadership gives the CEO hero status as the instigator and driver of change who saves the corporation. The popularity of what have been called 'hero-leader' books (Hucyzinski, 1993) over the last twenty years has reinforced the notion of the powerful leader as the source of organizational change. The cover blurb of one of the more recent examples illustrates the emphasis on the charisma, skills, and achievement of the heroic leader.

Jack Welch is perhaps the greatest corporate leader of the 20th century. As CEO of GE for the past 20 years, he has turned GE into the most valuable company in the world and his championing of initiatives like Six Sigma . . . and e-business have helped define the modern organization. But Welch is much more than a successful business leader. He has revolutionized GE's culture with his ground breaking management philosophy . . . His story – a telling testament to the power of the American dream—will inspire everyone interested in business, in achievement and in getting the best out of their lives. (Welch, 2001: cover copy)

Table 2.1 includes a few examples of this literature.

Not all subscribe to the value of such books; indeed one academic refers to 'the unending stream of self-congratulatory "I did it my way" blather from pensioned-off executives' (Grey, 2002: 9). Yet, as the business world becomes more competitive and more volatile, major changes become more and more necessary if organizations are to survive and compete. Kotter and Cohen (2002) claim that change always demands more leadership. Leadership from this perspective is seen as a way of an organization dealing with the many external trends and challenges explored in section 2.

There is also evidence that what may be important as a trigger for change is the presence of new people at the top, regardless of whether they are charismatic. The very fact of new people at the top often signals to the rest of the organization that change is likely to happen and that new courses of action are legitimate (Quinn, 1980). New members of the top team, coming from other industries or other organizations, can also bring new perspectives, often interpreting the potential impact of external trends differently from those steeped in the same industry or organization. New leaders' different experiences can thus reveal the perceived need for change in strategic direction. However, there is also a risk in such situations that leaders who are new to an organization believe that they must initiate change because it is part of their contract, or because others expect it, or because of their own ego needs and desire to leave their mark, without necessarily taking the time to understand the organization in its current state.

Table 2.1 Hero-leaders

Author	Book	Year of publication	Organization described
Lee Iacocca	*Iacocca: An Autobiography*	1985	Ford and Chrysler
A. Morita	*Made in Japan*	1987	Sony
Bill Gates	*Business @ the Speed of Thought: Succeeding in the Digital Economy*	2000	Microsoft
Jack Welch	*Winning*	2005	GE
Martha Stewart	*The Martha Rules: 10 Essentials for Achieving Success as you Start, Grow, or Manage a Business*	2005	Martha Stewart Living Ominimedia

Growth as a driver of change

An organization's own history, and its point in that history, may also illuminate the internal triggers for change. Organizations can be viewed as having **life cycles**, with periods of evolution and growth, during which time minor adjustments to working patterns are required (Greiner, 1998). These are punctuated by periods of revolution and crisis, during which management practices and habits are shown to be wanting and no longer appropriate for the size of the company—during which leaders tend to be frustrated and employees disillusioned, and the continued viability of the company can be under threat. These are what Greiner refers to as 'revolutionary periods' and it is these phases that prompt organizational change if the company is to survive.

The external environment plays a role too, in that the growth rates of the industry in which an organization operates affect the likely frequency of these crises. So, when in a slow-growth industry such as paper, Nokia remained in a reasonably steady state from 1865 to the 1960s. When it entered fast-growing industries such as electronics and, later, mobile telephony, there were significant crises and change.

Figure 2.2 illustrates Greiner's (1998) proposed phases of evolution above the diagonal line, with the revolutionary stages marked by jagged lines.

Phase 1: Creativity In phase 1, according to Greiner, the founders of a company are usually technically inventive or entrepreneurially orientated and often dismissive of the need for management. Their focus and energy is on creating the product and the market. Hours are

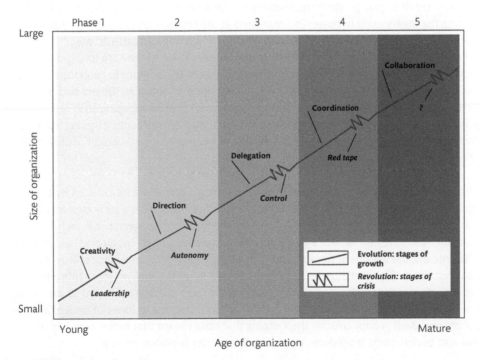

Figure 2.2 Five phases of growth
Source: Greiner (1998)

often long, communication is frequent and informal, and decisions are highly responsive to reactions from the market.

However, as the company grows and more employees join, these creative and individual-istic activities become problematic. More formal and systematic ways of making decisions and communicating are required; extra capital means that accounting systems are required, and yet such management activities are often constructed as burdensome and anathema to the free spirit of the founders. At this point, there is a *crisis of leadership*. A strong manager who has the knowledge and skills to introduce management systems is required, but, despite their dislike of management, founders are often reluctant to step aside.

Phase 2: Direction In this phase, there is often a period of sustained growth, with a functional organizational structure introduced and increasingly specialized jobs; accounting systems, proce-dures, and budgets are introduced; and communication becomes more formal and impersonal. Eventually, lower-level employees find themselves stifled by all of the heavy procedures and, despite knowing more about manufacturing or the customers than leaders, feel torn between following procedures and taking the initiative. The second revolution is thus the *crisis of au-tonomy*. The solution is often to move towards more delegation, yet this can be perceived as loss of control from those at the top; those lower down, who are not used to having to make decisions for themselves, can feel exposed. Many companies fail at this point, holding on to centralization, whilst lower-level employees remain disenchanted and leave the organization.

Phase 3: Delegation An organization that successfully manages to create a decentralized structure tends to give greater responsibility to managers by creating profit centres and mo-tivating managers using bonuses. Top managers at the centre manage by exception, focus on identifying other business to acquire, and manage in the same 'hands-off' way.

Eventually, there is a *crisis of control* as top executives feel that they are losing control over such a diversified range of operations. Some organizations try to return to centralized manage-ment, but this often fails because of the now-vast span of activities. Others find a solution through special coordination techniques. In Nokia's case, in 1986 it reorganized its management structure to simplify reporting and to improve central management control, going from eleven divisions to four industry segments, but later sought the more radical solution of divestment of all non-telecommunications businesses.

Phase 4: Coordination In this phase, formal planning systems are introduced by top man-agement for achieving greater coordination; head office headcount is increased to introduce company-wide programmes of control and review for line managers; some technical func-tions such as IT are centralized; and capital expenditure is carefully monitored and allocated.

Eventually, the volume of systems and form filling proliferates, and a lack of trust builds up between head office and those out in the field. A *red tape crisis* ensues. Head office typecasts the rest of the organization as uncooperative, while head office is perceived as increasingly distant and the latest piece of bureaucracy is seen as proof that it does not understand local conditions. Both groups criticize the systems that have meant that innovation has been sti-fled and bureaucratic procedures take precedence over problem-solving.

Phase 5: Collaboration Whereas phase 4 was managed through formal systems and proce-dures, phase 5 emphasizes the importance of teams, the skilful negotiation of interpersonal differences, social control, and self–discipline. It is sometimes characterized as the *move from roles to relationships*. This can be very difficult for experts who created the coordination systems and line managers who looked to the formal methods for answers. The focus is on solving problems quickly through: team action; matrix-type structures for getting the right people together; frequent conferences of key managers; educational programmes to train managers in behavioural skills for better teamwork and resolving conflict; fewer staff at head office; and economic rewards that are geared to team, rather than individual, performance.

This model seems to have much intuitive validity. Indeed, anecdotally, owners and managers of growing businesses speak of being at 'this stage of the business' or 'needing something to move the business to the next level' (Phelps et al., 2007). Greiner himself claims that the model is derived from research, but the details are sparse. To explore the usefulness of the model in helping to understand why organizations change, it is applied to Change in Practice 2.2.

 Change in Practice 2.2

The evolution of a consulting firm

CommCo was a Manchester-based consultancy firm specializing in internal communication, established in 1989 by Bill O'Leary and Marie MacNeil. In the early days, there was an almost missionary zeal about the place. Bill, the ideas man, was very entrepreneurial, slightly maverick, with huge energy and passion. Everybody worked very long hours, shared an office, and knew what was going on; the focus was on getting out into the market, building the name and reputation of the firm, and proselytizing the concept of internal communication, as few others were specializing in the area. Four years later, when the company was twenty-five strong, a finance partner was hired to tighten the accounting processes, and an HR manager was appointed to introduce a more formal recruitment system and appraisal system to ensure that bonuses were given on the basis of performance rather than personal favour (that is, pleasing Bill).

Bill could rationally see the need for management, but was bored by involvement in such 'trivia' himself. Marie, with her strong Presbyterian sense of duty, had filled the role of managing the day-to-day running of the firm, smoothing client or consultant feathers ruffled by Bill. Four years later, the company was sixty people strong. Marie came back from maternity leave, and decided she was tired of working long hours and shouldering all the management responsibility. She wanted to focus on client work. Given her desire and Bill's lack of interest in management, there was a succession crisis.

In 1997, Bill became executive chairman; Marie became managing director, and a management team of four was created from existing board members and became responsible for the day-to-day running of the organization. Although there was already some functional specialization lower down the organization, this was the first time that the top management of the organization was functionally organized, with a member of the management team responsible for each of finance, HR, knowledge management, and marketing.

Six months later, there was another crisis: several large consulting projects finished, a number of big proposals failed to convert into wins, and the forward order book looked weak. Bill returned from holiday, claiming that the management team had taken its eye off the ball and could not be trusted. He put himself in position of chairing the management team. A year or so later, CommCo was bought by an advertising and PR conglomerate. In the late 1990s, the consulting market was in recession and the organization now had to pay dividends to the new shareholder. Some of the newer people who had joined expecting to receive the traditionally excellent pay and bonus packages left the firm. More consultants started to leave, as did Marie. In 2000, the company made its first round of redundancies. It struggled on for a few more years and then what was left was absorbed by another subsidiary of the parent company.[4]

So, to what extent does Change in Practice 2.2 support Greiner's model? In the early years, the energy and focus spent on creating the product and the market, the long hours worked, and the frequent and informal employee communication certainly fit Greiner's phase 1 of creativity. The creation of an executive management team in 1997 could be seen as the result of a crisis of leadership and a sign of the firm entering phase 2. However, the appointment of a finance partner and an HR manager, and the creation of a functionally specialized support team, occurred before the executive management team was established. This raises the questions of how separate the phases are in practice and whether, in fact, the transition between phases is itself phased—that is, is a period of time rather than a point in time.

CommCo's employees were offered significant bonuses for individual performance very early on, so this was present in phase 1, not introduced in phase 3 as the model would suggest. From the start, everyone also received a bonus based on company performance, which is a phase 4 characteristic. So here, again, Change in Practice 2.2 suggests that not all of the characteristics predicted by Greiner may be present in the way the model would suggest.

Greiner commented: 'There is much more "death" in the life of organizations today. Few organizations make it through all the phases of growth. If they don't fail, as most do in the initial phase of creativity and entrepreneurship, they often get acquired by companies in a later phase' (1998: 64). The final chapter of the CommCo story seems to support this part of the model. However, such an interpretation may overplay the importance of the internal state of CommCo and underplay the role of external, industry-wide trends. The crisis that prompted CommCo to return to phase 1, with Bill taking back control, was not necessarily a failure to manage the transition from phase 1 to phase 2. It occurred when the whole consulting industry was in recession, so could equally be interpreted as being caused by changes in the external environment.

So how should Greiner's model of organizational life cycles be regarded? Lifecycle models like Greiner's are alluring because they simplify a myriad of facts associated with change and reduce the complex to a uniform, appealing, predictable, and deterministic pattern (Stubbart and Smalley, 1999). In our work as consultants, when we have shown the model to a top team, it often prompts a moment of real insight into where and why they, as an organization, may have got 'stuck'. However, as Change in Practice 2.2 demonstrates, growth is often only one of the many causes of change, and the phases and crises associated with growth may not conform exactly to the model's parameters.

Phelps et al. (2007) identify three main propositions about the nature of organizational growth from the notion of organizational life cycles: distinctly different 'stages' of development can be identified; the order in which organizations undergo these recognizable changes is predetermined and thus predictable; and organizations undergo the same sequence of developmental changes as they grow, just as all organisms do. From their extensive review of studies seeking to substantiate these claims, they conclude that there is inconclusive support for life stage models: 'All that is really clear is that over time, change along important structural and contextual dimensions is necessary and as these changes occur, important problems must be addressed and resolved in order to survive' (Phelps et al., 2007: 6). As well as internal factors, many of those problems relate to the need to manage the external environmental factors, which remains a significant problem for organizations whatever the stage of growth (Shim et al., 2000).

So, overall, current thinking has moved away from the idea of a fixed, linear, predictable sequence of growth stages to a more multidimensional concept in which crises and issues can occur at different points and can occur throughout the growth trajectory of an organization. Aldrich (1999) purposefully avoids using the term 'life cycle', with its deterministic implications, and uses instead the term 'life course' to suggest an evolutionary perspective in which an organization's direction, speed, and pattern of change are driven by the interactions with the internal and external environments.

 Exercise 2.4

Ask someone who has worked in an organization for a while to tell you how it has grown. Explore with him or her the changes in size, leadership, reward policies, and structure. Alternatively, reflect on your own experience of change in an organization.

● Were there any crises that prompted change in the organization and a shift from one phase to another?

● Could you identify causes of change other than those prompted by growth?

The resources of the organization

Another way of looking at internal reasons for organizational change is to take a 'resource-based view' (Boxall and Purcell, 2008). The **resources** of an organization are not only understood as assets in a formal accounting sense, such as factories, inventory, and debtors that would be disclosed on a balance sheet, but also include features with value-creating properties that are not actually owned by the organization, such as the talents and interactions of the people who work in the organization, the network of customer relationships, and the deep understanding of specific customer needs. The value of these resources can be a spur to organizational change as 'competitive success does not come simply from making choices in the present . . . but stems from building up distinctive capabilities over time' (Boxall and Purcell, 2008).This can help to illuminate why some organizations remain viable and thrive, and the reasons for the type of change on which they embark.

Organizations may develop resources as a defence against competition. The 'social complexity' (Barney, 1991) of deep networks of relationships, team working, and coordination can exist both within the organization and with external suppliers and customers. Successful organizations thus become strong clusters of 'human and social capital' (Goshal, 1998), generating valuable new combinations or 'bundles' of human and non-human resources for the organization. However, these connections are hard for others to imitate because they become deeply embedded in the social fabric of the organization. Because they are hard to copy, they can protect an organization from competitors, who cannot create or emulate the social complexity. However, in some cases, this may prompt a competitor to try to acquire an organization in its entirety, as Nokia did when it bought Technophone for its innovation capability. In other cases, a competitor may try to recruit a whole team from within a firm, wanting the team for its knowledge and client relationships. Industry sectors in which this tends to happen include law, investment banking, and creative industries such as advertising. However, acquired teams and individuals do not always thrive when part of a new organization with a different culture and ways of operating.

Organizations can change through building on existing strengths. From this perspective, organizations change by building on the assets and strengths that they already have, such as brand reputation, intellectual property, patents, experience, and key people. This means paying attention to an organization's historical strengths and capabilities, and then, based on this, exploring future opportunities. This is in contrast to first identifying opportunities in the external market and then trying to decide what is required for the organization to capitalize on them.

See chapter 8 for more on the resource-based view: p. 183

 Exercise 2.5

Consider the organization in which you work or your university.

- What would you describe as its resources, both physical and intangible?
- How do these differ from those of other institutions? And did any of these affect your choice to work or study here?
- How has developing or building on resources been a spur to organizational change over time?
- What future directions of change do you envisage, given your analysis of its resources?

 Section 3 Summary

In this section, we have:

- outlined the different ways in which the presence of new leaders can trigger change;
- examined the way in which growth can be a driver for change, looking in particular at lifecycle models of change;
- looked at how the resources of an organization can influence the direction of change.

 Integrative Case Study

Ben & Jerry's: The evolution of an ice-cream company

The first Ben & Jerry's ice-cream shop opened in a renovated petrol station in Burlington, Vermont on 5 May 1978 after Jerry Greenfield and Ben Cohen, who were high school friends, took a US $5 correspondence course on ice-cream making and borrowed US $12,000 from the bank.

Ben & Jerry's combination of super premium ice cream and innovative, socially orientated business practices created such a high profile that a 1999 *Wall Street Journal* poll found that Ben & Jerry's had the fifth best corporate reputation in America, behind Johnson & Johnson,

Coca-Cola, Hewlett Packard, and Intel, but ahead of such companies as Wal-Mart, Xerox, Disney, amazon.com, and AT&T. So, how did the organization change from its origins in a converted garage to a company with the fifth best corporate reputation in the US?

As Ben & Jerry's became famous locally for rich, all-natural ice cream with large pieces of biscuits, fruit, and nuts in it—what they called 'inclusions'—local restaurant owners started asking to buy Ben & Jerry's in bulk to serve in their restaurants. In 1980, Ben & Jerry's started selling ice cream packed in pint cartons to grocery stores and, in 1981, opened its first franchised scoop shop. By 1984, sales surpassed US $4 million and it was clear that it needed to build a factory to keep up with demand. To pay for the new factory, Ben & Jerry's sold stock to the public. An obscure law allowed the company to restrict the sale to residents of Vermont, and by the end of the stock sale, one out of every hundred families in Vermont owned Ben & Jerry's stock.

Haagen-Dazs, a far larger competitor, tried to limit distribution of Ben & Jerry's, prompting the company to file a lawsuit against its then parent company, Pillsbury. The famous 'What's the Doughboy afraid of?' campaign, is an early example of what Ben & Jerry's call 'guerrilla marketing'— highly creative ways in which to catch attention and challenge the power of larger competitors. The following year, it signed an agreement with Dreyer's to distribute ice cream throughout the US.

In 1985 the Ben and Jerry Foundation was formed to give 7.5 per cent of annual pre-tax profits to community building projects. In 1988, Ben & Jerry's formalized many of its beliefs about ice-cream making and social activism, creating a three-part mission statement that considers profit as only one measure of success. The product mission, economic mission, and social mission attracted national attention and differentiated the company from similarly sized food companies. The company's website gives many examples of its highly innovative marketing that targets both consumers and social and environmental issues. It includes: visiting twenty-eight UK universities with the National Blood service, giving a tub of ice cream to all students who gave blood; creating the world's biggest Baked Alaska and putting it in Capitol Hill on Earth Day in 2005, when the Senate was voting to allow oil drilling in Antarctica, deciding to go climate neutral; launching the world's first vanilla ice cream with exclusively Fairtrade ingredients; and renaming a flavour 'Yes Pecan' when Obama became US president. In the nineteen years between 1981 and 2000, Ben & Jerry's grew from a single scoop shop to a business generating over US $220 million in sales, with over 200 scoop shops across the US and another 100 outside the US.

However, there were problems in the mid-1990s. When the company went public, shares were at US $33; in 1995, they were down to below US $10. Some commentators argued that the issue was the company's practice of giving away 7.5 per cent of its profits. However, one journalist wrote 'the problem was much simpler than that. It was a couple of rough edged (ok hippie-freak!) entrepreneurs trying to run a company that had grown too big, too fast. To their credit, our boys actually realized this' (Serwer, 1999). The company hired a search firm and, as part of the recruitment, candidates were required to submit a hundred-word essay entitled: 'Yo! I want to be your CEO!' First prize was the job; second prize was a lifetime supply of ice cream. Robert Holland, who had good-naturedly submitted a poem, was named as CEO in 1995, but resigned in 1996. He was replaced by Perry Odal. Relations chilled between Ben & Jerry's and its US distributor, Dreyers, after Dreyers' offer of a buyout was rejected. The industry was surprised when Ben & Jerry's announced that it was going to increase its own sales force and turned to its arch-rival Haagen Dazs, which it had sued in the 1980s.

However, in April 2000, Unilever, the world's largest producer of ice cream, bought Ben & Jerry's, pledging to use its distribution muscle for overseas development whilst championing the company's socially responsible ethos. For some, it looked like a sell-out. The company's own publicity claimed that 'the same combination of ice cream, fun, business success and social values that made us popular with our consumers also made us attractive to Unilever'. Yves Couette, who had worked for Unilever for twenty-four years, was appointed the new CEO in November that year. The new European roll-out began in 2001, with the opening of the first scoop shop in Spain. However, the distinctive approach to marketing has remained the same—using brand humour to engage its customers in the serious business of the environment: 'We believe in milking happy cows not the planet' (Wills, 2008).

Questions:

1. Which external trends do you think help us to understand why Ben & Jerry's has grown so rapidly? Use the PESTLE framework to stimulate your thinking.

2. What other factors do you think may have been important?

3. Greiner talks of periods of evolution and revolution. How helpful is his model in understanding both the growth and the challenges the company has faced?

4. i. What resources do you think might have been key to Ben & Jerry's growth? ii. What resources do you think made Ben & Jerry's an attractive acquisition for Unilever? iii. Conversely, what resources did Unilever have that made it attractive for Ben & Jerry's to sell?

Conclusion

This chapter examined why organizations change. Some organizational changes are triggered by specific events or shifting patterns in the external environment; others by changes in the internal environment. A fundamental question for organizations is how to continue to be viable with such dynamics taking place around and within. A second question is how to take advantage of those changes and be able to thrive, not just survive.

External trends were examined in terms of their scope, which may be global, geographic, or industry-specific. Examples were also given of the content of trends, looking at current political, economic, social, technological, legal, and environmental trends. A historical view of causes of change is a reminder of both the complexity and interconnectedness of causes. Management fashions were also examined as a stimulus for organizations to embark on popularized approaches to change. Internal causes of change were examined in section 3, looking at the role of new leaders, growth, and the resources of the organization as drivers of change.

 Please visit the Online Resource Centre at **http://www.oxfordtextbooks.co.uk/orc/ myers** *to access further resources for students and lecturers.*

Change in Practice sources

1. Mobelitor.com (2008) 'Nokia Remade concept phone goes green', 9 Apr. http://www.mobiletor.com/2008/04/09/nokia-remade-concept-phone-goes-green/

2. Nokia Corporation website: http://www.nokia.com

3. Steinbock, D. (2001) *The Nokia Revolution: The Story of an Extraordinary Company that Transformed an Industry*, New York: AMACOM.

4. Wiggins, E. A. (2005) 'Making sense of consultancy: A qualitative analysis of the challenge of constructing a positive work identity for management consultants', Unpublished PhD, Birkbeck College, University of London.

Integrative Case Study sources

Ben & Jerry's website: http://www.benjerry.com

Datamonitor (2004) 'Ben & Jerry's case study: Developing premium food brands through innovative marketing', Aug: 1–13.

Serwer, A. (1999) 'Ben & Jerry's is back: Ice cream and a hot stock', *Fortune*, **140**(3): 267–8.

Thompson, S. (2001) 'Player profile: Ben & Jerry's puts Freese on global warming, sales', *Advertising Age*, 27 Aug. http://adage.com/article/people-players/player-profile-ben-jerry-s-puts-freese-global-warming-sales/53985/

Wills, A. (2008) 'Behind Ben & Jerry's "cool" brand values we find fresh environmental initiatives that work', *Travel Trade Gazette UK & Ireland*, 9 Dec: 22–3.

Further reading

Lawrence, P. (2002) *The Change Game: How Today's Global Trends are Shaping Tomorrow's Companies*, London: Kogan Page.
An examination of major trends and issues that are influencing the future of business.

Phelps, R., Adams, R., and Bessant, J. (2007) 'Life cycles of growing organizations: A review with implications for knowledge and learning', *International Journal of Management Reviews*, **9**(1): 1–30.
An overview of theories about the natural life cycle of organizations.

Intentions and Realities of Change

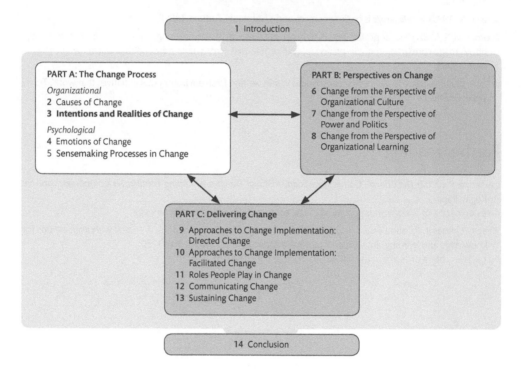

1 Introduction

PART A: The Change Process

Organizational
2 Causes of Change
3 Intentions and Realities of Change

Psychological
4 Emotions of Change
5 Sensemaking Processes in Change

PART B: Perspectives on Change

6 Change from the Perspective of
  Organizational Culture
7 Change from the Perspective of
  Power and Politics
8 Change from the Perspective of
  Organizational Learning

PART C: Delivering Change

 9 Approaches to Change Implementation:
   Directed Change
10 Approaches to Change Implementation:
   Facilitated Change
11 Roles People Play in Change
12 Communicating Change
13 Sustaining Change

14 Conclusion

Introduction

In the last chapter, we considered the issues that prompt change in organizations. The first purpose of this chapter is to explore the nature of organizational change, to examine the different scales of change and targets for change within organizations. We will then consider what happens in practice to change plans and explore the extent to which people can expect change programmes to deliver what is intended.

Main topics covered in this chapter

- Scales of organizational change: their size, span, and timing
- The focus of the change: what is expected to change
- Exploration of planned and emergent views of change

● Examination of the extent to which change can be planned and the implications of this for managing change

Section 1: **The realities of change—scale, span, and timing**

Organizations are never static: people join and leave; new processes are introduced; customers are lost and won; technology moves on. Some of these changes are of no significance to the majority of the employees, who barely notice them happening; others affect most people in the organization. Some changes result in little disruption to ways of working; others fundamentally change past practices overnight. These differences in pace and magnitude are what is meant by the **scale of change**: how rapid and substantial the change is. Scale ranges from small, focused, and bounded improvements, to radical changes to the organization. Small-scale changes, typically conducted step-by-step, are often referred to as **incremental change**, and large-scale changes, major shifts in strategy, or practices executed rapidly, as **discontinuous change** (Nadler and Tushman, 1995). So we are really comparing ideas of evolution versus revolution (Burke, 2008). Incremental change may be highly significant, but it is gradual (Holbeche, 2006). Discontinuous change is typically more dramatic and more demanding. One example is the change that was brought about by the collapse of financial institutions, such as Lehman Brothers Holdings Inc., a global financial services company that had to file for bankruptcy in September 2008, the largest bankruptcy case in US history. The overnight collapse and the subsequent fallout resulted in shock and, indeed, disbelief that this could happen, followed by changes in public perception of the financial industry and a return to part-government ownership of some banks. The scale of the change was sudden and significant, with the majority of organizations within the industry affected by events.

A related distinction is the **span** of change across the organization. Some changes affect the whole organization, as in the corporate collapse of Lehman's or the nationalization of other banks, while other changes are more local, limited to a particular section, department, or team within the organization. In discussing discontinuous change, Dunphy and Stace (1993) distinguish between modular transformation, limited to one section or department, and corporate transformation, involving the whole organization.

See Chapter 9 for more on Dunphy and Stace: p. 195

Organizations tend to create their own ongoing incremental changes during periods of relative stability and many undergo major discontinuous change when things happen in the external environment, often affecting whole industries (Mintzberg, 1991; Pascale et al., 2000). The challenge for those managing change lies in deciding how large any change needs to be at any given time, whether the change is a one-off event or needs to keep happening, and the speed at which it needs to happen. It is then a question of using the right tools or methodologies for the right task (Burke, 2008).

See Chapters 9 and 10 for more on possible methods and techniques

So what does this tell us about change? That change can occur in waves across a whole industry; that it is not easy to foresee or plan for such waves; that, in this case, apparently sound decisions can, with hindsight, be seen as dramatically flawed; that, at times, major radical moves, of a discontinuous scale, such as the acceptance of government funding, are

Change in Practice 3.1

Discontinuous change at RBS and Barclays: A tale of two banks

With a long history dating back to the 1700s, The Royal Bank of Scotland (RBS) was the first Scottish bank to install automatic cash machines and the first bank in the world to make its cash machines available to cardholders from other banks. In August 2005, RBS expanded into China, acquiring a 10 per cent stake in Bank of China for £1.7 billion. The bank was the 2005 recipient of the Wharton Infosys Business Transformation Award, given to enterprises and individuals who use information technology in a society-transforming way.

Barclays Bank similarly traces its origins way back to 1690. It launched the first credit card in the UK, Barclaycard, in 1967, developed some of the best-known products, and set out on international expansion, first establishing a US affiliate in San Francisco. Thus, by the mid-2000s, both banks were well-established players in the global market.

In March 2007, Barclays announced plans to merge with Dutch bank ABN AMRO, one of the largest in Europe, with operations in some sixty-three countries. In the past few years, ABN AMRO's stock price had stagnated and it had failed to break into the ranks of its top five peers. However, the financial market was at its peak of profitability and ABN AMRO was still seen to be a significant player, commanding a high value. Barclays was proceeding with merger talks when RBS put in a higher counter-offer, nearly 10 per cent higher than Barclays' offer. As a result, shortly afterwards, RBS was announced as the successful bidder and work began on the merger of the two entities.

Just one year later, the financial markets were in trouble. The price paid for ABN AMRO now looked ridiculous: vast losses, rather than opportunities for profit, had been acquired. On 22 April 2008, RBS announced the largest rights issue in British corporate history, to shore up its reserves following the purchase of ABN AMRO.

The markets continued to collapse and, in October 2008, the British Prime Minister Gordon Brown announced a UK government bailout of the financial system. The Treasury had to put £37 billion of new capital into RBS and two other banks, to avert financial sector collapse. As a consequence of this rescue, the chief executive of RBS, Sir Fred Goodwin, offered his resignation, which was duly accepted. In January 2009, it was announced that RBS had made a loss of £28 billion, of which £20 billion stemmed from ABN AMRO. The UK government now held a 70 per cent stake in RBS.

In the meantime, despite the global financial meltdown, Barclays rejected the need for any government assistance and instead turned to the China Development Bank and Qatar Investment Authority to increase their holdings. In 2008, Barclays bought another credit card (Goldfish), gaining 1.7 million customers. It also bought a controlling stake in a Russian retail bank, Expobank. In September 2008, with the dramatic collapse of the investment bank Lehman Brothers, Barclays was well placed to acquire a significant slice of its core business.

Within the space of twelve months, the tables were turned and the bank that failed to secure one merger was positioned to play an influential role in the future of the finance industry, backed by sources from the Middle East and China, operating without government constraints.[1-3]

needed to survive, even though they may appear unpalatable and fundamentally change the nature of the organization.

As Change in Practice 3.1 illustrates, the challenge lies in diagnosing what is happening and then deciding on the appropriate response. As discussed in Chapter 2, organizations need to be alert to what is happening in their industry and the wider business environment, as well as cope with the myriad of other internal and external issues such as trade union views, managers joining or leaving, and so on (Tushman et al., 1986). The senior leaders of an organization may need to consider both their own organization's place within its cycle of growth and the impact of the cycle of the industry within which it sits in order to decide whether incremental or discontinuous change is needed. The Schumpeter column of *The Economist*, 26 September, 2009, comments that:

> The business cycle continues to prey on the modern economy. The 2008 (financial) debacle might have come as less of a surprise if (students) had been taught that there have been at least 124 bank–centred crises around the world since 1970, most of which were preceded by booms in house prices and stock-markets, large capital inflows and rising public debt. (Ibid: 85)

The timing of change initiatives

Despite the difficulties in interpreting the external environment, organizations do make changes in *anticipation of* what might be needed, known as **anticipatory change** (Nadler and Tushman, 1995). Anticipatory changes can be incremental, such as making alterations to formal structures or particular processes, for example, in order to prepare for an increase in product volumes in a particular range. But anticipatory change can also be discontinuous, involving a fundamental redefinition of the organization to be ready to face future opportunities and challenges. While usually initiated by senior management, such changes can also begin with the actions of others in the organization. For example, at Sony, it was a mid-level engineer who challenged top management to overcome its prejudice against making 'toys' and developed the PlayStation, which, once launched, accounted for more than 40 per cent of Sony's profits (Hamel, 2000) and continues to be a leading product. This was a change that had enormous impact on the allocation of resources and structures—getting ahead of, and indeed changing, the focus of the market at that time.

Yet, sometimes, organizations are forced to *respond to* changes in their industry's environment and to respond immediately, such as in the collapse of the financial markets, when both RBS and Barclays were forced to effect significant change in how they were funded in order to survive. These responses are **reactive change** (Nadler and Tushman, 1995). Like anticipatory change, reactive change can be either incremental or discontinuous. For example, incremental reactive change can be driven by the need to offer the same type of product or level of service as a competitor. This was the case with Nokia's update of its own Internet-connected multimedia smartphone in response to the launch of the Apple iPhone. On its launch weekend, in January 2007, Apple sold 270,000 iPhones in the first thirty hours: the product was a clear success and competitors were left standing, needing to find a rival product fast. Discontinuous reactive change typically occurs in response to a crisis. This may involve deep changes in the organization's way of doing business. This was the case with the impact of RBS's suddenly imposed part-nationalization, which resulted in the departure of the chief executive and a fundamental review of the business operating model.

Burke (2008) suggests that more than 95 per cent of change remains rooted in incremental change, and Tushman and Nadler (1986) note that the most effective organizations take advantage of the relatively stable periods to continuously build incremental change, and that even the most conservative of organizations expect some ongoing small changes, both anticipatory and reactive, which do not make too many waves. They cite the commonly held view that almost any organization can tolerate a '10 per cent change' without disruption—that is, changes that are still compatible with the prevailing structures, systems, and processes. Romanelli and Tushman (1994) depict organizations as evolving through relatively long periods of stability with bursts of discontinuous change, and those bursts of discontinuous change, in turn, laying the foundations for new periods of equilibrium. They call this the **punctuated equilibrium** model of change. Others suggest that it is possible for organizations to continuously adapt themselves in a fundamental manner, such that they are constantly reinventing themselves (Burnes, 2009). This enables them to avoid discontinuous change. Indeed, it is easy to overlook the importance of the overall impact of incremental changes and the role of personal initiatives in making change happen (Frohman, 1997). The Sony PlayStation is such an example: whilst its creation brought about discontinuous change, the instigation of the initiative came from the determination of one engineer building one new product, which would typically be classed an incremental change, in terms of its small-scale beginnings.

 Change in Practice 3.2

Delivering mail: Change at TNT and Royal Mail

TNT operates a global distribution business through two divisions: Express (parcels) and Mail (letters). Born of a Dutch state-owned postal company, it was privatized in 1989 in response to the perceived threat of technology to the traditional mail industry. Following a series of mergers and takeovers, it was listed on the stock exchange in 1998. It now continues to expand and serves some 200 countries, employing around 160,000 people.

Royal Mail is the UK's national postal service, a limited company owned by the government. It employs over 155,000 people in the UK. It has invested significantly in new technology and continues to be the main mail delivery provider in the UK.

The principle issue facing both companies is the fundamental change in their external context. Online shopping continues to drive volume growth in parcels, whereas delivery of letters continues to decline, by some 9 per cent per annum.

Both organizations have been forced to change working practices, to reduce staff numbers and costs, to find new ways forward.

TNT has had to work hard to improve the margins of its parcel business and to deal with the decline in mail volumes. It has continued to invest in its parcels infrastructure, growing its intercontinental success in this field. In 2010, it announced its intention to lose 11,000 mailperson jobs. Discussions with the unions were difficult, but agreement was reached on a reduced number of redundancies at the end of January 2011. It is now operating its Mail and Express businesses as two separate entities, recognizing that Mail faces a continuously declining market.

Royal Mail has faced an uncertain future, with the ongoing question of privatization hanging over it. In the past decade, it has made many attempts to modernize its work practices, but without significant change. The Communication Workers Union has fought to protect employment, engaging in a series of disputes and strike action. Year after year, commentators have suggested that modernization is moving too slowly to save the service. Its future remains uncertain.[4-7]

Perhaps modernization at Royal Mail is moving too slowly to save the service; the incremental changes that it has managed to introduce have not been of a scale or speed to sufficiently impact profitability. Mintzberg (1991) notes that, during periods of growth and stability, incremental change is relatively easy to implement, but that this in itself can become a double-edged sword because the internal forces for stability develop self-reinforcing patterns, so that organizations may not register external changes that are a potential threat. Somewhat more dangerous is that, where they do recognize the threat, the response is frequently heightened conformity and commitment to 'what we do best' rather than response by changing—the shadow side of playing to one's strengths. Royal Mail continues to cite the quality of its delivery and its public service ethos, wanting to ignore the continuing fall in number of users and profit. This lack of recognition may exacerbate the situation, until the decline in performance is so severe that the organization risks failure and unwanted or unexpected discontinuous change is forced upon it, in order to survive. This could yet be the outcome at Royal Mail.

See Chapter 6 for more on Royal Mail: p. 122

In our experience, different changes may be taking place in the same organization at the same time: some may be anticipatory changes, while others may be in reaction to new external issues; some may be incremental and others discontinuous. It can be difficult for organizations to be clear about the scale of change that they anticipate versus that which they experience, particularly whilst in the midst of it. For example:

- Buchanan and Boddy (1992) note that change that is seen to be of strategic importance in one setting may well be considered a mundane adjustment to another organization;

- Beugelsdijk and Slangen (2001) report that, often, employees at lower levels in the organization experience the change as incremental, whereas senior managers tend to describe it as discontinuous and revolutionary.

See Chapter 5 for more on sense-making: p. 91

It seems that change may have many different, subjective interpretations; the realities of change are often contested and it is certainly clear that hindsight plays a significant role in defining the 'reality' that has taken place.

The depth of change: First-order and second-order change

The descriptions of incremental and discontinuous change focus on its pace and scale as well as its span. A further distinction is between what is known as **first-order** and **second-order** change. First-order change makes changes within an established way of doing things, whereas second-order change creates a completely different way of looking at the situation (Senge, 2005). But what does that mean in practice?

First-order change involves trying to improve how something is done. It can typically be measured in a comparative way by assessing how things are before and after, to see how much improvement has taken place. For example, a team-building day might help a group to get to know each other better, resulting in generally improved levels of trust. At an organizational level, the acquisition of ABN AMRO was a first-order change for RBS—continuing a familiar business expansion model.

Second-order change refers to a change that results in operating from a different perspective or frame of reference—that is, thinking completely differently about the issue. Hamel (2000) refers to the process of reorientation as 'learning to forget': finding ways of letting go of biases and assumptions about what is viable to allow the creation of something new. Taking the previous examples, the team may decide that trust has nothing to do with its effectiveness and focus on other aspects beyond the team, which result in going about its task entirely differently. At an organizational level, banking may be undertaken in an entirely different way: for example: the experiment undertaken by the Virgin Money company, which has launched a person-to-person lending service that allows individuals (or groups of individuals) to structure formal loans with people whom they know, using Virgin Money as the service provider rather than as the lender (Pritchard, 2009).

Despite the apparent logic, first-order change is not always automatically incremental, nor is all second-order change discontinuous.

- *Incremental, second-order change*   An organization's sales team may completely rethink its approach to working with the research and development (R&D) unit, so that, instead of trying to instruct the unit about areas of research that it must undertake and facing the same resistance time and again, it decides to listen and understand the R&D unit's interests, energy, and resources, enabling both parties to develop the research agenda together, collaboratively—a second-order change.

- *Discontinuous first-order change*   Looking back to Change in Practice 3.1—the tale of two banks—the Barclays' entity now appears largely unchanged despite a significant period of disequilibrium, changes in funding sources, and subsequent mergers. The change it has undergone is first-order in the sense that it builds on what already exists: the overall organization and its thinking remains largely intact.

It may be important to understand the nature of change in this way in order to assess what else needs to happen. Typically, organizations change their structures and processes (first-order change) and then wonder why employees are adapting old practices to the new circumstances, rather than rethinking their approach (second-order change). The informal systems in organizations are as important in achieving shifts in thinking as the formal ones; it is often the informal ways of 'how things get done around here' that hold an organization in its past ways of operating and prevent second-order change from occurring (Hatch and Cunliffe, 2006). In our experience, desiring second-order change, but achieving only first-order change, is one of the biggest organizational frustrations.

See Chapter 6 for more on culture and change: p. 115

 Exercise 3.1

Identify an organizational change with which you are familiar or interview someone else about his or her experience of an organizational change. Discuss your interpretation of this change.

- How great was the scale of the change—incremental or discontinuous—and to what extent did it span across the organization?
- Was this change brought about in anticipation of the need or in response to external changes or pressure?
- How deep was the change—first-order or second-order?
- How easy or difficult is it to classify the change in these ways? Why do you think this is so?

Section 1 Summary

In this section, we have:

- examined two key scales of change, incremental and discontinuous, and considered how change processes can be local or span the organization;
- explored the implications of anticipatory and reactive timing for organizational change;
- considered the depth of change—first-order and second-order organizational change.

Section 2: **What changes?**

Some change theories focus on the whole organization—the macro level—and others on the group or the individual—the micro level. Inevitably, these are not discrete groupings: all are interrelated and, indeed, organizations interrelate with other organizations and their external environment in ways that are crucial to understanding how change happens. However, it can be helpful from a practical point of view to understand the primary focus of the change intervention. This section explores change at the individual, group, and organizational levels.

Change focused on individuals

Some approaches to change begin with the individual, the assumption being that changing individuals' skills or views will help the organization to move in its new direction. Individuals have a sense of what they expect to do at work and get from being at work—and their own idea of whether their expectations are satisfied. Employers are generally trying to motivate people—to work harder or to undertake tasks in a different way, or with a different focus. Formal training and induction schemes are often as concerned with generating appropriate approaches to the work (in terms of flexibility or teamwork, for example) as they are with specific skills.

Many changes at the individual level are in the service of a limited change. An example of this is the training of the sales and marketing team in selling skills to improve its effectiveness at winning new business. Whilst crucial to business success, the training is directed at one team within the organization. On the other hand, NHS hospitals in the UK have focused the fight against the spread of 'superbugs' resistant to antibiotics at the individual level, with training in hygiene and hand-washing. They expect this to improve the success rate of containing the spread of superbugs at the organization level.

Less frequently, but significantly, change focused on individuals can be second-order in nature. For example, post-privatization, British Airways embarked on a change programme to put customer service at the heart of every activity. Whilst training took place at the individual level, the programme was expected to achieve a significant cultural shift across the airline through the creation of new ways of thinking about the customer, thereby achieving such quality in its customer service that it could claim to be 'the world's favourite airline'. Because the change was directly linked to the strategic intent of the organization, BA was able to reinforce its importance and model different ways of behaving towards the customer in many ways beyond the individual training, encouraging second-order change to take hold.

Training in new skills is just one intervention at the individual level. Others include the following.

Recruitment and selection   This involves getting the right people in the right jobs or changing the people within a team, taking on new hires with different skills or different motivation. It may include placing people in positions that are important to the overall change effort. The appointment of key people in strategically important roles may serve to plant new ways of working across the organization. As examined in Chapter 2, one of the more extreme examples is the appointment of a new CEO whose primary purpose is to deliver significant change—to fundamentally transform the organization in ways that the existing leadership is unable to do.

Executive coaching   This may be used, particularly at the more senior levels, to achieve a change in individual approach: it offers the individual space to think through the change that is required of him or her, perhaps in a new role, or to face new organizational demands.

Change at the group level

Work within organizations is increasingly delivered via project teams, comprising various representatives or specialists rather than individuals working on their own. The particular prevalence of self-directed groups or flexible project pools has resulted from the 'flattening' of old-style hierarchies and the organization's need to be flexible, to be able to bring a group together and disband it once the need has passed. Burke (2008) points out that the work group is the primary source of social relationships at work; as such, it plays a key role in determining the individual's sense of organizational reality. For this reason, working at group level may provide a powerful change intervention.

Change interventions at group level include:

See Chapter 5 for more on how change is understood: p. 85

- assisting with setting goals, defining roles and responsibilities within the group, and clarifying group purpose in relation to new or future needs;
- exploring decision-making, communication, and interpersonal processes, to improve ways of working.

Most of these interventions are likely to result in first-order change—that is, altering the response to the situation and each other, without fundamentally changing the thinking about the situation. Sometimes, our work with teams focuses both on how they work together and how they think together—to form their strategy, for example. Where that takes the team to a fundamental shift in thinking, such that it together creates a new strategy, based on different assumptions, for example, then the change in frame of reference is likely to constitute second-order change.

Change at organizational level

Alternatively, the intended focus for change may cover a large swathe of the organization. In the current market, changing the shape and structure of organizations is often seen as the route to corporate salvation, initially led by 'best practice' firms in Japan and Germany in the 1990s, and then propelled into a range of restructuring approaches as a result of the recession in 2009–11. Large-scale organizational change takes many forms including the following.

Delayering   There is a trend for the creation of leaner organizations by taking out layers in the hierarchy, for example delayering by creating a global matrix structure across countries and products. This approach first took hold in Europe in the 1980s and, by the 2010s, had become accepted practice across the private sector in Western Europe.

Such structural changes may require different job design and behaviours, with employees assigned new roles and responsibilities, typically at middle manager grades. Those who remain may find themselves more accountable, which can be a source of job satisfaction, but can also bring greater pressure to perform, which can be a source of stress (Lawrence, 2002).

Downsizing   Another significant change has been through reducing headcount to reduce costs—also often referred to as *rightsizing*. The global recession of 2008–11 created large-scale job losses, particularly in the US and the UK, as well as in Greece, Spain, and Portugal. Cost containment is not always triggered by revenue reduction, however, and has now become a common way of increasing profits and managing performance even in steady market conditions. Lawrence (2002) notes that investors respond positively to headcount reductions, even when profits are already good; typically, shares soar when a global entity announces major job cuts worldwide. Thus, the focus of the organization change is sometimes selected to impress external parties, such as investors, rather than to respond to perceived internal issues.

Outsourcing   Contracting out key services to a third-party provider remains a strong trend. The drivers are competitive pressures to reduce costs and to divest the company of all but its core business. In the first wave of outsourcing, the 'back office' functions such as physical security and catering were outsourced to specialist providers, followed by IT and parts of human resource management, and then other administrative tasks (airline ticketing), as well as manufacturing. Alongside potentially reducing costs, outsourcing offers ways of flexing resource to respond to needs.

It is common for organizations' outsourced call centres to be **offshored** anywhere in the world to service that organization's entire global client base, with India known as 'the back office of the world' for a period in the 2010s (Lawrence, 2002). The quality and predictability of offshored work has increased exponentially, so that the choice is no longer automatically between cost-saving and quality. A European retail client recently compared the difference between first moving manufacturing to China in the late 1990s and the move to new markets in Eastern Europe in 2010. He told this author that he believes that his managers have developed, through experience, the skills to manage such fundamental changes, which, in turn, has decreased the pain and increased the success of such ventures. Yet even this market continues to evolve: the dynamism of wage levels resulted in call centres moving from India to the Philippines and Malaysia, offering yet more choices and potentially new issues of skill and capability.

Process reengineering   This change focuses on reviewing processes or the technology to improve the performance of the organization. Specific methods, such as Lean or Six Sigma, are seen to produce significant cost savings by streamlining processes to maximize outputs. Such approaches tend to come in cycles of fashion. In global organizations, such as Dow Chemicals, GE, or Toyota, such methods are applied on a worldwide basis, compelling different countries and operating units to adopt standardized approaches, the outcomes of which can be compared across the organization.

See Chapters 9 and 10 for more on change methods

Merger and **acquisition**   Although the terms 'merger' and 'acquisition' are often conflated, they mean slightly different things. When one company takes over another and clearly establishes itself as the new owner, the purchase is called an acquisition, as happened when RBS acquired ABN AMRO. From a legal point of view, the target company ceases to exist, the buyer 'swallows' the business, and the buyer's stock continues to be traded. In the pure sense of the term, a merger happens when two firms, often of about the same size, agree to go forward as a single new company rather than to remain separately owned and operated. This kind of action is more precisely referred to as a 'merger of equals'. Both companies' stocks are surrendered and new company stock is issued in its place. For example, both Daimler–Benz and Chrysler ceased to exist when the two firms merged and a new company, Daimler–Chrysler, was created.

See Chapter 12 for more on the communication of mergers and acquisitions (M&As): p. 286

In practice, however, actual mergers of equals do not happen very often. The merger is often a defensive move to avoid being taken over by the biggest players. Being bought out often carries negative connotations, so, by describing the deal as a merger, deal makers and top managers try to make the takeover more palatable. Usually, one company will buy another and, as part of the terms, simply allow the acquired firm to proclaim that the action is a merger, even if it is technically an acquisition.

Holbeche (2006) points to the intense pressure on merged organizations to achieve discontinuous change in short time horizons; where this is not evident, the merger is seen to have failed. This change goes beyond financial results and is seen to encompass the idea of 'fit' between the two organizations in terms of their people, culture, and values—change of second-order. This requirement has brought focus firmly on the totality of the change effort, including the quality of the management and leadership. Research undertaken at Roffey Park Institute found that people working in merged organizations were subjected to multiple waves of change, which had a strongly destabilizing effect (Holbeche, 2006). Thus, achieving the second-order change needed to bring two entities together to create a successful new whole remains challenging.

Cisco is an example of an organization that is seen to have managed successfully the acquisition of a range of partners. Founded by a married couple in 1984, Cisco was one of the first companies to sell commercially successful routers supporting multiple network protocols, and expanded by acquiring a variety of companies to bring products and talent into the company. Acquisitions, such as Stratacom, were the biggest deals in the US at the time. Cisco has developed criteria for deciding whether or not to acquire a company and a process for managing the acquisition, such that this in itself has become a core competence. It remains one of the most valuable companies in the world (see http://www.cisco.com).

Strategic alliances   Strategic alliances reflect the increasingly boundless nature of new organization forms (Lawrence, 2002). A strategic alliance is a formal relationship between two or more parties to pursue a set of agreed-upon goals or to meet a critical business need. This is a way of extending the 'boundary' of the organization while each remains independent. Partners may provide the strategic alliance with resources such as products, distribution channels, manufacturing capability, project funding, capital equipment, knowledge, expertise, or intellectual property. The alliance is a cooperation or collaboration that aims for a synergy in which each partner hopes that the benefits from the alliance will be greater than those from individual efforts. The alliance often involves shared expenses and shared risk. In the UK, the Disasters Emergency Committee is an umbrella group comprising thirteen UK charities. These charities are all associated with disaster-related issues such as providing clean water, humanitarian aid, and medical care. It brings together a unique alliance of the UK's aid, corporate, public, and broadcasting sectors with the purpose of rallying the nation's compassion, and ensuring that funds raised go to DEC agencies best placed to deliver effective and timely relief to people most in need.

Sometimes, strategic alliances cross national boundaries and, increasingly, cross industries. They are sometimes formed between a company and a foreign government, or among companies and governments. These kind of alliances have the potential to impact significantly the shape of the market, as has occurred in the airline industry, where, for example, American Airlines and British Airways (along with several other smaller airlines) formed the One World Alliance sharing, amongst other things: advertising and marketing; coding; reciprocal lounge access; and consolidated frequent flyer programmes (Lawrence, 2002). This and other airline alliances have been formed because profit margins within the industry are thin for all and ownership of the assets expensive. They hope to increase their collective market share in all major world markets, in which there is now overcapacity. This illustrates the extent to which the environment influences change in organizations and, in turn, organizations move to shape the environment in which they operate.

All such structures can provide real challenges for the employees working within them, and the work of Hirschhorn and Gilmore (1992) highlights the issues of working in the 'boundaryless organization'. They consider the example of an engineer working on an inter-functional project who must play multiple roles, sometimes being the technical expert, sometimes acting as the representative of the engineering department to make sure that it does not get too much to do with too few resources, and sometimes needing also to be a loyal team member as part of this project team. He has to play all three roles, sometimes within one meeting, juggling 'hats' in ways that were unknown in traditional organization structures with clear roles and accountabilities.

 ### Exercise 3.2

Consider again the organizational change that you chose for Exercise 3.1.

- Was the change focused at the individual, group, or organizational level?
- What form did the change actually take?

 ### Section 2 Summary

In this section, we have:

- explored the distinction between change focused at the individual, group, and whole organization level;
- examined some of the many forms that organizational change can take.

Section 3: How intentions and realities of change relate

Implicit in deciding who or what is the focus of change and how large or fast the change needs to be is the belief that you can take such decisions, that change can be planned for and implemented in accordance with that plan.

The planning of change has played a significant part in change management theory from the 1940s to the present day, yet, in reality, change is rarely delivered totally in accordance with the plan, as noted in Change in Practice 3.1. Similar unexpected twists happen to us even in our day-to-day lives. For example, you may plan a barbecue to celebrate a relative's birthday, when the weather forecast is set fair and all of the family are free to attend; you are delighted, and decide upon champagne and cake to open the proceedings. However, on the day in question, the rain sets in early, two of the cousins quarrel, drink too much champagne, and behave badly, and the aunt providing the cake falls ill and cannot attend. The plan was sound, but a barbecue turned out to be an unwise choice in the context of the weather on the day and unforeseen issues produced unplanned outcomes.

This section will examine two contrasting views of change, planned change and emergent change, and consider how they inform change management. **Planned change** emphasizes the managers' deliberate intentions to achieve organizational change, with a clearly defined start and end point for the change. **Emergent change** emphasizes the view that *whether or not change is intended*, organizations are, in fact, constantly evolving. It focuses on creating the conditions for change to occur, to enable change through continuous ongoing processes of organizational experiment and adjustment, with no defined end state. The section then draws together the implications of these views for managing change.

Planned change

Over the past half-century, it has become accepted practice for most organizations, particularly medium-to-large-sized organizations, to undertake some kind of business planning, for example plans to meet budgets, for growth or market segmentation, or for specialization. Plans tend to encompass actions for the immediate year and sometimes strategies for, say, five years hence. Public sector organizations need to provide plans that are open to central authority scrutiny as part of the process of review of their performance; voluntary sector bodies face similar requirements from funders. So plans are used both in the service of achieving maximum effectiveness and in response to regulatory or governance requirements. Organizations may have dedicated planning departments and use formal planning techniques to assess the external environment as part of this process. This type of planning is often used to decide what needs to change in the business, with the underlying assumption that intentions will translate in to realities.

Important early work in developing a view of planned change was undertaken by Kurt Lewin, a German-American psychologist working in the early 1940s; indeed, the very term 'planned change' is often attributed to him. He distinguishes change that is consciously embarked upon from that which just seems to happen, and undertook research into the conditions that enable individuals and groups to change. He incorporates his research findings into his approach to change and two of his frameworks, force field analysis and the three-step model, are still used by practitioners today to decide what needs to change and to create plans to effect the change.

Force field analysis is a planning tool that provides a framework for looking at the factors (metaphorically described as 'forces') that influence a situation. The process requires a change agent to identify forces that are either driving movement towards the change (helping forces) or blocking movement towards the change (hindering forces). Thus, Lewin draws attention to the tendency of organizations to seek to maintain their equilibrium in response to disrupting changes. The underlying principle of the 'force field' is that helping forces must outweigh hindering forces if change is to happen.

Force field analysis: An example

A manager deciding whether to introduce new technology (called SAP) for his billing system across a global organization might draw up a force field analysis, as in Figure 3.1. In the diagram, the intensity of the 'forces' is represented by the thickness of the arrows.

Once the manager has carried out an analysis, he can decide whether the project is viable. In the example in the figure, he may initially question whether it is worth going ahead with the plan.

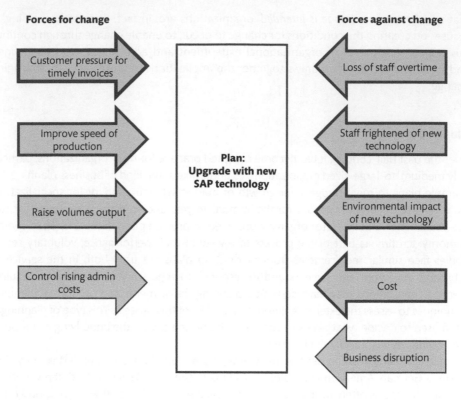

Forces for change

Customer pressure for timely invoices

Improve speed of production

Raise volumes output

Control rising admin costs

Plan:
Upgrade with new
SAP technology

Forces against change

Loss of staff overtime

Staff frightened of new technology

Environmental impact of new technology

Cost

Business disruption

Figure 3.1 Force field analysis

 Exercise 3.3

Trying out force field analysis for yourself

Now apply this approach to a change that you are considering making in either your work (such as reorganizing a team that you manage) or personal life (such as taking up exercising, starting a new course of study, or applying for a new job). Identify the forces for and against the change.

● What does the exercise tell you?
● How could that affect your decision and approach to the change?

Lewin's three-step model of change

1. **Unfreezing** the present
2. **Moving** to a new level
3. **Refreezing** the new level

This planning process has been adapted many times and continues to be widely used. It encompasses the following.

1. The first phase involves sound analysis of the internal and external environment to gain a clear focus for the *unfreezing*. Using the SAP example in Figure 3.1, unfreezing at the individual level may involve promoting employees with good IT skills; at group level, introducing new approaches to team productivity, which do not depend on individual overtime; at an organizational level, designing a new matrix structure to improve the information flow and to discourage units from operating in separate silos. Plans can then be aimed at helping employees to understand the need for change, so that they are ready to *unfreeze* from the present.

2. The second step in the plan is *movement*, when it is expected to see people behaving differently. Success depends on very careful planning, to ensure that all key parties who need to change are targeted, and that the process is lead by managers who have the skill and determination to overcome resistance from their teams.

3. The final phase, *refreezing*, involves stabilizing the changes, making them part of the system, so that people experience what is new as integral to what they do. For example, part of the refreezing may involve making changes to the recruitment process for the future, to ensure the hiring of more people with the new skills sets or behaviours, or changing the reward system to ensure that it reinforces the behaviour changes.

Lewin's original ideas of planned, participative change focused on the needs of small groups of employees to adopt change through being involved with the implementation. As noted in section 1 of this chapter, organizational change may encompass a whole range of different scales and spans of change, from the rollout of new technology, to the sale of part of the business. Once change is discontinuous and affecting the whole organization, the principles of 'unfreezing' and 'refreezing' become more complex. Some argue that Lewin's three phases are ill-suited to this purpose (Conger, 2000). In large-scale changes, the leader often has little connection with or control over the people affected or the actions of the incoming organization or provider, so that planned change now sometimes becomes top-down imposition of structural and process changes (By, 2005).

Many writers suggest that the planned view is most applicable to incremental changes (Burnes, 2009). Here, leaders can plan small-scale changes, try out new ideas to see which are likely to be effective (that is, where there is movement), and try to induce commitment within the organization through continual, but low-scale, change. This is sometimes called **logical incrementalism** (Quinn, 1980). So, as we noted in Change in Practice 3.1, the introduction of cash machines was an important change, probably planned well in advance in order to gradually install the machines. The resulting changes in how business was conducted, the reduction in counter service, and the subsequent reduction in the number of bank branches on the high street was a gradual shift, introduced through careful planning over a number of years. Had the customer shown no appetite to use the machines, cash machines might have died away and alternative plans might have been made.

Leaders who embrace the view that change must be planned for assume that they can be sufficiently certain in their analysis to decide what needs to change, and how, as well as sufficiently able to control the variables in the plan to achieve the outcome they want. Such views tend to pay attention to patterns of authority in an organization and expect that commands that are issued from the top (for example to introduce a new structure) will travel through the organization in a determined way to create a particular effect. Thus, the planned change view:

- anticipates a relatively predictable external environment, in which the economic conditions or government intervention or changes in competitors do not get in the way of the plans before they are exercised—that is, the assumption of a reasonable degree of predictability and control during the time span of the change;

- expects communication to be efficient and skilled, ensuring that there is minimal distortion within the system so that everyone understands the same picture of the future state;

- depends on a critical mass of people within the organization becoming quickly aligned to the change and working to create the new future state without resisting or refusing;

- believing that change is systemic and, in paying attention to the impact of key interventions in the system, changes in the overall system can be effected.

Most managers do adopt a planned view of change, for without it there seems to be little alternative, except to 'wait and see'. Large consultancies typically work with change models based on Lewin's three-stage principles, producing timetables, objectives, and methodologies for the different stages of change, so that the view remains prevalent in US and European organizations. However, the planned view is sometimes criticized for seeming insufficiently flexible to be helpful in unexpected, discontinuous change (Burnes, 2009).

Johnson (1993) suggests that managers often consciously pursue a planned incremental approach, aware that it is not possible to know about everything that could affect the organization, but recognizing the need to cope with uncertainty and to keep moving—that planning has its place, but cannot account for everything that happens. He suggests that the total pattern of action requires constant, conscious reassessment of the whole organization, its capacities, and its needs. We have certainly found this pragmatic, ongoing reassessment to be helpful: by so doing, organizations can find ways in which to shape the direction and to integrate the small changes. Allowing for this is a crucial part of the planning process.

Emergent change

In the last twenty years, some organizations have chosen to step back from strategic long-term planning because they perceive the inevitability of other events getting in the way, which renders it invalid. However, those who criticize the planned view do so from a range of different perspectives: there is not one single alternative view. Some comment on the complexity of modern organizations; others, the speed of change in a high-tech global environment; others still, on issues of power and politics that make plans unmanageable, and so on. What they largely share is a view of change as *emergent*—that is, as an ongoing process of organizational adaptation, with the organization being interdependent on the much larger external environment. The environment affects the organization in unpredictable ways, resulting in a complex mix of messy decisions, with no one right answer, such that decisions need constant refining (Dawson, 2003).

This section will now examine more closely what it means to work with an emergent view by examining three different lenses on emergent change.

1. Emergent change: Readiness for change

One view of emergence focuses on organizations developing the capacity to change, to be agile enough to change.

In examining the issue of readiness, Boxall and Purcell (2008) distinguish between **short-run responsiveness** and **long-run agility**. Short-run responsiveness includes being able to increase or decrease the headcount, for example, through use of fixed-term contracts to match cyclical needs, applying fixed salary base rates, with top-up bonuses to match the organizations results, adopting multi-skilling across roles, such as the BBC requiring radio studio managers to be able to perform some studio engineering tasks, as well as balance the sound. Long-run agility focuses rather on being able to change technology or products faster than competitors, for example by outsourcing some aspects of production (as discussed in section 2), whilst protecting the critical core workers, whose skills are crucial to a firm's core or distinctive capability.

To achieve agility, the organization needs the capacity to continually scan the environment for patterns or trends in order to inform the focus for experimentation and action. Scanning involves picking up small signals, making sense of an incomplete picture. For example, in 2008, a small number of property companies were able to recognize the signals of over-stimulation in the housing market before the crash, but the majority paid attention to the relative market share of their competitors and, because the competition continued to perform strongly right up to the moment of the crash, their narrow focus rendered them blind to other signals.

The emergent-readiness view defines the leader's role as the communicator of the long-term intentions and encouragement of employees to be alert to possibilities to move in that direction. It includes the acceptance of, and paying attention to, issues of power and politics. Experimentation is encouraged, with enough trust between parties to take some risks. This combination of experimentation, risk, and trust is used to convert opportunities into results, as in the example of the Sony manager's interest in the PlayStation; it is expected that change will emerge through starting where there is some interest to cultivate (Handy, 1994; Holbeche, 2006). This may require more skill on the part of the managers than simply offering instruction; it is a more sophisticated approach to leadership.

See Chapter 7 for more on power and politics

2. Emergent change: Renewal

Another way of thinking about emergent change is based on the principles of the *ecosystem*, explored by Hurst (2002: 2) who suggests: 'Modern business organizations advance strategically by accident, economically by windfall and politically by disaster. This does not mean that events in organizations are random or capricious or unmanageable.'

Hurst (2002) proposes that rational actions and plans are not wrong, but are not sufficient when organizations face complex dilemmas, that there are oscillations between the need for clear analysis and clear direction and the times when this will not work. He considers what it takes to renew or revitalize an organization and likens the patterns of oscillations to those of the *ecosystem,* describing the life cycle of the forest by way of example.

- Change is continuous, sometimes smooth and incremental, sometimes rapid and discontinuous—steady growth of trees, then huge bursts during which the forest spreads. In industry terms, this might equate to the exponential growth in the music industry from the 1960s to the 1990s, with the sale of CDs peaking in the early 1990s.

- Renewal requires destruction. The point is reached at which the only way to open up spaces is to creatively destroy the large structures within the forest that are eating up resources. In music industry terms, new sources of music became available—with some musicians moving cautiously to releasing their albums via the Internet and CD sales starting to decline. The music industry's first response was to try to block this change—expecting that it would destroy the industry.

- New plants and trees emerge from the open patches, surviving because they can cope with the constraints of that environment. They self-regulate to survive and renew in the new forestry conditions—that is, they have the capacity to **self-organize**. In terms of the music industry, a digital music report written in 2009 reported the emergence of new business models between the music industry and mobile phone operators, and revenue-sharing deals with Internet service providers (ISPs). They found that music companies were working on licensing arrangements with YouTube and MySpace, etc., such that the sites became part of the legitimate music economy (IFPI, 2009). The instigation of Spotify, a proprietary music streaming service that allowed free instant listening to any tracks, which was launched for public access in October 2008, was one attempt to take advantage of this new landscape. An experiment that raised funds through a combination of subscription and advertising, it represented one of the first 'green shoots' for the industry.

- Thus, it is the whole ecosystem that evolves. Organisms do not evolve by adapting individually to environmental changes. It is the *pattern*, not just the separate units comprising this pattern, that evolves.

Hurst suggests that it is at the point of decline that an organization needs to 'destroy' itself creatively by *creating* a crisis to shatter the constraints. The crisis serves to erase parts of the organization's memory—the framework of logic—so that it can be open to fundamental second-order change. At this stage, it is imperative that an organization is creative and bold rather than 'planful'. In our experience, many managers understand the role of crisis in galvanizing organizations into action, but find it difficult to do in practice; such 'creation' is often experienced by employees as manipulative or scaremongering. Yet it is apparent that crisis can be a valuable catalyst for change, especially in contexts that constrain effective action, as discussed in Change in Practice 3.2. The view further stresses the need to hold onto and return to the organization's original purpose and values as part of the renewal process. In so doing, it suggests that, unless leaders embody in their behaviour the ideals of the organization that they are trying to change, it is inevitable that their change efforts will be seen as self-serving.

3. Emergent change: Complexity theory

A third way of thinking about change as emergent has formed through the study of **complexity theory**. Complexity theorists suggest that complexity sciences have implications for how we think about our lives and our organizations. Whilst they point out that the science cannot be taken and simply applied to organizations (Stacey, 2011), they suggest that it can be used to provoke thinking about how we view organizations. Stacey (2002–03), Griffin (2002), Shaw (2002), and others invite us to think of organizations as social rather than physical objects. As such, they suggest that an organization is not an entity, but an ongoing self-referencing process of gestures and responses between people. People are constantly engaged in interactions with each other, from which overall behavioural patterns emerge. This way of thinking about organizations has become known as a **complex responsive processes perspective** (Griffin and Stacey, 2005).

Stacey (2002–03: 28) illustrates what he means through a description of the weather system:

> The weather is not just unpredictable . . . it's predictably unpredictable, or unpredictably predictable. It's not confusion. It has pattern. We predict seasons; we predict a lot of rain at this time, but just when and how it's going to take place we can't predict over more than a short time in to the future. So we're not talking about something that is completely unpredictable; we're talking about a system producing patterns that are recognizable and paradoxical.

He draws further on particular dimensions of the weather example to suggest principles to bear in mind in organizational life.

- The need to look for *patterns* means paying attention to patterns of interaction between people. He suggests this is often best achieved by focusing on interactions at the smallest local level—a group within a business unit, for example, noticing what is important for them, how they operate. When these interactions change, then a new pattern—or way of doing things—is likely to emerge. Griffin and Stacey (2005) call this the phenenomenon of **self-organization and emergence**.

- Griffin and Stacey (2005) note the issues of power relations in organizations, and how often people are included or excluded through the dynamics of power: 'these groupings establish powerful feelings of belonging' such that our identity is derived from the groups to which we belong, creating 'complex patterns of power relating' in our daily lives (Griffin and Stacey, 2005: 6).

- To achieve new patterns, the existing system needs to be *disturbed*. That means having the greatest diversity possible in the group. Difference in views can be uncomfortable and organizations often hire people who 'share values' or 'think in our way'. Complexity theorists believe that where there is enough difference and enough anxiety, then new thinking will occur. Often, in organizations, this sort of difference is introduced through the hiring of a new chief executive. But this does not create difference in the day-to-day relationships between people, which remain largely untouched by the new person at the helm. So diversity means encouraging people with different views and experiences at all levels of the organization to be equal partners, to express their views.

See Chapter 2 for more on new leaders: p. 25

- Patterns may change because people have the capacity to do what they think is best—to self-organize. People do the best they can in the organization, which is simultaneously full of cooperation and conflict. Not everyone gets on in the typical workplace, but, on the whole, people adapt and find positive ways of getting the work done.

- An important aspect of the complex responsive processes perspective is the understanding of the nature of leadership. If change happens through local patterns of interaction, then no one person can be 'in charge' of an organization. When a powerful person makes a statement, it may bring about many different responses throughout the organization. Leaders cannot control those responses, but they can pay attention to them and participate in the conversation as fully as possible, listening carefully to what is going on and trying to understand what sort of meaning is emerging. They can also encourage connectivity and feedback between different parts of the organization.

See Chapter 5 for more on sense-making: p. 91

This view of change acknowledges the complexity of organizational life, challenging previous assumptions about what happens in organizations. It assumes that individuals are self-directing, and want to be part of a shared vision and shared values, with leaders and followers mutually dependent. It also suggests leaders should be capable of simultaneously creating a general sense of direction, but not directing people in how to go there; managing performance yet encouraging diversity; creating enough tension to damage the status quo and provoke innovation, but not so much that people are completely destabilized. Evidence does suggest that creativity and innovation increase where there is a balanced distribution of internal power, and a strategy of continuous experimentation and learning (Pascale et al., 2000). However, a complex responsive process view of change is difficult to pin down. It certainly does take a leap of faith to embrace: this view is as much a way of thinking and being as it is a set of actions.

 Exercise 3.4

Reflect on Stacey's (2002–03) description of the weather and think back on events in your country in the past twelve months (what has happened to retailers, the housing market, car sales, or the sustainability agenda, for example).

- What examples can you find of 'predictably unpredictable patterns'—patterns you can see with hindsight?

- Can you identify any fresh thinking about key issues? Where has that come from? What might that tell you about the conditions needed to foster creativity?

- What are the pros and cons of this view of change?

Emergent change: Summary

In summary, proponents of emergent change are a broad group, each holding to important points of difference in their views.

Nevertheless, there are some key principles of emergent views of change that we find helpful in terms of:

- understanding change as a continuous, unpredictable process of trying things out and adapting, trying to match resources to opportunities in a dynamic way (Burnes, 2009);

- thinking about ways of human interaction and sensemaking as crucial to the creation of change;

- recognizing the impact of organizational culture and politics on what happens;

- the move from 'understanding individual persons as autonomous to thinking about them as interdependent' (Stacey, 2011: 464);

- seeing the leaders' role as one of shaping a general direction of travel, and facilitating the thinking and learning of everyone to create new ways forward.

See also
Chapter 5

Implications for managing change

Views of change have evolved alongside the development of leadership practice and theory. They have also had to adapt to the fact that, in many Western countries, manufacturing—where process improvement could bring about huge improvement in efficiency and productivity—has been replaced by service and creative industries, where success is much more dependent on the less tangible or measurable features of organizational culture and environment. Western leaders rely on planning principles to find a route through the highly uncertain situations and the majority still believe in a rational, planned approach. The planned view of change carves out a clear, traditional leadership role, whereas the emergent view perceives the leader to be a catalyst for change, creating conditions that enable others to change, rather as a coach or facilitator. This may be a less familiar role for leaders to take. Weick (2000) notes that if leaders take notice of emergent change and its effects, they can be more selective in their use of planned change.

Managing change offers real opportunity—to innovate, to refresh, or simply to achieve survival. So how then can a leader decide the best way of going about change? Which style is likely to give best chance of implementing change effectively? Table 3.1 overleaf summarizes some key dimensions examined in this chapter.

When reviewing this list, it is not surprising that managers are uncertain about which approach to adopt. Whether viewing change as planned or emergent, leaders do still find themselves responsible for ensuring that change takes place. Additionally, organizations increasingly need to manage through periods of both incremental and discontinuous change (Burke, 2008). If periods of business volatility become more commonplace, then change may need to be initiated and implemented rapidly. This all means that leaders are less likely to be able to rely on their own preferred approaches.

See Chapter 11 for more on the role of leaders: p. 244

Table 3.1 Views of change: Key features

View of change	Scale of change under consideration	Leadership role	Benefits and limitations
Planned	Incremental	• Decide priorities for the immediate future and create a plan • Target the parties that need to change, generally specific groups or individuals • Promote understanding of what is required • Manage any difficulties, such as resistance • Encourage participation in all aspects of the change	• Enables employees at all levels to be involved • Steady pace • May be considered slow • May be so incremental that no tangible change is evident
Planned	Discontinuous	• Create a plan and drive the change from the top • Create the vision of the future • Offer clear, efficient communication • Offer participation though formal workshops e.g. on specific aspects of implementation • Set the goals, monitor the project, control and manage any resistance and difficulties • Deliver to agreed timescales (generally tight)	• Clarity; clear picture of the future state • End state can be planned and worked towards • Can cause great disruption • Top-down approach may not achieve employee engagement • Unpredicted events get in the way of achieving the planned end state • Little opportunity to amend or respond to new circumstances
Emergent-readiness	Typically incremental—and cumulatively may lead to discontinuous change	• Actively involve employees in decision-making and problem-solving • Encourage experimentation • Recognize issues of power and politics—and encourage trust • Enable flexibility in staffing arrangements to better respond to changes • Coach, support	• Models empowerment, rewards reacting to the unpredicted • Can become self-serving—noticing and reacting rather than taking the initiative • Its iterative nature means there is no clear end state
Emergent-renewal	Typically discontinuous	• Notice the patterns in the environment • Provoke and create the crisis that leads to a return to values • Role model the change the leader wants to create	• Demonstrates possibility for fundamental renewal • Depends on the notion of crisis to create energy
Emergent-complexity	Either incremental or discontinuous dependent on outcome	• Encourage diversity • Facilitate, listen • Make things uncomfortable • Hold the tension • Notice patterns, and encourage experimentation	• Encourages self-organization • Difficulties of creating the appropriate levels of certainty/uncertainty and safety/tension • May feel directionless—no clear start or end state

Section 3 Summary

In this section, we have:

- examined different views of planned and emergent change;
- considered the views in relation to their intentions about change and the realities of the outcomes;
- drawn together the implications of the different views for approaching the management of change.

 Integrative Case Study

Nike: Emergent and planned change

The athletic footwear industry has experienced explosive growth in the last two decades. The branded shoe segment is dominated by a few large companies, including Nike, Reebok, and Adidas. The story of the Nike organization is often said to symbolize the benefits and risks inherent in globalization.

Nike was founded in 1964 by two young entrepreneurs, a track star and his coach, who wanted to improve the performance of running shoes for track competition. Hurst (2002) describes them as 'muddling along', testing and redesigning shoes without planning. The famous 'swoosh' logo was created by a graduate design student in 1972 for US $35.

A shared passion and purpose rather than financial reward held together the early team. Having established itself in track shoes, Nike developed products for other sports in a highly flexible way, with little plant or infrastructure. Hurst (2002: 41) describes the strategy as emergent through its sense of purpose—a mixture of 'planning and opportunism in an unexploited field'. Locke (2002) notes that Nike was the first to outsource shoe production to lower-cost Japanese producers.

In time, the trial-and-error approach evolved in to set ways of doing things and, as the company grew, there was a need for structure and hierarchy. Objectives and financial rewards became routinized. Performance and profits continued to increase, although some of the early founders left the organization, perhaps 'bored' by its professionalization. But sustained success reinforced the appropriateness of more of the same. When Japan became an expensive source of labour, Nike moved production to Korea and Taiwan. When costs began to rise in these countries as well, it began to urge its suppliers to relocate their operations to other lower-cost countries.

However, in subsequent years, Nike was shaken by a series of scandals about the treatment of its workers, the factory conditions, poor wages in Indonesia, and the use of child labour in Pakistan. In 1996, *Life* magazine published an article with a 12-year-old boy stitching a Nike football. At first, Nike managers tried to deflect these criticisms, arguing that the Indonesian factories were owned and operated by independent contractors, not by Nike.

However, as pressure grew, this hands-off approach changed as Nike formulated a code of conduct for its suppliers that required them to observe basic labour and environmental/health standards. Nike created new departments, which became organized under the corporate responsibility and compliance department, with some eighty-five people specifically dedicated to labour and environmental compliance, all located in countries in which Nike products are manufactured. It developed a new incentive scheme to evaluate and reward managers for improvements in labour and environmental standards amongst its supplier base.

Nike also became actively involved in environment issues, virtually eliminating the use of petroleum-based chemicals in its footwear production and taking the initiative in organizing an industry-wide organic cotton consortium.

Today, Nike's products are manufactured in more than 700 factories, employing 500,000 workers in fifty-one countries.

Questions

1. Can you identify the key points of change in Nike's history?

2. Specifically what changed and what do you think was the scale of that change, using Nadler and Tushman's (1995) dimensions?

3. Read the case, applying first a planned view of change. Re-read it, applying an emergent view of change. What do you notice about the application of these different views?

Conclusion

In this chapter, we have examined what really happens when implementing change in organizations, exploring the extent to which intentions become realities. We began by considering the scale, span, and timing of change, and the issues involved in deciding on the scale of change needed at any given time. We then looked at examples of first-order and second-order change, noting the challenges of achieving second-order change across organizations.

In section 2, we considered the different targets for change, from the individual to groups and, indeed, the whole organization. This provided the backdrop for section 3's exploration of different views of how change happens, focusing on planned change, which has been the dominant approach to change management for the last twenty years, and emergent change, which, in contrast, sees change as an open-ended and continuous process of adaptation, a view of change that is beginning to gather ground in organizations.

In our own practice, we continue to approach change in a planned way because it enables us to explore the decisions we are making at any given time, not because we expect the change to be delivered exactly in accordance with the plan. We recognize the power of some of the processes adopted by those holding an emergent view of change in harnessing the input and energy of all employees, and will examine these further in Part C of the book.

 Please visit the Online Resource Centre at **http://www.oxfordtextbooks.co.uk/orc/ myers** *to access further resources for students and lecturers.*

Change in Practice sources

1. BBC News (2000) 'NatWest merger's mixed fortunes', 11 Feb. http://news.bbc.co.uk/1/hi/business/639201.stm

2. Sutherland, R. (2007) 'Barclays boss: RBS overpaid for ABN Amro', *The Observer*, 7 Oct: 1.

3. Wilson, A. (2008) 'RBS now 58% owned by UK government', *The Telegraph*, 28 Nov. http://www.telegraph.co.uk/finance/newsbysector/banksandfinance/3532604/RBS-now-58pc-owned-by-UKgovernment.html

4. BBC News (2009) 'Q&A: Royal Mail disputes', 5 Nov. http://news.bbc.co.uk/1/hi/business/8260701.stm

5. Royal Mail website: http://www.royalmail.com/portal/rm

6. TNT Group (2010) *Annual Report*. http://group.tnt.com/annualreports/annualreport10/

7. Wearden, G. (2010) 'Royal mail to be privatized or sold', *The Guardian*, 10 Sep. http://www.guardian.co.uk/uk/2010/sep/10/government-privatise-sell-royal-mail

Integrative Case Study sources

BBC (2000) *Panorama: Gap and Nike: No Sweat?*, 15 Oct. http://cdnedge.bbc.co.uk/1/hi/programmes/panorama/970385.stm

Hurst, D. (2002) *Crisis and Renewal: Meeting the Challenge of Organizational Change*, Boston, MA: Harvard Business School Press.

Locke, R. (2002) *The Promise and Perils of Globalization: The Case of Nike*, IPC Working Paper 02–007, Cambridge, MA: Massachusetts Institute of Technology Industrial Performance Centre. http://web.mit.edu/ipc/publications/pdf/02-007.pdf

Nike Inc. (undated) 'Responsibility at Nike Inc.'. http://www.nikebiz.com/responsibility/cr_governance.html

Further reading

Beer, M. and Nohria, N. (2000) *Breaking the Code of Change*, Boston, MA: Harvard Business School Press. Particularly chs 10–12, which further explore planned and emergent change.

Stacey, R. (2011) *Strategic Management and Organisational Dynamics*, 6th edn, Harlow: FT Prentice Hall. A comprehensive review of approaches to change.

Tushman, M., Newman, W., and Romanelli, E. (1986) 'Convergence and upheaval: Managing the unsteady pace of organizational evolution', *California Management Review*, **29**(1): 29–44. Explores why organizations may make incremental changes for a long time and then make painful discontinuous shifts.

4 Emotions of Change

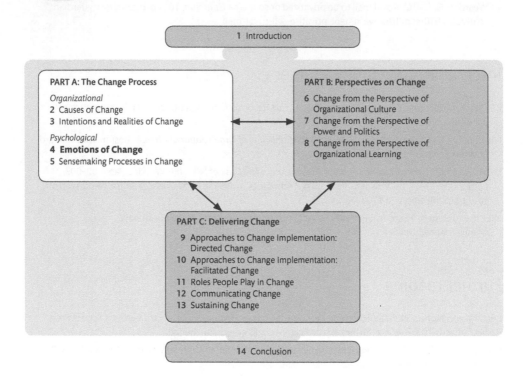

1 Introduction

PART A: The Change Process

Organizational
2 Causes of Change
3 Intentions and Realities of Change

Psychological
4 Emotions of Change
5 Sensemaking Processes in Change

PART B: Perspectives on Change

6 Change from the Perspective of
   Organizational Culture
7 Change from the Perspective of
   Power and Politics
8 Change from the Perspective of
   Organizational Learning

PART C: Delivering Change

 9 Approaches to Change Implementation:
   Directed Change
10 Approaches to Change Implementation:
   Facilitated Change
11 Roles People Play in Change
12 Communicating Change
13 Sustaining Change

14 Conclusion

Fancy what a game at chess would be if all the chessmen had passions and intellects . . . if your knight could shuffle himself on to a new square by the sly; if your bishop, in disgust at your castling, could wheedle your pawns out of their places; and if your pawns, hating you because they are pawns, could make away from their appointed posts that you might get checkmate on a sudden . . . you might be beaten by your own pawns. You would be especially likely to be beaten, if you . . . regarded your passionate pieces with contempt.

George Eliot

 ## Introduction

In Chapters 2 and 3, our focus has been on organizational aspects of the change process. In Chapters 4 and 5, we turn to examining psychological aspects of change and their implications. In this chapter, we consider emotions and change, before focusing on sensemaking and change in the next chapter.

Emotions—both positive and negative—are part of the everyday experience of change for everyone, from those people who lead change initiatives, to those who feel that change has been imposed on them. But textbooks on organizational change have often neglected the emotions involved. We are setting out to remedy this because, in our experience and that of our colleagues, knowledge and practical skills associated with emotional aspects of transitions are essential in dealing with change.

 Main topics to be covered in this chapter

- Different views of emotion, with different implications for emotions in organizational change
- The expression and suppression of emotions during change
- Stage models of emotions of organizational change
- Capabilities to support people through transitions

Section 1: The relevance of emotions to organizational change

The impact of emotions

As you are likely to appreciate from your own experience, the emotions people feel affect them intensely. Emotions in organizational transitions matter not only in terms of employee well-being, but also because they affect behaviour dramatically. Feelings of despair or fear are unlikely to foster cooperation or effective work, but feelings of compassion or enthusiasm may do. Envy, anxiety, or loneliness are unlikely to foster innovation or high performance, while hope, curiosity, or excitement may do. Employee emotions also affect others: colleagues, customers, and clients (not to mention friends and family). So emotions impact directly on the successful navigation of change, whether the change is planned or emergent. A successful restructuring not only involves getting the right people with the right capabilities in the right roles, but also entails establishing commitment and morale, which are underpinned, or can be undermined, by emotions.

When changes are made, everybody involved is undergoing a transition. It is important to appreciate that emotions are not just experienced by those on whom change is imposed. Those who lead change, and those such as middle managers and HR professionals with responsibility for implementing organizational change, may experience transitions as equally emotional. Workplaces develop their own norms regarding which emotions can be expressed—and in which way—with some emotions seen as unacceptable to display. Nevertheless, the emotions of change that people actually feel are not constrained by these organizational norms. Alongside openly expressed excitement and anxiety, for example, might be concealed feelings of fear, hatred, joy, compassion, or fury.

See Chapter 1 for more on change and transition: p. 5

Change in Practice 4.1

Emergent change driven by anger and contempt

In 2003–04, a process of emergent change at the BBC was driven by an emotional dispute between the broadcaster and the UK government about a contentious BBC radio broadcast at the end of May 2003. Early in the dispute, on Friday 6 June 2003, Alastair Campbell, a senior adviser to the Prime Minister, sent an indignant fax to the BBC Head of News:

> I am writing to complain about [your journalist's] irresponsible reporting . . . With regard to the report on the BBC Today programme last Thursday at 0607 (transcript enclosed), can you explain to me how it conforms with the BBC's own producer guidelines . . . You will, I imagine, seek to defend your reporting, as you always do. In this case, you would be defending the indefensible.

In an email to his manager, the editor responsible for the contentious broadcast referred to Campbell's fax contemptuously as 'all drivel' and, in a further email later in the afternoon, suggested that he may have 'gone bonkers', adding:

> For what it's worth, I don't think [he] has anywhere to go on this - he isn't going to shift our story: not by endless transcripts, not by regurgitating producer guidelines.

Similarly, the BBC Director-General was given a copy of the fax and later commented that Campbell 'clearly suffered from verbal diarrhoea'. Emotions like this, of indignation and contempt, were the backdrop to continued escalation of the dispute; government communications were belligerent and, at the BBC, both senior management and the governors failed to investigate the complaints properly. The dispute led to the apparent suicide of a government weapons inspector, followed by a judicial inquiry. Only then did the reporter who had presented the original story admit that his most serious allegations had been 'slips of the tongue'. The inquiry led to a change of leadership and new training procedures at the BBC in 2004, and also contributed to a later restructuring of its governance.[1]

Sadness during planned change

In 2008, the chief executive of a large European law firm made a speech to all employees at the corporate headquarters on the day it was announced that the company was being taken over by a major multinational. His opening words were 'Today is a day of mixed emotions', and he began by acknowledging the end of an era for the organization. So, despite apparently speaking to professional colleagues on a matter of business, his opening words were on the subject of emotions and loss. At the end of his speech, many were in tears—the majority too choked to speak.[2]

Perspectives on emotion

The examples in Change in Practice 4.1 show how emotions can be both drivers of change and consequences of change. But what is an emotion? Frankly, psychologists disagree about this (Fineman, 2003) and we are not going to try to resolve the debate here. However, we will introduce three different views on emotion and discuss why they matter for organizational change practitioners.

Firstly, the **social constructionist perspective** emphasizes that even though emotions may feel like they come from deep inside the individual and represent their authentic self, in fact emotions draw on 'scripts' from societal cultures. The way in which they are expressed, and the settings in which they are felt, are part of these cultures and vary across the world (Heelas, 1996; Lutz, 1988), and indeed from one historical era to another (Stearns and Knapp, 1996).

Moreover, there are often sharp contrasts between the social acceptability of expressing different emotions, not only from one society to another, but also from one organization to another. This view of emotions is important to organizational change practitioners because it highlights: i) that emotional reactions to change may vary internationally and depending on the organization; ii) that employee emotional reactions may be inhibited by conformity with what they see as the norms of acceptable expression; and iii) that modifications in these norms are sometimes one of the objectives or consequences of organizational change.

This perspective would highlight the way in which the dispute between the BBC and the UK government follows quite a familiar pattern in British public affairs of angry, indignant voices and contemptuous responses with little meeting of minds. At the law firm, the social constructionist perspective would suggest that the chief executive's speech shifted the context from one of practical work issues to one of loss and legitimized the voicing of sadness by expressing how he himself felt.

A second perspective on emotions, probably the most dominant in psychology today, is **appraisal theory**. This perspective asserts that an emotion is an internal state triggered by a particular interpretation (an 'appraisal') of a situation, and these emotions in turn trigger behaviour (Lazarus, 1982; Roseman and Smith, 2001). So although this does not say a great deal about the nature of emotions, the principle is that emotions follow after a situation has been understood via a *thought* process, and they prepare us for certain kinds of action in response to the resulting interpretation. In terms of organizational change, emotions would be seen from this perspective as a reaction to the way in which changes or the prospect of change have been understood by people. This view of emotions is important to organizational change practitioners because it highlights how employee interpretations of transitions (and therefore also change communications) influence emotions.

This perspective would suggest that, in the dispute between the BBC and the UK government, people on each side interpreted what was going on—thought that, for example, they were under attack and had been treated unfairly—and that this led to emotions such as anger, indignation, and contempt. These in turn led to unhelpful behaviours such as belligerence or failure to consider the other side's point of view, driving the emergent transition process. At the law firm, appraisal theory would suggest that interpretations of the situation as one of loss, encouraged by the chief executive's speech, led to the outbreak of employee sadness and a temporary suspension of 'business as usual'.

The third perspective that is particularly significant for organizational change practitioners has been referred to by Griffiths and Scarantino (2009) as the **situated perspective** on emotions. The situated perspective views emotions as distinctive ways of engaging with situations—particularly social situations. They are experienced as involuntary (which is why people talk about people *losing* their temper, or *falling* in love) and adjust how people relate to each other (de Rivera, 1977; Parkinson et al., 2005; Griffiths and Scarantino, 2009). This perspective departs from appraisal theory in viewing the interpretations associated with emotions as an aspect of the emotion and not necessarily its cause. That is, instead of always understanding what is happening and *then* becoming, say, angry, happy, hopeful, compassionate, sad, fearful, or indignant in response to this assessment, an approach to understanding the situation can be *part of* the pattern of the emotion (Parkinson, 1997). For instance, as part of getting angry, people are able to critically condemn in a way that might otherwise be alien to their character; or, as part of feeling compassion, a person might realize that somebody needs help.

This view of emotions is important to organizational change practitioners because it draws attention to emotions as a form of engagement with transition—not just a reaction to it—and highlights how, during transitions, emotions influence interpretations and communication as well as the other way around.

The situated perspective suggests that Campbell's anger was a way of organizing a condemnatory stance, just as contempt among counterparts at the BBC was a way of dismissing his protests. It suggests a view of both these emotional reactions as a way in which UK government and BBC protagonists engaged with, and shaped, the emergent changes in the BBC. At the law firm, the situated perspective would draw attention to sadness as a way in which employees allowed the loss to 'come home to them' and could acknowledge the need for support from one another.

The spread of emotion

As well as emotions leading to different patterns of behaviour and interaction and therefore impacting on other people, there is another route through which emotions may influence colleagues and customers. Research evidence suggests that emotions can be directly picked up from other people. This is called **emotional contagion** (Barsade, 2002). Emotional contagion is not fully understood, but it seems that simply being in the vicinity of others' hopelessness or anger or delight can result in those emotions being mirrored in oneself. This has crucial implications for change processes in which, very often, the trajectory of employee emotions is in the balance. If emotions can be 'caught' from one another, there can be a tendency for emotions to resonate right through an organization with impacts—for better or for worse—on which the success of a change programme or, indeed, the future of an organization can depend. For example, at the law firm, widespread sadness in the chief executive's audience may have been only in part directly in response to his speech. When some people became 'choked up', others were likely to follow.

Suppressing and expressing emotions

As a social constructionist perspective emphasizes, societies as well as organizations have regulative **display rules** that establish norms regarding which emotions should be felt and shown, and how they should be shown in particular settings and situations (Averill and Nunley, 1992). Elation displayed at a funeral would be likely to be met with disapproval. Anger in the midst of a family quarrel is often suppressed when the phone is answered to someone outside the immediate family. Similarly, 'displays' of emotions are also required of employees in the workplace, so that this can be regarded as part of what employees are paid for. This is referred to as **emotional labour** (Hochschild, 1983). In Hochschild's original research on emotional labour, she studied airline stewardesses, who were required to smile even when passengers were being abusive. Equally, debt collectors may be rewarded for appearing angry and suppressing feelings of compassion that they have for debtors. Contemporary concerns with customer service, teamwork, and employee well-being mean that changing the boundaries around acceptable—and valued—expressions of emotion may be an important aim of organizational change (Meyerson, 2000). But, in this chapter, we are concerned with the expression or suppression of emotion in the organizational change process itself.

Bryant and Wolfram Cox (2004: 588) give examples from interviews with employees in organizations that have undergone large-scale change, which illustrate the emotional labour involved in transitions:

> I couldn't give a shit about the company before change … but then management dangled a carrot in front of me and offered me a better job and higher pay. But I reckon that was only because I kept my mouth shut when the changes were taking place and for that I was a more worthy employee to have … only after that time did I even contemplate feeling any sort of ties to the place. (George)

> While my manager continues to promote me I'll continue to say how good organizational change was and how great the place is to work for. It's as simple as that! (Jessica)

There is evidence that deliberate displays of apparent emotion may not always remain false. Over time, in some cases, they can lead to genuine feeling (Ashforth and Humphrey, 1993; Parkinson, 1995). George's last sentence in the interview extract above suggests that this may have been the case with him.

Hochschild's research found that employees conduct emotional labour by conforming to display rules in two distinct ways. The first of these is called **surface acting**, which simply means pretending to feel. For example, it would be surface acting if an employee were to smile when he or she is actually annoyed, anxious, or contemptuous; or equally if an employee were simply to hide his or her contempt or, for that matter, his or her compassion. George and Jessica, in the interview extracts above, seem to be describing surface acting.

The second way in which Hochschild found employees complying with display rules is called **deep acting**. This means making an effort to actually experience, or not experience, required emotions. Hochschild describes two approaches to deep acting. One is that employees sometimes exhort themselves, either individually or in conversation with others, to feel a certain way. For example, an employee might try to put his or her cynicism about a change programme to one side and to feel enthusiastic about it; an HR director might try to persuade himself or herself to put compassion to one side and focus dispassionately on the implementation of a redundancy programme 'because it's my job to do so'. Alternatively, Hochschild found that employees sometimes use their imaginations to evoke required emotions. The HR director might try to imagine that he or she was just playing a game, rather than dealing with people's livelihoods, while 'red circling' employees for redundancy.

If emotional labour is a valued aspect of a role to which an employee is committed, then it will lead not to damage, but to enhanced psychological well-being. But emotional labour that is inconsistent with what the employee believes in can create a sense of being inauthentic—of living a lie—with demoralizing consequences (Ashforth and Humphrey, 1993). So, emotional labour can be a source of stress for employees, and whether it is or not depends on the degree to which employees themselves identify with the emotional labour that they are performing. Depending on the values of the employee, emotional labour can have a beneficial *or* a detrimental effect. In research that underscores this, Bryant and Wolfram Cox (2006) find that if employees feel that their negative emotions about organizational change have been suppressed *against their will*, this heightens retrospective negativity about the transition:

> We moved into a new site … before it was [properly] finished … it was like working in a third world country. The paging system wasn't working … we didn't have stock … the bloody phone system didn't even work. So professionally it was frightening … the whole thing was a goddamned nightmare! And if we complained or voiced our anger or annoyance, we were verbally abused.

I got to the point where I no longer cared about what I was actually doing . . . I just acted like everything was okay otherwise I would have been in all sorts of trouble with my boss for not acting in the right ways. (Ibid: 124)

In this way, maintenance of organizational display rules for emotions during transitions, which may be intended to nullify negative feelings, can instead result in negative emotions associated with loss becoming ingrained among an organization's employees.

 Exercise 4.1

Consider a recent experience of yours of organizational change in your workplace, university, or another organization to which you belong.

- Which emotions did you experience during the transition? Make some notes, recalling as many as possible. Here are some to jog your memory (but do not be limited by this set of emotions):

- Select a few of the emotions that you have identified. What were the circumstances in the change process in which you felt these?

- During the organizational change, were these emotions expressed or hidden? Why? How did this affect the situation?

 Section 1 Summary

In this section, we have:

- introduced the social constructionist, appraisal theory and situated perspectives on emotions, and considered how each highlights different implications of emotions in organizational change;

- explained that emotions associated with change can spread within an organization or business unit through emotional contagion;

- examined the emotional labour involved in organizational change, how it is accomplished, and its consequences.

Section 2: Models of adaptation to transition

In Exercise 4.1, you were asked to consider your own emotional experience during organizational transition. We agree with Härtel and Zerbe (2002) that it is a myth that so-called 'negative' emotions have bad consequences and 'positive' emotions have good consequences. You may be able to identify this yourself from the exercise. In this section, we describe theories that look at emotions, including those commonly regarded as negative such as anger and sadness, as natural *reactions* to organizational change or the process of transition. In this sense, these theories are informed by the appraisal theory perspective on emotions. But, as we examine the theories, we will use the situated perspective on emotions to see how the same emotions can also be regarded as adaptations that actually *enable* organizational transitions.

In most models of adaptation to organizational transition, it is recognized that the emotions associated with adaptation to change vary from one individual and one organizational transition to another. There can be many factors that influence differences between individuals' experiences. For example, responses may vary depending on how the particular change affects the individuals, how they themselves are involved in the change process, their personality and resilience, their recent experiences of organizational change, their past experiences of loss, and the extent of their support network inside and outside the workplace (Schlossberg, 1981). For some people affected by an organizational transition, there may be simply an unreserved welcome for change, with loss being experienced with pride, joy, or relief (Stuart, 1995; Wolfram Cox, 1997). An employee's particular responses to organizational change may be idiosyncratic. For example, an employee might be delighted and thrilled with a new direction being set for the organization because it fits with what he or she believes the organization should stand for, or disgusted because it does not. An employee might come to hate his or her manager for making a particular colleague redundant, or be deeply envious of the outcomes of organizational change for other staff. Some employees, throughout the course of a transition, might be in awe of a leader who is taking their company in a new direction.

On the other hand, there are two factors that mitigate individual differences and can establish a tendency for some synchronization of emotional journeys among staff. The first is that members of staff are dealing with shared circumstances of organizational change, and the second is the phenomenon of emotional contagion. As discussed in section 1, emotional contagion means that if some people are experiencing an emotion, say anger, sadness, or excitement, others around them are more likely to experience similar feelings.

Stage models of transition

Is there a pattern of emotion through which people typically progress in response to organizational change? Curiously, much of the exploration of this question originates in a completely separate domain—the experience of death and dying—with the work of Elisabeth Kübler-Ross, a Swiss-born psychiatrist who worked in the US. Kübler-Ross (1969) found that patients with a terminal illness went through a pattern of emotionally charged psychological responses—stages in facing up to their future, as follows.

1. Denial—carrying on as if nothing is wrong
2. Anger—rage, frustration, and resentment
3. Bargaining—acknowledging the situation, but attempting to negotiate more time
4. Depression—mourning for things already lost and lost prospects
5. Acceptance—preparation to move forward

Later, Kübler-Ross found similar patterns in patients who had experienced bereavement. She emphasized that these steps do not necessarily come in this order, can vary greatly in the length of time they last, and some of her patients experienced only some of the stages. Kübler-Ross' work has been picked up by those studying other personal changes that involve loss including, in particular, the study of responses to *organizational* change (Freeman, 1999; Stuart, 1995; Zell, 2003). We discussed in Chapter 1 that organizational change always involves loss or the threat of loss (Bridges, 2003)—whether of a familiar working role, of working relationships, of power or influence, of status, etc. In addition, if people experience change being imposed on them against their will, the loss of autonomy and control can be felt particularly acutely. Many authors have developed models of stages of employee response to organizational change based on Kübler-Ross' work. So what are the personal and emotional impacts of change according to these models?

See Chapter 1

Denial stage

Freeman (1999) points out that, while the word 'denial' sounds like active rejection of information that an employee knows, denial in the context of organizational transition in most cases amounts more to simply ignoring changes or the possibility of impending change. Denial can last hours, days, weeks or even months. Kübler-Ross (1969: 35) herself writes that denial 'functions as a buffer after unexpected shocking news' until the individual can mobilize other resources. Sometimes, employees simply turn a blind eye to the full implications of new developments or hesitate to accept that they themselves will be affected. Stuart (1995: 30) refers to a similar process as 'minimizing':

> 'it's a mistake', 'it could be temporary', 'this wasn't deliberate', 'I don't believe they'll go through with it', 'I can't believe it', 'this isn't happening!', 'it won't have a big impact', 'it won't affect me', 'it's still the same job'

Several authors point out that denial is often preceded by a state of shock. Although this could be regarded as another form of denial, the experience is distinct. When there is sudden news of change, whether good or bad for the individual, the first response may be that of feeling stunned, dazed, or immobilized (Stuart, 1995; Hopson, 1981).

Anger stage

As news of organizational change is absorbed, anger is commonplace. Implicit in anger is a judgement that expectations have not been met—expectations that staff should be able to work without disruption, or of job security, or that people should not have to choose between relocating and losing their job, etc. A related emotion is indignation, which involves a more specific negative evaluation of other people: there has not been only an accidental offence; someone is judged to be culpable or reprehensible. From an appraisal theory perspective, it is these judgements that lead to the anger or indignation. From the situated perspective, it may be emotions of anger or indignation that themselves enable people to 'step out of role' and make harsh judgements.

Should people have the opportunity to express negative emotions such as anger or indignation during organizational transitions, when this may run counter to prevailing display rules? The alternative is to implicitly or explicitly reinforce the requirement for emotional labour. As explained in section 1, unless the employees themselves respect and value the requirement to suppress their emotions, this is likely to lead to a sense of inauthenticity and demoralization, and can lead to an increase in subsequent negative emotions about the transition. So, in the case of either anger or indignation, there is a strong case for change practitioners giving people a chance to vent their grievances. If there is no opportunity to communicate these feelings, or if people feel that candour will be penalized, then the chances of people instead conveying their anger or indignation through rumour, sabotage, and defiance are greatly increased.

Depending on the circumstances, the organization and the losses experienced, the appropriate forum for expression of anger might be a one-to-one or a group meeting. Further considerations are as follows.

1. In order that people realize they have been heard by those who organize or implement the change, it can be helpful to encourage them to be specific, and to acknowledge their grievances with responses that summarize and reflect back what has been heard. For instance: 'In a way you feel that you've ended up in the very tough situation of having an increased workload, but with less opportunity to advance your career.' Often, apologizing is helpful too: 'Understandably, you feel that we've let you down, and I'm sorry.'

2. An advantage of spoken communication over written communication (such as email or intranet) for expressing anger or indignation is that people are likely not to feel so bound by what they have said. They can change their minds as temporary emotions fade and the transition process progresses.

3. It is helpful to clarify the boundaries for expression of feeling. If these are clear, then, often, they will not be resented: for example no raised voices, no swearing, but all views can be put on the table.

4. It can be unhelpful to argue: once you have understood the views to which the transition is giving rise, there will be opportunities for further communication and clarification. If you argue, that may serve only to convince people that you do not care about *their* experience.

Bargaining stage

Attempts at bargaining are another way in which change or the need for change is not faced up to (Freeman, 1999). People may propose unrealistic deals such as higher production levels if plans for outsourcing can be put off for *this* year. Equally—because it is not only at the front line that change can be traumatic—an executive might dwell on the possibility of achieving unrealistic sales targets so that a planned plant closure can be postponed. However, some researchers who have developed stage models of adaptation to organizational change based on Kübler-Ross' work have questioned whether a distinct stage of bargaining can, in fact, be identified (Stuart, 1995; Zell, 2003).

Depression stage

Overall, Stuart (1995) describes the depression stage as 'holding on', referring to holding on to the past, while Freeman (1999) describes it as 'reorientation', reorienting oneself in order to be able to leave the past behind. They are identifying complementary aspects of the experience: the past is held on to, while reorientation takes place. Depression as a stage in individual adaptation to organizational change can, in fact, incorporate a variety of emotions: anxiety, loneliness, sadness, despair, anger, and guilt, as well as depression itself (Freeman, 1999; Stuart, 1995; Hopson, 1981). Here, we focus on sadness and depression because they are characteristic of adjustment to loss and of this stage of adaptation in particular.

If in anger, people identify grievances; in *sadness*, they tend to focus on loss itself. Sadness enables people to reach out for support and comfort, again (as with anger) often stepping somewhat outside the bounds of usual role relationships. Sadness may, or may not, find direct expression in the workplace depending on the individuals involved. Many people may instead find outlets with family and friends outside of work. But many people can reach out to work colleagues, and this can help to build or maintain cohesion during a difficult transition.

According to Solomon (1976: 297), *depression*, despite being a debilitating, painful experience, is people's way of 'shuffling the structures' of their lives:

> Our depression is our way of wrenching ourselves from the established values of our world, the tasks in which we have been unquestioningly immersed, the opinions we have uncritically nursed, the relationships we have accepted.

Viewed like this, depression may be an adaptive and beneficial—if painful—response to important organizational changes. In depression, immediate productivity may suffer: people may be stepping out of the role of diligent focus on business as usual to 'shuffle the structure' of their working life, tasks, and values. As with sadness and anger, willingness to listen is important during depression, but people may not want to let others get too close, so sensitivity to an individual's boundaries is important too.

Acceptance stage

Acceptance is a stage at which losses due to organizational change are accepted and people let go of past realities so that they are ready to move on. Stuart (1995) points to the role of hope, as well as interaction with other people, in shifting from the depression to the acceptance stages. The role of hope here reflects that it is an emotion that enables people to act with conviction when there can be no certainty of success. Kübler-Ross writes that acceptance itself 'should not be mistaken for a happy stage', but, in organizational change, relief is frequently experienced at this stage.

Further stages

Further stages are often added to this kind of model, such as 'testing', 'searching for meaning', and 'moving on/moving away' (for example, by Hopson and Adams, 1976; Stuart, 1995). These stages look beyond the experience of loss to how people take up the challenge of engaging with new organizational realities or roles, or, for that matter, roles in other organizations. During these stages, emotions such as curiosity, confidence, hope, excitement, and enthusiasm may take hold. This does not mean that feelings such as nostalgia and sadness cannot be present; just that they do not inhibit engagement with a new organizational context (Hopson, 1981). Again, from the point of view of appraisal theory, 'positive' emotions could be regarded as reactions to new interpretations of the organizational environment. But from the situated perspective point of view, they would also be regarded as a way in which the transition is achieved. That is, curiosity and confidence allow people to step away from familiar ground to which they might otherwise cling. Hope, as explained in discussion of the acceptance stage above, allows people to believe in and try out new ventures when there is no way of guaranteeing success. Excitement and enthusiasm allow people to put aside inhibitions to committing to goals and task collaboration.

Are stage models 'true'?

The simple answer is that this is an open question. At the beginning of this section, we discussed how individual emotional responses to change may be idiosyncratic, apparently completely at variance with the patterns that stage models propose. Among organizational researchers, there are different views as to whether stage models developed from Kübler-Ross' work, or indeed any models that attempt to find universal patterns in individual responses to organizational change, are valid (Freeman, 1999; Archer and Rhodes, 1987; Fryer, 1985). It is certainly our experience that, when these patterns are in evidence, the stages can span anything from minutes to years. In addition, when changes are coming thick and fast—as they are for many employees in today's organizations—it is often difficult to disentangle the impacts on individuals of a multitude of simultaneous change processes. There are, in fact, clear discrepancies between different stage models, and some authors have changed their minds over the years about the stages through which people go and the order in which they go through them. This suggests weakness in the research underlying the models. It is also difficult to disprove any specific theory since discrepancies between employee experience and particular models can usually be explained by saying that people do not always go through every stage, or can go through stages in different orders. Stuart (1995), whose research is especially thorough in this area, proposes a model of 'change journeys' that is so intricate that it could encompass almost any sequence of emotional responses. Later in this section, we will discuss emotions typically experienced by particular groups (change agents and 'survivors'), but, within those groups too, individual experiences may differ from the patterns described.

Practitioner use of stage models

See Chapter 1 for more on Bridges model: p. 7

Despite doubts about the validity of stage models, they are nevertheless widely employed within organizations and by consultants. Stages of emotional response to transition are sometimes discussed in association with Bridges' (2003) model of phases of transition, which we explained in Chapter 1. Broadly speaking, Bridges' *ending* phase can be associated with

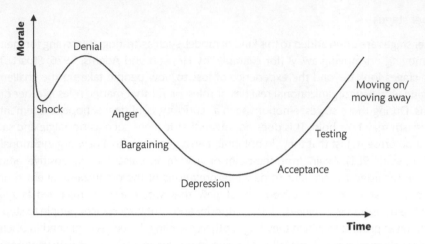

Figure 4.1 Change curve

stages of denial, anger, and bargaining, and the start of the depression stage; Bridges' *neutral zone* phase, with the completion of the depression stage and with the acceptance stage; and Bridges' *new beginning* phase, with the further stages such as testing and moving on/moving away. Often, though, practitioners represent stage models of individual adaptation to organizational change as a '**change curve**' or 'coping cycle', which dips during the initial stages of transition until a low point corresponding to the depression stage, before rising in the acceptance stage, and further stages of individual adaptation to change (see Figure 4.1). Sugarman (2001) points out that there has been considerable confusion over what is represented by the vertical axis in these diagrams. Morale, confidence, competence, performance, self-esteem, and mood have all featured in various published versions.

In our experience, discussion of a stage model with employees—including visual representations in the form of this change curve—can be useful in helping people to adapt to organizational change, even though it is not established that the models are scientifically valid. This is because such models:

See Chapter 12 for more on the change curve: p. 277

- reassure employees that it is normal to experience emotional responses to change;
- may subtly shift the display rules for emotions that are in place, implying that a degree of emotional expression will be accepted;
- may nudge those people who are ready out of denial, by reinforcing the message that change is really happening;
- communicate to staff that it is understood within the organization that they may be feeling and reacting quite differently later on in the transition from the way in which they are feeling and reacting currently;

See later in this chapter and Chapter 12 for more on the interpersonal role of managers: pp. 78–81, 273

- in the context of this 'progression through stages', convey that different employees may currently be experiencing different emotional reactions (which is particularly helpful for managers to recognize, since they may have known about impending change well in advance of their staff and have had time to adapt to it while their members of staff are still struggling);

- give managers a structure within which to appreciate the importance of their interpersonal role during the change process (see section 3).

The example in Change in Practice 4.2 shows how academic scepticism concerning training about emotions was overcome by observing the benefits in practice (see also the end-of-chapter Integrative Case Study).

 Change in Practice 4.2

Training about change emotions

Huy (2002), as part of a study of large-scale organizational change, describes how a line manager had to close five out of nine service centres working with business customers and relocate employees to the other service centres. There was a great deal of anger and also tearfulness among employees, interspersed with periods of calm. Absenteeism increased rapidly. People were 'living on the edge' (ibid: 52). In response, the line manager organized training sessions that addressed emotion and which were delivered to small, separate groups of between twenty and forty employees. Huy asked to observe one of these sessions:

> Employees were encouraged to verbalize in small groups, outside the scrutiny of their superiors, their private feelings about the ways in which change had affected them. Then each group was invited to make a drawing about how it felt collectively, and drawings were displayed around the room. There were drawings of anxious-looking people in lifeboats, of caravans lost in the desert, big thunderstorms, and of a small sun hiding behind black clouds. It was only then that individuals started to realize how similar their feelings were, and they started to laugh and joke about them. (Ibid: 52)

The consultant running the sessions then introduced Bridges' transition model and explained that such emotions were normal. Huy writes that his initial scepticism about the effectiveness of the training sessions subsided as he discussed the effects with participants. People told him that the sessions had helped them to accept their emotions, while actually tending to augment emotions such as calmness and sympathy, and to diminish feelings such as fear and helplessness. The sessions also helped to reduce absenteeism.[3]

 Exercise 4.2

Reflect on the results of Exercise 4.1 in the light of the discussion in this section. Try drawing a 'timeline' of the organizational change and placing the emotions you felt on the timeline.

- How does the pattern of emotions you have noted correspond to, or differ from, the emotions in the stage model described here?
- Can you position your emotions on the change curve diagram, Figure 4.1?

Change agent emotions

Are there distinct experiences that change agents, those responsible for planned change, undergo? Change agents would include those leaders, managers, and HR staff who make or implement key decisions concerning change. Huy (2002) describes the emotions that can be experienced if managers are committed to an organizational change, such as enthusiasm, excitement, hope, and frustration with obstacles. We take this up again in the discussion of 'emotional balancing' in section 3. There may also be anxiety and fear for change agents associated with their personal and professional vulnerability; often, future career prospects are contingent on success (Buchanan and Boddy, 1992). In practice, change agent communication often involves emotional labour.

However, research has also uncovered further aspects of the experience of being a change agent when there are perceived to be detrimental effects on other employees. Clair and Dufresne (2004) and Wright and Barling (1998) conducted research on agents responsible for downsizing programmes and found recurring patterns of emotional responses. Clair and Dufresne (2004: 1608) describe the particular emotionally taxing experiences that 'downsizers' faced:

Deceiving others

One woman came in and said, 'I know I'm going to lose my job.' She was an Office Support Manager. It was a position we could easily do without and she knew that, and I couldn't say anything and she was a good friend of mine too.

Making tough, uncertain decisions

Very difficult . . . when you're making decisions that are as serious as those . . . not having a lot of time to evaluate people . . . a lot of anxiety on my part and the other manager's part because it was not as clean a decision as you probably would have liked to have.

Dealing with others' emotional pain

People—they get upset, they get defensive, they get angry, they cry—it's just very difficult to sit here, at this table, with somebody across from me and tell them the bad news and have them go through all those feelings.

Empathy for victims

I sort of put myself in their shoes. And you know, felt 'Jeez, how would I feel if the same thing happened to me' is really what I kept dwelling on.

Being stigmatised

People stare at you funny, they won't even say 'Hello' to you. You know, they think you made the personal decision yourself . . . What was my name for it? A grim reaper . . .

Wright and Barling (1998) found that, in a first stage of response to these pressures, change agents responsible for downsizing experienced guilt and role overload. In a second stage, the strains of this would create conflict between downsizers' roles at home and at work, and family relationships would suffer. This resulted in emotional exhaustion, and guilt would become ingrained and be accompanied by depression. In a third stage, downsizers would experience loneliness as they isolated themselves from colleagues in the workplace (partly due to the stigmatization described above). Wright and Barling do suggest that if downsizers believe that they have been fair and just throughout the lay-off process, this can ameliorate some of these damaging effects. On the other hand, Clair and Dufresne (2004) present the same phenomenon in a less positive light, seeing a preoccupation with fairness and justice as just one of a number of ways in which, in practice, downsizers distance themselves from their situation in order to cope. These are:

1. Emotional distancing—avoiding compassion and other feelings

2. Telling oneself that harsh outcomes such as redundancy are 'normal' in the commercial world

3. Denying to oneself that injury has actually been caused to the other person

4. A preoccupation with justice and fairness

5. Isolation—physically distancing oneself

6. Sanitizing—dealing with making employees redundant in a routinized and businesslike manner, with minimal opportunities for interaction

If these are the experiences of those responsible for implementing downsizing programmes, what about those others who remain in post after such an organizational 'cull'?

Survivor syndrome

Survivor is a term used to refer to those who remain working for an organization following a disruptive change programme, particularly one involving redundancies. Research suggests that there are particular patterns of emotions and attitudes that are typical of survivors, and these are sometimes called **survivor syndrome**. Brockner et al. (1987) describe studies of the effects on survivors of witnessing other employees being laid off. Their conclusion is that reactions depend on:

- the extent to which the organization (or change agents within the organization—see above) are perceived as having been fair or unfair to dismissed staff;

- the extent to which survivors consider themselves to be similar to the dismissed staff—for example, in terms of role, status and values.

If dismissals, or the procedure leading to dismissals, are considered to be unfair by survivors *and* if survivors identify with dismissed staff, then both survivors' performance and their commitment to the organization are undermined.

As well as undermining performance and commitment to the organization, perceived unfairness in the treatment of dismissed staff can create a sense of guilt among survivors (Stuart, 1995). In some cases, like guilt experienced by change agents, this can be focused on the survivor's actual actions or inaction. However, it can also be concerned simply with the survivor staying while others had to go: 'I'm safe, but, oh God, what about the others . . . I felt guilty . . . what do I say to them?' (Stuart, 1995: 47).

The depth of emotional disturbance that can be experienced by everyone involved in organizational change means that capabilities to support people through transitions are especially important. We turn to these in the next section.

 Section 2 Summary

In this section, we have:

- introduced stage models of emotional reactions to organizational change, and discussed how these emotions may also facilitate change;

- considered aspects of good practice in terms of handling emotions of change;

- examined the validity of stage models and also their use in practice;

- looked at the particular emotional effects of change on change agents and those who are survivors of change events involving redundancies.

Section 3: Capabilities to support people through transitions

Supporting people through loss

See Chapters 5 and 10 for more on involvement in change: pp. 94, 219

See Chapter 12 for more on making the case for change: p. 267

In the previous section, we explained how open discussion of emotions by sharing, for example, stage models or the 'change curve' can have many benefits in preparing people at all levels for change. The approach taken to change communication more generally is also vital, and we will be coming back to this in Chapter 12. As discussed above, the first response to information about an impending change is frequently shock and denial. It can be far easier for people to get over their shock and move through denial if they are involved in planning for change. Establishing a clear case for the changes—that is, a perspective on the organization's internal and external environment that makes change critical—also mitigates shock and denial. However, sometimes, when immediate change is imperative or where changes are emergent and unplanned for, neither of these approaches is possible.

Bridges (2003) recommends anticipating the losses that will be involved in a proposed or imposed change. These may be specific to an individual, and might concern a seemingly minor change such as needing to move his or her office or to join a different team. Other losses may be much less tangible: an aspiration for promotion, a sense of ownership over particular tasks, or a sense of security derived from trusting relationships. Some losses impact everyone in the organization and, again, these may not be immediately tangible: for example, the change might represent a modification or abandonment of familiar organizational values or vision. If ways can be found to compensate people for their losses, then this may be an important symbolic communication even if it does not truly make up for their loss. In any event, it is usually important to treat the past with respect (Bridges, 2003) and not to denigrate previous practices. We have already noted the practical use of the change curve or other representations of stage models to help people through emotions of loss. If a loss is shared widely within an organization, it can be beneficial to acknowledge that in a shared way, through a formal event, ceremony, or ritual (Huy, 2002). The chief executive's speech at the law firm, described in the second part of Change in Practice 4.1, was one instance of this. Here is another, more elaborate, example:

> when a Canadian company was acquired and folded into a former competitor from France, managers from the acquired business invited employees to a church-like ceremony where the company was eulogized by executives and hourly workers alike. Afterward, people went outside and, one by one, threw their old business cards into a coffin-shaped hole in the ground, which was then covered by dirt as a dirge played on a bagpipe. The event may sound ridiculous, but it did serve a healing purpose. Employees said later that they had buried their old company and were ready to embrace the new one. (Frost and Robinson, 1999: 105)

See Chapter 5 for more on ethical evaluations: p. 89

If some people are conspicuous as 'victims' of a change process, those made redundant for example, there are multiple reasons to treat them fairly. Managers may feel that there are ethical reasons to treat staff fairly, and it may also be important for the external reputation of the organization that they are seen to be treated well. But Brockner's research on survivors (Brockner et al., 1995; Brockner et al., 1987), which we discussed in the previous section, implies that it is also important because otherwise remaining members of staff who identify with those who have had to leave will tend to be less committed to the organization and perform less well. Fairness need not be especially costly from an economic point of view (Brockner et al., 1995). It can mean, for instance, providing clear information about how decisions have been reached, treating people with respect, and supporting them with finding new employment. Since the response of survivors depends on their *perceptions* of fairness to dismissed staff, it is important not only that people are treated fairly, but also that the fairness of their treatment is communicated effectively to those who remain with the organization (Brockner et al., 1987).

Dealing with 'toxic' emotions

Frost and Robinson (1999) highlight the danger of ingrained negative emotions in organizations, which they refer to as **toxic emotions**. These originate in prolonged negative experiences, and emotional contagion then supports the ongoing entrenchment of these negative feelings to the detriment of individual employees and the organization. Frost and Robinson highlight organizational change as a common cause of toxic emotions. For example, Eriksson (2004) describes how, after years of radical change programmes, an organization can end up with depressed employees who 'see no future within the organization, they tend to concentrate on failures instead of successes' (ibid: 110):

> I've worked for this company more than ten years and I've seen it all. I can't say that it makes me feel motivated and interested in what's going on in the company. I've felt quite the reverse. You know, there is always something 'new' that has to be done and something 'old' that should be thrown out. But most of it is just boring talk and I don't have much interest in that kind of talk any longer. I have heard it all before. How I feel about it? Nothing, really—just fatigue. (Ibid: 120)

In Eriksson's example, the result of ongoing attempts at transition had been an emotional climate that actually acted as a barrier to organizational change. This means that how transitions are handled is vital not only to the success of any particular change programme, but also to the ongoing capabilities and agility of the organization.

People vary in their capacity and willingness to listen to how other people may be suffering and support them. Frost and Robinson (1999) and Frost (2003) emphasize the important role played by **toxin handlers** (Frost, 2003): staff at all organizational levels who support and protect colleagues who are suffering emotionally, for example, during organizational change, and so prevent the development of toxic emotions. Toxin handling can involve, for example, listening empathetically and finding ways in which to protect other people or to ameliorate painful situations. According to Frost and Robinson's account, the presence of toxin handlers is usually an emergent development in organizations rather than planned. Toxin handlers are rarely acknowledged or supported, and often themselves suffer from stress due to their efforts on colleagues' behalf. So, one important intervention that organizations can make during transitions is to explicitly offer recognition, appreciation, and encouragement to individuals who support others.

Emotional intelligence

In a seminal article on **emotional intelligence,** Salovey and Mayer (1990: 189) define it as 'the ability to monitor one's own and others' feelings and emotions, to discriminate among them and to use this information to guide one's thinking and actions'. Their model views emotional intelligence as integrating abilities in four areas (Mayer et al., 2004; Mayer et al., 2008), as follows.

1. Accurately perceiving emotion
2. Using emotions to facilitate effective thinking
3. Understanding emotion
4. Managing emotions in oneself and others

Since Salovey and Mayer's original work, many alternative definitions of emotional intelligence have been put forward, so that it is not clear that different practitioners and researchers are talking about the same thing when they refer to 'emotional intelligence' (Matthews et al., 2004). Considerable claims have been made about the advantages of having high emotional intelligence, particularly in terms of career success, interpersonal skills at work, and leadership (Goleman, 1995). However, the evidence that has been put forward to substantiate most of these claims is weak or inconsistent (Matthews et al., 2004; Mayer et al., 2004). Nevertheless, it can be clearly seen from the previous sections of this chapter that these kinds of emotion-related abilities are likely to play a key part in enabling people to move through the transitions of organizational change and to support others in moving through those transitions (Huy, 1999). Opengart (2005) suggests that emotional intelligence is also needed to accurately perceive workplace emotional display rules and to manage emotions in order to *comply* with these constraints. In the context of organizational change, there is an additional point that is important too: emotional intelligence abilities may be needed in order to successfully *contravene* emotional display rules—or to enable other people to do so, as discussed in section 2, in order to support them through transitions (Huy, 2002). Overall, the abilities that Salovey and Mayer use to define the concept of emotional intelligence are likely to be valuable in building organizational agility—the capability to change—as discussed in Chapter 3. This is, therefore, a factor to consider in the development of recruitment, as well as training and development, policies.

See Chapters 3, 6, and 13 for more on agility: pp. 53, 123, 301

Emotional balancing

Huy (2002) describes the emotion-related capabilities that enable organizations to successfully undergo radical change. He has looked at the capabilities of middle managers collectively at the level of the organization or business unit. In order for radical change to be successfully achieved, his research suggests that **emotional balancing** is required. This means that:

- some middle managers develop and display emotions reflecting commitment to change, for example enthusiasm, excitement, and hope, as well as frustration with obstacles or those who obstruct change;
- other middle managers attend to the need for emotional support of those who report to them, for example listening to them, addressing their practical needs as change progresses, and helping subordinates to understand and deal with their own emotional responses (as shown in Change in Practice 4.2).

In Huy's study, emotional balancing was an emergent quality in some business units within a larger organization, and it was these units that navigated change most successfully. His research suggests that, in managing change, attention should be given to the *balance* of skills and sensitivities among management staff, rather than necessarily focusing on individual capabilities such as emotional intelligence.

Section 3 Summary

In this section, we have:

- examined organizational strategies for supporting people through loss;
- described toxic emotions, and explained the importance of offering support and encouragement to toxin handlers;
- discussed the value of emotional intelligence and emotional balancing for organizations undergoing change.

Integrative Case Study

With the programme—or not . . .

In 2008, a London-based trading company with offices worldwide decided to offshore to India a significant part of its core back-office capability. Such was the scale of the project that some fifty managers were responsible for different parts of the functions that were to be offshored.

   Although a small number of the managers had known about the plans for some time, most did not know until just days before the public announcement because it was a highly sensitive move that could—and indeed did—directly affect the share price. So the managing director informed the fifty managers simultaneously by conference call late on a Thursday evening. The call lasted an hour, but there were few questions as people struggled to absorb the information.

   The managing director invited the managers to be involved in the delivery of the offshoring change programme, which had to be executed within three months of the date of the announcement. He said it would be a highly pressurized three months, dealing with both the technical complexities and with the people in the roles to be offshored, who would face redundancy—few were likely to transfer to India with the work. He invited the managers to attend a two-day retreat the following week, to 'explore openly what would be involved in being part of the change programme'. The managing director stressed that all would have a truly free choice about whether to participate and that if they were to choose not to do so, their decision would not affect their jobs because there was a need to keep other projects on track over this period. He was clear that the most important thing was for each manager to decide whether he or she was 'with the programme' or not. If the manager were 'with the programme', he or she would need to commit wholeheartedly, work through the process, and 'stay on message at all times'. The managing director wanted their answers by the end of the retreat.

All of the managers attended the retreat. The managing director opened the meeting with a short speech, passionately declaring his determination to succeed in this change. He said nothing about how the planned change would impact on the futures of the managers themselves, and for the rest of the morning no one asked. The HR manager then took over the process. Her focus was the exploration of the emotional aspects of dealing with change on this scale. She used a stage model of adaptation to organizational transition based on Kübler-Ross' work to talk through the emotional responses that the managers might face as they informed their own teams of the change. Then she drew 'the change curve' in masking tape on the floor and invited the group to stand on the curve—to express how they themselves felt about the change at that moment in time. All fifty positioned themselves somewhere in the second half—that is, in the process of acceptance and being ready to move on, despite still knowing nothing about the implications that the change would have for them. The managing director expressed delight and left the meeting, promising to return for its close the following day.

The group worked on in a subdued manner. Finally, after lunch, someone stood up and asked the managing director's deputy if he knew the impact that the change would have on their own job security. The deputy conceded that he did not know, but that the managing director had gone to join the board, which was considering the issue that very day. This unleashed a torrent of questions. The anxiety in the room was palpable as people started to voice reservations about the plan, and horror at their lack of involvement until now. The HR manager gave them space to talk and try to make sense of the implications of the change. As they closed the session for the evening, she invited them to stand again on the change curve on the floor—to express how they felt in light of the afternoon's discussions. All fifty positioned themselves at the early stages of the change curve—they were confused, angry and anxious, and wanted to negotiate some holding position with the managing director.

The following day, as the group worked on, the HR manager helped them to examine what had happened, and to explore what it had been like to be asked to respond without knowing the implications of the situation for themselves, why they had suppressed their real emotions, and how difficult it had been for them to work effectively in doing so. They began to plan their meetings with their own teams in light of this experience. When the managing director returned that evening, all but two of the fifty managers were ready to sign up; they were 'with the programme'.

Questions

1. What do you think may have been the explanation for the managing director's silence about the managers' future in the conference call and his initial speech at the retreat? How would you have handled this?

2. How could the managers' own lack of questions about their future, and how they positioned themselves as in the process of 'acceptance and being ready to move on' during the first morning of the retreat, be explained?

3. At the end of the second day, assuming that the managers were frank about being 'with the programme' (that is committed to involvement in the delivery of the change), consider whether, in terms of the change curve, they were necessarily then at the stages of acceptance or being ready to move on.

4. Which aspects of behaviour described here would you see as reflecting emotional intelligence, or a lack of emotional intelligence?

Conclusion

Overall, in this chapter, we hope to have conveyed the importance and complexity of inter-actions between organizational change and employee emotions. We believe it is essential for all those involved in leading, managing, or implementing organizational change to develop their understanding of these interactions, and to use that understanding to guide their own behaviour.

 Please visit the Online Resource Centre at **http://www.oxfordtextbooks.co.uk/orc/ myers** to access further resources for students and lecturers.

Change in Practice sources

1. Myers, P. (2007) 'Sexed up intelligence or irresponsible reporting? The interplay of virtual communication and emotion in dispute sensemaking', *Human Relations*, **60**(4): 609-36.

2. Based on personal experience.

3. Huy, Q. N. (2002) 'Emotional balancing of organizational continuity and radical change: The contribution of middle managers', *Administrative Science Quarterly*, **47**(1): 31-69.

Integrative Case Study sources

Based on personal experience.

Further reading

Fineman, S. (2003) *Understanding Emotion at Work*, London: Sage.
Steve Fineman's book is a good, and very accessible, introduction to emotions in the workplace, and features a chapter on organizational change.

Stuart, R. (1995) 'Experiencing organizational change: Triggers, processes and outcomes of change journeys', *Personnel Review*, **24**(2): 3-87.
This three-part article is a classic account of research into people's emotional responses to organizational change.

5 Sensemaking Processes in Change

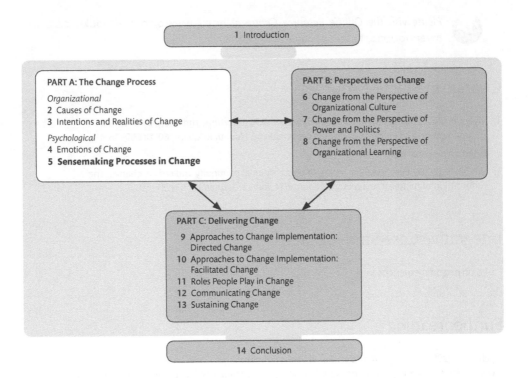

1 Introduction

PART A: The Change Process

Organizational
2 Causes of Change
3 Intentions and Realities of Change

Psychological
4 Emotions of Change
5 Sensemaking Processes in Change

PART B: Perspectives on Change

6 Change from the Perspective of
  Organizational Culture
7 Change from the Perspective of
  Power and Politics
8 Change from the Perspective of
  Organizational Learning

PART C: Delivering Change

9 Approaches to Change Implementation:
  Directed Change
10 Approaches to Change Implementation:
  Facilitated Change
11 Roles People Play in Change
12 Communicating Change
13 Sustaining Change

14 Conclusion

The hills are shadows, and they flow
From form to form, and nothing stands;
They melt like mist, the solid lands,
Like clouds they shape themselves and go.

                              Tennyson

 ## Introduction

Here, in the second of our two chapters exploring psychological aspects of the change process, we shift the focus from emotions in organizational change, how things are felt, to how things are *understood*— and how this relates to the way in which people in organizations behave. Change always involves people in the challenge of understanding what is happening: as in the poem above, solid lands in people's minds 'melt like mist' and new lands, new ways of seeing things, need to be established. The process of under- standing, the factors which influence it, and the impact that it has are our focus in section 1.

In section 2, we look at organizational sensemaking, the way in which behaviour and thinking interact. Sensemaking plays a fundamental part in organizational change because—as we explain—key aspects of change such as trust, choice, and engagement can be viewed as sensemaking. In section 3, we then consider strategy, deliberate and emergent, as a process of sensemaking.

 Main topics to be covered in this chapter

- How change is understood
- Organizational sensemaking
- Strategy as sensemaking

Section 1: 'What's going on?' How transitions are interpreted

People are continuously engaged in understanding or interpreting what is around them. Frequently, the same situation means very different things to different people. Most of you will know only too well, from your own experience, how this can lead to '*mis*understanding' and miscommunication, a topic we come back to in Chapter 12. In familiar situations, an individual can often understand the physical and social environment automatically using **mental models** (sometimes called 'schemata') (Harris, 1994; Walsh, 1995; Nonaka, 1991): habitual ways of understanding situations. You may find yourself easily able to interpret your manager's behaviour, and its implications for how you act; or to understand the meaning of a set of figures about the performance of your business unit (including implications for your own job security or promotion prospects), and to adjust your behaviour accordingly. Mental models also provide the basis for people's initial understandings of the context, content, and process of change.

See Chapter 1 for more on context, content, and process: p. 5

Understanding change over time

It is characteristic of change that, as people face unfamiliar situations, their mental models take time to adapt. In Chapter 1, we introduced Bridges' (2003) account of how people understand organizational transitions, in which employees are said to experience a phase of ending, then a phase of reconstructing their thinking that he calls the neutral zone, followed by the more solid lands of a new beginning. Isabella (1990) describes in more detail the patterns of understanding that people experience over time as they participate in an organizational transition.

Although Isabella's research focuses on managers in organizations undergoing change, we think that the stages she identifies—anticipation, confirmation, culmination, and aftermath—are applicable to employees more generally. In the first stage, **anticipation**, people pick up (and spread) rumours, develop and share hunches, gather scattered information, and, as they realize something is afoot, are left without a clear understanding of events. In a second stage, **confirmation**, they begin to relate what is happening to their past experience and develop explanations for what is happening now based on this, so that there is some standardization of understanding for individuals and in conversation between people. In the third stage, **culmination**, these understandings are amended as people compare past and present, and new explanations and mental models are constructed. In this stage, symbols

See Chapter 6 for more on symbols: p. 117

are particularly important in guiding and developing new understanding. According to Isabella, in a fourth stage, **aftermath**, people take time to evaluate the changes that have taken place in terms of their consequences, their strengths and weaknesses, the winners and losers, and so on.

Similar provisos apply here to the ones we discussed in Chapter 4 in relation to stage models of emotional responses to organizational change, and the 'change curve'. The stages Isabella identifies may not be present for everybody or in all episodes of organizational change. Real-world changes also often involve multiple adaptations in understanding, with interaction and conversation repeatedly leading to new mental models, so that the pattern of anticipation, confirmation, culmination, and aftermath becomes cyclical (Balogun, 2006; Balogun and Johnson, 2005). Moreover, in large-scale change programmes, mental models may alter in different ways and at different paces in various divisions of the organization (Stensaker and Falkenberg, 2007; Balogun, 2006).

But, when the model is applicable, there tends to be an association between patterns of emotion and patterns of understanding, which we show in Figure 5.1. From the appraisal theory perspective on emotions, the emotions are caused by the interpretations. That is, as people come to a view about what is happening and what they may be losing in the confirmation stage, they can respond with anger or depression. As they revise their understandings in the culmination stage, emotions such as hope or curiosity are triggered, which are hallmarks of 'acceptance' and 'testing'. From the situated perspective on emotions, new understandings are themselves an aspect of the emotions. As part of becoming angry, people are able to face up to the realities of what is going on. In depression, they are able to amend their understandings and move from confirmation to culmination. Curiosity, confidence, hope, and excitement can enable people to engage with what has altered, as well as with their new roles and opportunities.

See Chapter 4 for more on the change curve: p. 74

See Chapter 4 for more on appraisal and situated perspectives on emotions: p. 65

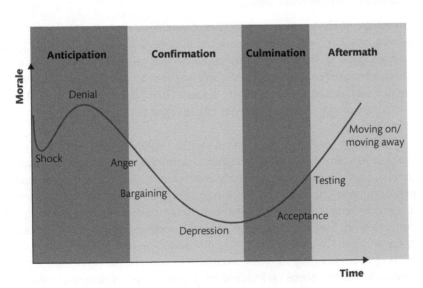

Figure 5.1 Stages in understanding

Change in Practice 5.1

One change becomes another

Greenberg (1995) described her experience at a small, but rapidly growing, US consultancy with 150 employees. In consultation with the chief executive, a decision was made by the senior vice president in charge of consulting to restructure because he 'could no longer effectively manage all the staff and the clients'. Prior to this, the consultants were managed in a matrix structure, with each consultant having both a career manager and reporting to a project manager during the tenure of specific consulting projects. Ten middle managers acted as both career managers and project managers. There was a considerable degree of unity and cohesiveness among the consultants. People worked in project teams, but also collaborated across teams, helping each other to meet deadlines and to ensure success, and they were rewarded with bonuses based not on success of individual projects, but on the organization as a whole achieving profit goals.

The restructuring plan was to divide the consultants into two groups. Adopting the corporate colours, these were called the 'Blue Group' and the 'Grey Group'. Two vice presidents were appointed to lead these groups: an internal appointee for the Grey Group and an external appointee for the Blue Group. At a meeting officially announcing the restructure, the senior vice president emphasized that he did not want competition between the groups, but one of the consulting staff asked whether the groups' names, Blue and Grey, referenced the Civil War (in the American Civil War, 1861–65, these were the colours of the uniforms of the opposing sides). In the months that followed, the vice presidents leading the two groups developed quite different meeting styles: the Blue Group meetings were relaxed and informal; the Grey Group meetings, formal and structured. The groups began to understand the situation in terms of 'disunity and competition' (ibid: 195). When there was a shortage of consultants, they engaged in a 'struggle over the borrowing and loaning of staff' (ibid.). The vice presidents stopped greeting one another even though their desks were close. When they met with the senior vice president, it was in a glass conference room and tensions between them were on full view to other staff. A rumour spread that the vice presidents' bonuses would be linked to the profitability of their individual groups. Strikingly, the senior vice president and CEO did not intervene in this way of understanding the new structure, and the competitive, antagonistic dynamic between the two groups became entrenched. A 'civil war' had indeed materialized.[1]

In Change in Practice 5.1, the importance of emergent understandings can be seen. In the confirmation stage, people understood the new formal structure of the organization and the *intended* outcome: division of the consulting staff into two collaborative groups for administrative purposes. But, in this case, the change did not work out as intended. In the culmination stage, mental models of the real, informal outcomes were developed: the working climate was dependent upon which group consultants had been assigned to, and there was a shift from unity and cohesiveness to division and competition.

In the next section, we will focus on the concept of 'sensemaking', which combines understanding and action. Before that, we highlight three specific aspects of employee mental models that impact on understanding change: the psychological contract; ethics; and the metaphorical 'framing' of change.

The psychological contract

One aspect of employees' mental models that influences how organizational change is interpreted is their **psychological contract**. In the developed world, at least, most employees have a formal contract of some kind. But as everyone knows, to our cost or our delight, the formal contract does not necessarily delineate the boundaries and expectations people face in the workplace, and what they expect from their employers. The psychological contract is a term for these real-world expectations: a subjective, implicit agreement between an individual and his or her employer. Rousseau (1995) points out that the psychological contract is a mental model that employees develop over time. From the employees' side, the development of the psychological contract begins to happen before people even enter a particular workplace, through the absorption of professional and societal norms. But it is during the recruitment process that people really lay a foundation for what they expect from their employers and, conversely, a foundation of commitment in terms of what obligations they feel they have toward their employers. Usually this mental model is refined rapidly during an employee's early days with an organization, both through his or her own active information seeking and through active induction efforts by his or her employer. People soon learn whether a 35-hour week in the written contract translates into a norm of working from early morning until 8pm. Later, once they have 'learnt the ropes', the psychological contract develops more slowly or more intermittently. At the consultancy described in Change in Practice 5.1, the original psychological contract of the consultants may have included unity and cohesiveness across the whole organization, and bonuses based on profit goals for the company as a whole.

People *experience* the psychological contract as if it were based on promises (Rousseau, 2001). Promises in this sense can be explicitly made, for example written down in the contract of employment, or verbally stated: 'I'm going to put you in charge of this project'; 'I will make sure you get away from work by 4pm on Thursdays and Fridays so you can pick up your child from school.' Or promises can be experienced as made implicitly. If you initiate and take charge of a project in its initial stages, you may feel implicitly promised that your leadership of it will continue. If you have been leaving work, with your manager's blessing, at 4pm on Thursdays and Fridays for the past year, you may feel implicitly promised that that can continue. Similarly, if other parents have been granted this kind of flexibility, you might feel implicitly promised that your employer will see that as part of its obligation to you when your child reaches school age. Significantly, it is in the nature of the psychological contract that it is believed to be mutual—that is, employees are likely to believe that their employer shares their view of what should be expected of them and what are the employer's reciprocal obligations, whether or not this is really the case.

See Chapters 1 and 4 for more on losses during charge: pp. 7, 78

When organizational changes occur, whether deliberate or emergent, people understand whether the impact on them—including losses—is reasonable or unreasonable through the prism of the psychological contract. When the implicit promises of the psychological contract (as understood by the individual) are broken, this is referred to as a **psychological contract violation** (Turnley and Feldman, 1999), and can lead to deterioration in the relationship between employer and employee.

The lesson of this for change agents is that they need to appreciate the nature of employee psychological contracts. In Chapter 4, we explained Bridges (2003) recommendation to *anticipate* the losses that will be involved in a proposed or imposed change. In order to achieve this, understanding employees' psychological contracts and potential associated losses is vital. Handy (1993) distinguishes between calculative, cooperative, and coercive psychological contracts. A **calculative psychological contract** is based on the exchange of work for the satisfaction of needs, such as money, social and career opportunities, promotion, training, and a sense of achievement. A **cooperative psychological contract** is based on employees identifying with the perceived goals of the organization, and having a voice in the selection of those goals and how they are achieved. A **coercive psychological contract** is established when individuals are working completely against their wishes. In, for example, an area with little other employment, people may experience themselves as simply forced to work on an employer's terms. In practice, psychological contracts are normally a blend of these different types. That said, the losses and gains that will be experienced by employees in an organizational transition are likely to be very different depending on which type of psychological contract is in play. In a calculative psychological contract, people's interpretations of changes are likely to be sensitive to issues of perceived fairness. In a cooperative psychological contract, people's interpretations of changes are likely to be sensitive to issues of influence and autonomy. In a coercive psychological contract, once established, people may interpret an employer's attempts at change simply in terms of compulsion and control. These interpretations of change in turn affect which kind of changes, or ways of handling transitions, are likely to evoke 'resistance'.

See Chapter 7 for more on resistance: p. 150

Ethics

Another key aspect of the mental models through which people interpret what is going on during a transition is their ethical framework—that is, they evaluate situations in terms of what they believe is morally right and wrong. According to Steare (2009), depending on the individual and the situation, ethical frameworks can be based on *ethical values*, on *rules*, or on *consequences*. If people in the consultancy company in Change in Practice 5.1 had used rules, such as legal or professional frameworks, in evaluating right and wrong, then the vice presidents' behaviour might have been judged wrong because senior managers feuding in public would be seen as unprofessional. If people had focused on consequences for the majority of people in terms of benefit and harm, then the impact on company value, or clients, or employee morale might be foregrounded. If people had applied ethical values, they may then have interpreted the behaviour of the vice presidents as wrong because it was disrespectful or irresponsible. Values—standards to which people aspire—can be pragmatic, based on what the individual considers preferable or effective, such as maintaining investment in research and development, or ethical, based on what the individual thinks is morally right (Dose, 1997), such as, in this case, respect and responsibility. In the next chapter, we discuss how individual values are influenced by organizational culture, and become shared values. But, whether or not associated with their organizational membership, people's ethical values strongly influence how they interpret what is happening during an organizational transition and how they respond to it. It has been suggested (Kidder, 2005, cited in Gentile, 2010) that some ethical values, such as honesty, respect, responsibility, fairness, and kindness, are more-or-less universal and would therefore influence everyone's understanding of organizational

See Chapter 6 for more on *shared* values: p. 118

change processes. Whether change is on a very small scale, such as relocating an individual's office, or on a large scale, each of these ethical values may be at issue.

In Change in Practice 5.1, ethical frameworks may converge, but there are other situations in which choices need to be made between two or more options, neither of which seems 'right' (Badaracco, 1997). For example, depending on the ethical framework adopted, the choice faced by an HR executive about whether or not to reveal to his or her best friend that the friend's job is in jeopardy (Steare, 2009) might be understood as a conflict between a value for loyalty or kindness and a value for responsibility. Or it may be understood as a conflict between values and rules, or between values and consequences for other employees.

See Chapter 14 for more on ethics and change: p. 320

These issues can be complex to resolve. But, in any event, even when their ethical evaluation is clear, standing up, or speaking up, for what they believe is right may not be easy for people. Gentile (2010) calls this the challenge of 'giving voice to values'. The apparent failures of respect and responsibility at the consultancy company in Change in Practice 5.1 may have been perceived as wrong by many people, including the senior vice president and the chief executive as well as junior staff, yet they were not addressed. As Gentile points out, actively responding to ethical concerns may require astute selection and timing of approaches: when, for instance, to question, to persuade, to insist, to negotiate, to lead by example, or to find allies. Your own approach, in the context of organizational change, may depend on your attitudes to risk, your preferred communication styles, your status, your role in the change process, the strength of your network, your loyalty to or dependence on the organization, and your communication skills and experience. As Gentile says, it usually becomes easier with practice.

 Exercise 5.1

Consider a time when you were dealing with change in an organizational, educational, or voluntary setting, and what you were expected to do was at odds with what you thought was right, and in one way or another you stood up for what you believed in.

- What did you do and what was the impact?
- How pleased were you with your response and what, if anything, would you have liked to have done differently?

Now consider a time when you were dealing with change, and what you were expected to do was at odds with what you thought was right, but you think you did not stand up for what you believed in.

- What happened?
- How pleased were you with your response and what, if anything, would you have liked to have done differently?

What made it easier or encouraged you to act in the first situation, and more difficult or discouraged you in the second situation? What can you learn from this about the factors that influence how you resolve ethical dilemmas during organizational change? (Based on Gentile, 2010)

Metaphors: Framing and reframing change

A **metaphor** is a description or a way of looking at a thing (or situation) as if it were something else. Morgan (2006) points out that use of metaphor frames people's mental models of organizations, even if they are not aware of it. For example, when people think or talk about an organization as *smooth-running*, it is implicitly being compared to a machine. When people think or talk about the *growth* of an organization, it is implicitly being compared to an organism. Each of these implicit metaphors directs people's thinking about their organization and organizational change. If, for instance, an organization is compared to a machine, that directs people's thinking towards one set of possibilities for organizational change. Where, for example, can the levers that control it be found? Are the cogs meshing together well? If, on the other hand, the organization is compared to a growing organism, that may direct people's thinking toward another set of questions around change. What will this life form be like when it is fully grown? How can we nurture it? How does it reproduce? The point is not that some organizations are machines and some are organisms: they are neither. The point is that any organization has some similarities to a machine, and some similarities to a living organism. Each metaphor highlights some features and obscures others.

Explicit use of metaphor is also extensive in the way in which people refer to organizations and organizational change. Over recent decades, there has been great interest in the use of these metaphors in organizations and how they can direct or constrain thinking about change. Metaphors used to describe change, the various components of change, the causes of change, and the players involved in change or impacted by it, affect how the need for change and changes themselves, are understood and acted upon. Dunford and Palmer (1996: 97) explain the impact in these terms: 'metaphors provide a central role in defining action as legitimate, necessary, maybe even as the only 'realistic' option for a given situation.' For example, in Change in Practice 5.1, the emergent metaphor of 'civil war' became embedded in mental models of the consultancy company, making it only too easy to view the developing situation and the options open to the protagonists in terms of competition and conflict.

 Section 1 Summary

In this section, we have:

- considered the phases of understanding through which people pass during organizational change;
- discussed understanding during organizational transitions against a background of psychological contracts, ethics, and metaphors.

Section 2: **Sensemaking—linking understanding and behaviour**

Some authors have used the term 'sensemaking' to refer to the process, discussed in section 1, of people coming to an understanding of what is happening around them (Greenberg, 1995)—that is, interpreting situations. However, in the way in which we will use the term, sensemaking is not simply a passive process of understanding change. How situations are understood by people informs how they behave, while their own behaviour can itself direct the way in which they understand situations. We now move from a simple focus on 'understanding' to a focus on *sensemaking*, this interplay of understanding and action.

What is sensemaking?

Weick (1995: 13) points out that as well as interpreting situations in organizations, people also 'generate what they interpret' through their actions and reactions. So, rather than referring simply to understanding what is happening, **sensemaking** has been adopted as a term for this more powerful concept, used to describe the way in which people establish interpretations *and* link them with their own actions. Through sensemaking, people create plausible explanations—explanations that seem reasonable to them—linking up their actions and their beliefs about what is happening (Weick, 1995; Maitlis, 2005). Crucially, these explanations do not need to be objective, but they do need to be credible to the people doing the sensemaking. In Change in Practice 5.2, we give an example in which this process of building plausible, but not necessarily objective, links between behaviour and beliefs is particularly clear.

 Change in Practice 5.2

Belief trumps potential for change

Kärreman and Alvesson (2001) described a 'news bill meeting' at a Swedish evening newspaper. These meetings were held once a month to discuss the content of the street billboards used to advertise the paper. Unlike every other type of meeting held at the paper, these meetings involved all senior editors, even those with the day off, together with the billboard copy-editors: about twenty people in all. Around the walls were placed examples of recent billboards that had been 'best-sellers' and 'disasters'. During the meeting, no correlation could be found between the quality of news bills and the resulting circulations. Other factors that might have affected sales were flagged up, including inclusion of a TV guide, the day of the week, proximity to paydays, celebrity gossip, unemployment, the weather, and competitor behaviour. However, discussion of these other factors was used only to mask the evidence that billboard headlines did not drive sales. Remarkably, Kärreman and Alvesson, one of them present in the meeting and with a complete tape-recorded transcript, could find no coherent attempts at analysis or decision-making. Instead:

> The premise around which the news bill meeting—at least on a superficial level—circles, is simple and is present in almost every utterance during the meeting, one way or another: *news bill content sells.* (Kärreman and Alvesson, 2001: 77)

In fact, at one stage the sports editor did question the premise, but heated interjections quickly restored the status quo. As another participant said: 'You simply can't say that [billboards] don't sell.' While, on the face of it, the meeting could have been used to analyse the situation and change the approach to newspaper marketing, it instead ensured the continuation of effort put into producing billboards and belief in their influence.[2]

For those involved in the evening newspaper meeting in this case study, focus on the billboards was reasonable given the belief in their importance, and belief in their importance was reasonable given that meetings to focus on them had been given such a high priority for so long. People did indeed have plausible explanations linking their actions and beliefs.

The sensemaking process

In practice, sensemaking is a social process (Weick and Roberts, 1993; Maitlis, 2005) in two respects. *Firstly*, explanations need to be socially acceptable (Shotter, 1989; Weick, 1995). At the news bill meeting in Change in Practice 5.2, this meant that people needed to construct a *business* case for the billboards. It would have been a socially unacceptable explanation that billboards must continue to be produced, and meetings held to discuss them, because that kept editors in a job or because the billboards were a fun bit of street furniture. In the consultancy company described in Change in Practice 5.1, each of the feuding vice presidents are likely to have justified his behaviour to himself and others, in terms of the failings, inadequacies, or misdemeanours of his adversary rather than, for example, in terms of hostilities simply being enjoyable. This depends on the social setting, of course: in a boxing match, for instance, other rules would apply to what makes a socially acceptable explanation for fighting. *Secondly*, sensemaking is a social process in that people's explanations linking their actions, and their beliefs about what is happening are shared, negotiated, and contested in the interactions between people (Currie and Brown, 2003; Sims, 2003; Weick et al., 2005). For example, in the consultancy company described in Change in Practice 5.1, an explanation that linked antagonistic behaviour patterns with a belief that the company had competitive consulting groups gradually prevailed in a contest for acceptance. Correspondingly, explanations that would have seen antagonistic behaviour patterns as anomalous exceptions, based on a belief that the consulting groups were still working collaboratively, lost ground.

People's own identity is intimately bound up with the processes of sensemaking. Faced with organizational transition, roles as a committed colleague, a compliant employee, a union activist, a change agent learning new skills, or a family breadwinner facing up to the threat of possible redundancy may all be accessible to you. Which of these is more salient will have a considerable effect on what is foregrounded for you as the transition progresses, on how you interpret events, and on how you respond. Weick (1995: 24) explains:

> What the situation will have meant to me is dictated by the Identity I adopt in dealing with it. And that choice, in turn, is affected by what I think is occurring . . . I derive cues as to what the situation means from the self that feels most appropriate to deal with it, and much less from what is going on out there.

Sensemaking is often routinized using mental models. This is clear in the case of the 'news bill meeting' described in Change in Practice 5.2. People knew how to understand what was happening, and how to 'go through the motions' of being an effective participant, with some coherence between beliefs and actions. But how do people cope with change or with other unfamiliar scenarios? According to sensemaking theory, these situations, characterized by uncertainty or ambiguity, tend to interrupt this habitual sensemaking (Weick, 1995). Then, individually or collectively, people re-establish links between what they are doing and what they are thinking (Helms Mills, 2003). Weick (1995) points to four ways in which this is accomplished. In two of them, people change what they do as a result of what

See earlier in this chapter for more on mental models: p. 85

they are thinking. In the other two, people change what they think as a result of what they are doing.

Changing what you do as a result of new thinking

● Discussion based on changed beliefs can lead to agreement on new actions.
  For instance, in response to figures convincing them that sales are falling precipitously, senior managers may decide to launch a marketing campaign, to cut back production, or to invest in new product development. Or, following discussion of the flaws in a proposed change programme, staff may agree on action to oppose it.

● Changed expectations can lead to active, but selective, information gathering as a basis for further action.
  For instance, after coming to the view that a project team is unlikely to succeed, a leader might take note of its shortcomings, but not its strengths, reallocate resources accordingly, and thereby ensure the team's failure. Conversely, having been convinced that there is a prospect of success, the leader may note the team's achievements, throw his or her weight behind its initiatives, and thereby ensure the expected success. This is often called a 'self-fulfilling prophecy'.

Changing what you think as a result of what you are doing

● Action is taken that leads to a clearer situation, more easily interpreted.
  For instance, unsure of which of two strategies to proceed with, a leader may proceed with one (or pilot one), revealing hidden flaws or benefits, clarifying his or her beliefs, and making decisions easier. Or, faced with the task of implementing a new IT system, people may try it out and, through trial and error, realize how it can best be used, the benefits it brings, and the pitfalls for which to watch out (Stensaker et al., 2008).

● People can *retrospectively* discover beliefs that justify their actions. Weick (1995: 135) puts it this way: 'Committed actions uncover acceptable justifications for their occurrence.'
  For instance, people who have worked very hard for change in an organization may, on finding that the primary benchmarks they set for success are not met, 'discover' new measures of success or new justifications for the programme.

Choice

This last sensemaking process, retrospectively discovering beliefs that explain or justify actions, is called **behavioural commitment**. Behaviour that is public, irrevocable, and voluntary forces people to explain themselves, so that they require explanations to justify it (Weick, 1995). This kind of sensemaking helps to explain why involving people in change leads to more commitment. It might be tempting to explain 'buy-in' to change of this sort by saying simply that people like to be involved. Sensemaking provides a powerful alternative explanation: involvement deprives people of an explanation for their behaviour. If changes are imposed on people, they can explain their participation by thinking: 'I had no choice about this.' In that case, loss of autonomy and control can be felt particularly acutely, especially if there are elements of a cooperative psychological contract (see section 1 of this chapter). But if somebody *chooses* to participate in taking change forward, then he or she needs to find

See earlier in this chapter for more on types of psychological contract: p. 89

another explanation for his or her behaviour. This is where behavioural commitment comes into play. The more choice they have about change, the more people rely on 'commitment' or 'interest' to explain their actions to themselves—even if the commitment and interest are discovered retrospectively when people see what they are saying and doing (Weick, 1995). In these instances, people become committed because they are working for change, rather than the other way around.

Escalation of commitment

However, there is a dark side to behavioural commitment. This kind of sensemaking process means that once people—typically managers and leaders—embark on a course of action voluntarily and in a clear and public manner, changing their minds becomes increasingly difficult. This phenomenon is called **escalation of commitment**: the more people go through for a particular course of action, the more convincing they make their reasons for pursuing it (Salancik and Pfeffer, 1978; Staw and Fox, 1977). If a change project is failing, it is commonplace for the decision-makers behind it to reason more fervently that it was, and is, the correct course to pursue; conversely, it is difficult for them to recognize that a mistake has been made. Paradoxically, the theory predicts that the more challenging and difficult a project has been, then the more likely people are to think that it was appropriate to pursue it. This is particularly the case if they are personally responsible for negative consequences. Even more seriously perhaps, ethical values may adapt to current behaviour, so that behaviour previously seen as unethical begins to be thought of as acceptable. We return to escalation of commitment in Chapter 8, when we look at barriers to organizational learning, and in Chapter 13, when we look at the sustainability of change.

See Chapters 8 and 13 for more on escalation of commitment: pp. 178, 308

For example, it may have been especially difficult for the newspaper employees in Change in Practice 5.2 to recognize that the billboard meetings were fatuous *because* they had been responsible for conducting them for so long. The vice presidents in the consultancy company in Change in Practice 5.1, whose conflict was doing so much damage, may have been continuing with their action partly because they were themselves responsible for the damage. Equally, the senior vice president and chief executive may not have seen the consequences of their passivity, precisely because it was so damaging. Or their ethical sense of responsibility may have diminished, so that their current neglect seemed justifiable. The key point here is that this is not just a matter of saving face; escalation of commitment means that sense is made of the situation in a way that is consistent with previous behaviour rather than current challenges (Staw and Ross, 1987).

Emotions and sensemaking

In section 1, we discussed how patterns in the *interpretation* of change set out in Isabella's (1990) model correlate with the stages in the emotions experienced during transitions discussed in Chapter 4. The situated perspective on emotions that we introduced in Chapter 4 helps to explain how the more complex concept of *sensemaking* relates to emotions experienced during organizational transitions. According to the situated perspective, emotions are experienced as involuntary and allow people to engage with situations and to relate to others in distinctive ways—making temporary adjustments in how they interpret situations and

See Chapter 4 for more on the situated perspective on emotions: p. 65

how they behave in them. Through anger or contempt, the vice presidents in the consultancy company described in Change in Practice 5.1 could refuse to talk to one another, row in public, undermine one another's work, and no doubt think of one another in very disparaging terms, and yet maintain a sense of their role as professional managers—the emotion providing an explanation for what they were doing when, otherwise, linking this with what they believe about the role of a professional manager might be difficult (Myers, 2007). Similarly, 'carried along' by curiosity, excitement, enthusiasm, or hope, people can engage with tasks they had previously rejected or in situations in which prospects of success seem minimal—the emotion providing an explanation for what they are doing when, otherwise, explaining themselves might be difficult. In practice, sensemaking and emotions usually intertwine as people explain their actions to themselves and others, so that the meanings that change has for people are infused with both thinking and feeling (Fineman, 2003; Myers, 2005).

 Exercise 5.2

Recall an occasion on which changes in an organization had a powerful emotional impact on you, positive or negative. It could be change in an organization in which you are an employee or customer.

● Write some brief notes that explain your conduct.

● To what extent does your account explain what you said and did in terms of voluntary choices, based on what you normally believe, and to what extent does it explain what you said and did in terms of emotions, experienced as involuntary?

Sensegiving

In the case of the consultancy company in Change in Practice 5.1, it is clear that unmanaged sensemaking processes within the company established new meanings for the split into two divisions. It illustrates how the 'best-laid plans' are subject to unmanaged, emergent sensemaking processes, impacting both individual experience and the organization. What had been notionally about a structural change and effective management had become about a shift from internal cooperation to competition. What was striking in this case is that, although the senior vice president emphasized at the outset that he did not want competition between the groups, the alteration in how the restructuring was interpreted was then neglected at all levels of management, from the chief executive and the senior vice president in charge of consultancy, to the vice presidents appointed to run the Blue Group and the Grey Group. This highlights the need for **sensegiving** (Maitlis and Lawrence, 2007; Gioia and Chittipeddi, 1991). Sensegiving, sometimes called 'the management of meaning', refers to active efforts to influence the way in which events are interpreted in organizations. This is a key leadership task that we discuss further in Chapter 11.

See Chapter 11 for more on sensegiving: p. 248

Trust and engagement

Trust

Trust is an important factor in successful change because voluntary change involves vulnerability in moving from familiarity into Bridges' (2003) 'ending' and 'neutral zone' phases. Rousseau et al. (1998: 395) define trust in this way: 'Trust is a psychological state comprising the intention to accept vulnerability based upon positive expectations of the intentions or behavior of another.' This definition combines both trusting beliefs (that is, the trustor's positive expectations of the intentions or behaviour of a trustee) and the intention of trusting action (that is, the trustor's intention to accept vulnerability) (McKnight and Chervany, 2001). Trust then is a form of sensemaking, a link people make between their actions and beliefs about somebody else. Likewise, distrust is a psychological state in which people link their *reluctance* to accept vulnerability to their *negative* expectations of the intentions or behaviour of someone else (Lewicki et al., 1998).

See Chapter 1 for more on Bridges' phases of transition: p. 7

Often, during transitions, breaches of trust create an ambiguous situation in which an employee's trusting beliefs are challenged so that the link between those beliefs and their own trusting behaviour is under threat. What happens then? According to S.L. Robinson et al. (2004), there tend to be two patterns that can emerge. In one, which Robinson et al. refer to as 'love is blind', the trustor's thinking adapts to his or her trusting behaviour, and he or she finds new ways to explain the trustee's actions, new beliefs that avoid seeing that the betrayal has taken place. For instance, an employee might trust his manager, and she may have promised to tell him if there are any plans in the offing that might affect his job security. Now he finds that she has known for the past three months that he would be made redundant this year and has not told him. However, he finds ways in which to maintain his trust. He finds it easy to accept her apology and to believe her explanation that legal impediments prevented her informing him. Or he comes to believe that she spent the last few months fighting for his post to be retained. In a second pattern, which Robinson et al. refer to as 'hell hath no fury', the trustor's beliefs change, and his or her behaviour adapts to this new thinking. The betrayed former trustor recognizes that the (former) trustee has not lived up to expectations; he or she switches into distrust, and selectively gathers information to support this view of the trustee. The employee in the previous example might follow this pattern not only by switching into distrust for his manager, but by selectively gathering information that demonstrates just how untrustworthy she is: indications, perhaps, that she has really been plotting against him for years while he has naively trusted her.

 Exercise 5.3

Think of a time when you trusted someone in authority, and he or she let you down.

- What was the nature of the issue and can you define how he or she let you down?
- What were your thoughts, emotions, and actions in response? Does this correspond to one of the patterns that Robinson et al. proposed: 'love is blind' or 'hell hath no fury'?
- What has happened to your attitudes to the person since?

Employee engagement

Kahn (1990) defines **employee engagement** as people expressing themselves in their work physically, cognitively, and emotionally, or being 'fully there', as Kahn (1992) put it. The degree to which involvement *in change* can be physical, cognitive, and emotional varies, of course, between change projects and from task to task within a change project. After Change in Practice 5.3, we discuss how engagement is associated with sensemaking involving *beliefs* that your work is meaningful, that it is safe to express yourself in the workplace, and that you have the personal resources to commit fully to your work, and *behaviour*, involving discretionary effort, support for colleagues, and proactivity.

 Change in Practice 5.3

'Diversity' in flux

In January 2010, IBM, the multinational technology conglomerate, was named employer of the year by Stonewall, the UK charity dedicated to campaigning for the rights of gay, lesbian, and bisexual people. Brendan Riley, the CEO for IBM in the UK and Ireland, said: 'At IBM, we pride ourselves on delivering a working environment which reflects equality of opportunity and experience for all. Diversity constitutes our character, our identity and ultimately our success—it is in our DNA.' This is an unusual statement of identity: what does it mean, and how did it arise?

IBM's commitment to equality of opportunity can be traced back to a policy letter, dated 21 September 1953, written by the company's then long-term president, Thomas J. Watson, Jr:

> The purpose of this letter is to restate for all of the supervisory personnel of the IBM Company the policy of this corporation regarding the hiring of personnel with specific reference to race, color, or creed . . . It is the policy of this organization to hire people who have the personality, talent and background necessary to fill a given job, regardless of race, color or creed. If everyone in IBM who hires new employees will observe this rule, the corporation will obtain the type of people it requires, and at the same time we will be affording an equal opportunity to all in accordance with American tradition.

At the time, Watson wanted to strengthen his hand in a negotiation with southern states of the US about siting a factory there without separating black and white employees. The focus changed from equal opportunities to valuing diversity following Lou Gerstner's appointment as CEO in 1993. This began with Gerstner's perception that his senior executive team did not reflect the diversity of IBM's customers and employees. In 1995, IBM established eight diversity task forces focused on distinct employee groups: Asian employees; black employees; employees with disabilities; white male employees; women employees; gay, lesbian, bisexual and transgender employees; Hispanic employees; and Native American employees. Each consisted of fifteen to twenty senior managers from within the group, but had a senior vice president as an executive sponsor who was not necessarily drawn from the group. They were to report back on what needed to be done in order for employees from the group to feel welcome and valued, and to maximize their productivity, and what IBM should do to persuade consumers from the same group to buy from IBM. This began a transition from seeing diversity as an internal issue to seeing diversity as a 'bridge between the workplace and the marketplace' (Thomas, 2004: 103).

Thomas (2004) records initial employee scepticism and conflicts over priorities within the task forces. Indeed, even Lou Gerstner had been sceptical when his vice president with responsibility for diversity had proposed the task forces. However, under the pressure of a six-month deadline to

report back, each task force came up with specific, agreed recommendations, which were subsequently implemented. The recommendations taken forward included providing benefits for partners
(from the gay, lesbian, bisexual, and transgender task force), improved access to company buildings
and technology (from the disabilities task force), groups for teenage girls to encourage their interest in
science and mathematics (from the women's task force), a marketing unit to focus on female and
minority-owned businesses, and an increased R&D focus on accessibility of technology. Following
this, IBM set up local and regional diversity councils. Grass-roots networks also emerged as employee
initiatives to address the needs of specific groups.

Subsequently, diversity as a core value and as a marketing strategy became increasingly central to
IBM's internal and external image. The fiftieth anniversary of Thomas J Watson's letter about equality
of opportunity within IBM was celebrated on its website and in a YouTube video. More recently,
those original equality initiatives are referred to as 'Diversity 1.0', while the changes based around
valuing diversity are described as 'Diversity 2.0'. In 2008, senior leaders launched 'Diversity 3.0', a
programme that again added new connotations to diversity in the company. Goals included: cultural
awareness; new community initiatives (such as a parent community and a cross-generational wiki);
addressing needs of local geographic and business units; and clearer employee–senior management
partnership structures to address diversity issues. [3-13]

Kahn (1990) and May et al. (2004) found three *beliefs* or 'psychological conditions' associated with engagement at work: meaningfulness; safety; and availability. **Psychological
meaningfulness** is a belief that you are making a difference by expressing yourself at work.
In the case of IBM, the change programme provided opportunities for people to involve
themselves in the diversity project and to make a difference through, for example, the task
forces and grass-roots networks, and also the outcomes of the project revolved around the
difference that people make through their diverse selves. **Psychological safety** is a belief that
you can reveal and be yourself without fear of negative consequences. At IBM, this seems to
have been a central aim of diversity policy over the years. **Psychological availability** is the
belief that you possess the physical, emotional, and psychological resources to personally
engage despite the challenges and distractions (Kahn, 1990). At IBM, this would have depended on whether people involved in change programmes, for example the task forces
that were set up, had the personal resources to focus on them.

Other researchers associate distinctive *behaviour* patterns with engagement, as follows.

- **Discretionary effort** (Macey and Schneider, 2008) means taking on work not is not
  strictly part of your job role.

- **Organizational citizenship behaviour** (D. Robinson et al., 2004) means going out of
  your way to help colleagues in the workplace.

- Proactivity or 'taking charge' (Morrison and Phelps, 1999) —voluntary and constructive efforts
  to proactively change the way in which you work for the better.

Harter et al. (2009) present evidence that engagement of employees is positively correlated
with organizational performance. Accepting the validity of this finding would not imply a
cause-and-effect relationship between engagement and performance. The connection
could be the other way around, with high levels of organizational performance fostering employee engagement. Equally, other factors might be bringing about both engagement and
high performance. Nevertheless, the behaviours associated with engagement—discretionary

effort, support for colleagues, and proactivity—are often associated with successful organizational change. So whether high performance is caused by, or causes, employee engagement, we think it is usually beneficial for the accomplishment of organizational change. But it is worth noting that employee engagement is not a panacea: it supports, rather than ensures, effective change. After all, people can be potentially as fully engaged in rearranging the deck chairs on the *Titanic* as in getting people safely in the life rafts or in building a whole new ship.

 Section 2 Summary

In this section, we have:

- examined the nature of sensemaking as a dual process of understanding and action;
- explained the implications of emotions, choice, trust and distrust, escalation of commitment, and sensegiving for sensemaking in transitions;
- looked at the concept of engagement and its relevance to organizational change.

Section 3: Strategy and sensemaking

It is not our intention here to give a full account of strategy, but simply to set out some key concepts that relate to strategy and organizational change, and to clarify the links between strategy, sensemaking, and change.

Strategy and change

A strategy is often regarded as an overall plan for the long-term direction of an organization or one of its business units 'that integrates an organization's major goals, policies and action sequences into a cohesive whole' (Quinn, 1998: 5). However, it has long been observed in organizations that patterns of strategic choices are only in part deliberate (Mintzberg, 1987; Quinn, 1998). While, sometimes, intended strategy defines and structures the direction of an organization, sometimes aspects of intended strategy are not taken forward, or are not implemented successfully. Moreover some of the patterns that can be found in the long-term direction of an organization are not deliberate: they emerge and can be retrospectively viewed as strategy, and indeed sometimes are adopted retrospectively as the official strategy (see Figure 5.2). Mintzberg (1994: 25) suggests that **strategy**, in practice, is a mix of deliberate plans and emergent patterns:

> few, if any, strategies can be purely deliberate, and few can be purely emergent. One suggests no learning, the other, no control. All real-world strategies need to mix these in some way—to attempt to control without stopping the learning process. Organizations, for example, often pursue what may be called *umbrella* strategies: the broad outlines are deliberate while the details are allowed to emerge within them.

From this point of view, strategy development can be regarded as sensemaking. That is, it is a combination of the retrospective interpretation of what is taking place, and planned or emergent courses of action that create the events which are subsequently interpreted. For

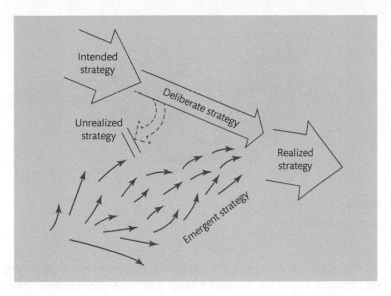

Figure 5.2 Intended and emergent strategy
Source: Mintzberg et al. (2009)

example, in the consultancy company in Change in Practice 5.1, the intended strategy of dividing the business into two cooperating units was overwhelmed by an emergent strategy of establishing competition. Change in Practice 5.3 illustrated a much more successful strategy development process at IBM.

Some models of the process of strategy formation focus primarily on careful planning, implementation, and evaluation (Mintzberg et al., 2009; Porter, 1996). The history of IBM's diversity strategy could superficially be viewed in that way—as the successful development of strategy over time through planning, action, and evaluation. However, this model of strategy formation is incomplete in several ways. *Firstly*, as we have described, strategy is often partially discovered retrospectively rather than planned in advance. This was the case in Change in Practice 5.3. At IBM, the intended strategy of promoting diversity to support innovation and marketing has been broadly realized and, in fact, has played an increasingly strong part in the identity of the organization. However, what 'promoting diversity' actually means at IBM has gone through a number of iterations—developed and refined by emergent factors—while, within the umbrella strategy of diversity, a plethora of projects have emerged.

Secondly, many authors have pointed out the importance of a **vision**, an image of the future of an organization, in inspiring and motivating the development of strategy and its implementation. For example, in Chapter 8, we explain how the capability to envision new futures is central to Peter Senge's (2006) concept of a 'learning organization', and in Chapter 9, we explain how John Kotter (2007/1995) sees a powerful coalition creating a vision for change as central to successful transition. Hurst (1986) highlights the part played by imagination in developing a vision.

Thirdly, Hurst et al. (1989) and Raelin (2006) point to the role that the leadership team in an organization can play in weaving strategic achievements (and failures) into coherent narratives—a storyline for the organization. This is a form of sensegiving in relation to strategy

See Chapters 8 and 9 for more on the importance of developing a vision: pp. 186, 212

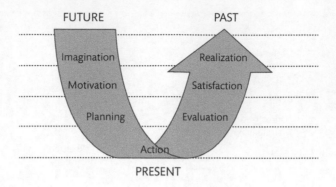

Figure 5.3 Strategy from future to past
Source: Based on Hurst et al. (1989)

that they call **realization**. The concept of realization augments Mintzberg's concept of **realized strategy**, shown in Figure 5.2. Realized strategy is not only about patterns of actions, but also about the patterns of actions that are actually highlighted in organizational conversations. These patterns can be seen as IBM developed and redeveloped its diversity strategy through stories told about the past as well as plans for the future.

Hurst et al. (1989) use the idea of vision as a precursor to strategic planning, and realization as a necessary conclusion to it, to develop the model of top-team involvement in strategy shown in Figure 5.3. This model shows the formation and implementation of strategy as a journey from a potential future to a remembered past. In the first stage, imagination plays a key role as a vision is developed. In the second stage, motivation plays a key role as the vision is translated into specific objectives. Then planning, action, and evaluation stages are followed by the emotional impact being taken on board and, finally, the 'realization' stage—that is, the responsibility to find a narrative on which further strategic cycles can rest.

Fourthly, as well as the role of emergent strategy, vision in strategy formation and realization—the role of the leadership team in highlighting the strategic story—others have pointed to strategy formation as a more distributed function in organizations. We explained in Chapter 3 how a complexity perspective on emergent change leads to a view that nobody can be really 'in charge' of organizations. Leaders can only provoke change, listen carefully to what is happening in response, and make sense of what is emerging. The role of realization is clearly present from this perspective too, but much less emphasis is put on leaders developing a vision and controlling the planning and implementation process. Mintzberg (1989; Mintzberg et al., 2009) describes this as a 'grass-roots' model of strategy formation, contrasting it with a 'hothouse' model of leadership only from the top:

See Chapter 3
for a complexity
perspective on
emergent change

> strategies can take root in all kinds of places, virtually anywhere people have the capacity to learn and the resources to support that capacity . . . [they] become organizational when they become collective, that is, when the patterns proliferate to pervade the behavior of the organization at large . . . New strategies, which may be emerging continuously, tend to pervade the organization during periods of change, which punctuate periods of more integrated continuity . . . To manage this process is not to preconceive strategies but to recognize their emergence and intervene when appropriate . . . Management must know when to resist change for the sake of internal efficiency and when to promote it for the sake of external

adaptation. In other words, it must sense when to exploit an established crop of strategies and when to encourage new strains to displace them. (Mintzberg et al., 2009: 205–6)

The impact of strategy on engagement with change

Do organizations need deliberate strategies and the planned change associated with them? While it has been argued that organizations with clear strategies are higher performing (Porter, 1996; Seurat, 1999), this does not necessarily mean that the former causes the latter. It could equally be that high-performing organizations develop clear strategies. According to Weick (2000), the importance of emergent change—incremental 'accommodations, adaptations, and alterations' (ibid: 237), which *add up* to fundamental change—is neglected because the small, often unnoticed, changes involved are not seen as 'heroic'. He argues that as much, or more, is achieved this way than is achieved through transformational change. He proposes that the requirements for successful change actually depend on its impact on people. In particular, he asks the following questions.

- Does the change programme get people animated and experimenting?
- Does it provide a direction for people?
- Does it encourage people to pay close intention to what is happening and to update their understanding?
- Does it facilitate respectful, candid communication?

This corresponds closely to aspects of *employee engagement*, but with an additional emphasis on candid social interaction—for which *trust* will be an essential precondition.

Weick goes so far as to claim that it 'makes no difference what [change] program they choose to implement, because any old program will do' (ibid: 233), so long as the change programme animates people, provides a direction, encourages updating, and facilitates respectful interaction. In Mintzberg's terms, the organization can then realize a strategy, discovered retrospectively. Weick explains that it is emergent incremental change that is more likely to create the conditions for this kind of sensemaking. His position is that while planned, transformational change may get people moving and provide direction, it will not encourage experimentation or facilitate candid communication, and will not necessarily encourage people to update their understanding.

At the heart of this perspective on strategy is the idea that it is not until action is taken that people realize what they are doing, or discover the information that they need in order to make informed decisions. In his 1987 essay, 'Substitutes for strategy', Weick illustrates this with a story adapted from an account by the Hungarian poet Miroslav Holub:

> The young lieutenant of a small Hungarian detachment in the Alps sent a reconnaissance unit into the icy wilderness. It began to snow immediately, snowed for two days, and the unit did not return. The lieutenant suffered, fearing that he had dispatched his own people to death. But the third day the unit came back. Where had they been? How had they made their way? Yes, they said, we considered ourselves lost and waited for the end. And then one of us found a map in his pocket. That calmed us down. We pitched camp, lasted out the snowstorm, and then with the map we discovered our bearings. And here we are. The lieutenant borrowed this remarkable map and had a good look at it. He discovered to his astonishment that it was not a map of the Alps, but a map of the Pyrenees. (Weick, 1987: 222)

He concludes that, perhaps, when you are lost, 'any old map will do', and when you are confused, 'any old strategic plan will do'. On this view, the challenge that leaders face is not to come up with a plan that is right in every respect, but to produce a credible plan and to enable people to develop it by experimentation. In our experience, leaders have found this story helpful in understanding that the primary importance of a strategy may not reside only in the planned outcomes, but also in engaging, and building trust among, employees who can then help to refine or revise the strategy over time. We take up these issues again in Chapter 8, when we look at organizational learning, and in Chapter 10, when we look at facilitated change programmes.

See Chapter 8 for more on strategy: pp. 181, 183

 ## Section 3 Summary

In this section, we have:

- discussed the connections between strategy, sensemaking, and change;
- looked at the impact of strategy on engagement with change.

 ## Integrative Case Study

Googling with China

Google was formed by two PhD students from Stanford University, Sergey Brin and Larry Page, who had developed new Internet search technology. With an initial investment of US $100,000, from one of the founders of Sun Microsystems, Google began as a start-up technology company in California in the autumn of 1998. Brin and Page rapidly gained investment of US $25 million from two venture capital firms. Google became a public company through an 'initial public offering' (IPO) in the summer of 2004, although Brin and Page maintained control through ownership of special shares. By this time, Google was by far the world's most popular search engine. From the year 2000, Google had a revenue stream from text-based advertising, which appeared in a separate column next to search results. In 2005, they introduced a system of placing adverts on other websites, sharing revenue with the content providers.

Google explicitly set out to be a business that was different from the norm. Its IPO letter to potential investors in 2004 began boldly: 'Google is not a conventional company. We do not intend to become one.' This letter also encapsulated the company's well-known 'Don't be evil' injunction, which had been proposed and adopted at an early staff meeting:

> **DON'T BE EVIL**
> *Don't be evil. We believe strongly that in the long term, we will be better served—as shareholders and in all other ways—by a company that does good things for the world even if we forgo some short term gains. This is an important aspect of our culture and is broadly shared within the company.*
> [Bold and italics in original]

Google's internal HR practices have been designed to engage employees in innovation. Famously, for example, engineers can take 20 per cent of their time to focus on their own projects. It is claimed that over half the company's product innovations each year, including Gmail and Google News, began life in this '20 per cent time'.

China was a huge potential market for Google, with a fifth of the world's population as well as a rapidly growing number of Internet users: 103 million by 2005. However, Internet information flow into and out of China had to pass through a state 'firewall' system that blocked connection with certain sites. In addition, the government had used the Internet to track down and prosecute dissidents. In the early 2000s, Google hosted its Chinese-language service from the US. However, the national firewall often slowed the connection from China to Google and contentious links in the search finds were blocked. In 2004, the Chinese authorities shut down the connection entirely for two weeks. Meanwhile, Baidu, a rival Chinese search engine company, had a rapidly growing share of the market, considerably exceeding Google's.

The Chinese government would agree to a mainland-based service only if Google censored search results at source. In a move that has been subject to much public criticism in the West, in January 2006, Google set up a Chinese language operation, Google.cn, acceding to the government demands. In a speech, Google CEO Eric Schmidt explained: 'We concluded that although we weren't wild about restrictions, it was even worse to not try to serve those users at all. We actually did an "evil scale" . . .' Of course, defining what 'Don't be evil' means in practice was never going to be easy. Once, when asked what it meant, Schmidt is said to have replied that evil is 'whatever Sergey says is evil'.

Four years on from the 2006 move, however, Baidu was still more successful than Google in mainland China. Then, on 12 January 2010, Google announced that the previous month:

> we detected a highly sophisticated and targeted attack on our corporate infrastructure originating from China . . . we have evidence to suggest that a primary goal of the attackers was accessing the Gmail accounts of Chinese human rights activists . . . We have decided we are no longer willing to continue censoring our results on Google.cn, and so over the next few weeks we will be discussing with the Chinese government the basis on which we could operate an unfiltered search engine within the law, if at all. We recognize that this may well mean having to shut down Google.cn, and potentially our offices in China.

The Chinese government did not agree to the operation of an unfiltered search engine and Google announced that it would redirect searches from Google China to Google Hong Kong. Hong Kong is a Chinese territory, but has a different political system from mainland China and an independent judiciary. The Google redirect went into operation on 23 March. However, the Chinese authorities duly threatened to withdraw Google's licence to operate as an Internet content provider if this continued. On 30 June 2010, Google compromised, stopped the redirect, and instead simply put a link to Google Hong Kong on its Chinese site. For the Chinese mainland public, while search results were not censored directly, some links were once again inoperable, as they had been in the early 2000s.

Questions

1. If you had 20 per cent of your work time to dedicate to projects of your own choosing, would that make you more engaged with your current work (as an employee or as a student)? In which ways might your organization change if everyone in your position had a day a week to work on his or her own projects?

2. What do you think is meant by doing an 'evil scale' as Eric Schmidt explained had been done at Google in relation to dealings with China? Have a go at drawing up a scale of good and evil yourself, and using it to assess the various ways in which the company did business in China.

3. Imagine you are Eric Schmidt and consider what processes of sensemaking were involved in the decisions about Google's China operation, in 2001, 2006, and 2010. What did you believe, how did you behave, and how did you explain how your actions and beliefs matched up?

4. To what extent can you identify Google's intended strategy, emergent strategy, and realized strategy in relation to the Chinese market during this period?

Conclusion

In this chapter, we explored how change disrupts the way in which people understand their organizations and their relationship with them, and how new understandings emerge during change. New understandings in turn drive and constrain the direction of change. We then looked at how sensemaking connects action and beliefs, and the part played by engagement, trust, and choice in sensemaking, during organizational transition. In the third part of the chapter we looked at strategy—intended, emergent, and realized—as a sensemaking process.

The four chapters in Part A of this book—two on organizational aspects of the change process and two on psychological aspects of the change process—should be seen as a cohesive whole. We have referred to the intimate associations between the emotional aspects of change discussed in Chapter 4 and the processes of understanding and sensemaking discussed here. In Chapters 2 and 3, we looked at causes of change, and at intentions and realities of change. The organizational dynamics we examined there drive the psychological dynamics we have been exploring, and are driven by them.

In the next part of the book, Part B, we re-look at organizational transitions through the prism of three theoretical perspectives: culture; power and politics; and organizational learning. Each perspective will illuminate different aspects of what change consists of, what makes it happen, and what hinders it.

 Please visit the Online Resource Centre at **http://www.oxfordtextbooks.co.uk/orc/ myers** *to access further resources for students and lecturers.*

Change in Practice sources

1. Greenberg, D. N. (1995) 'Blue versus gray: A metaphor constraining sensemaking around a restructuring', *Group & Organization Management*, **20**(2): 183–209.

2. Kärreman, D. and Alvesson, M. (2001) 'Making newsmakers: Conversational identity at work', *Organization Studies*, **22**(1): 59–89.

3. IBM (1953) 'Policy Letter #4'. http://www-03.ibm.com/employment/us/diverse/50/downloads/eo-policy-letter.pdf

4. IBM (2008) *2008 Corporate Responsibility Report*. http://www.ibm.com/ibm/responsibility/ibm_crr_downloads/pdf/2008_IBMCRR_FullReport.pdf

5. IBM (2009) *2009 Corporate Responsibility Report*. http://www.ibm.com/ibm/responsibility/IBM_CorpResp_2009.pdf

6. IBM (undated) 'Diversity 3.0: A new charter'. http://www.ibm.com/ibm/responsibility/diversity.shtml

7. IBM (undated) 'Diversity 3.0: Leveraging our differences for innovation, collaboration and client success'. http://www-03.ibm.com/employment/us/diverse

8. IBM (undated) 'Heritage'. http://www-03.ibm.com/employment/us/diverse/heritage_ibm_1990.shtml

9. IBM4diversity (2010) 'Why IBM works', Short film. http://www.youtube.com/watch?v=au8OIXXHnyk &feature=player_embedded

10. Stevens, M. (2010) 'IBM wins Stonewall equality list top spot: Technology company is first in diversity index for second time since 2007', *People Management*, 13 Jan.

11. Stonewall (2010a) 'Diversity champions Scotland: The journey towards LGB equality', PowerPoint presentation. http://www.stonewall.org.uk/other/startdownload.asp?openType=forced&documentID=2311

12. Stonewall (2010b) 'Stonewall Top 100 Employers 2010: The Workplace Equality Index'.http://www.stonewall.org.uk/at_work/stonewall_top_100_employers/default.asp

13. Thomas, D. A. (2004) 'Diversity as strategy', *Harvard Business Review*, **82**(9): 98–108.

Integrative Case Study sources

BBC News (2010) 'China condemns decision by Google to lift censorship', 23 Mar. http://news.bbc.co.uk/1/hi/8582233.stm

BBC News (2010) 'Timeline: China and net censorship', 23 Mar. http://news.bbc.co.uk/1/hi/world/asia-pacific/8460129.stm

Google (2004) '2004 Founders' IPO letter'. http://investor.google.com/corporate/2004/ipo-founders-letter.html

Google (2006) 'Google's "20 percent time" in action', *The Google Official Blog*, 18 May. http://googleblog.blogspot.com/2006/05/googles-20-percent-time-in-action.html

Google (2010) 'A new approach to China', *The Google Official Blog*, 12 Jan. http://googleblog.blogspot.com/2010/01/new-approach-to-china.html

Lawrence, A. T. (2009) 'Google, Inc.: Figuring out how to deal with China', in E. Raufflet and A. J. Mills (eds) *The Dark Side: Critical Cases on the Downside of Business*, Sheffield: Greenleaf Publishing, pp. 250–67.

Pink, D. H. (2009) *Drive: The Surprising Truth about What Motivates Us*, New York: Riverhead Books.

Radia, R. (2010) 'China renews Google's license', *The Technology Liberation Front*, 9 July. http://techliberation.com/2010/07/09/china-renews-googles-license/

Stone, B. and Barboza, D. (2010) 'Google to stop redirecting China users', New York Times, 29 June. http://www.nytimes.com/2010/06/30/technology/30google.html

Vise, D. A. and Malseed, M. (2008) *The Google Story*, Updated edn, London: Pan.

Further reading

Mintzberg, H., Ahlstrand, B., and Lampel, J. B. (2009) *Strategy Safari: The Complete Guide through the Wilds of Strategic Management*, 2nd edn, Harlow: FT/Prentice Hall.
A tremendously valuable strategy book—great background, but no specific change focus.

Rousseau, D. M. (2004) 'Psychological contracts in the workplace: Understanding the ties that motivate', *Academy of Management Executive*, **18**(1): 120–7.
A concise, accessible article on psychological contracts.

Weick, K. E. (1995) *Sensemaking in Organizations*, Thousand Oaks, CA: Sage.
The classic account of organizational sensemaking—wise and insightful, but a bit inaccessible. A book to dip into and chew over, rather than to read at one sitting.

Weick, K. E. (2000) 'Emergent change as a universal in organizations', in M. Beer and N. Nohria (eds) *Breaking the Code of Change*, Boston, MA: Harvard Business School Press, pp. 223–41.
A very thought-provoking chapter that links change, strategy, and employee attitudes.

Part B

Perspectives on Change

6

Change from the Perspective of Organizational Culture

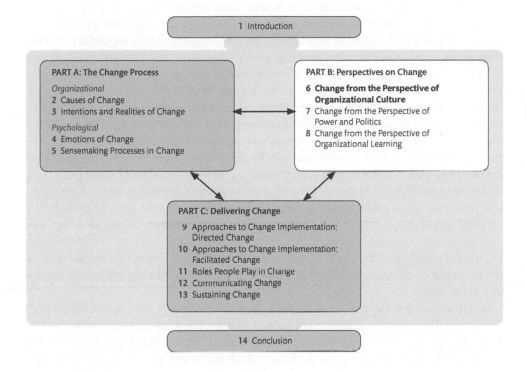

PART A: The Change Process

Organizational
2 Causes of Change
3 Intentions and Realities of Change

Psychological
4 Emotions of Change
5 Sensemaking Processes in Change

PART B: Perspectives on Change

6 Change from the Perspective of Organizational Culture
7 Change from the Perspective of Power and Politics
8 Change from the Perspective of Organizational Learning

1 Introduction

PART C: Delivering Change

9 Approaches to Change Implementation: Directed Change
10 Approaches to Change Implementation: Facilitated Change
11 Roles People Play in Change
12 Communicating Change
13 Sustaining Change

14 Conclusion

 Introduction

Viewing change from the perspective of organizational culture highlights the shifts in thinking, understanding, and patterns of behaviour that organizational change involves. It is a perspective that draws attention to what is actually happening in organizations, rather than what should be happening. It emphasizes the way in which informal patterns in organizational life can obstruct formal change strategies. This leads to a further issue: if those informal patterns are holding an organization back, can they be changed? Section 1 of the chapter introduces Part B of the book by discussing the contrast between the formal and informal organization. Section 2 looks at the contribution of the culture perspective to understanding organizations and organizational change. In section 3, we consider the challenges that organizational culture can present for change practitioners. Finally, in section 4, we examine the challenge of changing organizational culture itself.

Main topics to be covered in this chapter

- The informal organization: an introduction to Part B of the book
- The nature and dynamics of organizational culture
- Challenges of change from a culture perspective
- Culture change: planned and emergent

Section 1: **The informal organization—introduction to Part B**

Each of the three chapters in Part B discuss a distinctive perspective for understanding change: firstly, organizational culture; secondly, power and politics; and thirdly, organizational learning. Each of these perspectives provides an approach to analysing the need for change, selecting approaches to tackling change, and assessing deliberate and unintended change processes. It will become clear that each perspective highlights 'unofficial', as well as 'official', aspects of organizations and organizational change. These aspects of organizations are often distinguished in this way: the **formal organization** consists of hierarchy, structure, official communication channels, job roles, management and leadership responsibilities, and the processes for converting resources into goods and services that make the organization viable; the **informal organization** consists of those aspects that are not officially defined, are often less visible, and are characteristically human. For example, the informal organization includes networks, friendships, rivalries, gossip and rumour, meeting places, norms and idiosyncrasies of behaviour, commitments, beliefs, convictions, thoughts, and emotions—all of which greatly influence the way in which work is accomplished. The informal organization may enable or obstruct, enrich or frustrate, inspire or sometimes destroy formal organizational work. So, in working with organizational change, because this involves dealing with the way things are in organizations, rather than with the way they are supposed to be, we find that perspectives offering insight into the informal organization are crucial.

See Chapter 2 for more on organizational viability: p. 12

Like the iceberg in Figure 6.1, the formal organization is what is seen 'above the surface'. The informal organization is like the greater part of the iceberg, which exists 'below the surface'. Only by understanding the informal organization can the peaks and troughs of the formal organization's fortunes, and the way in which it changes, be understood; just as the strange shape of the iceberg in Figure 6.1, and the way in which it melts over time, can only be understood in the context of the much more substantial section of the iceberg existing under the sea. In this chapter, we see how change can be seen from the perspective of organizational culture, those aspects of the informal organization that establish some consistency in how events, and in particular changes, are interpreted among staff. Chapter 7 will focus on how change can be viewed from the perspective of power and politics, looking at change from the perspective of behind-the-scenes 'political' behaviour, largely in the informal organization. Finally, Chapter 8 will focus on change viewed from the perspective of organizational learning and, again, reveals that organizational learning and failure to learn is partly rooted in informal aspects of organizations.

Figure 6.1 The iceberg model
Source: Corbis

 Section 1 Summary

In this section, we have:

- distinguished between the formal and informal organization, and discussed the 'iceberg' metaphor;

- introduced the three chapters in Part B, highlighting that each of the perspectives we address—culture (this chapter), power and politics (Chapter 7) and organizational learning (Chapter 8)—is rooted, to a large extent, in the informal organization.

Section 2: **Organizational culture**

In this section, we begin by considering what is meant by taking a cultural perspective on organizations and then explore the significance of organizational culture as a perspective on organizational change in particular. We next consider the key aspects of an organization that make up the culture, allowing people to develop distinctive shared understandings of internal and external events and situations. Finally, we look at the way in which these different aspects interact in a dynamic relationship.

Culture as a perspective on organizations

Organizations differ from one another. Of course, they differ in many ways: in size; in business activity; in being for-profit, not-for-profit, or public sector; in success; in the morale of staff; and so on. But they also differ in the way in which people in the organization conduct themselves and, underlying that, the way in which people think—the way they understand and interpret their situation. This is where **organizational culture** comes in.

Many definitions have been given of organizational culture. According to Morgan (1997: 138):

> Shared values, shared beliefs, shared meaning, shared understanding, and shared sense making are all different ways of describing culture . . . a process of reality construction that allows people to see and understand particular events, actions, objects, utterances, or situations in distinctive ways.

See Chapter 5 for more on sensemaking: p. 92

Here, Morgan highlights that culture can refer to **shared meanings or understandings** that enable people to work together, or it can refer to the sensemaking processes that make those shared understandings possible—underpinned by shared beliefs and values. Brown (1995) focuses on these shared beliefs and values, which enable shared understandings, and also points out that the patterns of shared understanding are associated with distinctive ways of behaving, and with material objects:

> Organisational culture refers to the pattern of beliefs, values and learned ways of coping with experience that have developed during the course of an organisation's history, and which tend to be manifested in its material arrangements and in the behaviours of its members. (Ibid: 8)

Organizational culture establishes consistency in employees' thinking. For example, openness about the failings of a key project might be seen as wise or foolish, upright or mischievous—depending on the organizational culture. Seen from the perspective of culture, key challenges of organizational change occur because culture constrains new thinking, and therefore new behaviour, and change can itself be about shifts in culture—that is, new patterns of employee thinking (Schein, 2009).

 Exercise 6.1

Consider two organizations with which you are familiar, and which you regard as having different cultures (they might be where you work, study, volunteer, or worship, for example).

- what kind of *similarities* are there in how related events or situations are seen in these two organizations?
- what kind of related events or situations are seen in *different* ways in these two organizations?
- what effect do the differences that you have identified have on the way in which people behave and on the success of the organizations?

Culture as a perspective on organizational change

How does organizational culture affect the feasibility of strategies for change, and their implementation? As shown in Figure 6.2, culture has three effects on strategic planning.

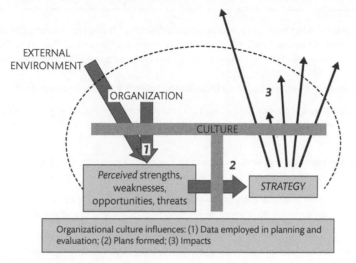

Figure 6.2 Culture and change strategy

1. Culture acts as a filter that influences perceptions of the internal and external environment of the organization. Perceived strengths, weaknesses, opportunities, and threats are a product not only of the internal and external situation, but also of the organizational culture through which the situation is perceived and assessed (Lorsch, 1985).

2. Culture influences the formation of strategic plans (Mintzberg et al., 2009).

3. Culture influences the implementation of plans and their consequent feasibility (Schwartz and Davis, 1981; Pant and Lachman, 1998).

This means that culture may discourage radical change and, in particular, second-order change; instead culture tends to foster first-order change in which shared understandings are unaltered by the transition (Gagliardi, 1986; Mintzberg et al., 2009). These issues are addressed in section 3. The reality is that sometimes a new strategy needs to be taken forward even though it is inconsistent with the organizational culture. In that case, the present organizational culture may have to be analysed in more detail and steps taken to alter it. This is taken up in section 4.

See Chapter 3 for more on first-order and second-order change: p. 41

In fact, processes of change can be analysed from the perspective of organizational culture whether they are regarded as planned or emergent. Change in Practice 6.1 illustrates this by discussing a change process of very rapid growth and spectacular collapse at Enron.

 Change in Practice 6.1

Growth and collapse at Enron

Enron, by 2000 a huge multinational with headquarters in Houston, Texas, started life in 1985 with the merger of two natural gas pipeline companies. It grew rapidly, especially during the 1990s, owning power plants, water companies, and oil and gas transportation infrastructure. However, by the end of that decade, Enron focused increasingly on commodity trading, involving gas, electricity, metals, coal, paper, Internet bandwidth, weather derivatives, etc. So much so that, in early 2001, its mission to be 'the world's leading energy company' was replaced by an aim to be 'the world's leading company'.

Enron claimed to be committed to communication, respect, integrity, and excellence.

Communication. We have an obligation to communicate. Here, we take the time to talk with one another . . . and to listen. We believe that information is meant to move and that information moves people.

Respect. We treat others as we would like to be treated ourselves. We do not tolerate abusive or disrespectful treatment. Ruthlessness, callousness and arrogance don't belong here.

Integrity. We work with customers and prospects openly, honestly and sincerely. When we say we will do something, we will do it; when we say we cannot or will not do something, then we won't do it.

Excellence. We are satisfied with nothing less than the very best in everything we do. We will continue to raise the bar for everyone. The great fun here will be for all of us to discover just how good we can really be. (Enron website, 2 December 2001)

However, many practices at Enron contrasted markedly with these stated values.

For example, internally, Enron operated a performance review process that came to be known as 'rank and yank' on which continued employment, as well as bonus levels, depended. Every six months, employees went through an appraisal process involving feedback from peers, and were then evaluated and given a ranking from 1 to 5 by their managers. It was a requirement that 15 per cent of all employees be given the lowest ranking of 1, facing certain redeployment and probable redundancy. Employees 'traded' positive peer assessments to secure their positions, and their managers 'traded' employee rankings in order that overall 15 per cent quotas could be met. This employee evaluation process was intimately interwoven with dynamics whereby staff colluded in inflating the value of Enron's financial deals because their rankings could be contingent on this complicity. Externally, Enron's accounts were audited by one of the big five accounting companies, Anderson's. Huge consultancy earnings, as well as reputational benefits from having Enron as a client, led Anderson's to sideline concerns about its largest client and to approve both these improper accounting practices and the use of nominally independent companies as vehicles to absorb and disguise Enron losses. The creation of such offshore partnership companies further obfuscated Enron's accounting practices by maintaining a false impression of corporate profitability. At board meetings in June and October 1999, Enron directors explicitly waived the company's code of ethics in order that the chief financial officer, Andrew Fastow, could continue in post at Enron while also running and profiting from some of these offshore partnership companies, which hid Enron's losses. So, ruthlessness rather than respect, deception rather than integrity, and withholding rather than communication were evident in at least some key facets of the business.

In March 2001, *Fortune* magazine published an article pointing to the lack of transparency in Enron's books and questioning its inflated share price. On 14 August that year, Jeffrey Skilling, Enron's famously abrasive CEO, resigned, having been in post for only six months. Kenneth Lay, the long-standing chairman of the company, reassumed the CEO role the following day. The next day, Enron accountant Sherron Watkins sent Lay a lengthy anonymous memo detailing dubious financial instruments the company was employing and the resulting precariousness of its position. Subsequently, Lay and other senior executives sold off some of their own shareholdings while continuing to talk up Enron stock to investors and employees. But, over the next few months, the share price collapsed.

On 2 December, Enron filed for 'Chapter 11' bankruptcy protection as vast off-balance-sheet debts came to light. Criminal proceedings were subsequently launched against senior Enron executives including Fastow, Lay, and Skilling. Numerous former employees had lost not only their jobs, but also the savings built up in pension plans invested in Enron stock; the sense of disillusionment among them was palpable. Yet many, after they had left, reported that Enron was the best place they had ever worked, even while describing feelings of betrayal.[1-5]

Aspects of culture

What is it in an organization that makes up organizational culture, allowing people to develop distinctive shared understandings of events and situations? The most immediately noticeable aspect of organizational culture is its observable features: the objects, structures, and patterns of behaviour that typify an organization. They include products, stories, logos, buildings, routines, hierarchy, reward systems, common ways of behaving toward subordinates, managers, and colleagues, jargon, types of speech, strategy documents, and so on. In the terminology of organization studies, these observable features are usually called **artefacts** (Hatch and Cunliffe, 2006; Schein, 2004), even though patterns of behaviour and stories are being included as well as objects. Figure 6.3 represents these observable features as the outer layer of culture. At Enron, for example, the notoriously plush offices in downtown Houston, Texas, were artefacts. But so were the sexist jokes that peppered email exchanges (Myers, 2008), the stories of spectacular deal-making that circulated (Cruver, 2002), and the 'rank and yank' system of performance review and associated informal 'trading' of rankings and assessments described in Change in Practice 6.1.

At a deeper level are symbols, and shared values and beliefs. These are not immediately evident, but they are accessible through discussion, observation, and reflection. **Symbols** are the particular established meanings associated with certain artefacts. For example, the open door of

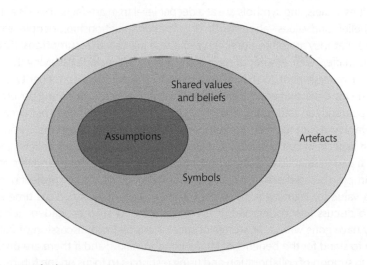

Figure 6.3 Aspects of culture

managers' offices may be taken in one organizational culture as a symbol of approachability. Alternatively, in another organizational culture, those open doors might be generally understood as a symbol of how managers constantly keep an eye on staff. At Enron, the share price—its meteoric rise and, later, spectacular collapse—became a symbol of success and, finally, of failure.

Shared values are the goals and standards to which employees aspire (Hatch and Cunliffe, 2006). For example, staff might aspire to support one other, to take on responsibilities, to build a diverse organization, to put customers' needs first, or to provide excellent service to customers—or, for that matter, they might aspire to exploit potential customers ruthlessly. Every individual has values to which he or she aspires. Values are part of an organizational culture if they are shared—that is, held in common among many staff. In Enron, a value for innovation appears to have become embedded—a shared value reflected and reinforced when, every year between 1996 and 2001, the company won *Fortune* magazine's accolade as 'America's Most Innovative Company'. **Shared beliefs**, views regarded as true by many staff, underpin shared values. They can be ethical or pragmatic in nature. For example, a value for diversity could be underpinned by a belief that reflecting the diversity of the wider society is the right thing to do, or it could be underpinned by a belief that a commitment to diversity will pay dividends in terms of staff commitment and the bottom line, or will build the reputation of the organization.

Sometimes, you might recognize values of an organizational culture from the way in which staff behave. A value for customer service, for example, might be evident because members of staff go the extra mile to make sure that you are happy with their service. These values, reflected in behaviour, are called **values-in-use**. Often, organizations make a point of proclaiming shared values, whether in internal documents, posters, advertisements, or websites. When organizations do this, the values are called **espoused values**. Espoused values in an organization may, of course, reflect actual values-in-use. But they may also differ considerably: what an organization claims are its principles may not correspond to reality as staff and other stakeholders experience it (Murphy and Mackenzie Davey, 2002). For instance, Change in Practice 6.1 contrasts the espoused values at Enron of communication, respect, integrity, and excellence with actual practices at the company. Privately, both employees and other stakeholders can often turn a blind eye to the differences between what is said and what is put into practice.

While values, beliefs, and symbols are at a deeper level than artefacts, there is a deeper level still. Some beliefs *and* values—about work, organizations, relationships, people, etc.—become so ingrained that they are often unrecognized; these are called '**assumptions**' (Schein, 2004; Hatch and Cunliffe, 2006). Assumptions in many enterprises include believing that it is a function of senior management to maximize returns to shareholders. In a charity, assumptions might include the belief that education is beneficial or a value for alleviating poverty. At Enron, there was apparently an assumption that the company would continue to be successful, which led many employees not to diversify their pension investments beyond the Enron shares.

All of the aspects of culture—artefacts, symbols, shared values and beliefs, and assumptions—play a part in establishing similarity between employees' understandings of events. To take an example discussed earlier, openness about the failings of a key project might be seen as *wise*: if a value for learning is prominent; if there are artefacts such as time set aside in meetings to discuss lessons learned; if there are symbols such as leaders acknowledging where they have gone wrong, or stories of success arising from discussion of failure, which have come to stand for the benefits of facing up to mistakes; and if there are underlying assumptions in support of collaboration and using resources to focus on the future. It might be seen as *foolish*: if there is a value for perfection; if artefacts such as project evaluation forms rate only how successful the work has been; if symbols, such as employees being put down in meetings or stories of rising stars who have got 'everything right', have come to stand for the importance of not putting a foot wrong; and if there are underlying assumptions in support of individual responsibility and continuity of working methods.

Dynamics of culture

Organizational culture is not simply a static amalgam of artefacts, symbols, values and beliefs, and assumptions. The various aspects of culture interact (Hatch, 1993; Hatch and Cunliffe, 2006). We now introduce two models of this interaction that we find helpful both in understanding how different aspects of culture affect one another, and in understanding how culture change occurs. Firstly, in Schein's (1985; 2004) model, organizational culture has three strata: artefacts; values and beliefs; and assumptions. Culture in the form of artefacts can be directly observed. In terms of the iceberg metaphor introduced in section 1, artefacts are above the waterline. But artefacts can be hard to assess in terms of their significance for the way in which events are interpreted. At an intermediate level, organizational culture in the form of shared values and beliefs is somewhat more difficult to discern. In terms of the iceberg metaphor, shared values and beliefs would be just under the surface of the water. But it is somewhat easier to see how values and beliefs influence the way in which events are interpreted. Finally, assumptions are generally hidden, and can be difficult to recognize even after careful reflection. In terms of the iceberg metaphor, assumptions would be concealed in the ocean depths. But assumptions underlie values and beliefs—and make them difficult to alter. For Schein, there is a mutual influence between these layers of culture. An assumption that employees avoid hard work when they can might lead to values for close control and monitoring of people, which might lead to artefacts such as time clocks or, for that matter, open-plan offices. Conversely, the open-plan offices or the time clocks may reinforce values for close control and monitoring, and these values may in turn reinforce the assumption that employees avoid hard work.

Secondly, the **cultural dynamics** model (Hatch, 1993) explains in more detail how the different aspects of culture interact. It incorporates artefacts, symbols, assumptions, and values and will be helpful when, in section 4 of this chapter, we examine how culture change is accomplished. The model is in the form of the cycle in Figure 6.4.

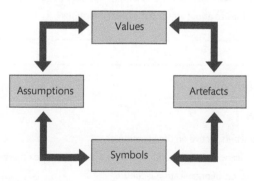

Figure 6.4 Cultural dynamics
Source: Adapted from Hatch (1993)

The model proposes that the aspects of organizational culture interrelate as follows.

- An assumption that employees avoid hard work when they can might lead to values for close control and monitoring of people, which might lead to artefacts such as time clocks or, for that matter, open-plan offices. Over time, these may become *symbols* of distrust in people, in turn reinforcing—for managers and staff—the assumption that employees avoid hard work.

- Moving the other way around the cycle, the assumption that employees avoid hard work makes it more likely that open-plan offices will become symbols of distrust. That distrust may lead to presenteeism as an additional artefact associated with the offices, in turn reinforcing a value for close control (are people working or playing on the Internet?), making it less likely that the assumption that employees avoid hard work will be questioned.

- *But change is also possible.* Whether intentionally or not, the open-plan offices may become symbols of fun at work or of productive interaction—rather than of distrust—which may, in turn, tend to undermine the assumption that employees will avoid work when possible.

Hatch's model not only clarifies how different aspects of culture interact, but also provides a framework for understanding different approaches to changing organizational culture. For instance, behaviour patterns and other artefacts, or values that inform behaviour patterns, or symbols—meanings associated with artefacts, or underlying, taken-for-granted assumptions, are all potential starting places for culture change. This is explored in section 4. Prior to that, in section 3, we turn to how organizational culture challenges and enables organizational change in general. Section 3 also introduces alternative points of view on organizational culture— 'differentiation' and 'fragmentation'—which shed further light on its implications for change.

 Exercise 6.2

Discuss with a colleague some of the observable artefacts of organizational culture in your own workplace, university, or another organization with which you are familiar. At a deeper level, identify some of the values and symbols that characterize the culture of the organization.

- Are the values really values-in-use or are they simply espoused (for example in marketing material)?
- Is it possible to hypothesize about any underlying assumptions?

 Section 2 Summary

In this section, we have:

- introduced a cultural perspective on organizations;
- considered the significance of organizational culture as a perspective on organizational change;
- looked at the key aspects of organizational culture;
- discussed different models of how the aspects of culture interact.

Section 3: The challenges of change from a culture perspective

How does organizational culture impact on organizational change? This section discusses how organizational culture and subcultures affect the course of planned and unplanned change processes, and can foster or undermine organizational agility—that is, the potential for successful change (Kotter and Heskett, 1992). We also explain how looking at culture from contrasting viewpoints gives insights into both planned and unplanned change.

Culture, subcultures, and change

In 2006, a *Wall Street Journal* article credited Mark Fields, a Ford executive, with the remark that 'Culture eats strategy for breakfast' (*WSJ*, 23 January 2006). In other words, organizational culture can render an apparently 'good' change strategy unworkable; the intended strategy will not be realized. Schwartz and Davis (1981) propose that, before plans for organizational change are finalized, a risk assessment is made, examining the degree to which each element of the proposed changes is compatible with the organizational culture. If an element of the change strategy is highly important to the success of the strategy and likely to be fundamentally incompatible with the values of the culture, then they strongly advise that an alternative strategy is adopted. Pant and Lachman (1998) have a rather different way of looking at this. They recommend identifying the values needed to take a change strategy forward. For example, in the case of Enron, the strategy of establishing new utility trading businesses may have *required* a value for innovation. A **strategy core value** is one that is central to the success of the strategy, while a **strategy peripheral value** is one that would be helpful, but which is of relatively minor importance to the success of the strategy. Pant and Lachman point out that an organization is unlikely to realize a strategy if its core values run counter to the values of the organizational culture. If its peripheral values are inconsistent with the culture, the strategy may be implementable.

See Chapter 5 for more on strategy: p. 100

Sometimes, however, strategy core values conflict with values strongly held within just one part of an organization. So far we have considered organizational culture from the point of view of *shared* values and assumptions. And for a very good reason: this quality of shared-ness is central to how organizational culture is usually conceived. But it is clear that values (and assumptions) are not always held in common across the whole organization. Of course, even in the most unified organization, there will be some people who overtly or covertly hold opposing views. In an organization with a value-in-use for diversity, there may be individuals who privately do not value the contribution of all sections of the workforce. In an organization with a value-in-use for customer service, there may be those inclined to sabotage that ethos. Sometimes, these differences between mainstream values of organizational culture and values of particular employees can be treated as individual anomalies. That said, often, groups of people who may be associated with one particular section or hierarchical level or function within the organization hold distinctive views—which they themselves hold in common—forming a **subculture** with values, beliefs, symbols, and assumptions that differ from those of other employees. For example, there may be a management subculture with values for maximizing profits and performance-related pay, and a front-line employee subculture with values for maximizing benefits and an egalitarian reward system.

If core values required for a change strategy conflict with subcultural values, a way forward frequently adopted is to avoid the conflict by subcontracting elements of the strategy that would normally be performed within that subculture (Pant and Lachman, 1998). In the UK, for example, this is often the case with organizations in which there is a frontline workforce value for a reasonably egalitarian reward system, but costs are being reduced as part of a change strategy. By subcontracting functions such as cleaning or catering, value-consistency can be at least nominally maintained, while labour costs are reduced. A similar dynamic is seen in the trend for offshoring product manufacture from Europe to Asia.

Sometimes, when organizational culture is discussed, subcultural differences are ignored or treated simply as irregularities to be eliminated. This is called the **integration** point of view on organizational culture (Martin, 1992; Meyerson and Martin, 1987). The integration point of view focuses attention on commonality in values, symbols, artefacts, and assumptions across the organization, leading to shared understandings—shared ways of viewing what is happening in the organization and its environment. Martin (1992) and Meyerson and Martin (1987) point to alternative points of view for understanding organizational culture and culture change. One of these alternatives is the **differentiation** point of view. Instead of seeing organizational culture as reflecting consistency across the whole organization, this point of view focuses on consistency within subcultures. Subcultural dynamics are highlighted that may support or obstruct change programmes. In particular, change initiatives can be undermined by one subculture even while being in keeping with another.

See Chapter 3 for more on Royal Mail: p. 40

 Exercise 6.3

In late 2009, there were a series of strikes in Royal Mail (the UK postal service) in response to perceptions of a change programme to 'modernize' the service. In the following short videos, Communication Workers Union members and Royal Mail managing director, Mark Higson, talk about the situation at the end of October 2009.

The view from the union subculture

Thursday, 29 October 2009: http://news.bbc.co.uk/1/hi/business/8332288.stm
Saturday, 31 October 2009: http://news.bbc.co.uk/1/hi/uk/8335528.stm

The view from the management subculture

Thursday, 29 October 2009: http://news.bbc.co.uk/1/hi/business/8331169.stm

● What differences do you notice between the union subculture and the management subculture in terms of values, beliefs, or assumptions?

● In 2009, do you think 'modernization' and 'the strikes' had become symbols in these two subcultures and, if so, what did they stand for in each subculture?

● How would you say the contrast between the two subcultures affected the prospects for planned change at Royal Mail?

It may be clear, watching the videos referenced in Exercise 6.3, that, in the culture of Royal Mail, seemingly intractable understandings—albeit contradictory ones—dominate the organization, the change initiatives under way, and the prospects for their success. In many organizations, the culture, when analysed from a differentiation point of view, is seen to be yet more complex because there can be many subcultures, overlapping and nested within one another. For example, in a university, there may be faculty subcultures, subcultures of lecturers and administrators that span faculties, subcultures associated with specific research groups, a management subculture, and so on. To an even greater extent, such an intricate array of subcultures can complicate the implementation of change.

A third point of view, **fragmentation**, does not focus on the notion of cultural unity even on a subcultural level (Feldman, 1991; Meyerson, 1991). Instead, it recognizes that the same event might be interpreted in contradictory ways even within a single subculture or, indeed, by a single person. Seen from a fragmentation point of view, multiple, often inconsistent values, assumptions, and symbols may be in play that come to the foreground for staff in different situations. Analysis might reveal that the introduction of a diversity programme was driven by ethical values for diversity among a minority of senior managers, a value for enhancing the reputation of the business among others, a value for personal profile and advancement held by some in the HR department, *and* a value for profit among specialist external consultants. Later, the emergent focus and direction of the diversity programme might be affected by values brought into play by specific situations that emerge. In hiring new managers, a value for looking after friends could undermine commitment to diversity; equally, if there were a perceived risk of ongoing discrimination in the organization being exposed, the values for business reputation among senior managers and advancement among HR professionals might lead to a cover-up. Seen from this point of view:

> an organizational culture is a web of individuals, sporadically and loosely connected by their changing positions on a variety of issues. Their involvement, their subcultural identities, and their individual self-definitions fluctuate, depending on which issues are activated at a given moment. (Martin, 1992: 153)

The fragmentation point of view highlights the role of leaders in bringing to the foreground situations that positively influence the values, symbols, and assumptions drawn into play. This is what is happening when leaders convey a sense of a 'burning platform' to put across the message that the survival of an organization depends on radical change. The purpose is to bring into play a value for the continued existence of the business.

See Chapter 11 for more on the leadership of change: p. 244

Culture and agility

As discussed in section 2, culture reflects alignment of interpretations (Harris, 1994). From this point of view, it makes sense to talk about the 'strength' of an organizational culture as the degree to which there is consensus on values and other aspects of the culture. A **strong organizational culture** (Chatman and Cha, 2003; Kotter and Heskett, 1992) is one in which there is a deeply held consensus on values, symbols, beliefs, and assumptions among the organization's people. By implication, subcultural differences are minor. Once consensus is established, it can be *reinforced* through two separate processes. The first is that the people tend to be attracted to work, selected to work, and more likely to stay in an organization when there is a good fit between their patterns of behaviour, values, and assumptions, and those of the organization (Schneider, 1987). The second is that employees become **encultur-ated** as they work in the organization, tending to adopt the behaviours, values, symbolic meanings, norms, and assumptions of the mainstream organizational culture (Schein, 2009).

Historically, many experts put forward the view that a strong organizational culture is not simply characteristic of some organizations, but is an asset that leads to success (Peters and Waterman, 1982; Ginsburg and Miller, 1992). However, it may be that success tends to strengthen culture as much as strong culture leads to success (Kotter and Heskett, 1992): for instance, doubts about shared values may be set aside as employees see apparently positive results from them. In fact, while organizations in which there is a strong consensus on values may sometimes be particularly successful, they can also fail spectacularly because of a lack of dissident voices to provide alternative perspectives when the viability of the organization is under threat. As Tom Peters writes, 'success is the result of deep grooves, but deep grooves destroy adaptability' (Peters, 1992: 616). Many successful organizations today have strong cultures, but many that have suffered catastrophic decline or failure in recent years after a period of success could also be said to have a strong organizational culture—for example, Enron and Lehman Brothers in the US, and Royal Bank of Scotland and Northern Rock in the UK. It seems that a strong organizational culture can both foster success and generate vulnerability.

Earlier in the book, we introduced the idea of organizational agility, the extent to which an organization maintains the capability to change rapidly. While some organizational change initiatives are intended to change the culture, which cultures themselves *enable* change? Dyer and Shafer (1999) help to address this by setting out a series of artefacts—patterns of behaviour—that contribute to organizational agility. These are:

See Chapters 3 and 13 for more on organizational agility: pp. 53, 301

- proactively spotting and addressing threats and opportunities;
- rapid redeployment of people as priorities require;
- spontaneous collaboration to pool resources for quick results;
- innovating; and
- rapid and continuous learning.

There are connections here with the discussion in Chapter 8 of 'learning organizations'

Schein (2004) calls a culture that favours agility a 'learning culture'. There is some common ground with Dyer and Shafer's work. Schein sets out assumptions underlying the behaviours that Dyer and Shafer list: assumptions that proactivity is appropriate, that learning is beneficial, and that solutions to problems derive from a pragmatic search for truth. But Schein also adds a *value* for full and open communication, and a *belief* that the world is complex and interconnected. To this, he adds three more assumptions favouring agility:

- that human nature is basically positive;
- that the environment can be dominated; and
- that it is valuable to focus on the *medium-term* future.

Finally, and significantly, Schein emphasizes the importance for organizational agility of a culture with *diverse subcultures*. Sometimes, as in the case of the Post Office considered in Exercise 6.3, subcultures are a source of friction. Nevertheless, after many years of study, Schein's conclusion is that diversity of subcultures is an important aspect of building agility, *provided* that the other characteristics, listed above, are in place. A strong culture is less likely to be agile—that is, less likely to be open to change—however successful it is in the short term. For example, a university could be expected to be *more* agile if diverse values, such as commercial success, teaching quality, reputation for research, and academic freedom were given different priorities in different subcultures. On this view, Enron, while displaying extraordinarily rapid growth, may have lacked true agility because of an increasingly consistent set of values across the company. The role of subcultures in building agility reinforces the importance of analysing culture from a differentiation, as well as an integration, point of view. While an integration point of view may provide a more or less complete picture when discussing a 'strong' organizational culture, in other scenarios it can lead to important elements of organizational culture being neglected.

 Section 3 Summary

In this section, we have:

- discussed the constraints and opportunities that culture and subcultures create for change strategies;
- considered the complementary implications for change of integration, differentiation, and fragmentation viewpoints on organizational culture;
- discussed the relationship between organizational culture and agility, including the impact of strong cultures.

Section 4: **How culture changes**

In the previous section, we discussed how organizational culture can support change or obstruct it. This raises the question of how an organization's culture can be changed if it is not conducive to the success of the organization or to change strategies that are deemed necessary. Over the past several decades, the importance of culture change has been widely recognized and promoted. On the other hand, there is considerable evidence that outcomes of culture change programmes are very variable (Smith, 2003). We think this is partly because culture is difficult to change, and partly because emergent culture change processes often outweigh the effects of intended culture change strategies. In this section, we begin by considering how the need for culture change can be diagnosed. We then look at planned culture change and emergent culture change. Of course, culture change in practice will often include both planned and emergent aspects.

Diagnosing the need for culture change

If change in organizational culture is to be deliberately initiated, then some kind of analysis or diagnosis of culture needs to take place. Often, this begins with observation by leaders, or internal or external consultants. There may be a clear cultural artefact, such as poor customer satisfaction, inadequate business performance, or a lack of speed in getting products to market,

See Chapter 11 for more on internal and external consultants: p. 257

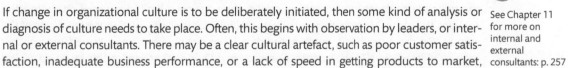

influenced by values and symbols, which highlights the need for change. However, usually, because much of culture is hidden from view, a more formal process of investigating culture is necessary in order to gauge what is going on.

There are different approaches to this. Schein (2009) recommends that organizational culture be analysed in relation to a goal of resolving a specific organizational issue—for example a business problem or the need to implement an organizational change. He suggests that groups of between ten and fifteen people from different levels in the organization, who share a concern about the issue, are facilitated through a process of identifying both artefacts and espoused values. Inconsistencies between these are used to surface values-in-use and assumptions. These shared values-in-use and assumptions are then assessed in terms of how they aid or hinder the goal that has been set out, and necessary changes in the culture can be identified. Our personal experience is different. People often find it difficult to fully understand the concepts. One way in which to help them with this is to encourage them to consider the culture of well-known brands first: in the UK, this might be Marks & Spencer, Virgin, or Royal Mail. Also, our experience of the politics of most organizations is that doing this in a single group with people from very different levels in the hierarchy can be problematic. Using workshops with separate groups, each drawn from similar levels, to analyse the culture may be more practical.

See Chapter 7 for more on the politics of change: p. 142

In any event, a programme like this is not only a cultural analysis, but also introduces a new artefact: the workshops themselves. In line with Hatch's model of cultural dynamics, the workshops in themselves may become a symbol of change that influences assumptions and which highlights new behavioural artefacts. For example, this may be the first time that some lower-level employees feel their views have been sought. Equally, established artefacts in the form of routines and habitual behaviour, and ingrained assumptions, may influence how the workshops are understood—as, for example, an unnecessary distraction or a historical blip. We have seen processes along both these lines in our work and, as Schein suggests, transformational leadership skills are likely to play the key role in tipping the process in one direction or the other.

See Chapter 11 for more on transformational leadership: p. 244

An alternative approach to analysing organizational culture is based on employee surveys as a diagnostic tool. Cameron and Quinn (2006), for example, set out a questionnaire that they called the 'Organizational Culture Assessment Instrument' (OCAI). This is intended to assess organizations in terms of various categories of artefacts and values, such as leadership style, management responsibilities, and success criteria. It is a much simpler approach to diagnosing organizational culture than that proposed by Schein. But can questionnaires capture the idiosyncratic characteristics of particular organizational cultures? Cameron and Quinn's measure assesses cultural values along just two dimensions:

- a focus on flexibility and discretion as against stability and control;
- a focus on competing with external rivals as against a focus on internal unity.

From this, organizational cultures are then evaluated according to the degree to which they resemble four archetypal cultures. Other commercial questionnaires are more complex, but the principle of 'measuring' organizational culture against a limited range of characteristics remains the same. Many of these products result in compelling visual representations of the culture. On the other hand, much of the detail that distinguishes one culture from another may be glossed over. To their credit, Cameron and Quinn acknowledge this by citing critical comments from John Van Maanen, an expert in organizational culture: 'Leaving readers with the suggestion that four and only four cultures represent the wonderful world of organizations is a mistake' (Van Maanen, cited in Cameron and Quinn, 2006: 20).

Nevertheless, we have found that, even though they cannot capture all of the detail of organizational culture, precisely because they are straightforward and accessible, these kinds of tools can be very useful in provoking *discussion* of cultures and subcultures in organizations. So they can make a very good starting place for analysing and changing organizational culture. Again, from the cultural perspective, questionnaires of this type are not only a diagnostic instrument, but they are also themselves a new artefact in the cultural landscape, which may become a symbol influencing or entrenching assumptions, patterns of behaviour, and values.

Planned culture change

Organizational culture change is never going to be a comfortable, quick, or easy process. There are several key reasons for this. *Firstly*, because culture change involves a change in thinking, it is always second-order change. *Secondly*, as explained, organizational culture incorporates different facets, all of which will need to change if culture change is to be achieved. Some of these—like artefacts—are more observable, some—like assumptions—are crucial to shared interpretations, but exist at a deep, unspoken level, which makes them hard to investigate, let alone alter. They are, as explained earlier using the iceberg metaphor, far below the waterline. *Thirdly*, organizational culture affects, and depends on, a range of other characteristics of the organization such as the formal structure, informal networks, planning systems, power distribution, and strategy (Johnson et al., 2008; Pettigrew, 1999). *Fourthly*, organizational culture has its roots in the history of the organization. Sometimes, when we work with an organization and ask 'why are these beliefs prevalent here?' or 'what makes these principles important in the company?', the answers begin ten, fifteen, or twenty years beforehand. If organizational culture is to change, then the perceived history of the organization may have to change (Pettigrew, 1999). Past 'successes' may later be viewed in a different light as, for instance, treading water or even unprincipled. What were once viewed as past 'failures' may later be regarded as the seeds of success.

Gagliardi (1986) suggests that, in practice, there are three kinds of culture change. The first of these is **apparent culture change**, in which the culture accommodates change and does not genuinely alter: for example, the maintenance of blame culture (based on an underlying assumption of individual responsibility/culpability), but with a shift of blame from one department or group to another, or explicit artefacts such as a pattern of accusations at meetings being replaced by more subtle ones such as gossip about individuals, or people being sidelined in decision-making following their 'mistakes'. A second form that supposed culture change takes in practice is what Gagliardi calls **revolutionary cultural change**. In revolutionary culture change, the organization is forced into abandonment of values by adoption of new, antagonistic ones. For Gagliardi, rather than genuine culture change, it would be more correct to say that the 'firm has died and that a new firm . . . was born' (Gagliardi, 1986: 130): for example, a turnaround or acquisition can result in this kind of abandonment of values. In the UK in early 2008, in the midst of a banking crisis, the Northern Rock bank was nationalized. The culture of the bank had been characterized by risk and rapid expansion. The Northern Rock trading results for the first half of 2007 showed that it had sold mortgages worth £10.7 billion, up 47 per cent on the same period a year before, and amounting to almost one in five of all UK mortgage policies sold in that period. In the year following nationalization, the bank adopted conservative

See Chapter 3 for more on second-order change: p. 41

lending policies, actively aimed to reduce its portfolio of mortgage customers, and chose to adopt a limit of selling 2.5 per cent of all UK mortgage policies. This is a revolutionary culture change in Gagliardi's terms: a new firm was born even though the name remained the same.

A third form of culture change is **incremental cultural change**: the incorporation of new values and assumptions (and usually corresponding symbols and artefacts) into an existing organizational culture. Although there is bound to be some antagonism between new and old values and practices, in this case new values, beliefs, and assumptions build on or modify those already established (Legge, 1995). For example, a value for customer service might build on a value for treating employees well. A value for investigating mistakes thoroughly to find out whom to blame might be adapted into a value for investigating mistakes thoroughly to learn and implement improvements, without blame. At Enron, a value for risk-taking was built on an established value for innovation that had been already inculcated into the way in which the corporation did business, as it deliberately diversified during the 1990s from a traditional utility business to focus on commodity trading. This association between risk-taking and innovation can be seen in a 1998 industry magazine article by Jeffrey Skilling, at that time the president and chief operating officer of Enron, entitled 'Competitive corporate cultures: Why innovators are leading their industries'. He wrote:

> **Maintaining an Innovative Workplace**
>
> While strategic recruiting is a critical starting place for building a competitive workforce, retaining experienced, creative people *who are effective at risk taking* and change is even more important.
>
> . . . By cultivating a corporate culture that encourages employees to act like entrepreneurs *and take greater risks*, energy companies will be well equipped to pursue the significant growth opportunities of the 21st century and customers will receive enormous benefits from their creativity and vision. [emphasis added]

So how is incremental culture change achieved in practice? It has already been suggested that each of the elements of the cultural dynamics model—values, artefacts, symbols, and assumptions—offers potential leverage for organizational culture change. Hope Hailey (1999) focuses on two of these: artefacts and values. A focus on artefacts includes altering observable features, such as patterns of behaviour, office layout, technology, routines, hierarchy, reward systems, responsibilities, appraisal measures, management style, and the kind of stories that are in circulation. New values can gradually be influenced by a focus on these observable manifestations of culture. A value for customer service could be developed by focusing on corresponding artefacts such as new technology to improve customer communications, measuring customer feedback and attaining year-on-year improvements, appraising and rewarding employees or teams on their service performance, and so on. At a major professional services firm with which one of us worked, linking reward to working in a way that was consistent with new values, alongside the traditional link with revenue generation, gradually achieved changes not only in behaviour, but also in thinking. This took more than three years. Hope Hailey discusses a similar process at Glaxo pharmaceuticals.

A direct focus on changing values, on the other hand, can be carried forward through training and development, role-modelling, and persuasive communication. Employee involvement in discussing and proposing appropriate values is a key tool not only in arriving at an appropriate value set, but also in building employee commitment to the new values (Schein, 2004, 2009). Another powerful tool is the use of recruitment, selection, and induction to build commitment to new values among employees. The replacement of executives and senior managers whose thinking is not in keeping with new values plays a key role (Cummings and Worley, 2008). Another, related, intervention is the systematic promotion of people from a particular subculture that reflects desired values and behaviours (Schein, 2004). Change in Practice 6.2 describes how both influencing values and influencing artefacts were used to modify the culture of a London-based charity.

 Change in Practice 6.2

Thames Reach

Thames Reach is a charity that has been working with homeless people in London since 1984. Since 1995, Thames Reach has been developing effective employment schemes for service users, including a painting-and-decorating course, a farm and conservation project, and a shoe-cleaning business. At Thames Reach, the central shared value is to work to end street homelessness. Among other shared values was a commitment to professionalism. This had been translated into a pattern of rarely employing people with actual experience of homelessness in Thames Reach itself, and clear-cut boundaries between employees and 'service users'. However, among statutory funding organizations, there was a value for rehabilitative working practices. In this context, the senior management team of Thames Reach initiated the GROW (Giving Real Opportunities for Work) initiative in July 2005. Its aim was to increase the number of Thames Reach employees with a personal history of homelessness. This was an innovative response not only within the organization, but also within the sector.

A steering group consisting of two members of the senior management team and three members of the human resources team, including a dedicated GROW manager, were responsible for planning and implementing the initiative. Initially, this involved ensuring that all structural barriers restricting the employment of homeless people were removed, for example by reviewing contracts and insurance requirements, and by adapting relevant policies, including recruitment procedures and the Thames Reach code of conduct.

The next stage aimed to transform the values of the majority of employees whose entrenched views about supporting the homeless had fostered strong professional boundaries within Thames Reach of 'us and them'. Initially, the scheme was communicated throughout the organization by the senior management team, steering group, and acknowledged champions who were either individuals who had been previously involved in service-user employment initiatives or current employees who had disclosed a history of homelessness. Through senior management team briefings, departmental and team meetings, the intranet, dedicated events, focus groups, and away days, employees were engaged, informed, and persuaded about the initiative, and success stories were promoted. Then, twenty-six employees with a history of homelessness were recruited through four trainee intakes. By July 2007, a GROW trainee had been on placement in almost all of the twenty-six different teams in Thames Reach, which enabled team managers and core staff to experience the value of having ex-service-user colleagues. The final approach was to involve employees in the development and delivery of the initiative, which helped to build organization-wide commitment. Eighteen months into the project, 85 per cent of Thames Reach staff had been directly involved. For example, each trainee had a supervisor, life coach, and buddy, who were selected from core staff volunteers, and team and service managers were involved in recruitment panels. After two years, in July 2007, the GROW initiative was mainstreamed, which meant, for example, that there was no longer a dedicated manager and the trainee scheme was harmonized with other similar schemes in Thames Reach. The initiative was viewed within Thames Reach and across the sector as a success, and an example of good practice. By March 2010, 103 staff—23 per cent of the total—had had experience of homelessness, compared with just 6 per cent in March 2005.[6]

Symbols also offer a leverage point for culture change. For example, a share option scheme seen as giving staff a stake in the success of a company might influence employee assumptions about profit and, in terms of artefacts, make the share price more salient and help to establish flexible working patterns. Change in Practice 6.2 also shows the part that can be played by new symbols in culture change: the new trainees and existing staff with experience of homelessness were promoted as symbols, capturing the importance of offering employment to ex-homeless people and the importance of experience of homelessness in serving other users. The introduction of key staff, particularly leaders, from outside an organization (Schein, 2004)—already discussed as a way in which to directly foster new values—can also be a potent symbol of cultural change. Shaping the shared meaning of symbols is a form of sensegiving, a concept that we introduced in Chapter 5.

See Chapters 5 and 11 for more on sensegiving: pp. 96, 248

Finally, it is worth considering the part played by *assumptions* in instigating culture change. Because assumptions are taken-for-granted beliefs and values, which are generally not reflected on and may not be recognized, we think that planned, deliberate organizational culture change rarely, if ever, begins with the reworking of assumptions. But as values, behaviours, and symbols change, assumptions are altered.

The discussion of planned change above implicitly takes an integration point of view on organizational culture. That view guides people to see cultural change in terms of uniform change across the whole organization. The changes, as Enron grew from a pipeline company to a major multinational energy and commodity trading conglomerate with a shift in values toward innovation, risk-taking, and ruthlessness, can be viewed from the integration point of view as a culture change across the whole organization, driven from the top. However, as already stated, there is considerable evidence that the majority of planned culture change efforts are not fully successful. The difficulty is that *emergent* processes of culture change or stability in culture often dominate planned processes. We now turn to culture change as an emergent process. Different factors in the emergence of culture change are illuminated from integration, differentiation, and fragmentation viewpoints.

Emergent culture change

See Chapter 3 for more on emergent change: p. 53

Culture change should not only be regarded as the result of strategic planning; it can also be regarded as an emergent process that happens with or without planning, or despite planning. We look at this first from the integration viewpoint, and then from the differentiation and fragmentation points of view. From an *integration* point of view, there can be a variety of causes of unintended culture change. One is that new artefacts, values, symbols, and assumptions filter into organizations from the societal and business environment. For example, new technological artefacts such as laptops and Blackberry devices can impact cultural dynamics; over time, they may weaken a value for presenteeism or strengthen a value for seven-day commitment. An assumption of gender equality, filtering in through societal influence, while far from universal or unopposed, has much more traction in many Western European organizations today than would have been the case a few decades ago. Assumptions and values can also filter into organizational cultures from their interactions in the commercial environment. At Thames Reach, as explained in Change in Practice 6.2, the instigating factor for culture change was the commitment of statutory funders to a value for 'rehabilitative working practices'. Equally, societal culture—or predominant cultures in the commercial environment of an organization—can have an inertial effect on culture change initiatives, tending to reinforce established values. For example, a value for linking rewards to performance might be more difficult to introduce in a company that operates in a heavily unionized industry.

The integration viewpoint also highlights culture change arising from growth, decline, or crisis in the development of the organization (Schein, 2004). In the first place, the predictable growth of an organization through stages of growth and crises (Greiner, 1998; Phelps et al., 2007) consists in part of changes in culture. Another cause of emergent culture change is scandal and reputational damage (Schein, 2004). Decline and failure also cause culture change (Schein, 2004).

See Chapter 2 for more on growth as a driver of change: p. 27

The differentiation and fragmentation viewpoints offer alternative insights into processes of emergent change. Seen from a *differentiation* viewpoint, alongside change led from the top, subcultures can influence one another. For instance, values can spread from one subculture to another, or there can be revolutionary, or apparent, or incremental change within a subculture. Seen through a differentiation viewpoint, an analysis of culture change at Enron as the company grew would require an examination of whether changes in the culture of the organization arose not from unified leadership, but, for example, from tensions between utility company and commodity trading subcultures.

In mergers and acquisitions, distinct subcultures are always present, at least on a temporary basis. Mergers and acquisitions often do not realize their potential. According to Harding and Rouse (2007), nearly two out of three companies lose market share during the first quarter after a merger; by the third quarter, this rises to nine out of ten. For a minority of mergers and acquisitions, it can be possible for the two former organizations to function independently, particularly if they operate in different markets. Cartwright and Cooper (1993) call this an **extension merger**. However, usually it is imperative—part of the aim behind the merger—to integrate aspects of the two organizations and, in so doing, to reconfigure the subcultures. Many experts recommend that, prior to merger or acquisition, cultural differences between the organizations are analysed. Some believe that there needs to be a certain degree of cultural fit as well as financial/business fit between organizations in order for a merger to be appropriate (Buono et al., 1985; Cartwright and Cooper, 1993; Harding and Rouse, 2007). Integration of cultures can take place through collaboration in building a new organizational culture (an incremental culture change). Cartwright and Cooper call this a **collaborative merger**. Alternatively, as in many acquisitions, integration of cultures can take place through annexation of one organizational culture by the other (a revolutionary culture change). Cartwright and Cooper call this a **redesign merger**. Harding and Rouse (2007) point out that, in the case of a redesign merger, the **cultural acquirer** may not necessarily be the larger organization. Sometimes, a smaller organization is acquired precisely because of the values, symbols, assumptions, and artefacts that it can offer a larger organization.

When does a collaborative merger succeed in building a new culture? Research suggests that, contrary to expectation, this does not necessarily depend on the degree of 'fit' between two organizational cultures. Instead, the single most important factor is the degree to which, formally and informally, there are cross-organizational **socialization activities**. According to Larsson and Lubatkin (2001), if the autonomy of each organization is respected, measures such as introduction programmes, joint training and retreats, employee visits, joint celebrations, and other rituals are likely to be sufficient for a joint organizational culture to be created *emergently*. If autonomy is restricted, as when savings are expected by eliminating replication of physical or human resources, then more formal measures such as transition teams, cross-organizational senior management involvement, and employee exchange/rotation are likely to be required. But, again, Larsson and Lubatkin's research suggests that such measures are usually successful. This research runs counter to the view of some practitioners that specific planed projects to build a new organizational culture are required (Schein, 2009).

Finally, seen from the *fragmentation* viewpoint, organizational culture change is not necessarily centred within or between subcultures. It can emerge simply from unpredictable individual and group understandings of specific issues. This viewpoint highlights how culture change can emerge from, for example, the actions of whistleblowers, and the conflicting emotions and interests of leaders at all levels. The fragmentation viewpoint would allow an understanding of the development of Enron's culture in terms of shifting commitments to values for growth and personal wealth accumulation, respect, and ruthlessness, as circumstances changed over time.

 Exercise 6.4

Identify an organization in which you consider that the culture has changed in the last five years. It could be where you work, or an organization you know well, or a well-known brand.

● Can this be regarded as a planned culture change? Can it (also) be regarded as emergent culture change?

● Whether deliberate or unintended, how do you think the change in culture was accomplished?

● In which ways, or from whose standpoint, has the change in culture been beneficial, and in which ways, or from whose standpoint, detrimental?

 Section 4 Summary

In this section, we have:

● considered how the need for culture change can be diagnosed;
● examined types of culture change and approaches to culture change implementation;
● discussed emergent culture change.

 Integrative Case Study

Culture change at Pace

Pace is a manufacturer of set-top boxes that allow reception of digital television. In 2006, when a new chief executive and HR director were appointed, Pace was close to bankruptcy. The company had debts of £30 million and was making a loss of £15 million on sales of £175 million. The HR director recalls communication being poor, 'mired in eight tiers of management' while 'engineering and sales "threw stones at each other over a high brick wall" rather than communicating or working together', hindering decision-making. According to the chief executive—who had previously been sales and marketing director—'engineers were questioning why we did things in a certain way because they weren't close enough to the customer to know what they wanted and why they wanted it'.

A key aspect of turning this around was a culture change programme. So-called 'Pace values' (passion, integrity, accountability, innovation, and appreciation) and 'Pace behaviours' (customer focus—external and internal, driving for results, leadership, communication, teamwork, and personal responsibility) were introduced. According to the HR director, focusing on customers led to the need to increase responsiveness and the removal of four of the eight layers of management. It was also decided that engineering and sales staff would work together in customer account teams rather than operate separately. She is quoted as explaining:

> Combining sales and engineering in the same team was a symbolic move. But actually it turned out to be incredibly successful . . . Staff were told they were 'jointly accountable' for delivery to the customer. (Churchard, 2010: 20)

The performance management and reward system was tailored to incentivize the desired behaviours. Each of the six behaviours was operationalized in more detail. For example, customer focus was operationalized as:

● Understands and supports our objective of putting the customer at the heart of the business

● Listens to the customer; understands and manages their expectations

● Responds appropriately, accurately and promptly to customer needs

● Develops and maintains effective customer relationships

● Thinks ahead, creating solutions to meet customer needs

(Pace Executive Committee, 2010: 11)

Assessment against the new behaviours made up 50 per cent of an employee's performance rating. Performance management also applied to members of the senior executive team, who were similarly reviewed and rewarded against the behaviours. Three 'critical success factors' for the change programme were established using the mantra 'on time, on margin and on quality'.

In 2008, following the success of these measures, Pace acquired the set-top box business of Phillips, the Dutch electronics manufacturer, for £68 million. Embedding the Pace culture at the new site was a major strategy in the takeover. At Pace, there were dramatic improvements in business performance, profitability, and employee satisfaction. The business rose from seventh place to second place in the league of set-top box manufacturers between 2006 and 2009, with revenues in 2009 of £1.1 billion.

Questions

1. Pace set out five values: passion, integrity, accountability, innovation, and appreciation. What would you need to know to establish whether these were espoused values or values-in-use? Are there other values-in-use that you can identify?

2. Can you judge whether culture change at the company was 'apparent', 'revolutionary', or 'incremental'?

3. In 2010, the leaders of Pace were certain that culture change at the company had contributed directly to radical performance improvement. Do you agree?

Conclusion

Although organizational culture can be difficult to analyse because it is rooted in the informal aspects of organizations, it provides a powerful perspective on organizational change. Central to this is the recognition that how an organization functions and changes depends on the way in which individuals understand and perceive what is going on around them. For this reason, organizational culture may constrain change or enable change to take place, whether change is regarded as planned or emergent. The chapter also addressed the challenge of analysing and changing organizational culture itself. It showed how the various models of culture and cultural dynamics provide insights into how to deal with both change in the context of culture and the challenges of culture change.

 Please visit the Online Resource Centre at **http://www.oxfordtextbooks.co.uk/orc/ myers** *to access further resources for students and lecturers.*

Change in Practice sources

1. Cruver, B. (2002) *Anatomy of Greed: The Unshredded Truth from an Enron Insider*, New York: Carroll & Graf.
2. Enron (2001) 'Enron values', 2 Dec. http://www.enron.com
3. Fox, L. (2003) *Enron: The Rise and Fall*, Hoboken, NJ: John Wiley & Sons.
4. Fusaro, P. C. and Miller, R. M. (2002) *What Went Wrong at Enron: Everyone's Guide to the Largest Bankruptcy in US History.* Hoboken, NJ: John Wiley & Sons.
5. Powers Jr, W. C., Troubh, R. S., and Winokur Jr, H. S. (2002) *Report of Investigation by the Special Investigative Committee of the Board of Directors of Enron Corp.* http://i.cnn.net/cnn/2002/LAW/02/02/enron.report/powers.report.pdf.
6. Based on interviews with Thames Reach staff.

Integrative Case Study sources

Churchard, C. (2010) 'In the top set', *People Management*, **16**(7): 18–21.
Gaydon, N., Hall, S., and Ezard, J. (2008) 'Pace analyst briefing'. http://www.pace.com/media/corporate/PDF/080619_pace_analyst_briefing.pdf
Pace Executive Committee (2010) 'Code of Business Ethics'. http://www.pace.com/media/corporate/PDF/bus_ethics_apr10.pdf
Pace plc (2008) 'Transaction overview'. http://www.pace.com/media/corporate/pdf/080331_transaction_overview.pdf
Palmer, M. (2010) 'Pace to take second set-top box slot', *Financial Times*, 1 Mar: 22.
Stafford, P. (2008) 'Change of channel for TV set-top boxmaker', *Financial Times*, 16 Apr: 24.

Further reading

Daymon, C. (2000) 'Culture formation in a new television station: A multi-perspective analysis', *British Journal of Management*, **11**(2): 121–35.
A case study of one culture change from three points of view—integration, differentiation, and fragmentation—showing what each reveals.

Schein, E. H. (2009) *The Corporate Culture Survival Guide*, 2nd edn, San Francisco, CA: Jossey-Bass.
A practical account of Edgar Schein's influential standpoint on diagnosing and changing culture.

7 Change from the Perspective of Power and Politics

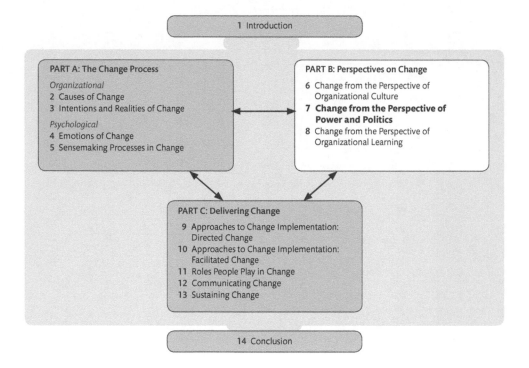

1 Introduction

PART A: The Change Process

Organizational
2 Causes of Change
3 Intentions and Realities of Change

Psychological
4 Emotions of Change
5 Sensemaking Processes in Change

PART B: Perspectives on Change

6 Change from the Perspective of Organizational Culture
7 Change from the Perspective of Power and Politics
8 Change from the Perspective of Organizational Learning

PART C: Delivering Change

9 Approaches to Change Implementation: Directed Change
10 Approaches to Change Implementation: Facilitated Change
11 Roles People Play in Change
12 Communicating Change
13 Sustaining Change

14 Conclusion

 Introduction

This chapter examines the three related phenomena of power, politics, and resistance, offering different theoretical interpretations as to what they mean, their role in organizational change, and the implications for both theory and practice. We call this a 'political' perspective on change. This perspective highlights the adversarial nature of change and is based on the assumption that organizations are formed of different interest groups, whose aspirations for a particular change are often incompatible. Indeed, one researcher describes organizations as 'a cacophony of complementary and competing change attempts, with managers at all levels joining the fray and pushing for issues of particular importance to themselves' (Dutton et al., 2001: 716).

Where there are competing change agendas, choices may not be straightforward about where and how to allocate time, money, people, and assets, or about what to change and what to keep the same. Rather than seeing those choices as being made through rational decision-making, a political perspective focuses on the way in which decisions are made through the exercise of power and influence, and the way in which those decisions may then be rejected through the exercise of a form of counter power, often referred to as 'resistance'. However, this exercise of power and counter-power is often seen as self-serving, which contributes to the largely negative view of power and politics: 'Most people perceive only the dark side of politics, and indeed there is a dark side, characterized by destructive opportunism and dysfunctional game playing' (Ferris and Kacmar, 1992: 113). This is a fundamental issue in working with organizational politics, which we will explore further.

A political perspective also suggests that the neatness and clarity of planned organizational change is a facade masking the interests and moves behind the scenes of different groups and individuals. Planned approaches emphasize rationality and logic. A political perspective on change allows for rationality and plans, but suggests that this on its own is insufficient. While groups bending the rules in their own interests may have perfectly logical reasons for doing so, the resulting behaviour by the organization may no longer appear rational (Davey, 2008: 651).

See Chapter 3 for more on planned organizational change: p. 49

Main topics to be covered in this chapter

- Power and politics and their relevance to organizational change
- Political interventions
- Alternative ways of understanding resistance
- Interventions to increase commitment or decrease resistance

Section 1: Power and politics and their relevance to organizational change

In this opening section, definitions of power and politics are examined, and their relevance to organizational change is explored.

Power

Power has traditionally been defined as the ability to change other people's behaviour so that they do what you want them to do. More recently, there has also been an interest in 'soft power'—the ability to get others to think the way you do. Whereas power is often described as a resource, politics tends to be seen as power being actively used.

There are three main ways of conceptualizing power in the literature (Buchannan and Badham, 2008): power as an individual property; power as a relational property; and power as embedded in organizational structures and procedures.

1. The most popular understanding of power views it as something that individuals possess. Sources of power can be structural, such as your formal position in an organization, your access to information, the centrality of your business unit, your physical and social place in the organization's communication network, or your role in resolving critical problems.

Sources of power can also be individual. Examples would be energy, the ability to 'read' other people, flexibility, and a willingness to engage in conflict and confrontation (Pfeffer, 1992). Managers who are able to draw from both sources can wield significant power.

2. The second and related view treats power as the property of the relationship between individuals rather than the property of one person and is a view associated with French and Raven (1958), who offer the categories outlined in Table 7.1.

Here, power is understood as a relational construct because it depends on the beliefs of others. For instance, a change agent may have superior knowledge and be able to control rewards and penalties, but if nobody believes that he or she has such attributes, others are unlikely to comply with his or her requests, so that, in fact, he or she has limited power. Another feature of this view of power is that individuals may use different power bases at different times and in different contexts, and these bases are interrelated. So, once a change agent has used coercive power, it may be hard to subsequently use referent power. Raven added the sixth power base, information power, in 1965.

However, these categories are arguably quite broad and it is questionable whether, in practice, power can be fitted into six neat categories, or eight, as later theorists proposed (Benafari et al., 1986). As Clegg and Hardy (1996) note, such sources are likely to be infinite, and highly dependent on what resources are available and appropriate in specific circumstances.

3. Proponents of the third view of power argue that a problem with both the first two approaches is that they focus on visible or semi-visible aspects of power. They suggest that power is pervasive and embedded in less obvious features of organizations, such as regulations, norms, and routines that perpetuate existing power relations. For instance, Davey's (2008) research shows that women continue to be excluded from existing informal networks and mentoring relationships, making it harder for them to progress their issues or their careers. This embedded view is valuable in alerting people to the way in which taken-for-granted patterns and practices in an organization, or indeed society, can serve to perpetuate existing power relations, rather than to encourage or allow change. As Buchannan and Badham say, 'invisibility and intangibility cannot be equated with insignificance' (1999: 57).

Table 7.1 Individual power bases

Positional power	Derived from your formal position
Coercive power	Your ability to threaten others and to carry out threats
Expert power	Derived from knowledge and experience
Reward power	Your ability to reward others
Personal or referent power	Based on others liking you and believing that you have desirable qualities and personality traits
Information power	Derived from access to data

Sources: French and Raven (1958; 1965)

Change in Practice 7.1 illustrates different uses of power and political behaviour.

 Change in Practice 7.1

Introducing a new IT system in a hospital

A large teaching hospital in the UK, with 1,500 beds, was the UK pilot for the implementation of a new hospital-wide IT system, costing £10.1 million. The team charged with introducing the new system was aware of the challenges generally experienced when trying to introduce IT, which is often seen as costly, difficult to implement, time-consuming to operate, and of marginal significance to the organization and its core purpose.

The same year, the hospital achieved Trust status, which meant that it became independent and self-governing, with a Trust board and chief executive, accountable directly to government ministers. The move to Trust status had strengthened the formal position of the executive directors and the chief executive, however in practice they were constrained by the need to meet the demands of the government, public opinion, and powerful internal groups, particularly doctors.

The IT implementation team explicitly recognized two key interest groups within the hospital i) clinicians, such as doctors and nurses, whose primary concern was the quality of patient care; and ii) managers, including the Trust board and finance managers, who were interested in control, economy, and efficiency. A third internal stakeholder group was support staff, consisting of porters, secretaries, and those working in medical records, but these were not thought to be critical to successful implementation of the new IT system.

Brown (1995), a researcher working in the hospital, perceived the new Trust board to be highly sensitive to internal or external criticism and that there 'seemed to be an active constraint on their willingness to force through change' (ibid: 957). So, in order to gain user acceptance for the new IT system, the implementation team had to 'engineer others' understanding of the system through calculated argument (and) control over the flow of information . . . so that they viewed it more favourably than might otherwise be the case' (ibid: 952). The implementation team did this by identifying the main benefits of the system, but then tailoring the message in conversation to meet the interests of those whom they were trying to influence. In the words of the project manager:

> The trick with those particular staff (clinicians) is that you don't go in there saying you could save them three nurses and whatever—it's the clinical benefits which again are easy to point out . . . (as for) . . . emphasiz(ing) the financial benefits . . . you talk about that when you're talking to the Trust Board and the finance directors and people outside the Trust. (Quoted ibid.: 959)

The team also deliberately withheld key information about the system that could have been used to help junior doctors with the diagnosis and treatment of patients, because the team did not want to be seen to be attempting to de-skill doctors. Another feature of the system would have allowed the hospital to evaluate the cost-efficiencies of different clinicians. This too was never mentioned, because the team did not want to upset the doctors.

The implementation team and its sponsors referred to all of these activities as 'marketing' or 'sales', denying for themselves and others the extent to which they were involved in political activities. 'Politics' was seen as a very derogatory word in the hospital, whilst at the time, marketing and sales had positive, private-sector connotations. The project manager was steeped in the culture and traditions of the NHS, and therefore adept at managing meanings of the new IT system, whereas the chief information officer, a recent joiner to the health sector, encountered considerable difficulties in articulating the benefits, building credibility, and influence. After a year, he was, in effect, sidelined, while the project manager was promoted.[1]

In Change in Practice 7.1, the implementation team did not perceive the organization as a monolithic entity, but as composed of different interest groups with different attitudes towards the proposed changes. The team also made a judgement about the degrees of power and importance that the team believed the different interest groups possessed: it paid significant attention to the concerns of clinicians and managers; no attempt was made to engage with support staff. The Trust board members had positional power because they were technically in charge of the organization. However, they were reluctant to push through any changes because they recognized the greater power of the doctors who had medical know-how (expert power) and knowledge without which the hospital could not survive (coercive power). This is the group that the implementation team targeted. The support services group was largely ignored by the implementation team because it did not regard the group as possessing any of these sources of power and the team was, therefore, not seen as a threat to the project. The implementation team itself used information power very carefully, sharing some information about the system and withholding other information.

The example illustrates another key feature of power and politics—its hidden nature. Although 'political behaviour sometimes takes the form of two or more armed camps publicly fighting things out, it usually is much more subtle. In many cases it occurs completely under the surface of public dialogue' (Kotter and Schlesinger, 1979: 108). In terms of the iceberg analogy, it is under the water, but significantly shapes what happens above it. Indeed, Lukes (2005: 1) suggests that 'power is at its most effective when least observable'. He looks at power in relation to decision-making. A one-dimensional view of power looks at whose view dominates in decision-making. A two-dimensional view of power is also interested in non-decision-making, because power can be used to veto and stop things happening. However, Lukes (1974; 2005) contends that even this is too simplistic. The third dimension of power is that of being able to limit the political agenda so that certain issues do not even get to the table to be discussed openly. In Change in Practice 7.1, the implementation team deliberately withheld information about the control features of the new IT system, so team members were using the third dimension of power to ensure that this aspect was never even discussed with the doctors.

See Chapter 6 for more on the iceberg model: p. 112

Politics

The word 'politics' comes from the Greek word *polis* meaning 'city state'. Aristotle advocated politics as a means of reconciling the need for unity in the city state (that is, the *polis*) with the fact that the *polis* was made up of diverse interests. Definitions of organizational politics fall into two broad categories (Zanzi and O'Neill, 2001). The first sees politics as negative and self-serving, leading to divisive, illegitimate, and dysfunctional behaviour and conflict. The second view sees political behaviour more neutrally, believing that it can sometimes be beneficial.

These two different views about politics derive from different views about organizations. Those with a **unitarist** perspective on organizations tend to emphasize cooperation and collaboration, and view politics as an aberration because any activity that is not directed to shared organizational goals is seen as both deviant and irrational. **Pluralist** approaches acknowledge the inevitability of politics in the activities of subgroups in an organization competing for limited resources. The implementation team in Change in Practice 7.1 recognized different interest groups, so was taking a pluralist view.

Defining political behaviour is challenging because the discussion is not purely theoretical. Definitions tend to carry with them an underlying criticism of those who act politically. Mintzberg (1985: 172), for instance, describes politics as 'individual or group behaviour that is informal, ostensibly parochial, typically divisive, and above all, in a technical sense, illegitimate—sanctioned neither by formal authority, accepted ideology, nor certified expertise'. The notion of politics being illegitimate or unsanctioned is a key element of many definitions (Poon, 2003), but who decides what behaviours are sanctioned or not and does that make some of them wrong, because they are not sanctioned? Whistleblowers' activities are, by definition, not sanctioned by those in authority within the organization, but may be regarded by others as morally right.

Definitions of politics do not just emphasize the unsanctioned nature of political behaviour. There is often an assumption that individuals playing politics do so for personal gain and individual career achievement, as well as sometimes for organizational benefit. It is this potential for politics to be self-serving that contributes to the 'taint' associated with politics. The following definitions both include this element.

- 'Organizational politics exploits unofficial networks and contacts to achieve personal gain.' (Ferris and Kacmar, 1991)
- 'Organizational politicking involves engaging in activities to acquire, develop, retain and use power, in order to obtain your preferred outcomes in a situation where there is uncertainty or disagreement'. (Huczynski, 1996: 247)

Political skill

However, of course, the really skilled politicians disguise their self-serving intentions. Ferris et al. (2000: 30) describe political skill as 'an interpersonal style that combines political astuteness with the ability to relate well, and otherwise demonstrate situationally appropriate behaviour in a disarmingly charming and engaging manner that inspires confidence, trust, sincerity and genuineness'.

Baddeley and James (1987) offer an interesting distinction in this respect, following their research into local government. They differentiate between the clever and the wise. Both types of people are skilled at 'reading' the politics of an organization, but whereas the former tend to be concerned primarily with their own self-interest, the wise are concerned primarily with what is in the interest of the organization and are predisposed to act with integrity. Whilst an interesting distinction in theory, this assumes that what is in the organization's best interests is clear and objective rather than dependent on whom you talk to. It also assumes that others' intentions and motivations are transparent, and that it is easy to discern those acting with the collective interest in mind and those acting with self-interest. In our experience, neither is always the case in practice.

 Exercise 7.1

Contemplate an example of what you consider political behaviour that you have noticed where you work or study.

- What do you imagine the individual was hoping to achieve through such behaviour?
- What feelings did this evoke in you?
- What circumstances or situations have, or would, encourage you to engage in political behaviour?
- What would stop you, personally, from involvement in political behaviour?

Colloquially people are referred to as 'playing politics'. Some theorists describe organizations as political or games arenas (Ferris et al., 1996; Mintzberg, 1985), in which some of the players are unknown and many of the rules are unclear. Others talk of 'winning the turf game' (Buchanan and Badham, 2008). In such games, organizational politics pits individuals or groups against each other, sometimes without all parties being aware of it. Tactics, according to Conner (2006), may be to outwit, outplay, or outlast. For instance, a co-worker may spread rumours to make a colleague's change proposal look badly conceived, simply so that he or she will have a better prospect of promotion. The colleague may be completely oblivious to such behaviour, as a feature of such games is creating a lack of transparency about what is going on. So groups of insiders and outsiders emerge, with not all organizational members having access to the necessary information, alliances, or understanding of the rules of the political game, which can subsequently lead to perceptions of organizational injustice.

This leads to another common theme in the organizational politics literature—the notion that, regardless of the actual existence of politics, the perception of politics is extremely important (Ferris and Kacmar, 1992). Gandz and Murray (1980) suggest that organizational politics is best understood as a state of mind rather than an objective reality. Judging political actions and their outcomes is therefore largely a function of the values and perspective of the evaluator, and what becomes important for the change agent is the meaning ascribed to their actions in their context by other organizational players. So behaviour can be seen as political if someone defines or rejects a behaviour as political (Connor, 2006).

The relevance of power and politics to organizational change

There are two main reasons to suggest that understanding organizational change through the perspective of power and politics is useful and important. The first is that, when an organization is in the midst of change, there is likely to be an increase in political behaviour, which affects everyone, whether leading change or on the receiving end of change. The second is that there is a view held by some that change agents need to engage in politics if they are to be successful.

To expand on the first point, organizational politics involves unsanctioned and informal forms of behaviour (Zanzi and O'Neill, 2001). These forms of behaviour are more likely when there is uncertainty because formal rules and procedures are no longer adequate guides to what should be done. Uncertainty and ambiguity increase when an organization is in the thick of change. The more complex the change, the harder it is to anticipate the potential consequences, which increases uncertainty, in turn amplifying the likelihood of political behaviour. Lack of trust is also associated with an increase in political behaviour (Poon, 2003). In a low-trust climate, people are more likely to be suspicious of the motives and intentions of others and, in such situations, informal and non-sanctioned behaviours are more likely to be perceived negatively and as political. Trust is likely to decrease during change because psychological and implied contracts are deemed to be violated, so an increase in ambiguity and uncertainty, and a decrease in trust, all contribute to the likelihood of increasing political behaviour during change.

See Chapter 5 for more on psychological contract violations: p. 88

However, this increase in political behaviour is neither inherently positive nor negative. Table 7.2 demonstrates the potential impact of political behaviour on change.

With flatter organizational structures and many change programmes being run as cross-functional project teams, change agents, whatever their particular roles, are unlikely to have line authority over those whom they need to influence. Hence, the argument goes, the need to use political skills. Such a view is anathema to proponents of organization development, who emphasize the value of trust and openness. We know from our own work teaching change that many leaders find politics distasteful too. However, 'the change agent who is not politically skilled will fail' claim Buchannan and Badham (2008: 18). 'You may find . . . power plays and the politicians behind them unsavoury—and they can be. But you'll have to get over your qualms if you want to bring about meaningful change' concurs another commentator (Pfeffer, 2010: 87).

See Chapter 10 for more on organizational development: pp. 222–8

Certainly, studies suggest that the perceived effectiveness of organization change is in part dependent on the political skills of change agents (Ferris et al., 2000). Indeed, an anonymous survey of 250 British managers (Buchanan and Badham, 2008: 27) found that:

- 60 per cent agreed that 'politics become more important as organizational change becomes more complex';
- 79 per cent agreed that 'politics can be used to initiate and drive useful change initiatives';
- 81 per cent that 'politics can be effective in dealing with resistance to change';

Table 7.2 Potential impact of political behaviour on change

Positive effects of politics	Negative effects of politics
Accelerates change when formal methods of influence are slow	Behind-the-scenes lobbying and building coalitions can absorb significant amounts of time and energy that could be used elsewhere
Stimulates debate and helps to ensure that all sides of an issue are aired and debated	Those with less real power may have their interests ignored and those with power may advance their own interests to the detriment of others or the organization
Can be a critical source of dynamic energy	Creates a climate of mistrust and suspicion
Keeps conversation about change 'in play', ensuring that proponents of change hone and refine their arguments	Distraction from organizational goals
Recognition and achievement for the change agent	Unproductive allocation of resources
Increases involvement of key political players, and so increases their engagement and ownership	Excludes those who are not able, or do not wish, to play politics, perpetuating existing inequalities

- 93 per cent agreed (21 per cent strongly) that 'politics can be used to slow down and block useful change initiatives';
- only 9 per cent agreed with the item 'change agents who avoid organization politics are more likely to succeed in their roles'.

Buchannan and Boddy (1992) offer a useful framework for change agents to think about their behaviour, introducing the metaphor of the **front stage** to describe the rational arena of action for change agents and **back stage** to describe the political arena. They suggest that:

> the change agent has to support the 'public performance' of rationally considered and logically phased and visibly participative change with 'backstage activity' in the recruitment and maintenance of support and in seeking and blocking resistance ... 'Backstaging' is concerned with the exercise of 'power', with 'intervening in political and cultural systems', with influencing, negotiating and selling, and deliberately tailoring messages. (Ibid: 27)

In times of change, holding onto the appearance of rationality may be an important source of security and reassurance, even if there is an intensification of political activity back stage.

 Section 1 Summary

In this section, we have:

- explored definitions of power and politics and the challenges associated with those definitions;
- explored the relevance of power and politics to organizational change and change agents.

Section 2: **Political interventions**

A political perspective on change assumes that people want to influence strategy or changes that are likely to impact on their interests. In this section, we examine a number of different political interventions from forming coalitions, presenting ideas for change and approaches to mapping the positions and power of different groups and individuals relative to a particular change.

Coalitions as political alliances

The coming together into groups of those who share particular interests, or who want to advance specific approaches to change, is described as the formation of **coalitions**. When more people are involved, and are organized, an issue can become more visible and the group potentially more powerful and influential.

See Chapter 11 for more on the role of leaders: p. 244

Leaders wanting to initiate change need to ensure that at least a majority of those on their own executive team are actively in support of the change. Without what Kotter and Cohen (2002) refer to as a 'powerful guiding coalition', it can be hard, if not impossible, to sustain the momentum and energy required for radical change. It can also be hard to convince employees that the leadership is serious about change. This is why many consulting interventions around change often begin with one to one interviews with the board or leadership team to identify whether or not there is indeed a sufficiently strong guiding coalition.

The word 'guiding coalition' tends to refer to coalitions formed of senior leaders. However, coalitions can be formed from different levels within the organization. For instance, we worked with a leading Asian airline, in which the impetus for organizational change came from a coalition of confident, highly qualified graduates who had been managers for three to five years. They threatened to leave unless there were changes to the very paternalistic ways of working in the organization, posing a significant risk to the company's reputation, in a country that takes 'loss of face' very seriously.

Coalitions also form against change. In 2010, British Airways cabin staff formed a coalition against changes to pay and conditions that they claimed had been imposed without consultation. In this case, the trade union, Unite, provided a critical catalytic role in targeting employees to join the coalition. Sometimes, there may be shared interests, but no coalition forms. In Change in Practice 7.1, members of support staff were all worried about losing control to the new computer system, but they never coalesced. Instead, in the words of the director of radiology, resistance was 'passive and quiet—the soggy sponge' (Brown, 1995: 961), absorbing what was happening, but not actively challenging it.

The formation of coalitions is the primary means by which individuals go from being on the same wavelength to being allies who recognize their common interest and are willing to devote resources (time, phone calls, and contacts) to a common effort (Bacharach and Lawler, 1998). So why do some individuals decide to collaborate to further their interests rather than go solo? Workers who have very standard, highly routine tasks may view themselves as potentially expendable and may therefore be motivated to join forces with others to create critical mass to influence a particular change. The decision to join a coalition is also often affected by social similarities such as departmental membership, professional affiliations, or demographics such as gender, age, and ethnicity.

Some coalitions, over time, become so entrenched they become explicit, openly acknowledged sources of political identities such as 'head office', 'the regions', 'the old guard', and 'the union', with reputations for, or against, change. In other cases, coalitions remain unacknowledged explicitly, but widely suspected or inferred. They can thus be thought of as subtle, informal 'institutionalized substratum of organizations' (Baccharach and Lawler, 1998: 73). In other words, they have continuing existence and influence, hence are institutionalized, but they are part of the organization that operates under the water, to return to the iceberg metaphor.

The politics of presenting ideas for change

Sometimes, managing politics around change is less about joining coalitions and more about the way in which proposals for change are drawn to the attention of senior people in an attempt to influence them. Rather than using the value-laden terms of politics, Dutton et al. (2001) use the term **issue selling** to describe the behaviour of people outside top management who compete for attention for their ideas about what should change and how. Understanding how attention is allocated inside an organization can provide insights into organizational change because some issues will come to be seen as more important and, through this, certain decisions will be made and others not made (Ocasio, 1997). This perspective thus offers a more emergent way of understanding organizational change, rather than a directed, top-down view, as it shows how the source and energy of ideas for change can come from people below top management, who may not even consider themselves to be change agents. However, in competing for senior managers' attention for their ideas to be adopted, 'issue sellers' are also recognizing the decision-making power of senior management and want their ideas to become accepted, legitimized, and resourced as part of any planned, directed change.

In an empirical account of issue selling, Dutton et al. (2001) found that managers who were successful in selling their ideas used a range of approaches to packaging the issue, and also drew on their knowledge of people and organizational norms. These included the following.

1. *Using the logic of the business plan*, which is also an example of what Buchanan and Boddy (1992) call a front stage activity.

2. *Persistence*: one respondent described how he tried to influence a vice president—'when you tell him about a concept, you sort of acclimate him to the situation and you repeatedly tell him about it for several months so he knows it is coming . . . and then you hit him with the big package' (Dutton et al., 2001: 722).

3. *Incrementalism*: packaging the issue as incremental refers to the way in which the size of a proposal is presented so that it appears more palatable to the target audience. Fincham (1999) also found that consultants frequently use incrementalism as a tactic when selling change projects, so that they appear more do-able.

4. *Bundling* is the term Dutton et al. (2001) use to describe managers' efforts to connect their issue to other issues or goals that had value and were salient in the organization, such as profitability, market share, or organizational image, or were important to key individuals whom they were trying to influence.

Three kinds of knowledge of the change context are important for issue sellers. An individual's ability to 'bundle' effectively is highly dependent on what Dutton et al. (2001) describe as **strategic knowledge**. Those who are aware of what has currency in their organization are, thus, better equipped to shape change. Strategic knowledge also includes a sense of the organization's competitive landscape and broader external context (Floyd and Wooldridge, 2000).

Relational knowledge refers to managers' understanding of individuals and social relationships. It enables them to answer questions such as: who will be affected by this change? Who has power to help or hinder this issue? When will people be ready to hear about this? This knowledge allows managers to anticipate and indeed to pre-empt responses, to work with the power structure, and 'to navigate the political aspects of a context' (Dutton et al., 2001: 727). The project manager in Change in Practice 7.1 showed evidence of using relational knowledge, tailoring what he said depending to whom he was talking.

Managers' understanding of the norms of expected or appropriate behaviour is what Dutton et al. (2001) refer to as **normative knowledge**. Those with normative knowledge know how data is normally presented, what kind of meetings would be legitimate for discussing a change, and how much challenge within formal meetings is tolerated. In Change in Practice 7.1, the project manager's boss, the chief information officer, was new to the sector. He struggled to gain credibility and influence because he could not read the signs of what was appropriate to say and what was not. Management consultants too are frequently unable to influence the internal politics around an organizational change because, as outsiders, they do not have access to normative and relational knowledge, so cannot 'play the game' and manage meanings with the same subtlety as those inside the organization (Fincham, 1999). In contrast, the project manager in Change in Practice 7.1 had relational, normative, and strategic knowledge, so could orchestrate the involvement of the right people in the right way at the right time. Arguably, such knowledge could also be described as understanding the culture of the organization.

See Chapter 6 for more on culture: p. 122

Understanding how middle managers can influence change by packaging their issues in ways that capture senior leaders' attention challenges the notion that change happens only because of the heroic efforts of those at the top. Senior management can facilitate this process if they provide opportunities for managers to deepen their understanding of contextual knowledge through involvement in conversations about strategy (Floyd and Wooldridge, 2000). Conversely, 'by failing to make sure that people are equipped with the knowledge to achieve effective selling from below, organizations rob themselves of this vital source of internal change initiatives' (Dutton et al., 2001: 731).

 Exercise 7.2

Think of an issue about which you feel strongly and would like to see changed in an organization of which you are a member. The organization could be where you work, the college at which you are studying, or a social organization to which you belong, such as a sports or voluntary organization. Imagine that you would like to bring this issue to the attention of 'top management'.

● How could you package this issue to gain the attention of those leading the organization?

● In what way does your relational, normative, and strategic knowledge influence your choices as to how to package the issue?

● Ask one or two people who do not know the organization what they would do to gain senior management attention. How different is their approach from yours and to what extent does this reflect their lack of relational, normative, and strategic knowledge?

● How do you think his or her approach would have been received? What insights does this give you into the politics around organizational change?

Stakeholder mapping and commitment planning

What should those charged with leading or implementing a change do when faced with different coalitions for, or against, change? How do they know how to tailor the message and to whom? Sometimes, change agents or leaders rely on their intuitive political judgement or what Dutton et al. (2001) would call relational knowledge. A more systematic approach to understanding the political dimension of a particular change is through stakeholder mapping (Scholes, 1998). Indeed 86 per cent of a survey of 250 British managers agreed with the statement that managing change is about managing stakeholders (Buchanan and Badham, 1999: 18).

The notion of stakeholders recognizes what we have referred to earlier as different interest groups. To ensure the successful implementation of a change and to minimize the likelihood of resistance, stakeholder mapping involves identifying, in advance, groups and key individuals who will want to have a say: groups who will be affected significantly and groups who may

	Low interest	High interest
Low power	A: Minimal effort	B: Keep informed
High power	C: Keep satisfied	D: Key players

Figure 7.1 Stakeholder mapping
Source: Scholes (1998)

need to make just minor adjustments. It involves careful consideration of views, motivations, power bases, and ability to help or to hinder the change.

One of the most frequently used tools is what Scholes (1998) refers to as a power–interest matrix. This is a two-by-two template, with level of interest along one axis and power on the other, as illustrated in Figure 7.1.

Change agents and leaders using this type of map need to decide whom to include and whom to leave out when populating the four quadrants. 'Avoid plotting long lists of stakeholders who "in principle" or "potentially" could have influence', counsels Scholes (1998: 155). In our experience, it is helpful to keep in mind that the focus is not about the general power of a group or individual, but their power in relation to this particular change. It is also helpful to subdivide groups if there are different levels of interest within those groups. So, when creating a stakeholder map for the implementation of a new IT system for customer relationship management, putting all of the executive team in the quadrant high power and high interest may not be appropriate if actually it is only the marketing director and the IT director who really want this change.

Once a stakeholder map has been created, using dimensions such as those suggested above, a stakeholder management strategy needs to be created. It should set out tactics in relation to the different stakeholder groups and identify who is responsible for implementing the activities in relation to each group. In some cases, managing stakeholders may occur through formal project management processes such as quarterly project reviews; sometimes it may be more of a 'back stage' activity (Buchanan and Boddy, 1992).

 Exercise 7.3

Take the example of a change you would like to initiate, which may be the same as the one you considered in Exercise 7.2.

- Create your own stakeholder map.
- Reflect on your experience of creating the map: What was easy? What may have been more difficult? What insights does this give you into the potential usefulness of such maps?
- What tactics come to mind for dealing with people in each of the quadrants?

Commitment mapping focuses on the commitment of the key players that have been identified. To create a commitment map, the names of target individuals or groups, whose commitment is needed if the change is to be successful, are written down. The focus is thus on the key players from Scholes' matrix. An estimate of their current position, attitude, and ability/power to influence the change is made, as is the position that you would like them to hold. An estimate of the critical mass of commitment needed to ensure the effectiveness of the change is also made and a created plan for getting this, with dates for reviewing progress.

Beckhard and Harris (1987) suggest there are three different kinds of commitment: 'let it happen' (that is, those who will not actively derail the change); 'help it to happen' (those who proactively support the change); and 'make it happen' (those who proactively drive the change). They also recommend settling for the minimum commitment required to effect the change, rather than trying to get as much support as possible, because it takes time and energy to convert people into supporters of the change. A fictitious example of a commitment map for Change in Practice 7.1 is shown in Table 7.3. The names of each individual or group who can have a major impact—that is, the key players—are written in the left-hand column. The letter 'O' is put in the appropriate column for the minimum commitment that the team assumed would be required for the change to occur and an 'X' put in the box that represents their current commitment. If the O and the X are in the same box, no further influencing is required. A plan is then put together to identify how the change team is going to try and influence each player's position.

Table 7.3 A commitment map

Key players	Opposed	Let it happen	Help it happen	Make it happen
1. CEO		X ·······························▶		O
2. Finance director		X ···········▶	O	
3. Medical director		X ···········▶	O	
4. Support staff	XO			
5. Clinicians	X ···········▶	O		
6. Managers	X ····························▶		O	

 Exercise 7.4

Taking the example of a change you would like to initiate, which may be the same as the one you considered in exercise 7.2:

- Create your own commitment plan, focussing on key players.
- What are the benefits you might gain from having created your commitment plan?
- What, if any, challenges did you experience in creating the plan?
- What might you do to mitigate these challenges?

The creation of stakeholder and commitment maps provide a forum for explicitly discussing the critical, back stage activity of influencing those who have the power to support or block the change. Without it, team members may gossip or moan about different stakeholders, but have no systematic approach for dealing with them. The creation of a map also gives team members the opportunity to check out or challenge their own and each others' perceptions of key players' interest and power. It also allows the team to think creatively about who is best placed to influence key players or groups. In one case, a team realized that none of them had the credibility to influence a particular individual, and that instead their job was to influence someone else outside the team and to persuade them to go and talk to this key player.

On the downside, some people feel uncomfortable in engaging in political activity so explicitly. Others find it frustrating because the positions on the map and judgements about the level of critical mass required are subjective and based on intuition, not hard fact. If stakeholder or commitment maps are to remain useful, they also need to be regularly reviewed and adjusted as unfolding events impact stakeholders' positions. In addition, it can sometimes be hard to identify all of the stakeholders. One of us worked with a project team implementing an IT system at an embassy overseas. The team had made a commitment map, but only after the project stalled did they realize they had missed off a key player, who was not even employed by the embassy: the ambassador's wife! At the social occasions she hosted, she heard staff's concerns about the project being expressed by their partners. She then passed on those concerns to the ambassador, who became more and more opposed to the change.

 Section 2 Summary

In this section, we have:

- examined the formation and role of coalitions as political alliances for or against change;
- examined the politics of presenting ideas for change;
- looked at stakeholder and commitment maps and explored their benefits and limitations.

Section 3: **Resistance**

This section begins with a brief overview of the nature of resistance and then explores three different ways of understanding it. Traditional views take an evaluative stance and assume resistance is something to be managed and 'dealt with'. Psychological approaches tend to adopt a non-judgemental stance. They see identity as key to understanding resistance, and seek to explore the complexities of individual and group responses. Although psychological approaches do not dismiss resistors as mad or bad, they still view them as being in opposition to the change. The last approach we will consider challenges this, and takes a more critical view, suggesting that 'resistance' is actually a creation of change agent sensemaking. The section concludes with a brief review of the potential value of resistance to organizations.

Introduction to resistance

Few organizational change efforts are complete failures, but equally few are complete successes. Most encounter some form of opposition to change, which costs time, money, and emotional effort, and may sometimes derail the change. One of the main reasons conventionally given to explain why change management proves difficult in practice is that of resistance to change. Indeed, resistance is often presented as *the* major difficulty (Grey, 2003: 14).

The term 'resistance' literally means a restraining force that attempts to maintain the status quo of the current situation. In the context of organizational change, **resistance** can be defined as 'intentional acts of commission or omission that defy the wishes of others' (Ashforth and Mael, 1998: 90). In other words, resistance may take the form of people actively doing something they should officially not, or, equally, deliberately not doing something they should.

Managers and change agents often perceive resistance negatively because it can get in the way of them achieving their goals. This can encourage a view of resistors as obstacles, shortsighted, insubordinate, and disobedient. As such, the label of resistance can encourage a dismissive attitude to potentially valid reasons for opposing a change. The convention historically has been to refer to acts by those in authority, for example leaders or managers, as acts of control and to refer to employee responses that are intended to oppose these acts as resistance. This may be because it was assumed that employees who were not part of the management or supervisory structure were more likely to be the targets rather than the instigators of change. More recent writers would regard managers, especially middle managers, as just as likely to resist as those with no management or supervisory role.

However, it is somewhat arbitrary to label one behaviour an act of control or power and the other an act of resistance. As Knights and Vurdubakis argue, 'acts of resistance are also act of power' (1994: 191). Indeed, a distinctive feature is that 'power and resistance are embedded in a dynamic relationship that tends to be mutually reinforcing' (Ashforth and Mael, 1998: 90). This can be seen in heavily unionized environments such as British Airways, in which leaders and unions follow a pattern of frequent threats and strikes. So, attempts to exercise control meet with resistance, which prompts an act of counter-resistance, inciting more resistance in a potentially never-ending cycle. Indeed Buchanan and Boddy (1992) talk of resistance as counter-implementation and change agents' responses as counter-counter implementation.

Traditional approaches

Traditional approaches to resistance encourage leaders to analyse resistance objectively. The dominant assumption is that leaders have the legitimate right to minimize, or even to 'mow over', resistance, to use Kotter and Schlesinger's (1979) term. They identify four sources of resistance.

1. *Parochial self-interest* suggests that people resist change because they focus on their own best interests and not those of the total organization. Note the heavily value-laden nature of the label, which assumes that leaders and managers occupy the moral high ground and know what is best for the organization. One could also argue that we all act in our self-interest, at least to some degree.

2. People resist change because of *misunderstanding and lack of trust*. This is particularly likely to occur when there is a climate of low trust, because managers are unable to surface

misunderstandings and clarify them before the mood has hardened to one of resistance. This type of resistance can catch managers by surprise if they assume that people resist change only when it is not in their best interest.

3. Sometimes, people resist because they have a *low tolerance for change*, and experience anxiety, insecurity, and fear that they may not be able to develop the new skills or behaviours required. Such resistance can apply to all employees, and may often apply to managers themselves, who may intellectually accept the change, but be emotionally unable to make the transition.

See Chapter 4 for more on emotions and change: p. 63

4. The last source of resistance identified by Kotter and Schlesinger is that of *different assessments*. Sometimes, individuals or groups interpret the facts or data differently from those initiating or explaining the change, or indeed may have access to different information. In doing so, they may conclude that there are more costs and fewer benefits to themselves and/or the organization itself than those presented.

The desire to analyse resistance objectively is taken a step further in Beckhard and Harris' (1987) formula:

C only if (ABD) > X
where

C = the change

A = the level of dissatisfaction with the status quo

B = the desirability of the proposed change or end state

D = the practicality of the change (minimal risk and disruption)

X = the 'cost' of changing

The factors, A, B, and D need to outweigh the perceived costs (X) for change to occur. If those whose commitment to change is required are not sufficiently dissatisfied with the present state of affairs (A), keen to achieve the desired end (B), and convinced that the change is feasible (D), then they will be likely to resist change.

In our experience, leaders are often drawn to this formula, perhaps because it appears to take the apparent messiness and unpredictability of people's response to change and summarize the potential level of resistance with logic and objectivity, the hallmarks of front stage activity. It can also potentially diagnose what type of intervention may be required to increase dissatisfaction with the status quo (A) or to convince that the change is possible (D). However, as with the commitment map, it relies on perceptions and judgements about people and their potential reactions, which are inherently subjective. It also assumes that an individual's responses will be very similar to those of others, can be standardized, and easily understood and evaluated by others, for example managers and change agents.

Psychological approaches

Psychological approaches to understanding resistance focus on the point of view of those resisting and tend to take a non-judgemental stance, maintaining that whether resistance is seen as positive or negative, rational or irrational, is largely a matter of perspective. The main contention is that acts of resistance are inherently meaningful to those carrying them out and to their peers, and that resistance is often prompted by a perceived threat to a valued conception of the self—that is, individuals' senses of who they are.

At a certain point, with all organizational changes, high-level plans become translated into changes to individuals' jobs. This might be changes to the role itself, to ways of working, or newly desired attitudes and behaviours. Any unilateral change to these terms is likely to be perceived as a breach of contract or a breaking of implied promises and commitments. It can, therefore, be a threat to face, inciting anger and a desire to retaliate. Resistance is more likely when people feel that change is imposed. This is particularly so when norms of **procedural justice** are not observed (for example there is perceived to be no warning or explanation of why terms or jobs are being changed), when the threat is perceived to be severe, and when the changes threaten individuals' identity. For instance, in the conflict between British Airways leaders and the union in March 2010, some of the latter's grievances were that the union and staff had not been adequately consulted on the changes and, therefore, norms of procedural justice had been breached.

As people tend to believe that bad things do not happen accidentally, they require a causal agent. The stronger the threat to their reputation and sense of who they are, the more likely individuals are to believe that the threat was deliberate and to personalize the blame onto the organization or management (Rousseau, 1995). In the British Airways dispute, striking staff, for instance, were vilifying the CEO, Willie Walsh.

Some individuals may choose not to resist a threat when it first appears, and may then be progressively less likely to resist as compliance creates strong norms for continued compliance, adopting identities as non-resistors (loyal employees or wimps, depending on the point of view.) Those with limited power, in their own eyes, may choose to resist through gossip, minor theft, non-cooperation, or simply tolerating the change rather than confronting managers directly (Tucker, 1993). 'Power therefore has a stronger impact on the form of the resistance than on its frequency' (Ashforth and Mael, 1998: 110).

Resistance often occurs with others, either in collusion with them, following the creation of coalitions or with their tacit support. The formation of coalitions can be prompted if the changes are targeted at groups rather than individuals. So a change to flexible working may impact everyone at a particular location. A sense of shared fate and shared threat can thus create a shared identity and cohesion, which can rationalize attitudes that an individual on his or her own may find hard to sustain. This can give a shared motivation for collective resistance, but recent commentators argue that a form of leadership is required to actually galvanize the collective into action (Zoller and Fairhurst, 2007).

See Chapter 11 for more on resistance leadership: p. 251

Ashforth and Mael (1998) provide a framework for examining different forms of resistance using three dimensions.

1. *Targeted versus diffuse resistance*   Resistance is targeted when it focuses directly on the perceived threat. So when a new computer system was being introduced, employees openly challenged the wisdom of computerization in computer training sessions, refused to do what the instructor asked, disseminated literature criticizing this particular system, and sabotaged the new computers (Prasad, 1993). Diffuse resistance is not targeted directly at the source of threat, but is displaced more generally in the workplace. An example would be employees starting to spend long periods outside smoking. Diffuse resistance tends to be more covert and passive, and is valued for its symbolic rewards, whereas targeted resistance tends to be used when the source of the threat is clear and

there is a reasonable chance of thwarting the change because the threat is remediable and the resisters have (or at least believe they have) a degree of power.

2. *Facilitative versus oppositional resistance*   Brower and Abolafia (1995) define facilitative resistance as acts that further the public or organizational interest, and define oppositional resistance as acts that serve narrow, self-interests. A parallel framing is offered by Baddeley and James (1987), which distinguishes between self-interested behaviour and behaviour in the interest of the organization. The problem with this distinction is that it assumes that self-interest is obvious and that there are unambiguous definitions of what is in the organization's best interest.

3. *Authorized versus unauthorized resistance*   This third dimension refers to the means of resistance rather than the purpose of resistance. Authorized resistance encompasses those acts that are within the norms of the organization, so might include complaining to one's manager, filing a grievance, legal strikes or sharing concerns during a focus group about a proposed change. Unauthorized resistance includes acts of violence and insubordination that go beyond the bounds of acceptable behaviour set by the organization. An example would be the workers in one of Unilever's factories in France who were angry at changes to working practices and locked the manager in his office for 48 hours, before he was released by police. Authorized resistance may be used for oppositional ends and unauthorized means be used towards facilitative ends.

 Change in Practice 7.2

Resistance as sabotage at a travel operator

As part of its strategy to appeal to more upmarket holiday makers, a mass-market package holiday operator bought a highly successful premium travel company specializing in art and culture tours. The company employed fifty people and was based in Wales. After the acquisition, the acquiring company decided to move all of the company's activities to its main site in the north of England. Some of the fifty employees were offered relocation packages, but none of them took up the offer. Just before the transfer of activities, employees stopped sending customers their tickets and destroyed all of the computer records. Believing that they had nothing to lose and much to be angry about, resistance took the form of sabotage. Using Ashforth and Mael's (1998) framework, this resistance was *targeted, oppositional,* and *unauthorized.*[2-3]

More recent psychological approaches suggest that the word 'resistance' is too blunt to capture the subtlety of employee responses to change. Piderit (2000) suggests capturing employees' attitudes to change along three dimensions: cognitive, emotional, and intentional. The cognitive dimension refers to an individual's beliefs about the change; the emotional refers to his or her feelings in response to it; the intentional dimension includes both an intention to resist at the attitudinal level (that is, a plan or resolution to do something) and a protest at the behavioural level (actually taking some action).

An employee's response to an organizational change along the cognitive dimension may range from strong positive beliefs (that is, 'this change is absolutely what the organization needs') to strong negative beliefs (that is, 'this change will sink the organization'). On the emotional dimension, responses may range from excitement, on the strong positive, to anger, anxiety, and despair on the negative. On the intentional dimension, an employee's response may be to support the change or oppose it.

According to this view, resistance to change is represented when there are negative responses along all three dimensions and support for the change is represented when there are positive responses along all three dimensions. Those with a mix of reactions are what Piderit would label ambivalent. The subtlety of this approach is that it recognizes that initial responses to change may not be consistently negative or consistently positive, but can be a mixture of the two.

 Exercise 7.5

Think about a change you have experienced recently that was not of your own choosing and which was imposed on you. It may be a change to your role or your work; it could be changes to your timetable or course at university.

- Make notes on your response to the change using each of Piderit's three dimensions: emotional, cognitive, and intentional.
- Now go and find a colleague or friend who has experienced the same change and explore his or her emotional, cognitive, and intentional responses.
- How easy was it to distinguish between the three dimensions?
- What might have been missed in simply viewing your response, and your colleague's response, in terms of resistance to the change or support for the change?

Piderit (2000) suggests that understanding resistance as ambivalence makes it easier to identify the most appropriate process for addressing employees concerns: active listening and support if employees have emotional concerns; exploring the reasons for change if their concerns are more cognitive. However, differentiating between the three dimensions of attitude requires well-developed people skills and takes time, as perhaps you found when undertaking Exercise 7.4. For change agents or leaders running sizeable change programmes, this work suggests the importance of ensuring that all dimensions are addressed rather than, for instance, focusing only on the cognitive dimension in change communication.

Reframing resistance as a product of change agent sensemaking

An alternative approach to understanding resistance claims that conventional views of resistance favour the perspective of change agents and their sponsors, by suggesting that the latter are doing the right and proper thing, whilst resistance is dysfunctional and irrational. This 'change agent-centric' point of view assumes that resistance is an accurate report of an objective reality by unbiased observers (change agents). On the other hand, resistance can be seen as an interpretation by change agents of the behaviours and communications of those on the receiving end of change (Ford et al., 2008). Ford et al. suggest that this can be a self-fulfilling prophecy, a creation of change agent sensemaking:

See Chapter 5
for more on
sensemaking:
p. 85

> Expectations, by shaping the very phenomenon to which change agents are paying attention, predispose change agents to look for and find resistance, thereby confirming its existence, validating their expectation, and sustaining the received truth that people resist change. (Ibid: 364)

This also allows change agents to claim that any unexpected problems in the change process are due to resistance, using others as a ready scapegoat, rather than examining any potential failings of themselves or the change programme (Meston and King, 1996).

Conventional approaches to dealing with resistance focus on doing things to or for those on the receiving end of change (Kotter and Schlesinger, 1979). Viewing resistance as a product of change agent sensemaking encourages change agents to review their own behaviour and actions. For instance, the way in which change agents communicate may unintentionally encourage resistance. Change agents may oversell the benefits of change, without necessarily intending to be deceptive or misleading. When the reality of the change experienced is different, those on the receiving end can feel that they were misled and promises were broken, which then leads them to resist change, in protest, thereby behaving as perceived resistors. So perhaps the question should no longer be 'why do recipients resist change?', but 'why do some change agents call some actions resistance and not others?' (Ford et al., 2008: 371).

The value of resistance

Even though conventionally dismissed as dysfunctional and irrational, some commentators have identified benefits to resistance. For instance, Kotter and Schlesinger (1979) recognize that resistors who have more accurate or up-to-date information can benefit the organization, stimulating a re-examination of particular aspects of the change. Yet if leaders and change agents assume that resistance is always negative and automatically try to overcome it, they, and the organization, may not benefit from these alternative assessments. Grey (2003) similarly suggests change agents need to countenance the possibility that resistors actually know what they are talking about and are not just defending their own economic or psychological interests. Failure to do so can lead to costly and embarrassing failures. He gives the example of a newly privatized electricity company in New Zealand that laid off so many staff that Auckland was blacked out for six months. Similarly, lay-offs in early days of the privatized rail companies in the UK led to subsequent safety problems and service cancellations, despite employees having said that more staff were required than the change programme predicted.

Organizational change entails introducing new conversations and shifting existing patterns of discourse (Ford et al., 2008). However, new conversations have to compete with existing and habitual discussions, which can be hard, because they are novel and ephemeral and not fully understood (Czarniawska,1997; Kanter et al., 1992). A challenge for change agents is, therefore, how to ensure that there is talk about the change in enough places and by enough people that it starts to have momentum and take root. Resistance can play a useful function in this respect because, even if it is negative in tone and content, it keeps the topic 'in play', allowing others to participate in the conversation. Paradoxically, resistance may thus help to ensure the ultimate success of a change (Ford et al., 2008). Recognizing the likelihood of cognitive and emotional resistance, or ambivalence, to use Piderit's (2000) terms, may also

See Chapter 8
for more on
conversations:
p. 175

encourage leaders to stop moving too hastily to congruent positions, and allow disagreement and discussion to improve initial change proposals (Floyd and Wooldridge, 2000).

 Section 3 Summary

In this section, we have:

- examined traditional approaches to resistance that view it as something managers need to 'deal with';
- explored resistance from the point of view of the resistors themselves, taking a more psychological stance;
- considered reframing resistance as sensemaking on the part of change agents;
- explored the potential value of resistance.

Section 4: Interventions to increase commitment or decrease resistance

This section explores some of the potential interventions open to leaders or change agents, if a more conventional understanding of resistance is adopted. It concludes with some interventions to consider if resistance is viewed as a product of change agent sensemaking.

Before planning what interventions are required, diagnosing the type and scale of resistance or the gaps between current and required commitment is often helpful, as discussed earlier. Frequently, managers use the same change intervention regardless of the context, so, the bully continually coerces, the cynic always manipulates, the people-orientated person always tries to involve, and the intellectual relies heavily on learning and communication (Kotter, 1977). We would also add that, in our experience, one intervention on its own is rarely sufficient. Of the approaches below, 1–6 are those originally proposed by Kotter and Schlesinger (1979).

1. *Communication*   This is one of the commonest ways to overcome resistance and is particularly effective when resistance is based on inadequate or inaccurate information. However, it requires a pre-existing atmosphere of trust, otherwise those resisting will not believe what they are being told. Bridges (2003) also reminds managers that they need to communicate ten times more than they would have originally thought.

2. *Participation and involvement*   The underlying assumption here is that involving potential resistors in the design and implementation of a change initiative can pre-empt resistance. Participation generally leads to commitment rather than compliance, and can allow people to take part of the old ways of doing things with them. Sometimes, participation is chosen not to neutralize potential resistors, but because employees have the information and knowledge required to design the change. Whatever the rationale for involvement, it takes time.

See Chapters 5 and 10 for more on involvement: pp. 98, 220

See Chapter 4 for more on providing emotional support: p. 78

3. *Education and support*   These can be alternative ways in which to deal with resistance. This might be listening and providing emotional support; it might involve training in new skills. Support may also take the form of respecting the past and marking endings (Bridges, 2003). These approaches also require investment in terms of time, money, and patience.

4. *Negotiation and agreement*   These involve offering incentives to actual or potential resistors. It is effective when it is clear that someone is, or a group are, going to lose out from a change and their power to resist is significant. Negotiation may compensate them for losses. The downside of such negotiations is that the deals struck can be financially costly. They can also create an unfortunate message to others in the organization that those wanting change will negotiate to avoid serious resistance.

5. *Manipulation and co-optation*   These involve covert attempts to influence others. Co-optation is one form of manipulation in which an individual or leader of a group is drafted into the design or implementation team. This is not a case of participation, because there is no interest in the individual's opinion; only their symbolic endorsement is required. Co-optation can be cheaper than negotiation and quicker than participation. However, if people feel that they are being manipulated or tricked into not resisting, their reactions can be extremely negative.

6. *Explicit and implicit coercion*   This means that managers force people to accept the change by explicitly or implicitly threatening them with loss of jobs, promotions, bonuses, or actually firing or transferring them. As with manipulation, it is risky using coercion because people resent forced change. However, in some cases in which changes are highly unpopular, it may be considered to be the only option left to managers. Sometimes, coercion is targeted at specific, outspoken, and seemingly intransigent leaders, who are fired. Their exit then is not just the removal of a resistor, but can also be a symbolic act, demonstrating the seriousness of those leading the change and providing a salutary lesson to others.

7. *Problem finding*   This is a neutral way of encouraging a wide variety of people to identify and clarify aspects of the problem. The purpose is not to identify solutions or to take actions, so this approach encourages people to listen and explore others' ideas and perspectives, without the need to adopt positions on what should or should not happen. It can be very helpful at the beginning of a change process, as it often enables employees to see or construct for themselves the need for change and ensures that those leading the change have a broad appreciation of the issues to which they will need to pay attention. When working with Xerox Europe, the change programme began with focus groups in all of the major markets to identify the problems as perceived by employees. Firm facilitation is required to keep people focused on scoping the issues rather than wanting to share their particular solution.

8. *Role modelling*   The importance of role modelling is premised on the idea that people are more likely to believe what they see rather than what they hear talked about. If leaders talk about the importance of changing to a more innovative culture, but then shoot down every new proposal as too risky, observers will draw their own conclusions and are unlikely to support or believe in the new culture. Whilst role modelling can be convincing, it is rarely sufficient on its own to convert doubters and resistors.

9. *Changing reward structures*   This is sometimes used when resistance is around a requirement for exhibiting new behaviours. This can be seen as a coercive measure to force change or at least to make resistors aware of the consequences of not embracing the new behaviours. Arguably, it too can be seen as a symbolic act, underlying the seriousness with which the leaders are taking the change. Whether it has an impact on resistors is largely dependent on whether rewards actually do change in practice. Sometimes, of course, changes to the reward structure may be the content of the change, rather than an intervention to support some other change.

In addition, the insights offered by Ford et al. (2008) into resistance as a self-fulfilling prophecy on the part of change agents suggest the importance of change agents becoming more reflexive and aware of the role of their own thinking and behaviour in the creation of 'resistance'. In our work coaching leaders, we often find ourselves helping leaders to revisit their own preconceptions, challenging their framing of individuals and groups as awkward and incompetent resistors. Becoming more aware can then help them to behave differently with those whom they had hitherto written off. As leaders, in giving a different gesture, they may allow 'resistors' to give a different response (Stacey, 2002), and allow a situation to become less stuck (Watzlwick et al., 1974). Ford et al. (2008) also emphasize the importance of change agents building trust, communicating honestly, and being clear about what action is required. These behaviours are less likely to trigger resistance in others.

 Section 4 Summary

In this section, we have:

- explored a number of different interventions designed to reduce resistance or to increase commitment to change;
- identified the importance of change agents being aware of their own assumptions and biases.

 Integrative Case Study

HBOS: Power and politics for and against change

Between 2003 and 2006, shares in HBOS rose by 53 per cent, far ahead of most of its competitors. The bank had a very strong sales culture, with even junior bankers receiving significant bonuses. Some people in the bank became concerned that the bank was 'going too fast', taking excessive risk because of the sales-driven culture, and without the appropriate balance of systems and controls. However, few people wanted to speak out because of fear of being branded troublemakers and concern that doing so would jeopardize them receiving large bonuses. The reward power of leaders thus quashed any emergent resistance and made it difficult for any coalition to form to challenge or change the culture or risk management practices. Paul Moore, head of global risk at HBOS from 2002 to 2005, was responsible for ensuring that the executives complied with the regulations of the Financial Standards Authority. He did speak out. He was subsequently dismissed: an example of a coercive approach to dealing with resistance and undoubtedly intended to silence any other resistance. Moore received a settlement for unfair dismissal under the Public Interest Disclosure Act 1998 (the 'Whistleblower Act'), but broke his gagging order in February 2009 when the bank nearly collapsed during the credit crisis, only to be saved with a taxpayer-funded bailout and a merger with the Lloyds Banking Group.

Moore gave evidence to the Treasury Select Committee investigating what had happened at HBOS. He paints an insider's view of the power of the guiding coalition and senior executives' use of politics to prevent changes to the status quo, which was making them personally very rich. Among the many incidents he describes are the following.

1. The company secretary failed to minute crucial comments he made at a formal board meeting, reporting his investigation that the sales culture at HBOS had got out of control.

2. He was strongly reprimanded by a board member for tabling the full version of a critical report at a group audit committee meeting, which made it clear that the systems and controls, risk management, and compliance were inadequate to control the 'over-eager' sales culture. 'Mysteriously, this had been left out of the papers even though I had sent it to the secretary', writes Moore (Comment 3.15).

3. After Moore was dismissed, an ex-sales manager who had no experience of risk management was appointed as group risk director.

4. A personal friend of the HBOS chairman was appointed to be the chairman of the risk control committee. Moore recounts that this individual 'admitted to me that . . . they met quite often socially. Of course, he was supposed to be challenging (the Chairman) . . . He obviously had no technical competence in banking or credit risk management to oversee such a vital governance committee' (Comment 3.15).

Questions

1. What types of power are being used by HBOS executives in this account, with what purpose?
2. In 2005, what would you have advised Moore to do to improve his chances of altering risk management practices at HBOS?
3. What lessons about power, politics, and resistance, in relation to organizational change, do you draw from this study?

Conclusion

This chapter shows that a political perspective on change draws attention to the dynamics of power and influence, which can become amplified during the uncertainty caused by organizational change. It introduces the idea of opposing interest groups that may form into coalitions for, or against, change. It highlights the different forms that resistance may take. The chapter also introduces the notion of front stage activity, which is rational and logical, and the rather more messy back stage world of power, influence, and politicking, and suggests that being able to read and work with power and politics is a critical skill for change agents.

Please visit the Online Resource Centre at **http://www.oxfordtextbooks.co.uk/orc/ myers** *to access further resources for students and lecturers.*

Change in Practice sources

1. Brown, A. D. (1995) 'Managing understandings: Politics, symbolism, niche marketing and the quest for legitimacy in IT implementation', *Organization Studies*, **16**(6): 951–69.

2. Ashforth, B. E. and Mael, F. A. (1998) 'The power of resistance: Sustaining valued identities', in R. M. Kramer and M. A. Neale (eds) *Power and Influence in Organizations*, Thousand Oaks, CA: Sage, pp. 89–120.

3. Based on personal experience.

Integrative Case Study sources

Bingham, J. and Porter, A. (2009) 'HBOS whistleblower Paul Moore breaks silence to condemn Crosby', *The Telegraph*, 11 Feb. http://www.telegraph.co.uk/finance/newsbysector/banksandfinance/4592025/ HBOS-whistleblower-Paul-Moore-breaks-silence-to-condemn-Crosby.html

The Guardian (2009) 'Daggers drawn: Conflict at HBOS' 12 Feb. http://www.guardian.co.uk/ business/2009/feb/12/pau-moore-james-crosby-hbos

The Telegraph (2009) 'HBOS whistleblower Paul Moore: Evidence to House of Commons' 'Banking Crisis' hearing', 11 Feb. http://www.telegraph.co.uk/finance/newsbysector/banksandfinance/4590996/ HBOS-whistleblower-Paul-Moore-Evidence-to-House-of-Commons-Banking-Crisis-hearing.html

The Telegraph (2009) 'Gordon Brown must go says HBOS whistleblower Paul Moore', 15 Feb. http://www. telegraph.co.uk/finance/financialcrisis/4629670/Gordon-Brown-must-go-says-HBOS-whistleblower-Paul-Moore.html

Further reading

Buchanan, D. and Badham, R. (2008) *Power, Politics and Organizational Change: Winning the Turf War*, 2nd edn, London: Sage.
A very readable account of the politics of organizational change.

8 Change from the Perspective of Organizational Learning

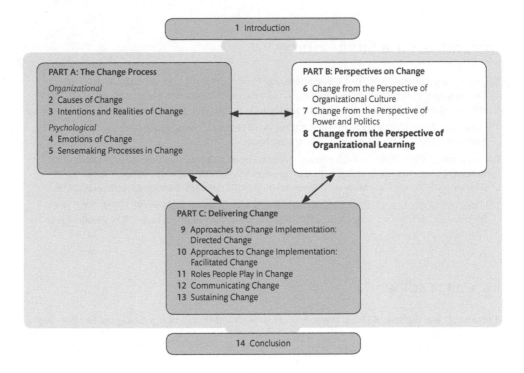

1 Introduction

PART A: The Change Process

Organizational
2 Causes of Change
3 Intentions and Realities of Change

Psychological
4 Emotions of Change
5 Sensemaking Processes in Change

PART B: Perspectives on Change

6 Change from the Perspective of Organizational Culture
7 Change from the Perspective of Power and Politics
8 Change from the Perspective of Organizational Learning

PART C: Delivering Change

9 Approaches to Change Implementation: Directed Change
10 Approaches to Change Implementation: Facilitated Change
11 Roles People Play in Change
12 Communicating Change
13 Sustaining Change

14 Conclusion

 ## Introduction

See Chapter 6 for more on the 'iceberg' model

The perspective taken in this chapter is to regard organizational change as learning. Often, when 'learning' is referred to in everyday life, it is as an adjunct to 'teaching'. The image evoked is that of an expert, transferring information and concepts to others, perhaps in a classroom situation. Learning, as a perspective on change, encompasses a much broader view of what is learned—that is, of 'knowledge'—and of how it is learned. The knowledge held in organizations includes capabilities of all kinds: hard data, know-how, insight, and skills, as well as collective capabilities reflected in an organization's routines, procedures, and practices (Akbar, 2003). Much of this knowledge and the learning that takes place in organizations, as well as the barriers to effective learning, lie in the informal organization, hidden from sight.

Learning is the third perspective on organizational change that we are introducing, following on from Chapter 6, which explored change from the perspective of culture, and Chapter 7, which explored it from the perspective of power and politics. Each of these perspectives provides new insights into change. Change in Practice 6.1 looked at the growth and collapse of Enron from the perspective of organizational culture. It could equally be viewed from the perspective of learning, examining the development of capabilities in the company, such as technical skills, learned patterns of extreme loyalty to the organization, acceptance of misleading investors, and lax attitudes to risk. Capabilities such as these underpinned and embodied both the company's growth and collapse. Change in Practice 7.1 described politicking in the implementation of new IT architecture in a UK hospital. Seen from the perspective of learning, it involved both IT skills and knowledge of the hospital bureaucracy in the implementation team, and it entailed the wide acquisition of new individual capabilities and new organizational routines and systems. This perspective focuses attention on the tension between assimilating new learning and using what has already been learned—that is, between novelty and continuity (Vera and Crossan, 2004).

Section 1 examines knowledge and learning in organizations and explores how change can be regarded as organizational learning. Section 2 examines the process of organizational learning in more depth and explores what this perspective reveals about how change can be enabled or blocked. Section 3 looks at the concept of dynamic capabilities to develop strategic knowledge and at the learning organization.

 ## Main topics to be covered in this chapter

- Knowledge, organizational learning, and change
- The organizational learning process, and barriers and enablers to change from the learning perspective
- Dynamic capabilities and the learning organization

Section 1: Knowledge and organizational learning

We begin this section with Change in Practice 8.1, another example of an organization changing—and learning: Dyson Appliances' move to offshore manufacturing in the early 2000s.

 ### Change in Practice 8.1

Dyson on the move

In February 2002, the British manufacturer Dyson Appliances Ltd, which specializes in the design and manufacture of vacuum cleaners, decided to move all of its vacuum cleaner production to Malaysia. The move cost 865 jobs. In the rural town of Malmesbury, only the manufacture of the CR01 washing machine, an ultimately unsuccessful product, remained—until the following year when it too was transferred, with the loss of a further sixty-five jobs.

Until that time, the owner and chief executive, James Dyson, had been a strong advocate of British-based manufacturing. Indeed, an interview with him had recently been published in *Director* magazine in which he bemoaned the decline of British manufacturing. The plant closure left many of the employees distraught. One told the BBC: 'I feel like I've been on death row for the last 7 months . . . Tonight, we're going into the actual execution, everybody is just sad, everybody's down.' Dyson himself, branded a hypocrite by some commentators, found the decision difficult. He said: 'I was presented with a stark choice—cling to a dream and go out of business frighteningly soon, or eat humble pie and survive hopefully to prosper and create more jobs [in the UK].' Dyson explained: 'I would prefer not to use the word "hypocrite" . . . I prefer to say that I had to do a volte-face.'

Dyson set out many of the issues in a later broadcast lecture. These included the rise in UK manufacturing costs while retail prices were declining and difficulties in obtaining planning permission for expansion to his manufacturing facilities, but according to Dyson (2004: 4):

> the biggest problem was that we had no local suppliers. Our British three-pin plugs were made in Malaysia. Our polycarbonate plastics came from Korea. Our electronics came from Taiwan. It was a logistical nightmare. We needed our suppliers on our doorstep so that we could drive them to improve their quality and keep pace with technology . . . In Malaysia, the biggest benefit has been that all our suppliers are within 10 miles of the factory. Some were there anyway. Others we developed, such as a tent pole maker. We got him to make our highly-engineered telescopic handles. And he turned out to be much better than our previous German suppliers.

In many respects, the move was a success. The following year, pre-tax profit per employee tripled as a result of the move to Malaysia. By 2007, three factories in Malaysia were making 4 million vacuum cleaners a year. The factory in which UK manufacturing had been based became a research and design centre. Remarkably, by 2007, Dyson Appliances employed more people in Malmesbury than had worked in the factory before the Malaysia move. Key innovations developed in the centre during the 2003–09 period, aside from continued progression of its world-leading vacuum cleaning technology (based on the 'double cyclone' system), included:

- a new form of hand dryer—slicing water off the hands with a 400 mph blast of air, rather than attempting to evaporate it with warm air;
- a form of fan operating without traditional fan blades;
- a 'Ball' vacuum cleaner with exceptional manoeuvrability.

There have also been innovations in the organization's approach to customer service and people management. For example, in the display of helpline telephone numbers, 'one of the team suggested putting our customer care number on the machine, instead of hidden in the user guide. Why hide it? If there is a glitch, people can find it easily and get in touch to find a resolution'. Additionally, the Dyson customer care team has access to all of its machines: 'Along the back wall of the room are lined all the machines we've ever developed so if you call them they know exactly which bit you're referring to.' This emphasis on knowledge of the core product range extends to all levels of the company: *every* new employee has to assemble a vacuum cleaner on his or her first day of work. In a 2010 interview, Dyson explained:

> They might be non-executive directors, who are knights of the realm, but they still have to [assemble a vacuum cleaner]. It gives them confidence in the technology. They know what's inside. And they keep the ones they build. It's to emphasize that what we do is make products that people use. (Beard, 2010: 172)[1-11]

Types of knowledge

A distinction is drawn between explicit and tacit knowledge (Polanyi, 1966; Nonaka and Takeuchi, 1995). **Explicit knowledge** is knowledge that can be formally expressed and easily articulated, the kind of knowledge that could be straightforwardly conveyed in a classroom situation, in a meeting, or in documents (Akbar, 2003): for example, the details of a proposed change programme or the results of a PESTLE analysis. In Change in Practice 8.1, staff at Dyson began with explicit knowledge of manufacturing and supply chains in the UK, and needed to develop explicit knowledge of how to build a successful manufacturing base in Malaysia, and of local suppliers there—including a tent pole maker, who turned out to be the perfect supplier for vacuum cleaner telescopic handles!

See Chapter 2 for more on PESTLE analysis: p. 17

Tacit knowledge, on the other hand, is knowledge that cannot easily be articulated, and is rooted in action rather than theory or information (Polanyi, 1966; Nonaka and Takeuchi, 1995). This can be skills such as running meetings, dealing with organizational politics, or giving effective presentations. Of course, there is explicit knowledge associated with each of these skills that can be taught, but knowing how meetings, politics, or presentations *should* be handled is insufficient to make someone skilled in practice. The converse is also true: someone who is a skilled presenter—who has the tacit knowledge involved—cannot necessarily articulate how it is done. At Dyson, new staff could have been given a manual full of explicit knowledge about how vacuum cleaners are put together on their first day, but instead they developed explicit knowledge and tacit knowledge in tandem, by learning how it should be done and also practising the skills of actually accomplishing the construction of a vacuum cleaner. Similarly, the skills developed to prosper effectively in the new Malaysian business context would again be tacit knowledge. As Nonaka and Takeuchi (1995) point out, ways of understanding the world, such as mental models and the values and assumptions associated with them, can also be tacit knowledge, put to use without being articulated. So, at Dyson, the concept of an electric hand dryer as a device that wafted hot air on hands may have been a tacit mental model that had to be revised in order that a hand dryer that 'sliced' water off hands could be developed.

See Chapter 7 for some of the techniques associated with dealing with organizational politics

So far, however, we have explained knowledge and learning as individual-level concepts. At this individual level, we have considered explicit knowledge, such as facts, concepts, and rules, and tacit knowledge, such as skills, getting the 'feel' for a role or tool or technique, and mental models. Knowledge can also be considered at a collective level in organizations (Cook and Brown, 1999). Stories, jargon, and metaphors—which might be treated as artefacts from a cultural perspective—can be thought of as **explicit knowledge at a collective level.** For example, stories of successes and failures, competitors, customers, or internal political infighting or collaboration, 'doing the rounds' in the informal organization can be a capability that supports effective working and organizational achievement. At Dyson, circulation of stories about Dyson's original development of the vacuum cleaner, as well as proud stories of its successful strategy as a UK-based manufacturer and later stories of ongoing UK-based innovation success were, in this sense, explicit knowledge at a collective level. On the other hand, routines, work practices, communication styles, patterns of decision-making, and social interaction not only between staff, but also with customers and suppliers, can be thought of as **tacit knowledge at a collective level**. At Dyson, both the practice whereby new staff and board members built a vacuum cleaner and the practice whereby helpline staff had available every previous vacuum cleaner model were tacit knowledge at a collective level. So were the practices, social interaction, and styles of decision-making that led to multiple innovations between 2000 and 2010.

See Chapter 5 for more on mental models: p. 85

See Chapter 6 for more on artefacts of organizational culture: p.117

Since knowledge includes not only facts, but also individual and group practices, learning—the development of knowledge—provides a perspective on organizational change itself. On this broad view of knowledge, organizational change not only involves knowledge being acquired

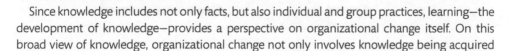

or lost by individuals, but also involves knowledge being acquired and lost at a collective level (Balogun and Jenkins, 2003).

Organizational learning

> Within the term 'organizational learning', the word 'learning' is a 'live metaphor' . . . that transfers information from the relatively familiar domain of individual learning . . . to a lesser known phenomenon in organizations. (Tsang and Zahra, 2008: 1443)

What does it mean for an organization to learn, rather than an individual? As Tsang and Zahra express it above, the concept of organizational learning is a metaphor. It is people who learn as their capabilities develop. But, *if* their learning is affected by the systems, structures, routines, and practices of the organization, and in turn *changes* these systems, structures, routines, and practices, this is called organizational learning (Crossan et al., 1999; Vera and Crossan, 2004). From this perspective, change always involves organizational learning, and organizational learning is always change. Within some companies, unlike Dyson, the chief executive might not have found himself or herself able to make a 'volte-face' about offshoring production; the loss of face in 'eating humble pie' might have been unacceptable, or the information systems needed to prevent the stark choice between going out of business or shifting production might not have been in place, or union opposition might have been allowed to prevent the move. In other companies, a creative alternative that allowed the firm to prosper, but perhaps with a lower growth rate, might have been found. So this learning at Dyson was affected by the particular systems, structures, routines, and practices of the company. And, in turn, the learning changed the company radically, and paved the way for future learning, for example new product innovation and knowledge of Malaysian supplier networks.

Single-loop and double-loop learning

A distinction can be drawn, however, between **single-loop** and **double-loop** learning (Argyris, 1990, 1994). In single-loop learning, planning, implementation of plans, monitoring the impact, and analysing how to improve performance takes place to meet a target, and is

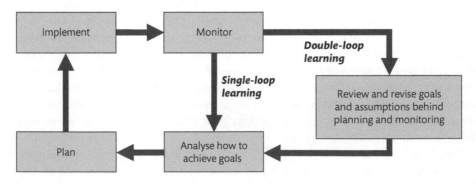

Figure 8.1 Single-loop and double-loop learning

based on pre-existing values and assumptions. Double-loop learning involves *reconsidering* targets, or *revising* values and assumptions (Argyris and Schön, 1996). Figure 8.1 outlines the two learning processes involved.

For example, prior to 2002, James Dyson's efforts to improve product design or to promote sales while extolling the virtues of British-based manufacturing could be regarded as a single-loop learning process. In contrast, his 'volte-face' in deciding to relocate the company's manufacturing base to Asia could be regarded as double-loop learning. Similarly, employee efforts to enhance vacuum cleaner user guides so that the appropriate customer care phone number stood out could be regarded as single-loop learning, while the idea of displaying the number prominently on the device itself could be regarded as double-loop learning. Single-loop and double-loop learning can be individual or organizational—that is, it may or may not change the organization. But double-loop learning is particularly significant for organizational change because it is required in order to achieve second-order organizational change, change that involves rethinking how things are done.

In reality, there is a continuum between single-loop and double-loop learning. Key values and assumptions can be reassessed to a greater or lesser extent. A single-loop learning response to declining applications for places in a university might be to intensify publicity, while a double-loop learning response might involve reconsidering the curriculum. But more radical double-loop learning responses would also be possible. The university could consider amalgamation with other institutions, international syndication of courses, or delivering courses online rather than face-to-face—revising assumptions about its 'independence' or the nature of the teaching relationship in the process.

One of the most challenging aspects of double-loop learning is recognized to be the abandonment of previous knowledge. This is sometimes called organizational 'forgetting' (de Holan and Phillips, 2003) or **unlearning** (Tsang and Zahra, 2008). Knowledge within Dyson that it was best to manufacture in the UK was unlearned, for instance.

 Exercise 8.1

Consider what you have learned in your work (or through a hobby or leisure activity) over the last year.

- Can you think of an example involving single-loop learning?
- Can you think of an example involving double-loop learning? Which of your values, assumptions, or targets were changed as a result, and what were the effects of this? Can you identify any unlearning involved?

The '4I' model

Crossan and her colleagues (Crossan et al., 1999; Vera and Crossan, 2004) have set out one of the most influential models of the processes involved in organizational learning: the **4I model**. According to this model, in achieving organizational change, four learning processes link individual, group, and organizational levels. They are: *intuiting*—coming up with initial ideas; *interpreting*—understanding their implications; *integrating*—developing cohesive action at the group level; and *institutionalizing*—incorporating learning across the organization. We discuss each of these aspects of organizational learning below.

Intuiting

In the 4I model, **intuiting** is the initial, individual-level process of coming up with new ideas or insights, for example a new way of viewing the business context or a new approach to tackling a workplace challenge. This may begin at a subconscious level (Crossan et al., 1999; Mazutis and Slawinski, 2008). In the next section of this chapter, we will revisit the issue of whether this is always simply an individual-level process. For now, two forms of intuiting can be distinguished in organizational change. Both rely on a foundation of pre-existing explicit and tacit knowledge.

1. **Expert intuiting** involves identifying patterns, for example in the internal or external business environment (Crossan et al., 1999). People are using expert intuiting every time they use what they know, and their skills and mental models, to understand what is going on in their organization. At Dyson, issues of product improvement and solving the practical problems of continuing to manufacture in the UK, or the practical problems of offshoring to Malaysia, are likely to have required expert intuiting.

2. **Entrepreneurial intuiting** involves finding a new way in which to view the business environment; it is double-loop learning. It involves using tacit knowledge—skills and mental models—to reconsider explicit knowledge. One of the most challenging aspects of organizational learning is the unlearning involved in entrepreneurial intuiting. New ways of thinking require past assumptions to be put to one side or 'suspended'. This suspension of familiar thinking patterns may involve simply bringing mental models to the surface so that they constrain thinking less (Senge et al., 2005). This may have been the case for James Dyson's rethink about UK-based manufacturing. But suspending a way of thinking may also involve purposely or inadvertently abandoning it. To develop a fan without fan blades, for example, involves letting go a conception of what a fan 'is'.

The opportunity for intuiting depends on the experiences that are focused on or attended to (Kleysen and Dyck, 2001), a point to which we come back later in the chapter.

Interpreting

Interpreting is the process of understanding an idea in more detail as an individual or through conversation with others. In the way in which the term is used in this model of organizational learning, it does not just concern understanding an organizational context, but also involves the way in which people behave in response to it: 'the focus of interpreting is change in the individual's understanding and actions' (Crossan et al., 1999: 528). So interpreting and intuiting together are closely related to the sensemaking process that we considered in Chapter 5, linking thinking and action coherently. But this is specifically the new thinking and behaviour that *initiates* organizational change, rather than just the sensemaking that occurs when faced

See Chapter 5

with unfamiliarity *as* organizations change. Figure 8.2 shows interpreting in action in Jack Dorsey's notebook from 2001, in which he was developing the idea behind the Twitter micro-blogging site. Five years later, this led to organizational transformation at Odeo, the struggling podcasting company at which the idea became a reality (see below).

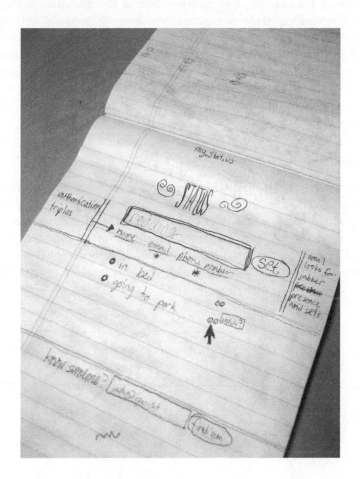

twttr sketch

Photo taken on 24 March 2006 by Jack Dorsey of his old 2001 notebook. Dorsey wrote:

> On May 31st, 2000, I signed up with a new service called LiveJournal . . . One night in July of that year I had an idea to make a more "live" LiveJournal. Real-time, up-to-date, from the road . . . For the next 5 years, I thought about this concept and tried to silently introduce it into my various projects . . . The 6th year; the idea has finally solidified (thanks to the massively creative environment my employer Odeo provides) and taken a novel form. We're calling it twttr (though this original rendering calls it stat.us . . .). It's evolved a lot in the past few months.

Figure 8.2 Intuiting and interpreting the Twitter concept

Sources: http://www.flickr.com/photos/jackdorsey/182613360; http://twitter.com/#!/jack/status/47069458363187200

Integrating

Integrating is the process of putting new understandings into action at the group and organizational level by doing things differently. In the integrating process of learning, changes become established as individuals align their understanding and adjust their behaviour to coordinate action. For example, the *implementation* of the offshoring strategy at Dyson would be the 'integrating' stage of organizational learning. Similarly, choosing a name, Twitter, for the microblogging site, programming the software for it, and launching the site were part of the integrating stage of organizational learning at Odeo. Programming was primarily accomplished in a two-week period in March 2006; the site was initially piloted among the Odeo staff and opened to the public that July. In the next section, we will look at how the quality of interaction between people, and the trust between them, can enable or block this stage of learning.

Institutionalizing

Institutionalizing is the organization-level process of incorporating learning back into other groups or work units, or across the organization, by embedding it in systems, structures, routines, and practices, including HR practices such as recruitment, reward, training and development, and leadership, which reinforces what has been learned. Crossan et al. (1999) call this last stage the 'feedback' organizational learning process, distinguishing it from 'feed-forward' processes of intuiting, interpreting, and integrating (see Figure 8.3).

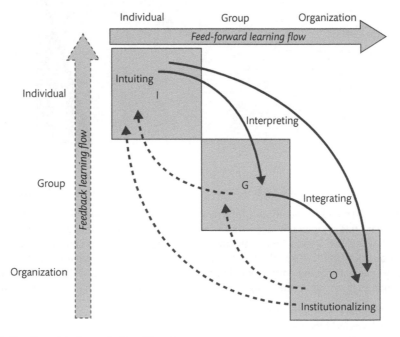

Figure 8.3 The 4I model of organizational learning

Source: Vera and Crossan (2004)

In the institutionalizing process, changes are embedded in the organization as normal ways of working. This, in turn, provides a new foundation for future intuiting, interpreting, and integrating. At Twitter, institutionalizing can be seen in the establishment of a professional interface and brand, of clear policies and ethical codes, of the computing power to handle an enormous number of 'tweets' (by the spring of 2011, this had risen to over 1 billion tweets per week, as many as were sent in the whole first three years of operation) and, in particular, through transforming the structure of the business. This was accomplished in stages. Twitter had been begun as a project within the struggling podcasting company, Odeo; in fact, in its initial 2006 logo, the strapline was 'Twitter—An Odeo Thingy'. That September, a letter from Odeo's chief executive, Evan Williams, to the company's investors offered to buy back their shares. Concerning Twitter, Williams wrote:

See Chapter 13 for more on institutionalizing: p. 298

> By the way, Twitter (http://twitter.com), which you may have read about, is one of the pieces of value that I see in Odeo, but it's much too early to tell what's there. Almost two months after launch, Twitter has less than 5,000 registered users. I will continue to invest in Twitter, but it's hard to say it justifies the venture investment Odeo certainly holds—especially since that investment was for a different market altogether. (Carlson, 2011)

In what must feel like a galling turn of events with hindsight, the investors agreed to be bought out. By the spring of 2007, Twitter had been spun off as a separate company, and by 2011 it was worth over US $5 billion.

One of the key strengths of the learning perspective on organizational change is the links made between the individual, group, and organizational levels of learning involved. In the next section, we look at the process of organizational learning in more detail, and at some of the key factors that impact on how learning and change proceed across these levels.

 Section 1 Summary

In this section, we have:

- examined different categories of knowledge—explicit and tacit; individual and collective;
- considered the nature of organizational learning and the distinction between single-loop and double-loop learning;
- introduced the 4I model of the organizational learning process.

Section 2: Key factors in organizational learning

Our focus in this section is the 'feed-forward' processes of intuiting, interpreting, and integrating. In accomplishing organizational learning, three aspects are key: the way in which people interact—that is, converse with each other; learning from the complexities of experience; and looking to the future through vision or aspiration (Senge, 2006). We examine each of these in turn, with a focus on the way in which organizational learning takes place, and some of the barriers that can impede it. We discuss the processes of institutionalizing in more detail in Chapter 13.

Quality of conversation

Conversation (not necessarily face-to-face) is at the heart of how intuiting, interpreting, and integrating take place in practice. In focusing on conversation, we depart somewhat from the view originally presented in the 4I model that intuiting 'must happen in a single mind' (Vera and Crossan, 2004). We would agree that sometimes change originates with one person's good idea. This clearly seems to have been the case with Jack Dorsey's idea for Twitter. But other authors (Baker et al., 2005; Senge, 2006) suggest that this original spark for learning and change can often originate in conversations between people, not clearly being attributable to one individual. This is our experience too. Change in Practice 8.2 describes a conversation in a software company—not, in this instance, Twitter—which illustrates this.

 ### Change in Practice 8.2

Software talk

Quinn and Dutton (2005) detail a conversation in a software company between Tony, a software interface designer, and Theresa, his manager, with Devin as a bit-part player. As they 'take turns' to speak in the conversation, first the definition of an issue and then a way forward are clarified.

Turn	Speaker	What was said
1	Tony	Theresa, when you get a minute could you come here?
2	Theresa	Sure. Just a sec.
3	Theresa	What's the problem?
4	Tony	The problem is that some of the files need to go on the web server, and some on the video server. On the web, these files [draws on the white board], on the video, these files.
5	Theresa	It used to be on one server.
6	Tony	Yeah, but how do you make it simple for the users? This has to go on this server [points], this on that server [points again].
7	Theresa	But even here [pointing] you may have these types of files.
8	Tony	Well, we may at some point, for tech support purposes, have to allow them to have this list [pointing]—or separate GIF and HTML folders. [Pause, both of them staring at the white board.] Here is the problem I see—the folders have to have different names, but you need a folder for each presentation to not override other types of files.
9	Theresa	We need to have it ask the users to give the presentation a name—we need to have Jim add some code that gives it a name. Devin [turning to face Devin]—does it make it easier for you if it has the same or separate folders?
10	Devin	Separate.

Turn	Speaker	What was said
11	Theresa	There's your answer. [Points at Devin.]
12	Tony	Okay. Then here are the folders. [Points at picture on the white board.]
13	Theresa	Is index.html your javascript?
14	Tony	No.
15	Theresa	I've got it! Make two starts! This will create two folders.
16	Tony	So that loads start and that loads index?
17	Theresa	You may want to not make it index, because that's the default presentation.
18	Tony	Having it up here screws you up either way.
19	Theresa	The problem is if you're doing many presentations . . . [pauses]. I'm not sure I understand the main issue anymore.
20	Tony	There's a lot of naming issues and overriding issues that need to be addressed.
21	Theresa	Let's name the issues. Folders need titles for the name of presentation to reduce erroneous overrides.
22	Tony	Plus ease of use for uploading stuff. So, rather than having fifteen folders . . . [draws on the white board].
23	Theresa	The options for multiple presentations are . . . [adds to the drawing].
24	Tony	Okay. So that would have a link to the presentation and the images!
25	Theresa	Great. Then Devin could point users here [pointing], and Jim could add the code that names the presentation.
26	Tony	Cool.

(Quinn and Dutton, 2005: 40)[12]

In Change in Practice 8.2, it seems to make more sense to say that both the issues and their solutions were developed in the conversation between Tony and Theresa (with a little bit of help from Devin), rather than that any one person came up with an idea. Examining a real conversation like this also illustrates how the distinctions between the 4I model's feed-forward learning processes of intuiting, interpreting, and integrating are dependent on context. Intuiting and interpreting are happening together in this conversation. What has been learnt may, of course, turn out to be a dead end, replaced by better ideas the next day. Or this may be intuiting and interpreting as *part of* integrating, with the software team working together to improve the implementation of changes that are already in the pipeline. Or this may turn out to be the start of something big: a whole new market and change of direction for the company. In that case, retrospectively, the conversation would be seen as intuiting and interpreting, followed by integrating later on with the *development* of these ideas.

In some ways, Tony and Theresa in Change in Practice 8.2 had it easy: the issue that they were discussing was not concerned with their own attributes or behaviour. Chris Argyris' (1990; 1994) research examines what happens when personal attributes or performance are at issue, and how learning and change can be obstructed because the issue is treated as undiscussable and, worse, its undiscussability is undiscussable, so that learning and change are prevented. Argyris' work suggests that people often interact as if they are guided by implicit rules called **Model 1 theories of action**, which are: to be in unilateral control over situations; to maximize winning and minimize losing; to avoid anxiety and embarrassment; and to be seen to be rational. Argyris and Schön (1996; Argyris, 1990) suggest that people's behaviour usually indicates the prevalence of these implicit rules, which create 'undiscussable' issues and inhibit double-loop learning. For example, Argyris describes how a 'total quality management' consultant in collaboration with the top management of a company used surveys and group meetings to help supervisors to identify areas in which procedures could be improved and costs reduced. The initiative was hailed a great success, meeting its goals and saving more money than expected. But Argyris discovered that the supervisors had known about the problems for years, and not taken action. He asked them why:

> They cited the blindness and timidity of management. They blamed interdepartmental competitiveness verging on warfare. They said the culture of the company made it unacceptable to get others into trouble for the sake of correcting problems. In every explanation, the responsibility for fixing the nine problem areas belonged to someone else. The supervisors were loyal, honest managers. The blame lay elsewhere. (Argyris, 1994: 78)

As Argyris points out, the first of the problems the company faced, cost reduction, is amenable to single-loop learning of the kind undertaken. Organizational change has taken place and there has been an improvement in the efficiency of production processes. But there was a second problem, 'a group of employees who stand passively by and watch inefficiencies develop and persevere' (ibid.), which prevented effective change through double-loop learning. Instead, both the senior management and the supervisors could see themselves as striving to achieve clear goals and doing everything that they could to prevail over obstacles, and they avoided expressing negative feelings about the years of inefficiency. Addressing this second problem would offer the opportunity, and the challenge, of double-loop learning.

See Chapter 5 for more on trust: p. 97

See Chapter 5 for more on engagement: p. 98

See Chapter 5 for more on candour: p. 103

What makes for productive interactions that contribute to double-loop learning and change? In Chapter 5, we discussed several factors that are important. First of all, *trust* (Hoe, 2007). Saying how you see things while welcoming someone else's point of view involves vulnerability (for example, you may learn that your previous ideas are not up to the mark). Trust, as we have seen, is about accepting vulnerability because you have positive expectations of others. Secondly, *employee engagement* is crucial: people who have the energy to apply their full resources to interacting (Quinn and Dutton, 2005), feel safe to do so, and believe that they can make a difference are more committed to learning. Thirdly, we also discussed Weick's emphasis on the importance of *candour*. As he argued, candid, respectful communication, along with engagement and trust, enables the incremental 'accommodations, adaptations and alterations'—the learning—that adds up to fundamental change.

Argyris suggests, though, that people will often espouse these kinds of principles while acting in line with Model 1 theories of action. Exercise 8.2 encourages you to consider how greater openness might contribute to a change situation in which you are involved.

 Exercise 8.2

Reflect on a change that you feel should take place in your organization (this could be at an individual, group, business unit, or whole organizational level) and which interpersonal issues have made difficult to take forward. Now recall a problematic conversation with someone about this, or imagine one that you would need to have in order to progress the change. Take several sheets of paper and draw a line down the centre. In the right-hand column, write out the conversation that occurred or which you think would occur if you were to raise the matter, as if you are writing a scene from a play, setting out your lines and the other person's lines. When you have finished this, in the left-hand column, write notes on the thoughts or feelings that you would keep to yourself. Now consider the following.

- Were the outcomes of the conversation beneficial to achieving the change that you want?
- How might your side of the conversation have contributed to any difficulties?
- Why did you avoid saying what was in your left-hand column? On what values is this reticence based?
- How could you have broached some of what was not said (that is, in your left-hand column) in a productive and beneficial way? You may find it helpful to discuss this with a trusted friend.

(Developed from Senge et al., 1994: 246–50, based on Argyris and Schön's work)

Isaacs (1999a) argues that the structures of conversations themselves also greatly influence the learning that can take place. Drawing on the work of Kantor, a family therapist, he examines four roles that are commonly played out in conversation:

- somebody makes a **move**, proposes an idea, advocates a way forward;
- someone may **follow**, supporting and developing an idea;
- someone else may **oppose**, challenging what has been said;
- another person may act as constructive **bystander**—standing back from the issue and providing perspective on what is happening.

The suggestion is that the quality of conversations is improved if all of these roles are in evidence. It is too easy for a conversation to get stuck in the dimension between moving and opposing, without the following or bystanding roles being in evidence. In particular, in productive conversations, there needs to be a balance between the *dimension of 'advocacy'*, moving and opposing, and the *dimension of 'inquiry'*, bystanding and following (see Figure 8.4). Having four roles does not mean that it needs four people to fulfil them. For example, in Change in Practice 8.2: Turns 4, 6, 8, 11, and 15 would be moves; Turns 12, 22, 24, and 25 would be following; Turns 5, 7, and 18 would be opposing; and Turns 9, 16, and 19 would be bystanding.

Isaacs (1999b) distinguishes between dialogue and discussion in conversation: discussion is about making a decision; **dialogue** is about evoking insight. This does not mean that decisions are not made in dialogue. Instead, it means that, in dialogue, decision-making begins

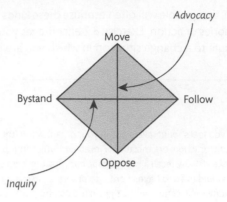

Figure 8.4 Balancing advocacy and inquiry

Source: Isaacs (1999a: 3)

 Exercise 8.3

Reflect on a recent meeting you have attended or a group conversation you have participated in.

- What role (or roles) did you take in the conversation (moving, opposing, following, or bystanding) and why?
- Were you aware at the time of the role(s) you were taking?
- Which of the four roles were adopted by different members of the group during the conversation?
- What was the quality of learning that occurred? Did people change their views? Did new ways forward emerge?

by really listening and understanding each other's points of view with a commitment to understanding one another's underlying assumptions and decision-making frameworks, so that double-loop learning can take place. Similarly Senge et al. (1994: 353) define dialogue as:

> *a sustained collective enquiry into everyday experience and what we take for granted . . .* a setting where people can become more aware of the context around their experience, and of the processes of thought and feeling that created that experience. [Emphasis in original]

The conversation becomes 'thinking together' (Senge, 2006; Isaacs, 1999b). In this case, advocacy needs to be distinguished by self-discovery and respect, and inquiry by suspension of certainties. Rather than seeing dialogue necessarily as a special kind of conversation, we think it is helpful to adopt Shaw's (2002) point of view that it represents a quality that supports learning in conversations and which can be present to a greater or lesser extent as the flow of conversation progresses. For example, in Change in Practice 8.2, Turns 19–24 have more of a quality of dialogue about them than the earlier part of the conversation, starting with Theresa's suspension of certainty and self-questioning in Turn 19. We return to the importance of dialogue in conversations for change when we examine facilitated approaches to change in Chapter 10.

See Chapter 10 for more on facilitated approaches and dialogue: p. 221

Learning from experience

Learning from experience, and understanding the complexities of experience, are vital aspects of organizational change, and are also difficult and often neglected (Kleiner and Roth, 1997; Szulanski and Winter, 2002; Carroll et al., 2004). In principle, both success and failure are rich arenas for learning. Kleiner and Roth (1997) recommend making a detailed written history of critical events, together with a commentary on the organizational dynamics. However, there is evidence that, in practice, people in organizations learn more effectively through organizational failures than successes (Madsen and Desai, 2010). Indeed, success, or solving problems successfully, may create complacency and lead to less learning (Tucker et al., 2002; Miller, 1993, 1994, cited in Baumard and Starbuck, 2005). One of the difficulties with success is discovering just what has gone right, when much of this may be tacit knowledge wrapped up in people's skills, relationships, and routines. Szulanski and Winter (2002) give examples of how this is achieved, in practice, through tacit, as well as explicit, staff knowledge. One example of good practice that they give is of a bank that was adept at converting acquired banks and their branches over to its own successful way of working:

> One tool the bank used to disseminate operating knowledge was traditional documentation, such as procedural guidelines . . . But it did much more. It also selected a sister bank . . . [that] had recently converted to a similar set of products and systems and served similar types of customers. The new staff could visit the sister bank to see how it operated. Having a living template helped the new bank make conversion-related decisions with more confidence . . . The sister bank relationship also reduced the likelihood that the new bank would repeat avoidable errors. If the sister bank's employees had resisted the shift from in-house to centralized processing, for example, the acquired bank's managers could use that information to anticipate the problem and circumvent it through superior internal communication. (Ibid: 66)

Despite the evidence that organizations learn more effectively from failure than success, failure is often associated with blame or shame, which militates against openness, frank discussion, and learning and change—at least, against double-loop learning (Tucker and Edmondson, 2003; Baumard and Starbuck, 2005). Change in Practice 8.3 illustrates this.

 Change in Practice 8.3

Paediatric heart surgery at the Bristol Royal Infirmary

In 2001, a UK public inquiry, set up to investigate a paediatric heart surgery centre at the Bristol Royal Infirmary, reported. The shocking findings led to key changes in practice. In particular, for the first time, mortality rates for heart surgery in different hospitals began to be published. Unbeknown to the parents of patients, for most of the period between 1988 and 1994, the death rate at Bristol for open-heart surgery on infants had been about double the rate of any other centre in England.

> At the time, however, there was a temptation for the clinicians to persuade themselves, even in the face of such evidence, that any poor outcome could quite plausibly be explained away . . . in terms of an expectation of improvement over time, notwithstanding the failure of Bristol's performance to improve in comparison with improvements reported in other units. Indeed, [one of the surgeons] spoke in terms of the 'inevitability' of a 'learning curve', by which it was meant that results could be

expected to be poor initially, but would improve over time with experience. They could argue that the small numbers of children who were treated meant that their figures looked worse when expressed in percentage terms, that they treated children who were more sick (albeit that there was no evidence to support this assertion) and that, once the hoped-for new surgeon was appointed, the pace of improvement would quicken. All of these arguments had sufficient plausibility at that time that they could be believed, and they could not readily be refuted, though they might be doubted. (Kennedy, 2001–public inquiry report: 247)

According to the report, the chief executive of the hospital, Dr Roylance, believed that clinicians 'at the bedside' should make decisions and it was not for management to interfere. So when Dr Stephen Bolsin, a consultant anaesthetist who joined the Bristol Royal Infirmary in 1988, complained about standards of care, first to colleagues and then to Roylance, his concerns were disregarded. Roylance insisted the issue was a clinical matter, which was in the domain of the paediatric cardiac surgeons. The Inquiry heard that a doctor's career at the Bristol Royal Infirmary depended on him or her fitting into a medical 'club', rather than on performance. Challenges to policy were perceived as disloyalty, so that a culture of fear had developed.

At the time, the consultants, particularly the surgeons, saw themselves as having very effective teams. But, in fact, they did not see *themselves* as part of their teams. And the Inquiry found that the teams were not organized around patient care. Instead the teams they referred to were teams of 'like professionals'–consultant surgeon leading surgeons, consultant anaesthetist leading anaesthetists, and so on–and these teams were 'profoundly hierarchical'.

Only when Bolsin eventually took his concerns to the press was paediatric heart surgery at Bristol stopped and the public inquiry set up. The findings, in 2000, were damning. Many children had died unnecessarily because the Bristol Royal Infirmary had failed to learn and to change in the preceding decade. In a telling postscript, Bolsin, who had brought the tragedy to light and in so doing saved many other infants, felt ostracized by the medical establishment in the UK, and had to move with his family to Australia to find work. On a more encouraging note, in 2010, a paediatric heart surgeon at another UK hospital himself raised concerns about a series of four deaths there over a two-month period, and surgery was suspended immediately and later halted altogether.[13-15]

What are the factors that encourage analysis of failings and the discovery of new ways of working? First and foremost that people can talk about organizational and individual failings without fear of negative consequences (Tucker and Edmondson, 2003), and are encouraged to engage with the double-loop learning required to address them (Tucker et al., 2002; Tucker and Edmondson, 2003). This plainly was not the case at the Bristol Royal Infirmary.

In fact, in a long-term case study that they conducted, Baumard and Starbuck found double-loop learning from failure unusual. Small failures tended to be regarded as demonstrating deviation from appropriate, established practice. Large failures were regarded as having idiosyncratic, external causes. Similar processes can be seen in the Bristol Royal Infirmary case. The terrible failure represented by the annual death rate of infant patients was explained away in terms of the supposed exceptional gravity of their condition. As Baumard and Starbuck point out, such external factors are rarely the explanation given for successes.

In Chapter 5, we discussed escalation of commitment. Problems and challenges encountered as a result of current mental models and actions can make it more difficult, rather than

See Chapter 5 for more on escalation of commitment: p. 95

easier, to adopt other ways of thinking and acting. At Bristol, unlearning the 'accomplished clinicians coping with complex cases' mindset would have involved discussions of clinical failure and unethical practice. The longer the situation continued and the worse the damage done, the *less* likely this was to occur. Dyson's relocation of its manufacturing operations to Malaysia in spite of a history of committing to UK manufacturing, described in Change in Practice 8.1, provides an example in which escalation of commitment was avoided: in that case, there was ongoing openness to organizational learning despite prior strategic commitments.

Systems thinking

A key way in which to broaden the focus of attention, in order to promote entrepreneurial intuiting and double-loop learning, is **systems thinking** (Senge, 2006): mapping out inter-relationships between different factors inside and outside the confines of the organization, and seeing their interaction as a whole system rather than as separate issues.

Senge (2006) points out that learning from experience can be illusory if a short-term perspective is taken. Bristol surgeons thought they were 'learning from experience' as they examined the lessons of each individual operation, without seeing the longer-term systemic picture of failure. There is also a danger of not noticing that gradual changes in, for example, the political, economic, social, technological, environmental, and legal contexts have major strategic implications for the organization. Senge refers to this as the 'parable of the boiled frog', drawing an analogy between the fate of organizations and the (reputed) fate of frogs slowly heated in a saucepan of water. The story goes that while frogs dropped into a pan of hot water will jump right out again, frogs placed into a saucepan of cold water enjoy themselves swimming around as the pan is gently heated, until they finally succumb. The idea is that, like frogs, people are insensitive to the need to learn in response to gradual changes in their situation. In the terms we discussed in Chapter 3, this leads to the avoidance of second-order *anticipatory* change. This was, for example, a very clear dynamic in the banking crisis of 2008–09.

See Chapter 3 for more on anticipatory change: p. 39

In addition, people often focus on their own roles, rather the purposes and performance of the whole organization, seeing themselves in a system in which they have little power and no need to take responsibility for failure. We think that the Bristol case illustrates how this constrained thinking can affect both those who experience themselves as having little power, and those with a great deal. Nursing staff avoided facing up to their responsibility for what was happening; even Roylance, the chief executive, in a powerful position and aware of his own power, continued to defer to the consultant surgeons. Alternatively, individuals or groups may blame others—other employees, other business units, equipment, competitors, etc.—when things go wrong, without acknowledging that these are all likely to be aspects of a system that is affected by their behaviour too. At Bristol, the surgeons made sense of recurring fatalities by blaming the supposed complexities of their patients' conditions, and the 'inevitability' of the learning curve. Blaming others can lead to self-fulfilling prophecies. At Bristol, belief that the infants with whom they were dealing had particularly complex heart problems prevented the surgeons attending to the possibility that their own skills were inadequate, which, in turn, did lead to dangerous, often fatal, complications for their patients.

See Chapter 5 for more on self-fulfilling prophecies: p. 94

To avoid locking organizations into these kinds of chronic problems and 'stuck' situations, issues facing organizations can be viewed as systems in action. For example, the Bristol Royal Infirmary case might be viewed as in Figure 8.5.

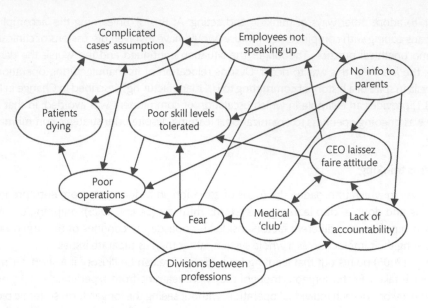

Figure 8.5 A rough map of the Bristol Royal Infirmary system

In Figure 8.5, various aspects of the system are mapped out and the arrows between them represent cause and effect. For example, divisions between the professions, the lack of information to parents, the toleration of poor skill levels, and the assumption that the Bristol cases are especially complicated are all contributory causes of the poor operations. And the poor operations themselves are contributory causes of fear, the assumption that the Bristol cases are especially complicated and, of course, the tragic deaths of the infant patients. All parts of the system needed to change—and the map provides an opportunity to think about what are the most effective interventions to change it. Tragically late though it was, the provision of more information to parents (and patients in general)—specially published hospital mortality rates for specific operations—has been a really significant NHS intervention in similar systems following the public inquiry.

Looking to the future

Alongside past experience, organizational learning takes place by focusing on future possibilities and potential. Strategy development is often supported by formal processes such as analysing strengths, weaknesses, opportunities, and threats facing an organization. This is one way in which to look to the future; the difficulty is that reliable data about opportunities and threats is frequently scarce. An alternative approach is **scenario planning** (de Geus, 1999). Rather than being based on definite information or predictions about individual opportunities and threats, scenario planning involves the development of 'coherent and credible alternative stories about the future . . . designed to help companies challenge their assumptions, develop their strategies and test their plans' (Cornelius et al., 2005). The use of scenario planning in business was pioneered by the Royal Dutch/Shell Oil Group. Famously, this enabled Shell to anticipate the possibility of a dramatic increase in oil prices prior to it actually transpiring in the early 1970s.

In some organizations, only senior leaders or a strategic planning group undertake such work. However, in our work as consultants, we have also found that some organizations involve employees from all levels and all parts of the organization in scenario planning. They often do this by running workshops, giving people data on external trends, and encouraging them to add their own knowledge and insights and to think about the likely impact on their part of the organization. Such involvement can make the case for organizational change much easier to 'sell' internally; it may also be part of encouraging a culture that is externally orientated and alert to changes in the external environment.

In Chapter 5, we discussed Henry Mintzberg's concept of strategy formation as a distributed function in organizations, with leaders promoting change by encouraging—and recognizing—strategy development across the organization. This highlights the importance of *experimentation* as another way of looking to the future. Gary Hamel put it this way:

See Chapter 5 for more on the 'grass roots' model of strategy formation: p. 102

> The only way you're going to see the path ahead is to start moving. Thus strategy is as much about experimentation as it is about foresight and passion. In many organizations, the quest for efficiency drives out experimentation. One question I often ask managers: 'Can you point to 20 or 30 small experiments going on in your company that you believe could fundamentally remake your company?' In most cases, the answer is no, there is nothing to point to. (Hamel, 1997)

This is the kind of approach to product development strategy through decentralized experimentation that Dyson Appliances, described in Change in Practice 8.1, claims to take (Dyson, 2005).

On the other hand, Senge et al. (2005) and Scharmer (2009) emphasize learning through an 'inner knowing', confidently *intuiting future potential* or possibilities for an organization—or oneself:

> Theorists have argued that we learn from the past through cycles of action and reflection that lead to new actions. [There is] a different type of learning process where we learn instead from a future that has not yet happened and from continually discovering our part in bringing that future to pass. (Senge et al., 2005: 86)

This process of intuitively discovering future possibilities Senge et al. (2005) call 'presencing'. It is something akin to this process that seems to have been in action in the repeated anticipatory radical changes that Apple Inc. made through its development of new products and markets in the 2000s. This is described in Change in Practice 8.4, which we also discuss in the final section of this chapter on dynamic capabilities and the learning organization.

 Change in Practice 8.4

Learning to change at Apple

Apple Computers was originally a highly successful manufacturer of innovative desktop computers during the 1980s. However, with the dominance of Microsoft's Windows operating system during the 1990s, Apple lost market share. Its operating system was, for many years, considered superior to Microsoft's, but was not licensed for use by other manufacturers. However, during the 2000s, Apple made a series of inspired moves into new markets. First, in 2001, Apple moved into MP3 players with its iPods. In 2003, it moved into music retailing with the opening of the iTunes Store. In 2007, the

iPhone was launched, and in 2010, the iPad tablet computer. Each product launch was a manifesta-
tion of learning that transformed both Apple and the market it was entering—in fact sometimes
practically creating a new market from scratch (as with the iPhone and iPad).

Figure 8.6 shows how the resulting sales had radically altered the profile of the company by 2011.
Desktop computers (Macs) were no longer its primary product line; sales were dominated by mobile electronic devices, particularly the iPhone, which by then accounted for 50 per cent of revenues. As described
in Chapter 1, in 2007, Apple Computers changed its name to Apple Inc. to reflect this transformation.[16]

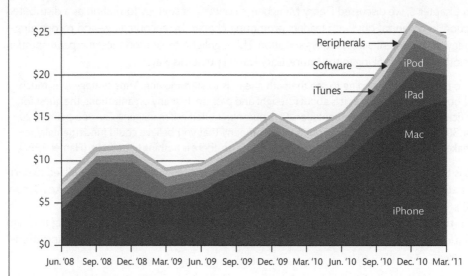

Figure 8.6 Apple revenue by segment (US $ bn)

Source: Frommer (2011)

 Section 2 Summary

In this section, we have considered three key factors that contribute to organizational learning:

- the quality of conversations;
- learning from experience;
- looking to the future.

Section 3: 'Dynamic capabilities' and the 'learning organization'

If organizations learn, do some learn better than others? This question has been approached
in recent years from two directions. One is to focus on the ability of organizations to adapt
their core strengths to changing circumstances. The other is the study of 'learning organizations'. We look at each of these in turn.

Core competencies and dynamic capabilities

In Chapter 5, we discussed strategy as deliberate and emergent patterns of choices and behaviour. An alternative standpoint, the **resource-based view of strategy**, focuses instead on strategic internal resources of the organization (Barney and Clark, 2007). This provides insight into what kind of knowledge is vital to an organization. Bundles of knowledge form **core competencies** (Prahalad and Hamel, 1990; Eden and Ackermann, 2010), which are also referred to as 'core capabilities' (Leonard-Barton, 1995). Representing the 'collective learning' of the organization (Prahalad and Hamel, 1990: 82), core competencies are the organization's collective skills that provide a unique competitive advantage—not in any one particular situation, but in a sustainable way over time. A core competency forms an *interdependent system* (Leonard-Barton, 1995), including, for example: employee experience, capabilities, and values; routines, work practices, and use of technology; patterns of social interaction, innovation, and decision-making; communication processes and managerial systems; and stories, everyday language, and metaphors.

See Chapter 5 for more on strategy: p. 100

But what kinds of collective knowledge provide competitive advantage over the long term in changing business environments? The resource-based view suggests that resources, whether financial, physical, or knowledge-based, provide potential advantage if they are valuable, rare, and difficult to imitate or replace with substitutes. Physical, financial, and asset-based resources may sometimes provide this kind of advantage, but resources based on collective knowledge are particularly well placed to achieve it. For example, while Dyson's intellectual property in terms of patents on vacuum cleaner technology was valuable and rare (in fact, unique), other companies attempted to substitute alternative technology to achieve 'bagless' vacuum cleaners. But Dyson's mix of a highly involved workforce at all levels, passion for vacuum cleaning, nimble manufacturing strategies, customer responsiveness, and product functionality, as well as the brand centred on James Dyson himself, proved much more resilient to attempts at imitation. It is this interdependent system that made up Dyson's core competence in high-quality vacuum cleaner technology.

See Chapter 2 for more on resources: p. 31

 Exercise 8.4

Consider which is your favourite organization at the moment—any organization at all. It might be a retail chain where you shop, a social media site, a charity for which you volunteer, your employer, or the university where you study.

- What tacit or explicit knowledge provides a competitive advantage in terms of serving customers, users, stakeholders, or beneficiaries especially well? Remember that, alongside explicit knowledge and tacit skills, collective knowledge can include routines, work practices, communication styles, patterns of decision-making, and social interaction, and the stories, jargon, and metaphors in use.

- Does this knowledge form a bundle that is valuable, rare, and, for other organizations, would be difficult to imitate or to find a substitute for? Could it be described as a core competency of the organization?

Recent research has focused on the ability of organizations to *adapt* their core competencies and how they are applied in rapidly changing environments. These kinds of abilities to adapt strengths are called **dynamic capabilities**:

> The firm's processes that use resources—specifically the processes to integrate, reconfigure, gain and release resources—to match or even create market change. Dynamic capabilities thus are the organizational and strategic routines by which firms achieve new resource configurations as markets emerge, collide, split, evolve and die. (Eisenhardt and Martin, 2000: 1107)

> A dynamic capability is a learned and stable pattern of collective activity through which the organization systematically generates and modifies its operating routines in pursuit of improved effectiveness. (Zollo and Winter, 2002: 340)

For example, core competencies of Apple could be regarded as innovative, user-friendly, high-technology design and building customer brand loyalty. These core competencies can be traced through years of great early success for Apple, and also during its years of relative decline as a niche computer brand. In recent years, it has demonstrated a *dynamic capability* to apply these core competencies to different markets and, indeed, to establish entirely new markets. Its extraordinary successful moves into MP3 players (the iPod), music downloading (the iTunes Store), and smartphones (the iPhone) illustrate this dynamic capability. From this perspective, it is this dynamic capability to restructure and apply its core competencies that has made Apple so successful in this period. Dyson's core competence lay in high-quality vacuum cleaner technology, but it has also demonstrated the dynamic capability to adapt this competence. It was able to broaden its focus to air-flow equipment in general (new forms of hand dryer and fans) and, as explained in section 1, to reconceive the company as a manufacturer with a UK innovation hub rather than as a UK manufacturer per se. In Chapter 3, we discussed Cisco Systems' capability to manage acquisitions. Cisco's core competency probably lies in the technology of networking (its technology underpins much of the Internet, for example). But the dynamic (and rare) capability to manage acquisitions successfully has been a key way in which it has refreshed this core competence, acquiring new technology and entering new markets. These three examples demonstrate how dynamic capabilities allow organizations to 'achieve new resource configurations', as Eisenhardt and Martin put it above.

The learning organization concept

The second approach that has been taken to exploring whether some organizations learn especially well focuses more on learning in the organization as a whole rather than on learning with regard to specific core competencies. The idea is that a learning organization is one that learns especially effectively and therefore, as well as organizational learning being a perspective on organizational change, the **learning organization** may be an appropriate strategic objective for organizational change. This concept has been operationalized in two distinct ways. Some authors have sought to discover methods by which organizations learn effectively and have set these out as guidelines for learning organizations (Garvin et al., 2008; Pedler et al., 1996; Pedler et al., 1998). Others have set out broad aspirations for 'the learning organization' without specifying precisely how those aspirations should be achieved (Senge, 2006).

Garvin (2000), who takes the first route, defines a learning organization as:

an organization skilled at creating, acquiring, interpreting, transferring, and retaining knowledge, and at purposefully modifying its behavior to reflect new knowledge and insights. (Garvin, 2000: 11)

This definition emphasizes the nature and impact of organizational learning, mirroring closely the 4I model of organizational learning. Garvin et al. (2008) take the view that becoming a learning organization requires strength in three sets of parameters.

1. *A supportive learning environment*   These parameters emphasize the significance of the quality of interaction or conversation and of double-loop learning.

   - Psychological safety to be open about expressing views, asking questions and owning up to mistakes
   - Valuing differing viewpoints
   - Being open to new ideas
   - Time for reflection

2. *Concrete learning processes and practices*

   - Formal, systematic, and clear processes for the generation, collection, interpretation, and dissemination of information
   - Experimentation with new products and services
   - Intelligence gathering
   - Identifying and solving problems
   - Focus on education and training

3. *Leadership behaviour that reinforces learning*

   - Leaders who actively question and listen to employees, prompting dialogue and debate
   - Leaders who, through their behaviour, show they value differing viewpoints and time spent on identifying and solving problems

These authors have developed a learning organization survey, available online at http://los.hbs.edu, which can be used by individuals or groups of employees to benchmark their organization against average scores from other organizations. Exercise 8.5 invites you to consider the usefulness and objectivity of this learning organization survey.

 Exercise 8.5

Go to **http://los.hbs.edu** and complete the learning organization survey based on Garvin et al. (2008). Or, alternatively, if you are not currently working, complete the survey as you interview a friend about his or her organization.

- How, according to the survey, does your (or your friend's) organization measure up as a learning organization against the norms set out on the site?
- What practical steps could be taken in the organization to remedy any weaknesses?
- Do you think that this is an objective analysis, or might it say more about your (or your friend's) own experience than the organization as a whole? Do you think other employees in the organization would see things the same way?

A second definition of the learning organization, from Peter Senge, emphasizes allowing the organization—or those within it—to have more control over their destiny: 'an organization that is continually expanding its capacity to create its future' (Senge, 2006: 14). Senge set out a series of broad aspirations—'five disciplines'—to achieve this.

1. *Personal mastery*

   A focus on personal mastery means people creating and maintaining a clear vision for their own futures, and facing up to current realities honestly (that is, not pulling the wool over your own eyes about the current state of affairs).

2. *Mental models*

See Chapter 5 for more on mental models: p. 85

   A focus on mental models means people making continuing efforts to clarify and to test their mental models, including assumptions, beliefs, values, and habitual patterns of reasoning, their psychological contracts, and so on. Because mental models, while they can be explicit, can also be unacknowledged, unrecognized or out of awareness, this can be challenging. In section 2, we explained Chris Argyris' theory that people's espoused mental models often do not match up with those that they actually make use of.

3. *Shared vision*

See Chapters 5 and 9 for more on developing a vision: pp. 101, 212

   This means a focus on building a common sense of purpose and commitment by developing shared images of future. In Senge's framework, a shared vision is not imposed, but is developed jointly by employees.

4. *Team learning*

   This means the capacity to collectively reflect, learn, and mobilize action as a team—in other words, in terms of the 4I model, a focus on integrating. Senge sees the quality of conversations, and dialogue in particular, as central to this discipline.

5. *Systems thinking*

   We have discussed systems thinking, mapping out interrelationships between different aspects of organizational situations, in section 2. For Senge, this skill is fundamental to developing a learning organization.

We would emphasize that, whether viewed in terms of specific guidelines or broad aspirations, the concept of the learning organization should be considered as a direction of travel rather than a destination that can be arrived at. It is unlikely that an organization would be rated perfectly on Garvin et al.'s survey in every respect by any employee, let alone all of them. Similarly, we cannot imagine ever saying: 'Okay, that's it, we got there, this is a learning organization—all five disciplines are lived up to here.' Instead, becoming a learning organization is a direction to which organizational change can aspire.

There is also a paradox at the heart of ideas about the learning organization: success can be assessed only retrospectively. In 1990, Senge used Apple Computers, as it was then, to illustrate many of the aspects of learning organizations. At that time, it was highly successful. By the mid-1990s, Apple was in relative decline, and was seen as a company that had made a fundamental mistake in not licensing its operating system as Microsoft had done so successfully. At that time, few would have seen Apple as an exemplar of a learning organization. The 2000s, on the other hand, was a period of phenomenal growth for Apple as it returned to focusing on design and diversifying into new markets. Once again, Apple was cited as a learning organization. The next episode in this tale is, of course, still to be told.

Section 3 Summary

In this section, we have:

- explained core competencies and dynamic capabilities;
- discussed the learning organization concept.

 Integrative Case Study

Toyota's learning

In 2010, Toyota, the Japanese and international automobile manufacturer, had to recall an unprecedented number of vehicles with brake and other faults, and attracted a great deal of negative publicity. Prior to this, however, Toyota had been lauded as a learning organization. In fact, according to Liker (2004), of all of the companies of which he knew, Toyota was the best example of a learning organization. Lawler and Worley (2006) pick out Toyota as one of three examples of organizations 'built to change'. By 2007, research firms had rated Toyota among the top car brands in terms of reliability, initial quality, and long-term durability for almost fifteen years, and Toyota was also the most profitable car manufacturer (Stewart and Raman, 2007).

Some Toyota practices are notably in keeping with the five disciplines that Senge and his colleagues set out.

- Quality circles are used at the end of each week for production workers to analyse any problems in quality, productivity, or safety and to identify 'countermeasures' that they then test. These quality circles are said to have played a major role in the evolution of the famed 'Toyota production system', which we discuss in Chapter 9. There is, equally, an emphasis on the dissemination of know-how gained across the organization.

- There is an eagerness to experiment and to set (almost) impossible goals. For example, Toyota launched the Prius, the first mass-produced hybrid car powered by petrol and electricity, in Japan in 1997 and worldwide in 2001. In a 2007 interview, Toyota's then president, Katsuaki Watanabe, explained his vision:

  I don't know how many years it's going to take us, but I want Toyota to come up with the dream car – a vehicle that can make the air cleaner than it is, a vehicle that cannot injure people, a vehicle that prevents accidents from happening, a vehicle that can make people healthier the longer they drive it, a vehicle that can excite, entertain, and evoke the emotions of its occupants, a vehicle that can drive around the world on just one tank of gas. That's what I dream about. . . . Our engineers are working right now to develop the technologies we need and to incorporate them into vehicles. If we accelerate our technology development, we can realize the dream car. (Stewart and Raman, 2007: 82).

- Teamwork is central at Toyota (Stewart and Raman, 2007): 'each member of the team is accountable and has the authority and responsibility to find a solution. The practice started on the factory floor and has spread throughout the corporation' (Takeuchi et al., 2008: 102). Without formally adopting dialogue as an approach to communication, open communication is emphasized, with face-to-face interactions a priority, freedom to express contrary opinions across the hierarchy, and refusal to listen to colleagues being seen as a 'serious transgression' (ibid: 103).

However, in October 2009, 3.8 million vehicles were recalled in the US following floor mat problems, which had led in some cases to stuck accelerator pedals. More recalls over safety concerns followed, totalling 8.5 million worldwide by February 2010. The faults had, by then, been linked to hundreds of injuries and reports of a number of deaths.

On 24 February 2010, Akio Toyoda, president of Toyota Motor Corporation, appeared before the US Congressional Committee on Oversight and Government Reform, in a gruelling three-and-a-half-hour session. As part of his opening statement, he acknowledged that the company had got its priorities wrong:

> Toyota has, for the past few years, been expanding its business rapidly. Quite frankly, I fear the pace at which we have grown may have been too quick. I would like to point out here that Toyota's priority has traditionally been the following: first, safety; second, quality; and third; volume. These priorities became confused, and we were not able to stop, think, and make improvements as much as we were able to before, and our basic stance to listen to customers' voices to make better products has weakened somewhat. We pursued growth over the speed at which we were able to develop our people and our organization, and we should sincerely be mindful of that. I regret that this has resulted in the safety issues described in the recalls we face today, and I am deeply sorry for any accidents that Toyota drivers have experienced.

In April 2010, the US authorities levied a record fine of over US$16 million on the company, amid claims that recalls over faulty pedals had been delayed, initially being reported within the company as 'customer satisfaction' issues rather than safety concerns. Toyota's reputation for quality had suffered enormous damage.

Questions

1. In view of the 2010 safety problems with Toyota cars, and the way in which recalls were handled, which of the following conclusions seem more appropriate to you, and why?

   - The organization never really was a 'learning organization'.
   - Toyota was once a learning organization, but became less so during the first decade of this century.
   - As a learning organization, Toyota is in the process of learning from its safety mistakes.

2. What changes might Toyota need to make to learn more effectively and rapidly from customer safety concerns?

3. From the case, and other information that you can find out about Toyota, can you identify a 'dynamic capability' of the company?

Conclusion

The three perspectives on organizational change that we have introduced—organizational culture, power and politics, and organizational learning—present different views of the main issues in change management. But these views are complementary rather than contradictory. We recommend analysing situations from multiple perspectives to provide a more detailed picture of the challenges and opportunities of change. Part C of this book considers how change is delivered in practice. As you turn to these implementation issues, each of the three perspectives at which we have been looking offers a framework for considering how interventions may encourage or inhibit effective change and for the ongoing evaluation of transitions.

 Please visit the Online Resource Centre at **http://www.oxfordtextbooks.co.uk/orc/ myers** *to access further resources for students and lecturers.*

Change in Practice sources

1. BBC News (2002) 'Dyson plant shuts up shop', 26 Sep. http://news.bbc.co.uk/1/hi/england/2282809.stm

2. Beard, A. (2010) 'Life's work', *Harvard Business Review*, **88**(7/8): 172.

3. Collins, N. (2005) 'Dyson is making pots of money for Britain by going to Malaysia', *The Telegraph*, 28 Feb. http://www.telegraph.co.uk/comment/personal-view/3615244/Dyson-is-making-pots-of-money-for-Britainby-going-to-Malaysia.html

4. Dyson, J. (2004) 'The Richard Dimbleby lecture: Engineering the difference'. http://news.bbc.co.uk/1/shared/bsp/hi/pdfs/dyson_10_12_04.pdf

5. Dyson Ltd (undated) 'Inside Dyson'. http://www.dyson.co.uk/insidedyson/default.asp

6. *The Economist* (2007) 'Suck it and see: The hazards of being an entrepreneur', 1 Feb. http://www.economist.com/node/8582349

7. Gribben, R. (2003) 'Dyson production moves to Malaysia', *The Telegraph*, 21 Aug. http://www.telegraph.co.uk/finance/2860995/Dyson-production-moves-to-Malaysia.html

8. Hirst, C. (2005) 'James Dyson: Dyson cleans up in America, but has he brushed a few things under the carpet?', *The Independent*, 27 Feb. http://www.independent.co.uk/news/business/analysis-and-features/james-dyson-dyson-cleans-up-in-america-but-has-he-brushed-a-few-things-under-the-carpet-484994.html

9. Mesure, S. and Beard, M. (2002) 'The appliance of science sucks Dyson eastwards', *The Independent*, 6 Feb. http://www.independent.co.uk/news/business/news/last-month-james-dyson-said-the-decline-of-british-manufacturing-was-a-tragedy-659618.html

10. This is Money (2004) 'Survival, Dyson style', 21 Mar. http://www.thisismoney.co.uk/news/article.html?in_article_id=322783&in_page_id=2

11. Uhlig, R. and Litterick, D. (2002) '800 jobs to go as Dyson goes to the Far East', *The Telegraph*, 6 Feb. http://www.telegraph.co.uk/news/uknews/1383870/800-jobs-to-go-as-Dyson-goes-to-the-Far-East.html

12. Quinn, R. W. and Dutton, J. E. (2005) 'Coordination as energy in conversation', *Academy of Management Review*, **30**(1): 36–57.

13. BBC News (1999) 'Bolsin: The Bristol whistleblower'. http://news.bbc.co.uk/1/hi/health/532006.stm

14. Kennedy, I. (2001) *Learning from Bristol: The Report of the Public Inquiry into Children's Heart Surgery at the Bristol Royal Infirmary 1984–1995*. http://www.bristol-inquiry.org.uk/final_report/the_report.pdf

15. Weick, K. E. and Sutcliffe, K. M. (2003) 'Hospitals as cultures of entrapment: A reanalysis of the Bristol Royal Infirmary', *California Management Review*, **45**(2): 73–84.

16. Frommer, D. (2011) 'Chart of the day: The iPhone is now half of Apple's business', 21 Apr. http://www.businessinsider.com/chart-of-the-day-apple-revenue-by-segment-2011-4

Integrative Case Study sources

BBC News (2010) 'Q&A: Toyota recalls', 18 Feb. http://news.bbc.co.uk/1/hi/business/8496902.stm

BBC News (2010) 'Toyota boss Akio Toyoda apologises for faults', 24 Feb. http://news.bbc.co.uk/1/hi/business/8533352.stm

BBC News (2010) 'Toyota faces record $16m fine from US over pedal recall', 5 Apr. http://news.bbc.co.uk/1/hi/business/8604150.stm

BBC News (2010) 'Toyota agrees to pay $16.4m fine', 20 Apr. http://news.bbc.co.uk/1/hi/business/8630447.stm

The Guardian (2010) 'Toyota president Akio Toyoda's statement to Congress', 24 Feb. http://www.guardian.co.uk/business/2010/feb/24/akio-toyoda-statement-to-congress

Lawler, E. E. and Worley, C. G. (2006) Built to Change: How to Achieve Sustained Organizational Effectiveness, San Francisco, CA: Jossey-Bass.

Liker, J. (2004) The Toyota Way: 14 Management Principles from the World's Greatest Manufacturer, New York: McGraw-Hill Professional.

Sanchez, R. (2005) Knowledge Management and Organizational Learning: Fundamental Concepts for Theory and Practice, Working Paper Series, Lund, Sweden: Lund Institute of Economic Research.

Spear, S. and Bowen, H. K. (1999) 'Decoding the DNA of the Toyota production system', Harvard Business Review, **77**(5): 96–106.

Stewart, T. A. and Raman, A. P. (2007) 'Lessons from Toyota's long drive', Harvard Business Review, **85**(7/8): 74–83.

Takeuchi, H., Osono, E., and Shimizu, N. (2008) 'The contradictions that drive Toyota's success', Harvard Business Review, **86**(6): 96–104.

Webb, T. (2010) 'Toyota recalls 1.66m cars worldwide amid fears over brakes and engines', The Guardian, 21 Oct. http://www.guardian.co.uk/business/2010/oct/21/toyota-recalls-166m-cars-faulty-brakes-engines

Webb, T., Booth, R., McCurry, J., and Harris, P. (2010) 'How did Toyota veer so far off course?', The Guardian, 7 Feb. http://www.guardian.co.uk/business/2010/feb/07/toyota-veer-off-course

Further reading

Senge, P. M. (2006) The Fifth Discipline: The Art and Practice of the Learning Organization, 2nd edn, New York: Random House Books.
This is a classic introduction to organizational learning and the learning organization.

Part C

Delivering Change

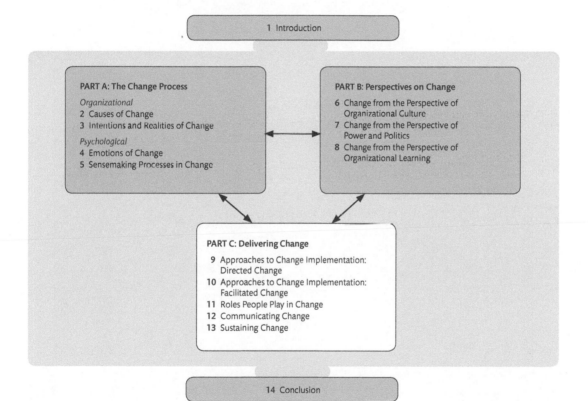

1 Introduction

PART A: The Change Process

Organizational
2 Causes of Change
3 Intentions and Realities of Change

Psychological
4 Emotions of Change
5 Sensemaking Processes in Change

PART B: Perspectives on Change

6 Change from the Perspective of
  Organizational Culture
7 Change from the Perspective of
  Power and Politics
8 Change from the Perspective of
  Organizational Learning

PART C: Delivering Change

9 Approaches to Change Implementation:
  Directed Change
10 Approaches to Change Implementation:
  Facilitated Change
11 Roles People Play in Change
12 Communicating Change
13 Sustaining Change

14 Conclusion

9

Approaches to Change Implementation: Directed Change

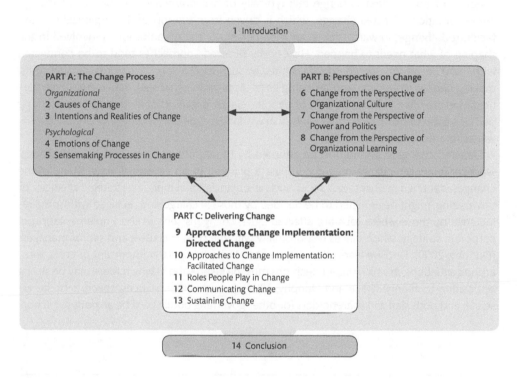

```
                        ┌─────────────────────────────┐
                        │       1 Introduction        │
                        └─────────────────────────────┘

┌─────────────────────────────────┐        ┌─────────────────────────────────┐
│ PART A: The Change Process        │◄──────►│ PART B: Perspectives on Change    │
│                                   │        │                                   │
│ Organizational                    │        │ 6 Change from the Perspective of  │
│ 2 Causes of Change                │        │   Organizational Culture          │
│ 3 Intentions and Realities of     │        │ 7 Change from the Perspective of  │
│   Change                          │        │   Power and Politics              │
│                                   │        │ 8 Change from the Perspective of  │
│ Psychological                     │        │   Organizational Learning         │
│ 4 Emotions of Change              │        │                                   │
│ 5 Sensemaking Processes in Change │        │                                   │
└─────────────────────────────────┘        └─────────────────────────────────┘

            ┌─────────────────────────────────────────┐
            │ PART C: Delivering Change                  │
            │                                            │
            │ 9 Approaches to Change Implementation:     │
            │   Directed Change                          │
            │ 10 Approaches to Change Implementation:    │
            │    Facilitated Change                      │
            │ 11 Roles People Play in Change             │
            │ 12 Communicating Change                    │
            │ 13 Sustaining Change                       │
            └─────────────────────────────────────────┘

                        ┌─────────────────────────────┐
                        │       14 Conclusion         │
                        └─────────────────────────────┘
```

Introduction

This chapter and the following one explore the range of choices that senior managers face in deciding their approach to the implementation of change. The spectrum extends from change that is driven from the top and imposed upon staff, to change that is developed through wide involvement of staff at all levels. In this chapter, we will first explore the nature of both directed and facilitated change, before turning our attention to a more detailed examination of directed change, looking at some of the methods deployed to effect directed change. Chapter 10 will then pursue this in respect of facilitated change, examining those methods that aim to maximize involvement of all in the change process.

See Chapter 10 for more on facilitated approaches

Main topics covered in this chapter

- Exploration of directed and facilitated change
- A sample of directed change methods, examining their relative strengths and weaknesses in enabling change
- A framework for implementing change with a directed approach

Section 1: Directed or facilitated change implementation?

Exploring directed and facilitated approaches

Theories of organizational change talk typically of two distinctive approaches to change implementation: **directed change**, which is driven from the top of the organization; and **facilitated change**, in which the wider membership of the organization is involved in the shaping of what needs to happen. Historically directed approaches tend to be connected with 'hard', economic-based change strategies such as changing structures, closing units, making people redundant, and reducing costs. Approaches that seek active employee participation are often linked with 'soft', or people-related, organizational strategies, concerning perhaps team performance, cross-divisional working, or the development of organizational values (Bradford and Burke, 2005).

See Chapter 3 for more on planned and emergent change: p. 48

Directed change is assumed to be adopted by those holding a planned view of change, whereas facilitated change may encompass a planned or an emergent view. Many of the changes identified in Chapters 2 and 3, such as organizational mergers, strategic alliances, or downsizing, might be expected to be decided by those in charge and received with some reluctance by those whose jobs are affected. Such change is seen as the implementation of corporate strategy, which places responsibility with the chief executive and senior managers (Dunphy, 2000). Decisive leadership can be seen to be particularly important in crisis, turnaround situations, in which urgent decisions must be taken—and in which there may be strong opposition to change (Stace and Dunphy, 1991). In such circumstances, speed is of the essence, and both staff and shareholders (or other governing bodies) will be anxious for action.

Change in Practice 9.1

Directed change at Marks and Spencer

In May 2004, when Stuart Rose first took over as chief executive of Marks and Spencer, the major UK retailer, the company was in a vulnerable state and fending off a range of takeover bids. Within two months, by July 2004, Rose had announced a recovery plan that involved selling off the financial services business to HSBC bank, buying control of the Per Una clothing range, which was one of the best-selling lines, closing the experimental concept store known as 'Lifestore', stopping the expansion of its 'Simply Food' line of stores, and cutting 650 jobs. As a result, Philip Green, a key competitor, withdrew his takeover bid after failing to get sufficient backing from shareholders.[1-2]

Change in Practice 9.1 demonstrates the power of Rose's decisive leadership, bringing about change swiftly and with confidence; there was no expectation from management or share-holders that staff should be consulted about the strategy.

Where facilitated change approaches are adopted, there is a greater intention for staff at different levels in the organization to input to and shape the change. By implication, senior management have less control of what gets decided, as employees have the op-portunity to influence and negotiate some aspects of the outcome; change is seen as more of a collaborative venture. Dunphy (2000) points out that, particularly in knowledge-based organizations, for example financial services or high-technology-based compa-nies, the workforce is likely to be skilled and well informed, understanding their segment of the market better than the senior executives may do. In such circumstances, exclud-ing staff from the planning of change does not make sense. Equally, where organizations are organized around complex global structures or strategic alliances, there may no longer be one clear central management structure or power base to take and control decisions.

In reality, there is not necessarily a sharp dividing line between directed and facilitated approaches. Many organizations that expect senior management to be in charge of the change process do not assume this to be at the expense of employee participation. For ex-ample, some organizations create the vision of the future in a participative way, with senior management taking key decisions that emerge from those conversations; others set the change in motion from the top and then engage smaller units in how they implement the changes in their areas. The culture of the organization and the context in which it operates may affect the range of approaches that are suitable.

 Exercise 9.1

Identify an organizational change with which you are familiar or interview someone else about his or her experience of an organizational change.

- To what extent were you and your colleagues able to give your views about the change before it was implemented?
- Would you classify the approach taken as directed or facilitated?
- How did that make you feel?
- Do you think the approach was the right one for the circumstances?
- How might you have led it differently?

A model of approaches to change

Dunphy and Stace (1993) suggest the choice of approach is dependent on the circumstances the organization is facing, so that the overall business context and the scale and the span of the change directly affect the nature of the change approach to be employed. Through a study of thirteen service-sector organizations, including high, medium, and low-performing organizations, they identify four styles of change management: two **facilitated** styles, namely **collaborative** and **consultative**; and two **directed** styles, **directive** and **coercive**.

Facilitated and Directed Styles

Collaborative   Involves widespread participation by employees in important decisions about the organization's future and about the means of bringing about organizational change.

Consultative   A more limited involvement. Employees are asked for their views on proposals and management may be influenced by their input.

Directive   The senior management team take key decisions about the change agenda and direct the efforts to deliver the change. They offer a vision of the future and employ firm persuasion to engage those affected to ensure that it is implemented.

Coercive   An extension of directed change, change is imposed on staff without attempts to persuade them, or to gain buy-in or understanding of the idea. Threats, sanctions, or force are used to gain compliance.

(From Dunphy and Stace, 1993)

See Chapter 3 for more on the scale and span of change: p. 37

They note also that organizations face changes of differing scale and span, from **fine-tuning**, involving gentle adjustments, often affecting one team or small unit, through to **corporate transformations** (also known as discontinuous change), affecting the whole organization in some fundamental way.

Scale and Span of Change

Fine-tuning   Gentle change at unit level, for example refining procedures.

Incremental adjustment   Adjustments made in response to the changing environment. Such modifications are distinct, but not radical, for example adapting structures or strategies at unit or departmental level.

Modular transformation   Major realignment of one or more department (and not the whole organization).

Corporate transformation   Organization-wide change fundamentally affecting ways of thinking and operating.

Through plotting the styles of change against the scale and span of the change, they identify four key change approaches, depicted in Figure 9.1.

1. **Developmental transitions** require constant gentle, incremental adjustment of the organization in response to external environmental changes. The primary style of change management is *consultative*, which aims to gain voluntary commitment to the need for continual improvement. There is widespread involvement in the communication process to develop trust.

2. **Task-focused transitions** require constant adjustment of the organization to redefine how it operates in specific areas, for example to realign a department. The change management style is *directive*, with the change leader seeking compliance. Whilst this

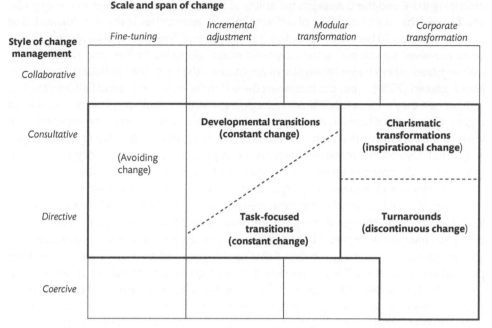

Figure 9.1 Approaches to change

Source: Adapted from Stace (1996)

means that the change is driven from the top, managers further down the organization may adopt a more consultative approach. Nevertheless the emphasis is on formal communication, with instructions, memos, and emails.

3. **Charismatic transformations** refer to change needing a more radical shift that may involve the whole organization. It is led by a *charismatic* senior management team, both to drive the change and to gain commitment through consultation. The aim is to use key managers to gain inspirational, emotional commitment of the staff to the vision, such that there may be top down communication, but with built-in feedback loops and the use of key role models to disseminate the change.

4. **Turnarounds** are fast discontinuous changes to recreate the organization, needing *directive* change management with some *coercion* to radically challenge existing practices. The aim is to communicate the sense of crisis in a formal and authoritative fashion, with no time to engage staff in the thinking.

Dunphy and Stace (1993) report that each approach is seen to have a key purpose and, over time, to have limitations; one approach will not serve for ever, and leaders need to constantly reappraise the circumstances and requirements.

   An alternative view is held by Beer and Nohria (2000), who propose that two primary approaches to change, Theories E and O—where change driven by economic imperative is known as Theory E, and change focusing on organizational culture and capability as Theory O—should be integrated to improve the success of change management. They argue that polarizing the E and the O weakens the ability of the organization to adapt in the long run, and believe that the integration of different change approaches is the way forward: that organizations would benefit by considering economic and organizational factors simultaneously. However, by comparing the integrated model identified by Beer and Nohria (2000) with eighteen other change management approaches, the limitations of their model are exposed. Leppitt (2006) points out that whilst there is some common ground between the two approaches, they do support different strategic alignment. For example, Theory E is suited to urgent, turnaround situations, which may not be well served by an integrated approach. This leads to the conclusion that a more comprehensive integrated model should be developed and tested. Overall, the research reinforces the importance of a contingency approach to achieving sustainable change rather than searching for one 'best practice' way.

Our experience in implementing organization change endorses the need for a true integration of approaches, both leading from the top *and* facilitating the involvement of people in all aspects of the change—in doing so, implementation success is much increased. However, such integration implies a united and skilful management team who, collectively, are able to operate across the spectrum of change styles, as well as an absence of conflicting political interests, and staff who have skills to make a genuine contribution; in reality, this is often difficult to achieve. Other practical considerations, such as the time available to make pressing decisions or the geographic spread of managers, can get in the way of achieving wider involvement. Technology is now proving to be a key enabler in this respect.

 ### Change in Practice 9.2

Alfa Laval: Directed change using technology to increase participative input

Alfa Laval is a global organization that focuses on energy optimization, environmental protection, and food production through heat transfer technology. With production units in Europe, Asia, the US, and Latin America, it has 11,400 employees and customers worldwide.

In 2008, Alfa Laval, a client of Ashridge Business School, needed to take swift decisions in order to create a change plan. In the past, the chief executive and the group board had worked on such plans. This time, they experimented with gaining the input of a wider range of their key senior managers, based around the world, in China, India, the US, and Europe, in a just-in-time virtual involvement process.

Ashridge worked with the CEO, eight members of the group board, and thirty senior leaders. From this group, five virtual project teams were set up and the work culminated just four months later, in March 2009, with a virtual conference involving all five teams and other contributors. Each of the project teams met via the IT platform five or six times during the four-month period, and the structure of the meetings was designed to maximize the input of all of these senior managers, to strengthen their connectivity, and hence to increase the effectiveness of their work during the session. Additional cross-team virtual workshops ensured critical cross-group exchanges.

The final four-hour virtual conference had many of the elements of a traditional conference, such as an opening address from the CEO, group presentations, breaks for coffee, and interactive feedback processes, but was completely virtual, again using the IT platform to create separate small-group discussions as well as whole-group forums.

The results of this mixture of direction and facilitation included:

- the development of skills in working virtually and involving a wider range of key stakeholders in business critical change projects via a virtual environment;

- a set of clearly defined and agreed change implementation plans and critical success factors (CSFs) for the plans.

- a group of senior managers with a high level of involvement in, and commitment to, the plans, prepared to lead and champion the changes.[3-4]

In this example, the CEO and group board needed to take decisions with speed, yet they found the confidence to take a risk and experiment, involving senior managers who were close to the business operations, without losing pace or focus. This, in turn, enabled those senior managers to describe the vision and champion the change within their own operations, creating the conditions for charismatic transformation (Dunphy and Stace, 1993).

 Section 1 Summary

In this section, we have:

- considered the difference between directed and facilitated change;

- applied a framework developed by Dunphy and Stace (1993) to identify directed and facilitated approaches to change in relation to the scale and the span of change;

- considered the ways in which directed change approaches can achieve wider levels of involvement.

Section 2: Directed change methods

This section will examine three of the frequently used directed change methods. They have been selected both because of their popularity over the past twenty years and because they are typical of their genre. We will consider the extent to which their growth has resulted from their established effectiveness or to organizations being attracted to them because they are 'of the moment'—the latest fashion that others are adopting, as explored in Chapter 2. They will be examined to consider their relative strengths and weaknesses in enabling change in terms of the cultural, political, and organizational learning lenses that were identified in Part B.

See Chapter 2 for more on management fashions: p. 23

Business process re-engineering

Business process re-engineering (BPR) is an approach to corporate transformation that first came to prominence in the early 1990s and still informs more recent versions of re-engineering that have been adopted since. The term was adopted by Hammer and Champy, who define BPR as:

> The fundamental rethinking and radical redesign of business processes to achieve dramatic improvements in critical, contemporary measures of performance, such as cost, quality, service and speed. (Hammer and Champy, 2001: 35)

Note the use of strong, determined language to describe BPR: *radical redesign* and *dramatic improvements*, which can be achieved by *fundamentally rethinking* how things get done—in effect, starting over. This rhetoric implies powerful change, not to be taken on as an experiment or on a small scale; it is an 'all or nothing' description. The implications of this positioning will be explored through the examination of BPR implementation examples.

The redesign of **core processes** is the main focus of the re-engineering. These are the processes that are at the heart of what the company does and which cut across organizational boundaries to include, for example, the wholesaler and distribution, through to the retailer and consumer. Hammer and Champy (2001) suggest that this encourages a focus on ultimate performance, rather than the performance of any one aspect of the business. By implication, narrow specialists are replaced by multi-skilled workers, often working in self-managed teams across organizational divisions.

There are four key steps involved in implementing BPR.

1. Prepare the organization—involving assessment of the strategic context and communication throughout the organization of reasons for re-engineering.

2. Fundamentally rethink the way in which work gets done—identify and analyse core business processes from start to finish, define performance objectives, and design new processes, in accordance with the following guidelines.

    -   Simplify the current process by combining or eliminating steps.
    -   Attend to both technical and social aspects of the process.
    -   Prevent past practice from being a constraint.
    -   Perform activities in their most natural order.

    In doing this, it is expected that all assumptions about how things are done will be challenged to achieve the promised *radical* redesign.

3. Restructure the organization around the new business processes. This is important: restructuring and the associated disruption are an expected part of BPR.

4. Implement new information and measurement systems to enforce change.

(From Hammer and Champy, 1993: 85)

Information technology is seen as the essential enabler of BPR and many new processes would not be possible without it. Hammer and Champy (2001) cite the example of Kodak's re-engineering of its product development. Kodak had a largely sequential process: individuals who work on one part of the product, such a camera body designers, did their work first, followed by the shutter designers, then the digital mechanism designers, and so on. The introduction of new technology enabled all individual engineers to work simultaneously, with technology combining all of the inputs on a daily basis so that any issues of incompatibility were immediately recognized. It also enabled the manufacturing engineers to begin their tooling design ten weeks into the development process—as soon as the product designers had given the prototype some shape. The re-engineered process cut across design and manufacturing, reducing the time taken to get from concept to production by 50 per cent. In this way, technology can impact the scale of the redesign that is possible. In recent years, the IT element has become the focus of many re-engineering programmes and we will return to this in the end-of-chapter Integrative Case Study.

Change in Practice 9.3

Business process re-engineering at Cigna Corporation

Cigna, a leading provider of insurance in the US and globally, has undertaken a range of business process re-engineering programmes over many years, starting as far back as 1990, when BPR was just gaining ground, estimating savings of some US $100 million in the first three years of the changes. Its application of BPR is one of the best-known re-engineering case studies.

The inception of BPR was prompted by the organization facing difficulties, plus the arrival of a new chairman, who initiated a new corporate planning process. In response to the chairman's plans, one of the organization's divisions initiated a BPR process, aimed at changing the mix of the business in the portfolio to meet the needs of the new strategic plan. The division downsized by 40 per cent and staff had to reapply for their own jobs. Within eighteen months, new work processes were implemented and cross-functional customer service teams, as well as team-based pay incentives, were introduced. It is claimed that a two-week underwriting procedure was compressed into fifteen minutes. The division's changes succeeded beyond expectations and Cigna's chairman became a strong advocate of re-engineering.

Other BPR initiatives were adopted in different parts of the organization. Some delivered, others did not, with some 50 per cent succeeding at the first attempt. The chairman encouraged people to learn from the successes and did not punish those who needed to try again or differently.

Sometimes, where programmes foundered, the executive commitment was not fully in place—that is, they were interested in the results, but not in personally driving the change. On other projects, the transition from ownership at the top to front-line personnel failed to happen.

Subsequently, CIGNA International successfully applied re-engineering in two countries where it did business, but decided that re-engineering would not automatically work in all countries; some cultures would need any change programme to be managed in a more collaborative way.

The CIGNA's experience suggests the advantages of gaining re-engineering experience and competency by starting with less complex initiatives.[5-6]

When applying BPR, the direction for the radical rethinking is expected to come unequivocally from top management. Hammer and Champy (2001) assert that re-engineering cannot happen from the bottom up, because a broad perspective is required to decide what to change and because, invariably, the changes cut across organizational boundaries, such that a middle manager would not have sufficient authority to insist on the transformation. Hammer (1990: 105) suggests that, whilst the process is undertaken in a planned way, the radical nature of BPR means that the outcome does not lend itself to meticulous planning; rather that it is 'an all or nothing proposition, with uncertain result'. This echoes some of the findings in Chapter 3 about managers' capacity to absolutely control complex change plans.

As can be seen in Change in Practice 9.3, issues of power and resistance may affect the implementation. At Cigna, where the process did have the full backing of the chairman, there were still pockets of the organization in which the management allegiance was weak and implementation failed. It may be expected that such groups will apply their managerial or status power to push back against such initiatives, which are often driven solely from the top until the point of implementation. It reinforces the need to make deliberate effort to win the confidence of managers and to create champions for the project in the field, whatever the scale of the programme (Hall et al., 1993). Jarrar and Aspinwall (1999) found that a directed approach and top management commitment, *plus* the establishment of cross-functional teams, are all critical. Stoddard and Jarvenpaa (1995) describe the need to target a small group of gatekeepers and to allow the change to take hold in that group, because, otherwise, communication becomes a unilateral directive. Failure to address this may result in the misunderstanding and lack of trust, which may further contribute to resistance.

BPR aims to achieve changes in thinking, to break out from assumptions that underpin current approaches to work, to effect second-order change. So changing processes cannot be separated from changing how people think (Grover et al., 1995). As Hammer (1990) points out, beliefs such as 'local inventory is needed for good customer service' may be deeply held and not readily given up: '[Re-engineering] is confusing and disruptive and affects everything people have grown accustomed to' (Hammer, 1990: 112). Often different roles emerge from the redesign, along with a need for skills training, all of which may require some very different thinking about the role or the customer. Indeed, the very first Cigna BPR project resulted in everyone having to apply for their own jobs and learn new skills. This is a key issue: changing views and assumptions can take a long time, yet BPR is considered a fast turnaround methodology; the speed of implementation may not allow for people to really adjust, to truly understand the change. This may be one of BPR's key weaknesses.

See Chapter 3 for more on second-order change: p. 41

Re-engineering assumes that an organization's performance is limited because of its processes. It further assumes the need to start the process of performance improvement by discarding what is and starting afresh. It is positioned as an 'all or nothing' approach: the change must be radical and happen across the organization, such that both the scale and the span of the change and the size of the organization are implicitly large. Yet, in the Cigna example, the first BPR experiment started as a pilot in one division, without which there would have been no buy-in from the top, or indeed, from other divisions. McNulty and Ferlie (2002), who studied the application of BPR in a UK hospital, found that whilst the change programme started out as radical and revolutionary, it was tempered by reality and reshaped to meet the needs of the key stakeholders.

Overall, organizations that have previously undertaken some form of process review or change report less anxiety and resistance from their people, lower training costs, and generally gained greater improvement in performance through BPR. This suggests that cultures that accept continuous change, improvement, and learning are better placed to deal with such fundamental and radical rethinking. Cigna understood that the expectation of the style of leadership in some of its operating countries militated against the likelihood of successful BPR implementation and left them to one side.

For these reasons, in recent years, BPR has been criticized for its neglect of some of the cultural and political aspects of organizational life. Even at the peak of its popularity, Davenport (1996) stated that it has become associated with 'massive lay-offs' and that no one wants to be 're-engineered'. He suggests that consulting firms, which grew fast on the back of the initiative, were seen to overpromise and underdeliver. Whilst finding some of the principles very useful, he believes it to be the fad that forgot people—the people aspects of process performance—which, whilst espoused in the methodology, do not explicitly form part of the approach to implementation.

Hammer and Champny (2001) acknowledge the criticism and attribute the backlash to the excessive enthusiasm with which the press and public first embraced the concept, but find that BPR does continue to be needed as the pace of technology-enabled change persists. They claim the possibilities are so great that, without fundamental rethinking on a regular basis, companies simply get left behind. Whilst our recent experience largely upholds Davenport's (1996) view, we do find that the principles of BPR, whilst not always labelled as such, can be found in many company turnaround strategies.

 Exercise 9.2

Imagine that you are charged with undertaking a BPR review of your organization or university. Your particular interest is in the link between facilities management, human resources, and your department or school.

- Where would you suggest the BPR review starts?
- What might be the problems you encounter in implementing this method?
- Why might BPR be a useful method for you to employ?

Lean: 'The Toyota system'

The second of the methods to be examined is called Lean. Lean is a process management philosophy derived mostly from the Toyota production system (TPS). In the 1990s, the steady growth of Toyota from a small company to the world's largest car manufacturer grabbed attention, with organizations wanting to understand how it had achieved this. The approach was identified as 'Lean' in the mid-1990s; the term 'Toyotism' has also been prevalent, although events in 2011 may alter this.

Lean's focus is on examining process flow and streamlining existing processes (Shah et al., 2008). It aims to reduce any activity that does not *add value*. Unlike BPR, which purports to dismember the process, Lean's purpose is to examine the whole process chain and to identify key **wastage** within the process.

There are a number of likely points of wastage in a typical process. One area that is often the focus for process review is that of production—and overproduction. **Overproduction** means making too much of the product, or making it too early, before the customer needs it (Bicheno, 2004). Overproduction in turn leads to increases in the amount of space needed for storage—sometimes storage of raw materials, as well as finished goods. Whenever goods are not in transport or being processed, they are **waiting**, another form of waste. In traditional processes, a large part of an individual product's life is spent waiting to be worked on. Goods may deteriorate whilst they are waiting to go to the customer; operators may be waiting for goods; deliveries may be waiting for the goods to arrive. **Transporting** is in itself another form of waste: any movement of materials is a waste that must be reduced to an absolute minimum. Goods should be produced in time (but not far in advance)—just soon enough to meet the customer demand, which is known as the **pull** of the customer. **Defects** in the product offer the ultimate form of waste, so that achievement of zero defects is a key theme of Lean (Bicheno, 2004).

Lean undertakes to review the process and to eliminate those points of wastage, for example smoothing demand where it can be smoothed and increasing flexibility to respond to fluctuations in demand that cannot be smoothed, perhaps by processing smaller volumes more frequently.

A toolkit of techniques for practical use at the operational level has been developed to support 'Lean thinking'. Tools include, for example, **value stream mapping**, which is used to analyse the flow of resources and highlight areas in which activities consume resources, but do not add value from the customer's perspective. This map is used to generate ideas for process redesign.

As can be seen in Figure 9.2, the simple act of mapping the stages in a process quickly identifies steps—in this case, within the investigations and tests stage—which do not add much value.

In application, key aspects of Lean include the following principles.

● Customers are better for the changes that Lean identifies.

● Lean's purpose is to pull service through the system in order to meet customer requirements, so that the product or service flows continuously.

● Lean is not overly analytical and statistical—it requires simple observations to identify visible problems.

● Lean is not 'big bang'; it is a continuous, long-term approach to achieve flexibility.

● Lean emphasizes including and empowering employees through change; its underlying philosophy is a respect for people and society, and senior management's leadership of the methodology should reflect this.

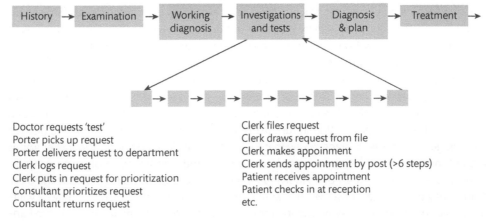

Doctor requests 'test'
Porter picks up request
Porter delivers request to department
Clerk logs request
Clerk puts in request for prioritization
Consultant prioritizes request
Consultant returns request

Clerk files request
Clerk draws request from file
Clerk makes appoinment
Clerk sends appointment by post (>6 steps)
Patient receives appointment
Patient checks in at reception
etc.

Figure 9.2 Value stream mapping in the NHS

Source: Adapted from Jones and Mitchell (2006)

Change in Practice 9.4

Undertaking a Lean review of a hospital pathology laboratory

The pathology department of a large UK hospital employs over a hundred staff in many specialisms. They conduct thousands of tests each day using specialist equipment and are vital to the running of the hospital. Two years ago, they were also seen to be the source of bottlenecks and delays, with tests taking longer than they should.

As a result of the problems, a review of the whole process was undertaken. Blood samples were tracked from the moment they left the patient, through the haematology, biochemistry, and microbiology laboratories. Points of delay were identified, for example a sample could not be analysed before the information had been put on the computer, but inputting delays were common because the samples often arrived in large batches. There were physical distances to travel because the department had laboratory space in two buildings, across two floors.

From the initial review, a range of possible improvements were identified.

- Knock two rooms together to cut down physical travel time.
- Place all analyser machines together, so that there is no need to go up and down stairs to access them.
- Change the inputting process with a standard form that can be scanned in.
- Analyse each rack as it is filled rather than accumulate a whole batch.

As a result of such simple suggestions, a process that had 309 steps was reduced to fifty-seven steps and the time taken for sample results from 24–30 hours to two or three hours. Staff were freed up for more productive work and, overall, less space was needed once the department had been reconfigured.

The changes improved quality, safety, and delivery, providing clear standardized procedures and engaging the enthusiasm of front-line staff.[7]

Lean's roots may be in manufacturing processes, but Lean principles have been applied across a range of industries, from the pathology example in Change in Practice 9.4, to call centre services to improve live agent call handling, to software development and maintenance, and other areas of information technology. For example, Unilever has applied Lean across its finance functions. Because one unit can be 'Leaned' at a time, the process can be applied in a small business or one unit of a larger organization, or across complex global organizations.

Although typically initiated as a top-down change, the nature of Lean means that people who understand the detail of the process need to be involved at an early stage. Senior management's role is to understand and explain what is driving the change (Radnor and Walley, 2006), and to engage others quickly in that understanding. Lean is most suited to organizations with high-volume, repeatable tasks, which lend themselves to standardization and integration, coupled with a less hierarchical management structure, which allows staff to be engaged in effecting the changes (Womack and Jones, 2005). Proponents of the Lean approach believe that it can be applied anywhere, provided that its underpinning philosophy of respect for people and society is clear, and that time is given to embed the change. They refer to the 'three secrets of successful implementation' (Jones and Mitchell, 2006).

1. No redundancies as a result of Lean exercises
2. Involve staff at all levels
3. Show and practice respect for people

These 'secrets' differentiate Lean from BPR under which a directive approach to the implementation and job reductions arising from the change are considered key success factors. However, implementation of Lean faces many of the same issues of power, politics, and resistance as noted in our discussion of BPR. Research into Lean implementation by Warwick Business School highlighted the need to establish a critical mass of people who are comfortable working with Lean practices (Radnor and Walley, 2006). Should managers who are not interested or do not want to look outside their part of the process, or people who are unfamiliar with the detail of the process be selected for the team, then Lean is significantly less likely to succeed. Expert consultancy support, which encourages skills transfer, is found to be necessary.

In a review of a service industry implementation process, Hanna (2007) reports the findings of Upton and Statts, who researched the experience of Indian software services providers:

> It was interesting to talk to some of the less senior team members, because they were getting involved in much bigger-picture issues than they ever had before . . . In the case of value stream mapping, every member of the team was able to get a sense of the overall picture of what they were doing and spot problems they wouldn't have been able to see before. (Hanna, 2007)

In this way, Lean expects to achieve culture change. At its best, the process serves to get people participating, and encourages a sense of innovation up and down the organization, such that the impact of the change begins to affect ways of thinking as much as processes. Lean encourages the use of a whole range of techniques, such as quality circles to keep employees continuously involved in improvement beyond the life span of the immediate review. A **quality circle** is a group of employees who are trained to identify, analyse, and solve work-related problems, in order to improve the performance of the organization and enrich their own work. Quality circles have the advantage of continuity: the circle remains intact from project to project. They encourage the concept of knowledge-sharing and learning within an organization. As with BPR, organizations with a history of managing change and the ability to build multidisciplinary teams typically have the greatest capacity for Lean improvement (Radnor and Walley, 2006).

In examining the move of Lean to the public sector, the Warwick Business School study found that the sector engaged with the principles of Lean, but less with the full range of tools and techniques, with most organizations applying just a few of the tools (Radnor and Walley, 2006). One aspect that was popular was the application of a '**rapid improvement event**'. This uses rapid improvement workshops to make small, quickly introduced changes via three phases.

1. A two-to-three-week preparation period
2. A five-day event to identify changes
3. A three-to-four-week implementation period

The managers found that this approach helps to overcome some of the public-sector cultural and political inhibitors, for example the slow responses to the changes, where consultation with unions and staff is customary. Here, they can experience a faster return for effort.

Equally, the disadvantage is that quick wins are difficult to sustain because they are not integrated into the overall organization strategy. Whilst all those who participated in the study reported some improvements, most had not achieved all of their objectives, in part because of a lack of engagement once the 'rapid improvement event' was complete.

Despite the largely positive reporting of Lean implementation, in 2011, Toyota itself faced much publicized issues with the safety of some of its cars, having to recall millions of vehicles in the US, Europe, and China, as well as suspending sales of eight popular US models, because of the potential for the accelerator pedal to stick (*Sunday Times*, 7 February, 2010). The issues attracted much adverse publicity, and Toyota's brand reputation for quality and reliability was seriously damaged by the problems. A BBC documentary suggested that Toyota had increased production by 50 per cent in five years and, in doing so, had significantly extended its chain of suppliers. This, coupled with driving down costs of key car parts by 30 per cent, may have prevented Toyota from being able to control all aspects of the process, to ensure that 'Lean' standards were adhered to (BBC1, 25 March 2010, *Panorama: Total Recall, The Toyota Story*).

See Chapter 8 for more on Toyota: p. 187

Lean has some evident success in improving processes and, indeed, in affecting the culture of an organization. The Toyota story serves to reinforce very publicly that all aspects of the process need to be addressed: the 'human factors' such as training are just as important as any technology; the process factors that affect quality are as important as the human factors; there is not an end to the need for continuous quality improvement.

Exercise 9.3

Think of a process with which you are familiar or which you can observe: for example, your selection for your place at university from the point of application; your induction to your new job; a hospital referral.

- Using Figure 9.2 as your guide, create a value stream map of the process.

- Identify points of frustration (that is, waste) from your perspective.

- Consider how that waste may be eliminated.

- Identify key people involved in the delivery of the process and consider the effect of your changes on their roles. How might you manage this?

- What does this tell you about the application of Lean?

Six Sigma

Six Sigma is the third method to be considered in this section and is the most recent of the three. Its focus is on reducing unwanted *variation* in processes by applying statistical methods in order to eliminate the causes of errors or defects (Bicheno and Catherwood, 2005).

Sigma is a Greek symbol and is used in the field of mathematics to denote the measurement of variation or **standard deviation** (Pande et al., 2000). Examples of variation might be differences in getting a good or bad cup of coffee at the university cafe from one day to the next, or waiting ten minutes for your train one day and forty minutes the next. Clearly, such variation can cause annoyance for customers: you do not know whether it is worth waiting in the queue for coffee or not—whether this will be a good or a bad coffee day. Variation can also accumulate, for example, in construction or electronics, where one variation adds to another, causing serious issues (Pande et al., 2000). Six Sigma experts claim that looking at variance rather than average performance helps companies to fully understand what is going on: averages mask the ups and downs in quality and standards that are often the very issues on which organizations are judged.

The purpose of Six Sigma is to reduce variation such that it is held within a narrow band, with limits defined by the customer specification, to 'remove the variation, hit the target' (Bicheno and Catherwood, 2005). So, where BPR starts by dismantling the existing processes, and Lean emphasizes process flow and streamlining, Six Sigma concentrates on process *defects*, aiming to eliminate the root causes of problems (Shah et al., 2008).

The application of Six Sigma includes:

1. defining what the customer needs;
2. counting the **defects**—that is, the instances in which the product or process does not meet the customer requirement;
3. calculating the percentage of items without defects;
4. calculating then the number of errors that would be experienced if the activity were repeated a million times **(defects per million opportunities, or DPMO)**;
5. working to reduce the incidence of defect.

(Pande et al., 2000)

Defects per million opportunities (DPMO) is the way in which Six Sigma measures performance: 3.4 DPMO is the goal and is close to perfection (Bicheno, 2002).

Defects per million chances/opportunities

- 2 sigma = 308,537
- 3 sigma = 67,000
- 4 sigma = 6,200
- 5 sigma = 233
- 6 sigma = 3.4

Clearly, different processes require different standards: an airline may find losing passengers' bags 3.4 times per million luggage transfers to be a very high standard to reach; it may not see that as appropriate in terms of the number of times its planes fall from the sky. Six Sigma works to the customer specification (this may be an internal or external customer).

Six Sigma was developed by Motorola at a time when the company was experiencing serious quality issues (Frahm, 2003). Through its application, Motorola witnessed dramatic results including a 40 per cent reduction in errors, and a 60 per cent reduction in the time it took to design a new product (Frahm, 2003). Having witnessed its power, General Electric began using Six Sigma with the backing of its CEO Jack Welch. Six Sigma then became the latest management method with high-profile blue-chip CEO backing and organizations began to adopt it rapidly: for example, Bombardier, Johnson and Johnson, and Dow Chemicals use the method

Exercise 9.4

Identify two or three services of which you are the customer and where you experience variation in the quality of the service.

- What degree of variation do you experience—how much and how often?

- What is the impact of that variation?

- How much would the variation need to be reduced by to impact your experience?

- On the basis of your experience would you recommend that the provider invests in Six Sigma to review its processes?

on a global basis; in the UK, it is in use primarily in the automotive sector and in services such as British Telecom and banking.

Other features that set Six Sigma apart from previous quality improvement initiatives include:

- a clear focus on achieving measurable and quantifiable financial returns from any Six Sigma project (most advanced Six Sigma organizations employ finance personnel to track project benefits—Shah et al., 2008);

- a commitment to making decisions on the basis of verifiable statistical data (rather than mere observation or assumptions) and, therefore, a high degree of project rigour (Bicheno and Catherwood, 2005);

- application of Six Sigma through fully trained Six Sigma experts, who are ranked using martial arts ranking terminology (for example, black belts, green belts, etc.), which defines a

Table 9.1 Six Sigma roles

Six Sigma role	Training (days)
Executive leadership, which includes the CEO and the executive team, responsible for creating the Six Sigma vision and providing the empowerment and resources for others to act.	2
Champions, who take responsibility for Six Sigma implementation across the organization and who mentor the level below (black belts).	5
Master black belts, who act as in-house coaches to other levels and work on Six Sigma for 100 per cent of their time. They identify and scope projects, and ensure consistency of application of the method across different functions.	20
Black belts apply the method to specific projects, working 100 per cent on Six Sigma work.	20
Green belts undertake Six Sigma implementation alongside other work, under the guidance of black belts.	9
Yellow belts are trained in the use of practical tools in order to be team members.	2

Sources: Harry and Schroeder (2000); Pande et al. (2000)

professional career path for anyone involved in the application of the method, whichever organization they work in (see Table 9.1).

Yet, by the late 2000s, the application of Six Sigma was beginning to slow and criticism to emerge. Some suggest that it really adds nothing new, that it is a limited analytical tool with a narrow focus, and that its application can, in fact, have a negative impact on the organization. Hindo and Grow (2007) cite the rigorous application of Six Sigma at retailer Home Depot, where staff morale dropped although productivity soared. The next chief executive started to undo some of the Six Sigma application to allow store managers some leeway to make decisions on their own. Bicheno and Catherwood (2005) claim that, after twenty years, Six Sigma is fully embedded in relatively few organizations, that often training is undertaken and projects tackled without quality levels being attained.

 Change in Practice 9.5

Six Sigma at 3M

3M is a global science-based company. It has over 70,000 employees in more than sixty countries. It is known as the company of innovation, one of its early developments being masking tape and then the Post-It note, and, more recently, films that brighten the displays on electronic products.

In the late 1990s, the company's financial performance began to weaken and it was deemed to have lost its creative edge. In 2001, James McNerney was brought in from General Electric (GE) as CEO, the first outsider to lead the company. The stock market expected him to take decisive action and he did, making redundant 8,000 workers, reducing other expenditure, and introducing the application of Six Sigma, the success of which he had witnessed at GE. The directive approach to change management won 'accolades for bringing discipline to an organization that had become unwieldy, erratic and sluggish' (Hindo, 2007: 1).

McKerney introduced the two main Six Sigma tools:

- the five-step approach to problem-solving, namely 'define, measure, analyse, improve, and control' (known as **DMAIC**); and

- the systematizing of product development, so that the product can be made to Six Sigma standards from the start (known as 'design for Six Sigma' or **DFSS**).

The methodology was applied with rigour: almost all staff undertook the green belt level training and several thousand were trained to full black belt standard. Operating margins went from 17 per cent in 2001 to 23 per cent in 2005 (Hindo, 2007).

Yet, when McKerney left four years later, 3M did not appear to have rediscovered its creative roots as a result of the Six Sigma improvements. Hindo (2007) quotes the next CEO, George Buckley, as pointing out that innovation is, of itself, a disorderly process that can not fit into a Six Sigma schedule.[8]

As Change in Practice 9.5 suggests, pushing product development into a 'DFSS' process may reduce the capacity to think differently. The CEO of 3M was left trying to manage the tension between innovation and efficiency, to allow space to think without damaging quality and profits. The tight control of Six Sigma may serve to enforce conformity, not to encourage experimentation.

From a cultural perspective, the application of the martial arts career path is interesting. In effect, when fully implemented, it creates a parallel organizational structure, which has the potential to exert power through its specific technical knowledge and expertise. Its statistical basis and the nature of the language and acronyms (DMAIC; DFSS—see above) are symbolic of this being a difficult, expert field, which the average employee will not understand. The explicit nature of the rankings introduces a formal hierarchy, with the capacity to offer different levels of reward, making measurement the primary issue, as evidenced at 3M.

Equally, by keeping the martial arts group as a separate entity, there is less opportunity for others to engage in the work in the way in which Lean expressly aims to do. The sustainability of the approach depends upon the black belts meeting with peers, often outside of the organization, having refresher training, and being supported by senior management on an on-going basis (Bicheno and Catherwood, 2005). This impacts also the opportunity for organizational learning as the development is positioned with external training bodies rather than within the organizational structure. Six Sigma may also suffer because those who are selected for the training are chosen for their competence to work with the statistical tools, whilst lacking sufficient organizational power to drive major projects (Bicheno and Catherwood, 2005). The martial arts labels leave the approach open to being criticized as a gimmick, and where it is not wholly endorsed by the top team, it can fall into disrepute. It has certainly served to foster an industry of training and certification, with all of the large consultancies offering programmes to achieve the different levels of belt. This in itself impacts the application. Small companies may not have the resources available or indeed be able to afford to adopt this model. Such a company, sending one employee on a Six Sigma programme, will have no understanding or support back in his or her organization on which he or she can draw and existing authority and ideas will prevail (Bicheno and Catherwood, 2005).

Less has been reported about Six Sigma in recent years. Where companies are still using it, trends include:

- organizations, such as Dow Chemicals, sharing Six Sigma with suppliers;
- an ongoing shift to businesses outside of manufacturing;
- combining Six Sigma with Lean to create Six Sigma Lean. For example, KPMG offers the Lean Six Sigma Performance Improvement Framework. Most researchers agree that there is more commonality between Lean and Six Sigma tools and practices than differences (Shah et al., 2008). Lean emerged as a concept before Six Sigma, but it is possible to combine both to good effect, thereby paying attention to overall flow of the process, as well as to the root cause of specific problems.

This last joint application of methods may be useful, both because each addresses different aspects of the process and because the combination enables a wider range of change management styles to be adopted in their application. We believe that, in order for change to succeed, style cannot simply reflect the chosen method, but must take account of the prevailing culture, the organizational power and politics, the scale and span of change, and other contextual issues. The combined offering of Lean with Six Sigma has the potential to drive the change from the top, using expertise to address specific issues of variation, whilst engaging a wider group of staff in overall reviews of processes.

Section 2 Summary

In this section, we have reviewed the application of:

● business process re-engineering (BPR);

● Lean; and

● Six Sigma.

Section 3: **A framework for directed change**

To conclude this chapter, an overall framework for the management of directed change will be considered. Amongst a number of well-known writers in this field, John Kotter (1996) developed a framework that identifies the key challenges in bringing about a planned change process, which has been used widely by organizations as a guide to implementation. It is not in itself a method and does not intend to provide a prescriptive solution, but may be used to ensure that key aspects of implementation are not overlooked.

The framework positions change as being both owned by top management *and* seeking to achieve wide staff participation as an integral part of the process, specifically in order to overcome resistance and to achieve buy-in to the changes. Kotter (2007) asserts that challenges can be overcome if approached in a planned, methodical way.

Figure 9.3 outlines Kotter's (1996) eight critical steps for leading change, from establishing a sense of urgency across the organization for the change, to mobilizing a coalition that is able to describe the vision of the new future, creating short-term wins and, ultimately, changing the culture by embedding the new ways of working such that they become the accepted way of doing things.

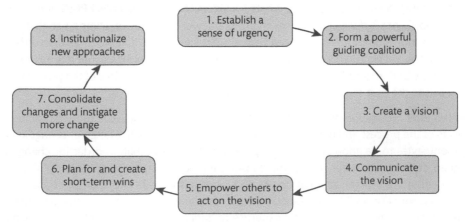

Figure 9.3 Facing eight challenges of change

Source: Adapted from Kotter (1996)

Kotter's steps relate directly to Lewin's three phases of change discussed in Chapter 3:

- unfreezing occurs through stages one to four;
- moving the organization in stages five and six; and
- refreezing though the consolidation processes of stages seven and eight.

See Chapter 3 for more on Lewin: p. 49

Kotter (2007) suggests that the CEO and his or her team need to create urgency for change by spelling out the dangers of not changing; to be successful, some 75 per cent of a company's management needs to be convinced that change must happen. Once this is achieved, successful transformations require a strong coalition of key figures in management, from all levels in the organization, to get behind the change: managers who are powerful in terms of titles, information, expertise, reputation, or relationships in the organization. If sufficiently influential managers choose to become involved, they are likely to overcome the political manoeuvres of their colleagues. This relates to issues highlighted in section 2: the BPR need to manage potential resistance from middle managers at the point of implementation; Lean's need to engage managers who are able to think beyond their own process; Six Sigma's enrolling as black belts managers with sufficient organizational power to deliver the change.

Kotter focuses specifically on using a coalition of key managers to create and communicate a vision in order for the change to become accepted and embedded in the organization (Kotter and Cohen, 2002). His stories of doing this are vivid and offer insight into the nature of the challenge. Relating this to the three methods, the Lean process mapping offers the obvious vehicle for people to achieve understanding of what can be different. Six Sigma's challenge is to move away from the technical language to bring alive the possibilities. In the case of BPR, the likely issue is creating a picture at local unit level, bringing the change back close to home such that people can appreciate the difference it may make to their part of the business. Kotter (1996) points out that skipping steps in the change process creates an illusion of speed, without achieving new behaviours, as described earlier in the Lean rapid improvement events (Radnor and Walley, 2006).

In our experience, organizations find Kotter's framework to be extremely helpful in managing the change process. Much of the appeal of Kotter's (1996) work comes from the sense of rational certainty that it offers: a certainty that change can be planned for and the outcome predicted. The tenor of engagement that Kotter describes is closer to 'directive' influencing than 'collaborative' exploration. However, there is a danger that, by dividing the work into 'steps', the process becomes mechanical and the nature of engagement superficial. It does not allow for greater levels of exploration, tending to move quickly towards achieving congruent positive attitudes and avoiding the sort of disagreement that can play a key role in supporting organizational renewal (Floyd and Wooldridge, 2000). Randall (2004: 138) notes that such frameworks offer 'uncritically an explanation of change couched in mechanistic terms'. As such, they address what goes on **front stage** (in terms of formal processes and relationships), but do not pay attention to the **back stage** political arena, as discussed in Chapter 7. In following these eight steps, if the plan hits unexpected challenges, the process may be derailed. The danger of all three methods examined in section 2 is their potential to be rigid, not allowing for the unplanned or emergent change, and Kotter's (1996) framework does not offer help in this respect. So Kotter offers a sound guide for directed change, but slavish application will not automatically achieve success.

See Chapter 7 for more on front and back stage: p. 144

Exercise 9.5

Identify an issue about which you feel strongly—something that you would like to see changed in your organization, your university, or your community.

● How many people would you need to influence to create a sense of urgency about the issue and how could you go about this in a way that would help those people to understand the issue?

● Write down your vision for the future—what the situation can be if the change is realized. Imagine yourself reading this to people affected by the issue. How does this affect your description or the language you use to paint the picture of the future?

● Now plan your change implementation, using Kotter's stages five to eight as a guide.

● What do you discover about the application of Kotter's framework?

 Section 3 Summary

In this section, we have:

● examined Kotter's framework for planned change implementation;

● considered the strengths and limitations of the framework.

 Integrative Case Study

HMRC: Culture change and Lean

Her Majesty's Revenue and Customs (HMRC) is a department of British government, responsible for the collection of taxes and the detection and prevention of smuggling. It was formed in 2005 by the merger of the Inland Revenue (Revenue) and Her Majesty's Customs and Excise (Customs). The two departments had very different histories, cultures, and legal powers. The joint organization employed some 80,000 people. It was expected that 12,500 jobs would be lost as a result of the merger by 2008, with further job losses to result from the closure of smaller local tax offices.

Against this backdrop, HMRC declared that the level of service to its customers would be increased by the implementation of Lean process reviews alongside the introduction of new technology and stronger focus on the needs of the taxpayer. It planned to spend £2.7 billion in the period 2007–11 on a transformation programme with the aim of becoming the UK government's processor of choice, to:

● redesign service delivery processes;

● implement the appropriate management infrastructure;

● change thinking and behaviour in staff to support the new approach.

The application of Lean within HMRC was known as the Pacesetter programme. Pacesetter embraced Lean, along with development in leadership, with the aim of achieving a top-down and bottom-up approach to improving performance: 'Lean drives performances up in to the wider organisation. [Operational management and senior leadership] drive performance from the leadership team down in to the wider organization' (Radnor and Bucci, 2007: 3).

When Lean programmes were first introduced, the organization was still in the aftermath of its merger. Staff were preoccupied with grading issues resulting from the combining of two different structures, with proposed office closures, and grappling with the instigation of a raft of new roles, such as the customer relationship manager, whose purpose was to offer one face to the customer, thereby straddling Revenue and Customs. Lean was one more change. Stories of clear desk policies, of not being allowed any personal possessions, and of depersonalized ways of working spread rapidly when Lean was first applied. Despite this, HMRC aimed to use 'Pacesetter' to motivate and empower staff. It hoped to integrate reviews of processes with cultural and behavioural changes, to ensure the ongoing sustainability of Lean.

Alongside Lean, the key IT programmes were managed centrally, focusing on large systems data storage changes. It was decided to implement Lean locally in strategic HMRC sites, which would incorporate the work of smaller sites over time, using Lean as *the* way of working. To implement Lean across these sites, a number of dedicated central and local experts were based in the offices. Lean was introduced by a series of workshops, helping people to understand the possibilities for performance improvement and encouraging their input to the changes.

In 2007, an evaluation of Lean was undertaken by A to Z business consultancy, assisted by Warwick Business School, which found the following.

- There was a direct correlation between senior management engagement and staff attitude towards Lean: the more committed the senior team, the more positive the attitude towards Lean.

- Lean resulted in an increase in the quality of work at all sites. This was partly to do with quality checks being instigated, so errors were caught before the work left the team. They noted that, in time, there was a need for front-line staff to become directly responsible for quality.

- Lean created more reasons for front-line staff to speak to managers, which was welcomed by many staff. The evaluation recommended supporting this shift with training to meet the new needs of the roles.

- Senior managers had a better understanding of Lean than front-line staff, for whom perceptions were influenced by union documentation. The evaluation suggested better handling of communications to overcome this.

- Some of the new key performance indicators (KPIs), under which individual productivity was recorded hourly and then aggregated to team productivity, worried staff and the reasons for having such indicators were not understood. Despite this, overall team working was acknowledged to be better under Lean, with better team spirit and problem-solving.

Lean continued to be implemented successfully in further areas and, from 2008, HMRC claimed the best ever quality improvements in processing, with improvements in customer service and productivity increases of at least 30 per cent in areas in which Pacesetter was operational. As a result, HMRC remained committed to continuing to update its IT systems, to working with Lean, and to continuing to strive for the culture change that it desired.

Questions

Consider the size of the HMRC organization, and the scale and span of the change that it wants to achieve.

1. In light of the context described here, what style of management do you think was needed to make the changes for which HMRC hoped?

2. What part does Lean play in effecting change at HMRC?

3. What are its limitations and why?

Conclusion

This chapter examined approaches to the implementation of change. The first section considered the range of styles that can be adopted and when they may be most successful. Section 2 focused on three change methods that are typically associated with directed change, because they are typically instigated and led by senior management. These methods focus first on changing structures and systems, and, whilst employee participation in the change process is offered in a range of different ways, management is expected to retain overall control of the process and key decisions. The final section considered one of the best-known frameworks of planned change to examine the change challenges and success factors that it identifies. We will continue the examination of choices and methods in Chapter 10, turning our attention to facilitated change methods.

 Please visit the Online Resource Centre at **http://www.oxfordtextbooks.co.uk/orc/ myers** *to access further resources for students and lecturers.*

Change in Practice sources

1. Marston, R. (2009) 'Sir Stuart Rose's legacy at M&S', BBC News, 18 Nov. http://news.bbc.co.uk/1/hi/ business/8366635.stm

2. *The Telegraph* (2006) 'How M&S was turned around', 10 Jan. http://www.telegraph.co.uk/ finance/2929807/How-MandS-was-turned-around.html

3. Alfa Laval (undated) 'Our company'. http://www.alfalaval.com/about-us/our-company/pages/our-company.aspx

4. Ashridge Business School and Alfa Laval (2008) 'Submission paper for the EFMD Excellence in Practice Award 2009 "Partnership in Learning & Development"'. http://www.ashridge.org.uk/Website/IC.nsf/ wFARATT/Partnership%20in%20Learning%20%26%20Development/$File/PartnershipInLearning&Dev elopment.pdf

5. Caron, J., Jarvenpa, S., and Stoddard, D. (1994) 'Business re-engineering at Cigna Corporation: Experiences and lessons learned from the first five years', *Management Information Systems Quarterly*, **18**(3): 233–50.

6. Hayes, J. (2010) *The Theory and Practice of Change Management*, 3rd edn, Basingstoke: Palgrave Macmillan.

7. Jones, D. and Mitchell, A. (for the Lean Enterprise Academy) (2006) *Lean Thinking for the NHS. Report Commissioned by the NHS Confederation.* http://www.nhsconfed.org/Publications/reports/Pages/ Leanthinking.aspx

8. Hindo, B. (2007) 'At 3M, a struggle between efficiency and creativity', *Business Week*, 6 June. http://www.businessweek.com/magazine/content/07_24/b4038406.htm

Integrative Case Study sources

Financial Times (2004) 'The joys of crossing a terrier with a retriever', 9 July.

HMRC website: http://www.hmrc.gov.uk

Neveling, N. (2007) 'Tax bosses look to boost staff morale', *Accountancy Age*, 24 May. http://www.accountancyage.com/accountancyage/news/2190607/tax-bosses-look-boost-staff

Radnor, Z. and Bucci, G. (2007) *Evaluation of Pacesetter: Lean, Senior Leadership and Operational Management within HMRC Processing—Final Report September 2007*. http://www.hmrc.gov.uk/about/pacesetter-final-report.pdf

Tax Advantage (2010) 'HMRC tax code fiasco', 15 Sep. http://www.tax-advantage.co.uk/news/hmrc-tax-code-fiasco.html

Further reading

Bicheno, J. (2004) *The New Lean Toolbox: Towards Fast, Flexible Flow*, Buckingham: Picsie Books.

Bicheno, J. and Catherwood, P. (2005) *Six Sigma and the Quality Toolbox*, Buckingham: Picsie Books.
For clear accounts on the Six Sigma and Lean processes, respectively.

Kotter, J. and Cohen, D. (2002) *The Heart of Change: Real-life Stories of How People Change Their Organizations*, Boston, MA: Harvard Business School Press.
For examples of directed change undertaken with the purpose of engaging people in understanding and accepting the change.

10 Approaches to Change Implementation: Facilitated Change

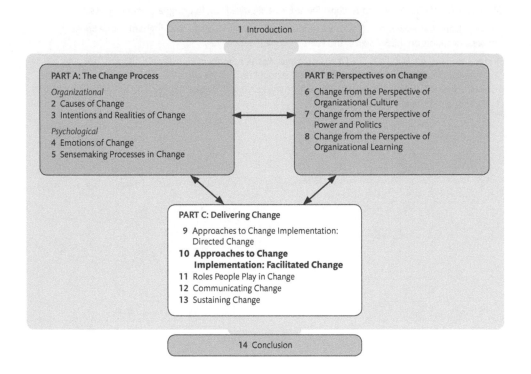

```
                    ┌──────────────────────────┐
                    │      1  Introduction      │
                    └──────────────────────────┘

┌────────────────────────────────────┐      ┌────────────────────────────────────┐
│ PART A: The Change Process          │      │ PART B: Perspectives on Change      │
│                                     │      │                                     │
│ Organizational                      │      │ 6  Change from the Perspective of   │
│ 2  Causes of Change                 │◄────►│    Organizational Culture           │
│ 3  Intentions and Realities of      │      │ 7  Change from the Perspective of   │
│    Change                           │      │    Power and Politics               │
│ Psychological                       │      │ 8  Change from the Perspective of   │
│ 4  Emotions of Change               │      │    Organizational Learning          │
│ 5  Sensemaking Processes in Change  │      │                                     │
└────────────────────────────────────┘      └────────────────────────────────────┘

            ┌────────────────────────────────────┐
            │ PART C: Delivering Change           │
            │                                     │
            │  9  Approaches to Change            │
            │     Implementation: Directed Change │
            │ 10  Approaches to Change            │
            │     Implementation: Facilitated     │
            │     Change                          │
            │ 11  Roles People Play in Change     │
            │ 12  Communicating Change            │
            │ 13  Sustaining Change               │
            └────────────────────────────────────┘

                    ┌──────────────────────────┐
                    │      14  Conclusion       │
                    └──────────────────────────┘
```

Introduction

This chapter continues the exploration of the range of options available to senior managers when deciding their approach to the implementation of change. Having considered those in which the change is largely directed from the top of the organization, this chapter focuses on **facilitated change**—that is, change in which the approach is designed to maximize the involvement and contribution of people.

A variety of methods sit under the umbrella of facilitated change, from those, still largely under the control of senior managers, which encourage greater levels of consultation with staff, to others in which the widest membership of the organization is involved in deciding what needs to happen. In this chapter, we will concentrate largely on those that are intended to maximize involvement, sometimes to the extent that senior managers let go of their control over decisions, and, indeed, in some cases in which the change is co-created with the involvement of all interested parties, where no one party is seen to be 'in control'. In previous chapters, we have discussed the different views of change, from planned to emergent: planned change emphasizing senior managers' deliberate intention to achieve organizational change, with clearly defined start and end points; an emergent view emphasizing that, whether or not change is intended, organizations are, in fact, constantly evolving such that change cannot conform to a plan and has no end state. Facilitated approaches to change are adopted to enable both planned and emergent change. We will consider both perspectives in exploring a sample of the range of facilitated methods, examining their structures and their relative strengths and weaknesses in enabling organizational change.

See Chapter 3 for more on planned and emergent change: p. 48

 Main topics covered in this chapter

- The range and purpose of facilitated change approaches
- A sample of facilitated change methods, exploring their place in planned and emergent change, and evaluating their relative strengths and weaknesses in enabling change

Section 1: Why choose a facilitated approach?

Facilitated approaches and planned change

Chapter 9 established that, even in large-scale structural change, where methods such as business process re-engineering (BPR), Six Sigma, or Lean are applied, successful implementation requires people on the ground, those doing the work, to have the opportunity to explore and understand the proposed change in order to adopt new ways of working. The chapter explored Kotter's view (1996) of the eight crucial challenges for managers in leading change, which focus on communication with and involvement of employees, *in order that* employees have sufficient understanding and motivation to adopt the changes that are planned. So, one key reason for involving people is, paradoxically, to enable managers to maintain control of the programme of change that they have planned, by reducing the risk of resistance to change.

See Chapter 7 for more on resistance: p. 150

So what then is the motivation for further involving employees? Dunphy and Stace (1993) suggest that, in planned change approaches, the choice of approach is dependent on the circumstances that the organization is facing. They identify two facilitated approaches: collaborative and consultative. When adopting consultative approaches, managers may seek employees' views, typically about gentle, incremental adjustments in how things are done, which, whilst they may be significant, are gradual, not dramatic or instantaneous (Holbeche, 2006). Collaborative approaches are aimed at much greater involvement, offering employees ways of participating in important decisions, such as the major realignment of a unit.

See Chapter 9 for more on Dunphy and Stace: p. 195

In our experience, such involvement is not often evident in matters of organization strategy or structure, but rather in relation to people-related organizational objectives, such as team performance, organizational values, or the development of increased trust or well being, as illustrated in Change in Practice 10.1.

 Change in Practice 10.1

Creating a high engagement culture for a global facilities services organization

The organization, which operates facilities services for organizations across 150 countries, wanted to achieve sustainable behavioural change in its customer-facing staff, to deliver a more responsive level of customer care. Specifically, the executive team believed that employees would offer customers the same quality of care and attention as they themselves received within the organization, so that if they were to alter the everyday experiences of employees to improve their sense of well-being, the positivity would be passed on to the customers.

Following advice from change consultants, the executive team agreed that high-profile speeches from senior leaders and formal events would not have sufficient effect on people's day-to-day working lives, that employees had limited confidence in what they were told, and that rather they believed what they actually experienced. They therefore designed change activities so that they minimized speeches from the top and maximized active participation on the ground. They brought people together from across the range of countries to work on important organizational issues, to experiment and to collaborate with possible solutions, working across organizational boundaries. Some 150 cross-organizational change agents were trained to support local experiments. Experimentation was focused on things people wanted to change in their day-to-day work, for example being able to take decisions about an aspect of the service without referring upwards, and having their ideas listened to and respected by senior managers.

After the first quarter of the change programme, there was concern amongst the executive team about the low-key nature of these activities. The lack of events, plans, and timeline created discomfort and uncertainty about whether anything was happening. The executive had little say in which local experiments were taken forward. Yet, for the people involved in the experiments, change was being experienced in an immediate, local way, as team leaders offered more freedom in the taking of day-to-day operational decisions and team meetings were put to good use to explore people's issues and ideas.

Gradually, over the coming six months, employees began to feel an increased sense of well-being as they worked with changes that they themselves had instigated and grew more confident in having ideas, knowing that they could be implemented. The business evaluation showed improved quality in interactions with customers.

Despite this, there remained a sense, from employees and the executive team, that this was not a true 'change programme'.[1]

Change in Practice 10.1 illustrates change that remains the responsibility of senior management and which encourages collaboration to achieve commitment to behavioural change. Methods that encourage involvement are often believed to contribute to the development of employees' commitment and engagement. It is hoped that, in turn, engagement gives people the enthusiasm and will to change for the good of their own role and the organization's future (O'Reilly, 1996). Vanstone (2010: 2) suggests that true engagement means 'excitement, anxiety, ideas, disagreements, diversity, discontinuity, innovation, experimentation, localized decision-making and power sharing across all levels of the organization'. This description conjures up something much more complex and messy than a cascade briefing or a team meeting to elicit responses and ideas to a planned change. Hence, there may be a

See Chapter 5 for more on engagement: p. 98

point at which, if senior managers are serious about the involvement and engagement of staff in the change process, they must go beyond collaboration to relinquish their control over the outcomes. In Change in Practice 10.1, despite understanding the need to involve staff, the executive team did find it difficult to leave the change to a series of local experiments, led and managed by people on the ground. They had little control over the nature of the things that were tried out and found this to be a source of tension. This 'letting go' is one of the key issues in adopting such a method within a planned change programme. The example highlights also the difficulty of taking seriously something that has less structure than say, a business process re-engineering (BPR) plan: this too is a recurring issue for facilitated methods and may result in them being discounted or, indeed, going unrecognized.

Facilitated approaches and emergent change

Facilitated change approaches may also be adopted to enable the process of emergent change. As explored in Chapter 3, an emergent view suggests that change is inherently unpredictable. As such, organizations need to be ready to respond to external environmental changes in an agile way, through enabling organizational experiment and adjustment, to see what may emerge, rather than defining a specific change outcome. We have already noted the importance of organizational relationships in effecting emergent change; change is enabled by stimulating new forms of social interaction. To achieve this, there is a need to maximize the diversity in decision-making, so that different patterns of thinking have space, and fresh ideas surface (Stacey, 2002–03). A leader's role is to offer no more than a general framework for direction. He or she then needs to stand back, to put aside his or her power, so that all employees, wherever they sit in the hierarchy, have the space to collaborate as equals, to have difficult conversations; he or she needs to make it safe enough for people to disagree in order that novel ideas may emerge. The seeds of this approach are evident in Change in Practice 10.1. Whilst set in train by senior managers, the change itself occurred through people working in new formations, across the normal department boundaries, not just with teams in their own country.

See Chapter 3 for more on agility: p. 53

Many of the facilitated approaches to change are influenced by **social constructionism**, the view that 'reality' is socially constructed through what people do and say together (Lewis et al., 2008). From this viewpoint, there can be no fixed definition of the change that the organization wants, because it will evolve as people are able to feel it and describe it to one another. In Chapter 8, we discussed the concept of dialogue, an inquiry-based generative conversation. Dialogue offers the possibility for new behaviours, which last, coming from being with others, 'listening . . . suspending one's views' to come to 'new ways of seeing, from new awareness' (Issacs, 1999a: xviii). Dialogue entails frankness about emotions, as well as thinking, and is an approach in which feelings are welcome (Lewis et al., 2008: 117). As Isaacs (1999b) points out, this is not the normal approach to conversations in organizations, where people come to meetings well prepared, ready to represent their own department's policy, to advocate a position and to defend it (the 'ping-pong' of the advocate and the opposing party at committee meetings). It requires people to be authentic and honest in their views. We will examine the role of social construction and dialogue in the facilitated methods we explore in the next section.

Section 1 Summary

In this section, we have:

- considered when leaders may adopt facilitated approaches to change;
- considered the merits of facilitated approaches in relation to planned and emergent views of change.

Section 2: **Facilitated methods**

In this section, we will explore a sample of the best-known facilitated change methods, some of which are rooted in planned change, others of which are adopted to create the conditions for emergent change to occur. They are chosen because they represent the complexity of managing change in modern organizations. The range of methods is illustrated in Figure 10.1 and we will consider a sample from **organization development**, to **Open Space Technology** and **virtual conferencing**. As the diagram illustrates, the purpose of the approaches ranges from collaborating to solve problems, through full engagement of all parties, to senior managers relinquishing control so that employees co-create the vision of the future, co-design organization processes or structures, and ultimately organize themselves and their ideas without senior management intervention.

Organization development (OD) is one of the best-known methods in the field of organizational change. It has developed over many years, has been in fashion, then ill-regarded, and is now seen once again as a valuable approach to change. Its purpose is to work collaboratively across the organization in order to engage people and to effect change.

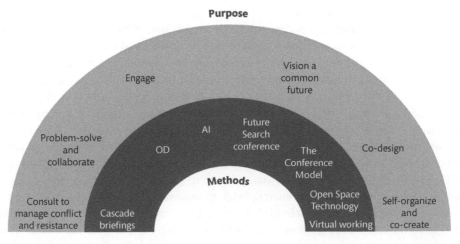

Figure 10.1 Facilitated approach methods

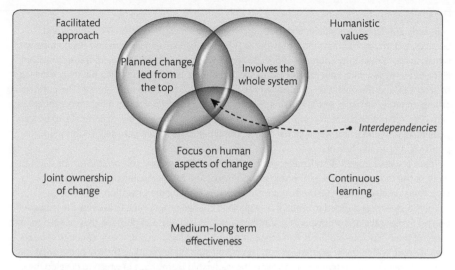

Figure 10.2 What is organization development?

What is Organization Development?

- It is a *planned* approach to change that takes in all parts of the organization (the whole system), from the individual to the group to inter-organizational, noticing how they interrelate (French and Bell, 1999).

- It is *managed from the top* of the organization (Beckhard, 2006).

- Although the emphasis is on planned change, much of OD work focuses on dealing with the *human reaction* to the planned steps to achieve *organizational effectiveness* (Bradford and Burke, 2005).

- It typically takes a *long-term* (say, two years plus) approach (Beckhard, 2006).

- The work is rooted in a set of key *humanistic values* related to openness, honesty, involvement, and the capacity to grow, these aspects positioning it firmly across the 'facilitated change' arena (French and Bell, 1999).

Burnes (2009) cites the findings of Hurley, who undertook a survey of OD practitioners and established five key principles that are used in their work: empowering employees; creating openness in communications; facilitating ownership of the change; promoting collaboration; and continuous learning. The tone of such descriptions is strikingly different from that used in directed change examples, which used language such as driving performance, eliminating cost, maximizing speed, and optimizing service. The key dimensions of OD are illustrated in Figure 10.2.

 Change in Practice 10.2

Taking an organization development approach to change: Outsourcing at NS&I

National Savings and Investments (NS&I) is a UK savings organization, the purpose of which is to provide a secure establishment in which people can save, backed by the government. It has over 26 million customers and almost £100 billion invested (2011).

In early 2000, NS&I entered into an outsourced partnership with Siemens IT Solutions and Services, a German-founded global provider of IT infrastructure management and IT solutions, with offices in more than forty countries and 35,000 employees. Over 4,000 staff were transferred from NS&I to Siemens, which now manages all of the operational business, including the service delivery of products, and the operation of customer call centres, IT and systems upgrade, etc. The partnership arrangement was a major test of working collaboratively across two entirely different organizations, with different national cultures and different business models: one to grow, to compete, to be lean and efficient to make profits in a global market; the other to be a stable, trusted, UK-only, not-for-profit savings establishment.

There are now some 150 staff employed by NS&I, based in London, responsible for the development of the business, for the partnership with Siemens, and for the quality of service that its customers receive through Siemens, but no longer busy running the operation.

The NS&I leaders decided to embark on a planned change programme to address the issues left behind in the wake of the outsourcing: they had lost their old sense of purpose, they needed to make sense of their new role and understand their responsibilities for the contract—in effect, to recreate their identity within the new arrangement. This meant starting the work at the top of the organization, with key planned interventions to allow the leadership team space in which to develop the organization's strategy together and to better understand their own contributions within that strategy. Once greater clarity had been achieved, the leaders engaged the wider organization. Further interventions were undertaken at team level, specifically aimed at enabling people to explore the values of the organization in its new form. The quality of people's engagement and purpose improved enormously. Yet somehow the leadership team still could not fully make sense of the difference between itself and Siemens: they continued to have expectations of the relationship that were not fulfilled. Finally, the programme was extended to include Siemens representatives. This wider group undertook project work that required Siemens and NS&I leaders to present joint outcomes to a challenge panel. In doing so, it quickly became clear that the different parties held fundamentally different views of what comprised good partnership decision making, in terms of the number of people to involve, attention paid to issues such as cost-effectiveness or quality of service, and the extent to which decisions affected the roles of employees. Their views were born of different underlying assumptions, reflecting their different organizational cultures. Whilst these differences had been understood at an intellectual level, exposing how it *felt* through an experiential exercise brought the issue to life. The clarity enabled change to occur in the relationship; each party began to adjust its expectations of the other, to allow a professional partnership to grow that respected their differences.

The change programme started in 2004 and continued over a period of some three years.[2-4]

The organization development process

See Chapter 3 for more on Lewin: p. 49

Often, senior managers will call on OD practitioners to undertake the programmes of change rather than do it themselves; it is seen as an expert field. The traditional OD approach is underpinned by Kurt Lewin's framework of 'unfreezing' the situation, 'moving' it to a new way of being, and 'refreezing', or consolidating the change that has occurred.

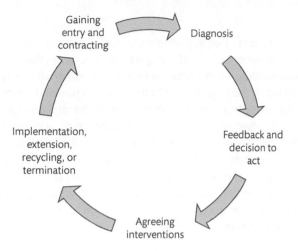

Figure 10.3 The consulting cycle

The process is illustrated in Figure 10.3. According to Burke (2008) and French and Bell (1999), it involves the following.

Unfreezing

1. *Gaining entry with the client*   This is important to the approach: gaining entry means getting alongside the client, understanding the issues through their eyes, and developing a working relationship based on this understanding. It is expected that the practitioner will be curious, open, and 'value neutral' (Palmer et al., 2006: 194). In Change in Practice 10.2, it was important for the consultants to gain entry with both Siemens and NS&I, and to be open to both views of the situation, without judgement.

2. *Contracting with the client to agree the scope of the work*   The first task is to agree what the issues are to be explored. This is known as 'raising the question', identifying and prioritizing issues of concern to explore. It is seen as crucial to being able to diagnose correctly: if the wrong issues are identified, the root cause of what needs to change may not be discovered. The client and the practitioner plan ways of getting answers to the question through the involvement of others.

3. *Undertaking diagnosis*   This comprises interviews with individuals and groups, sometimes using a questionnaire, or observing groups in action. All data is collected through a participatory approach, so that solutions come from the organization, not from the consultant. The practitioner's role is that of 'helper', helping the client to make sense of the diagnosis data, deciding where to intervene within the system (Holbeche, 2009). At NS&I, board meetings were shadowed and managers interviewed individually and in small groups to explore their challenges. It is fundamental that the very act of exploring the issues generates thinking and creates learning. This serves to develop the 'felt-need' for change (Burnes, 2009).

4. *Feeding back the data collected and making sense of the organizational issues*   It is important that this is done with the client, so that the outcomes are jointly owned. At NS&I, the leadership group was involved in making sense of the findings at an off-site workshop. There was no expert 'diagnosis', no written report; rather, a joint exploration of the issues.

Moving

1. *Agreeing the interventions*—that is, planning the change process   In this, the representative involvement of the **whole system** is important—that is, representation of all parts of the organization and its key stakeholders. Traditionally, OD practitioners work with a diagonal slice of the organization to develop a picture of the whole system (Mirvis, 2006)—that is, with people drawn from all levels of the hierarchy, across different divisions and geographies. In doing so, they pay attention to, and explore with participants, the interdependencies between the different parts of the organization. Sometimes, the work starts with the top team, but this is generally with a view to involving a wider cross-section of the organization, as happened at NS&I. In fact, the NS&I programme succeeded only when the 'whole system' was represented—that is, when Siemens and NS&I managers worked together on the issues, and invited views from customers and stakeholders.

2. *Implementing the interventions*   In NS&I, a series of strategy days, workshops, individual coaching, **action learning** (in which small groups of peers tackle organizational issues), and experiential simulations were used (for example, using actors to represent key stakeholders; holding challenge panels to assess joint project outcomes). These techniques were a crucial part of people gaining new insights, starting to think differently about the situation.

Refreezing

1. *Evaluation and/or extension of the intervention*   NS&I chose to evaluate the change through use of 'pulse checks' (informal staff feedback processes) and staff surveys.

The process of contracting and diagnosing has its roots in **action research**. This recognizes that successful action comes from analysing the situation accurately and choosing the most appropriate solution (Burnes, 2009). The cycle of data collection, diagnosis, feedback, intervention, and evaluation may be iterative: the action research cycle. The act of diagnosis involves the system; the diagnosis results in further action to effect change (see the discussion about action research in Chapter 14).

A feature of OD practice is the recognition that all interventions have consequences for the client (Schein, 1999). For example, the very act of asking a question prompts thinking in the direction of that question; this may result in a change in focus, an opening up of thinking or closing down of other avenues. In this way, every move counts.

Tolbert and Hanafin (2006) distinguish the OD practitioner's role from that of a technical expert, because the focus of the work is on how the task is to be accomplished in terms of roles and relationships rather than on the task itself or its technology, and so on. Practitioners need to understand how groups work and work with the 'back stage' of organizations—the power, the politics, the culture of the organization to effect change. Whilst the change programme at NS&I was led from the top, it was important that the positional power of the executive team did not overshadow or inhibit the contribution of the wider group as the work progressed. This proved difficult: despite the collegiate behaviours of the leaders,

See Chapter 11 for more on roles: p. 254

people still held back in their presence and it was the role of the practitioner to manage the **group process** to overcome this, to create the conditions for people to feel safe enough to speak out.

 Exercise 10.1

Consider an issue in your organization or university that requires review and impacts what employees do. Imagine yourself to be the OD consultant. Explain the issue to a colleague and, as you do so, think about the following.

- Notice the extent to which your mind is made up about what is going on, and the extent to which you feel open and curious about possible ways forward. See whether you can identify your own vested interest in the issue.

- Identify who is needed to explore the issue to ensure a good cross-section of stakeholders. Consider how interested you are in their views.

- What does that tell you about the skills required to be an OD practitioner when gaining entry and contracting with the client, and when undertaking the initial diagnosis?

There are conflicting views about the primary purpose of OD. For some practitioners, the term 'organization development' is an umbrella for thinking about the behavioural aspects of change as the primary approach to changing organization culture (Bradford and Burke, 2005). As such, it is well placed to sit alongside other methods such as BPR, to deliver organization-wide behavioural change to meet the needs of new technologies and processes. Indeed, at NS&I, is was the OD programme that sustained the delivery of a major outsourcing initiative.

Yet, perhaps because it is rooted in the humanistic values, it is often associated with the notion of making organizations ' "better" places to work' (Schein, 2006: xvii) and is sometimes described as a 'movement' focused at the individual level, with interventions focused on interpersonal relationships. As such, it spread quickly, taking on a 'faddish quality' (Greiner and Cummings, 2005: 87) and, through its success, began to attract more attention and then criticism for putting the individual above the organization, for lacking business focus, and for failing to deliver quantifiable outcomes. This demonstrates just how difficult it is to intervene across a whole organization system to effect culture change in a sustainable way. Marshak (2005) asserts that OD has failed to play a central role during times of extensive organizational change worldwide. Because it takes time (at NS&I, the programme stretched across three years), it cannot have the same up-front impact as some of the more tangible instantaneous changes in structure or process.

Despite this criticism, many of OD's techniques have now become mainstream. Schein (2006) cites improving communications, team building, and having processes to manage change as examples that are rooted in an OD perspective, yet now are simply part of organizational life and key interventions to aid individual and group learning. We find the key dimensions of OD (see Figure 10.2), such as paying attention to the interdependencies between different parts of the organization system and taking a longer-term view, helpful in most change situations. We also generally apply the processes of involvement, such as working with cross-sections of the organization, as we find this offers a deeper under-standing of the issues and the opportunity to effect change that can be sustained by all parties. We regularly deploy key tools and techniques such as coaching, feedback, and action learning simultaneously, as Change in Practice 10.2 described, and find that their cumulative effect helps where the organization's capacity to think differently has got stuck. We find that, overall, OD does serve to address the human aspects of the business trans-formation agenda.

Appreciative Inquiry

The second method that we shall examine is **Appreciative Inquiry** (AI) (see Figure 10.1). This is a planned change method, led from the top, yet the aim of which is full participation and engagement of the whole organization system. It is based on everyone participating in an inquiry to focus on the 'strengths' that exist in the organization. Its purpose is to facilitate the development of organizational capacity in those strengths.

See Chapter 8 for more on dialogue: p. 175

AI is used with groups, often large groups, drawing on the process of dialogue (see sec-tion 1) to build consensus around the positive aspects of the organization. Storytelling is used to recall the best examples of what is (or has been) in the organization, for example leadership or customer care at its best. These stories form the basis for visioning what could be in the future. Sharing the stories creates the energy and enthusiasm to develop more of what works well.

The approach was first experimented with by David Cooperrider, Frank Barrett, and colleagues as a complement to the conventional forms of action research described as part of OD practice (van der Haar and Hosking, 2004). Cooperrider and Srivastva (2008) describe a shift from problem-solving to appreciation and a shift from advocacy to in-quiry, believing that the problem-solving view is the world's 'primary constraint on its imagination and contribution to knowledge', because our assumptions and choice of method impact our findings. They suggest that a traditional action research approach of critiquing gets in the way of being completely open to something novel, inhibiting the capacity to 'marvel' and 'wonder' (Cooperrider and Srivastva, 2008: 354). Therefore, un-like OD, those adopting this approach choose not to analyse what is wrong and find remedies, but rather to focus on what works well, on the basis that we 'get more of whatever we inquire into and talk about' (Vanstone, 2010: 6; Austin and Bartunek, 2006). The claim of AI proponents is that AI is not about wishful thinking, but rather is grounded in the reality of what already exists. It is typically used to change the culture of an organization, to solve conflicts, and to create renewal (van der Haar and Hosking, 2004).

Most AI practitioners are influenced by social constructionism (see section 1), believing that change is created with and between people. Taking this as a central premise of AI, they believe that 'by getting people to unite on a central theme or idea, Appreciative Inquiry al-lows people to construct their future' (Cooperrider et al., 2008: 14). This concept is explored further in Change in Practice 10.3.

Exercise 10.2

Work in a group of four to six people whom you know reasonably well. Sit in a circle, each person turning to face the person on his or her left and tell them:

- what you appreciate most about them;
- when you see them at their best;
- what they do that you would like them to do more of.

Move on to the next person to your left and repeat the exercise.

- How easy or difficult was the task?
- How did you feel (embarrassed/energized/foolish/happy, etc.)?
- What happens within the group during the process?
- What does this tell you about taking an appreciative stance?

There is a core structure to the AI method, which follows broadly five phases (often known as the 'five Ds'). Phases two to five are often worked though at a conference or summit, generally lasting three days (Lewis et al., 2008).

1. A *definition* phase The goals, the project management structure, and the approach to enabling people to participate are agreed, as well as the broad topic of inquiry such as innovation (Watkins and Mohr, 2001).

2. A *discovery* phase Participants inquire into the times when the organization is at its very best in human, economic, and organizational terms, in terms of the topic of choice. For example, participants may interview each other in pairs, using questions to guide them through the telling of real stories. Sometimes, stakeholders such as customers and suppliers are included in the process. From this, the whole group identify themes and patterns to understand what they valued most about themselves, the nature of their work, and the organization at those moments in time when things were at their very best, during the 'high point' experiences (Cooperrider et al., 2008).

3. A *dream* phase Participants now start to describe their picture of the future. They are encouraged to take the best of the past and to break any rules they need to create a new future. Cooperrider et al. (2008: 133) understand the dream stage to be strategically significant, leading to 'higher levels of creativity, commitment and enthusiasm for the organization and its future'. Sometimes, the dreams are acted out as a short play at the end of the afternoon, which creates a sense of energy to take in to the third day (Lewis et al., 2008).

4. A *design* phase The participants now take their dream and translate it into reality by considering the aspects of organization life that they need to change: policies, structures, processes, etc. It is expected that the senior leaders will be in the room as this work happens, so that ideas can be agreed to or negotiated as the work is being done, to ensure that it remains part of the real organization, not just a fun away day. Much of the thinking is undertaken in small groups, with a whole-group discussion to identify who else needs to be involved to make it happen; the phase requires 'widespread dialogue' thereby

'co-constructing the organization's future' (Cooperrider et al., 2008: 164). The small groups then prepare design statements about what is going to happen (Lewis et al., 2008).

5. A *destiny* phase   A range of projects is agreed upon to take the ideas forward.

 Change in Practice 10.3

Appreciative Inquiry at Nokia

Chapter 2 explored the origins of Nokia, the technology and mobile phone provider. By 2002, Nokia had around 60,000 employees worldwide. In that year, the executive board decided that, given the enormous growth in employees and resultant changes in working practices as new people and new ideas came on board, they needed to revitalize the Nokia values that had guided them through the previous ten years. They decided to undertake the programme through a process of Appreciative Inquiry (AI). The board believed this to be the appropriate choice because it was neither top-down nor bottom-up, so that senior leaders could be involved, yet were not in the role of deciding what to do and cascading those decisions through the organization. They felt that the process itself paid attention to aspects of organization life that Nokia believe are important, emphasizing involvement and respect for others.

Twenty people, including four members of the executive board, drawn from different countries and functions and different levels in the hierarchy, came together to form a core team for the AI project. They spent two days together gaining an understanding of the approach and agreeing the specific topics of inquiry for this change intervention under the banner of 'revitalizing the values'.

This core team then embarked on the *definition* phase. Over the next four months, each member of the team carried out AI interviews, collecting stories and quotes, which were used to create a hundred posters. One recurring theme was that of values-based leadership and it was agreed that this would be the focus of the next phase of the work, to take place at a summit.

The three-and-a-half-day summit was designed for 200 people in Helsinki, the purpose of which was to undertake the entire process of the rest of the 'Ds', from *discovery* through to *destiny*. The participants were chosen to represent the maximum diversity within Nokia. The posters of quotes were used to decorate the walls of the conference room—to bring the inquiry into the room.

The summit days had many ups and downs. One of the issues the core team faced was enabling people to engage with the process and stay with it over such a lengthy period. The executive board had chosen to give the event a high profile, which in turn made the core team want it to be a success. It needed to be carefully facilitated by the external consultants to ensure that the group stayed with the process, avoided responding to people's concerns in the moment, thereby hurrying it along or predetermining the outcome, or changing tack when people got restless. By the final day of the summit, those participating were immersed in the work and felt that they were achieving new understanding of the issues and identifying ways forward. Eighteen groups formed to take forward key actions, focusing on bringing life to Nokia's core values. These were values-in-action, to be demonstrated through acts of leadership in everyday life.

Some of the ideas of the eighteen groups did not survive the transition from the high energy event to the work needed to take them forward in the workplace. The 'relight the fire' team developed and presented an updated communication of the values to the executive board, which experienced the work as 'lively and relevant output' (Vanstone and Dalbiez, 2008), which was adopted and followed through. The primary aim of the intervention, to refresh the values, was delivered.

Looking back, people still remember the energy of the summit and their sense of being part of creating new ideas. Nokia reports that the appreciative approach has become part of many leaders' and teams' ways of working, and that subsequent AI projects have happened since in other parts of the organization, including the Far East and Latin America.[5-6]

AI is sometimes seen as a subset part of OD—a technique to be drawn on as one aspect of an OD change programme (Watkins and Moor, 2001). AI practitioners typically feel strongly that it is a method in its own right. Where it is well received, it is best known for the amounts of positive energy that it releases during the process, as evidenced at Nokia, and its capacity to set innovative change in motion (van der Haar and Hoskins, 2004). AI practitioners believe that the process enables learning and change to take place simultaneously, because patterns of thinking shift through a high involvement process (Whitney, 1998).

Van der Haar and Hosking (2004) note that although AI has become increasingly popular, there are few published evaluations. What is unclear is how much of the learning and involvement continues in the workplace *and* has an impact on the business. Vanstone and Dalbiez (2008) report that the work undertaken with Nokia focused heavily on the summit and suggest ensuring that this aspect does not become too stand-alone, and that there is both sufficient preparation and follow-up to make what happened at the summit survive back in the workplace. Other AI interventions have undertaken more work with the teams on the ground, focusing on relationships that are happening daily between managers, taking up to a year to work informally and locally before a summit and putting more support in place to enable ideas to flourish after the summit (Vanstone and Dalbiez, 2008). Nevertheless, it remains difficult to find evidence that AI can produce organization-wide change.

One of the concerns of the process is its apparently rigid structure: the five Ds suggest a process of inputs and outputs, a method that is applied and then comes to an end (van der Haar and Hosking, 2004). It might be expected that change occurring through organizational relationships is ongoing; the structured AI process may, in fact, act as a constraint to the relational flow. The structure offers a framework that can lend itself to clear outputs, and managers can get impatient with the process and want to speed up and control the choice of such projects, as they did at Nokia. The day-to-day patterns of power and politics in the organization may be unaffected by the process. Vanstone and Dalbiez (2008) suggest that managers need support and coaching through the informal phases of the work in order to comfortably let go of their control and to enable the full participation of everyone.

As noted in section 1, methods such as AI link positive emotions with well-being, through which it is hoped to improve employee engagement and ultimately productivity. Yet many comment on the determined repression of negativity in the process as a problem in itself. Vanstone and Dalbiez (2008) report the findings of Fredrickson and Losada that, without appropriate negativity, the experience may become ungrounded and ineffectual. Van der Haar and Hosking (2004: 1026) suggest that to insist on only positive ways of relating does not fit with typical relations, that 'such an injunction could hinder the openness of the process and therefore the realities that can be "made"'. Vanstone and Dalbiez (2008) did not find this to be a problem in their work with Nokia, although the process needed careful facilitation because they were working with managers trained in problem-solving and critiquing, so that staying in appreciative mode did feel forced at times. The process encourages also some deep thinking and reflection. For the first day or so of the Nokia summit, managers more accustomed to task and action found the process at times 'slow and ponderous' (Vanstone and Dalbiez, 2008: 189). They caution against AI becoming a dogma and note the skill required by the facilitator in deciding when to hold the line and insist on an appreciative stance, and when it is helpful to speak or act from a different stance.

New approaches to organizational psychology and HR practices, which encourage people to play to their strengths, now form part of performance appraisal and development planning in some organizations. Organizations are therefore more familiar with taking an appreciative approach. However, the time and expense involved in delivering an AI summit, and the uncertainty in transferring the energy and learning from the summit to the workplace, mean inevitably that the full five stages of AI are less frequently adopted.

Large-group methods

AI is one of the best-known approaches that adopt a large-group process and dialogue as an integral part of the design. However, since the 1990s, facilitated approaches have concentrated increasingly on using the large-group process as an intervention in its own right (Bunker and Alban, 1997). There are now a range of methods, which sit under the 'large group' banner, drawn from the assumption that change happens when representation of the whole system is present and that dialogue enables people to work together with high involvement and sustainable commitment to change (Holman and Devane, 1999; Lewis et al., 2008). Most aim to encourage the freeing up of leaders from the ownership of a planned process and create the environment in which people can self-organize, vision a future together, and co-create solutions to organizational issues (see Figure 10.1). Because relevant stakeholders are in the same place at the same time, change can happen in the system immediately, rather than slowly over several months (Bunker et al., 2005). This has the potential to move a facilitated approach from incremental change to rapid-response organization-wide change.

See Chapter 3 for more on incremental change: p. 37

 Exercise 10.3

Think about the last time you were required to attend a conference or large-group meeting at which you did not know everybody.

- How did you feel when you arrived in the room?

- Did you expect to be able to join in? What were your assumptions about what might happen?

- Did you behave differently because of the large-group setting?

- Was your experience positive or negative and why?

- What does that tell you about the facilitation needed to manage large-group processes and to achieve dialogue?

Table 10.1 Large-group methods

Purpose	Method
Creating the future, strategic planning	The search conference Future Search Real-time strategic change
Work design or structuring (when strategic plan already exists)	The Conference Model™ Fast-cycle full participation work design Real-time work design
Work on current issues, problem identification, or process improvement	Simu-real Work-out Open Space Technology World Cafe
Maximizing involvement on day-to-day issues through application of IT	Virtual conferencing using IT platforms Organization–wide social networking

Sources: Bunker and Alban (1997); Holman and Devane (1999); Lewis et al. (2008)

Table 10.1 lists some of the most prevalent of large-group methods currently in use, grouped according to their primary purpose.

These large-group methods have developed on the back of each other and, like AI, are seen by some as simply techniques to be deployed under the umbrella of OD, rather than methods in their own right (Bunker et al., 2005). We outline below one example of each of the above four categories, starting with *Future Search,* in more detail to illustrate a whole process.

1. Future Search: Creating the future, strategic planning

Future Search was created by Martin and Mary Weisbord and Sandra Janoff. It is one of the best known of the large-group methods and is focused on planning the future with everyone who has an interest (see Figure 10.1).

The process is run as an action-planning conference. The participants may include employees and senior leaders, suppliers and customers, etc. The group can range from twenty-five to over a hundred people, with around seventy being considered a good number to create the necessary diversity and energy, yet maintain a sense of community (Bunker and Alban, 1997). This differentiates it from another approach, called the search conference, which typically takes input from stakeholders, but has only those directly responsible for the issue at the conference. There is a clear structure for the conference (Lewis et al., 2008), designed around five key tasks.

i. Reviewing the past

ii. Exploring the present

iii. Creating future scenarios

iv. Identifying common ground between all parties

v. Creating action plans

Whilst it is expected that the group will have divergent views and interests, often over dilemmas about future choices, the emphasis of discussions is on establishing where there is already common ground on which to build, not on solving issues of difference; the conference moves forward on actions on which the group can agree (Lewis et al., 2008; Bunker and Alban, 1997). The group works together without external input to the discussions from consultants or facilitators, who are typically there to oversee and ensure that the overall process is adhered to.

 Change in Practice 10.4

Future Search at Ikea

Ikea is a privately owned international furniture and home products retailer. Founded in Sweden in 1943, it was the first to offer modern flat-packed, self-assembly furniture at affordable prices. It has over 300 stores in thirty-seven countries, largely in Europe, North America, Asia, and Australia, with over 12,000 products. Ikea stores have a 'one-way' layout, which guides the customer through the store so that they see the products showcased in 'rooms' and are led through the store in its entirety. The stores have long opening hours, restaurants, and crèches, designed to attract families who work, who have young children, and who are managing on a tight budget. Products are largely manufactured outside of Europe, with suppliers in some fifty countries, a third coming from Asia.

In 2003, the company decided to reprocess its product flow, from the drawing board design in Sweden, through to factory and assembly distribution points, and then to customers. It decided to adopt the Future Search process to initiate the work because it felt that its approach fitted with its 'Simply Ikea' principles: teamwork; challenge; enthusiasm; possibility; humbleness; responsibility; simplicity; coaching; and cost consciousness.

The Future Search focused on one sofa—the Ektorp—as the prototype for all product lines and the task was to reimagine its journey from the design centre to the customer. The conference was held in Hamburg over three days in March 2003. Fifty-two key stakeholders attended, including suppliers from Poland, Mexico, and China, the company's president and other staff from Sweden, Canada, and the US, plus a range of customers. For the greater part, they had not met previously nor did they know each other well.

The conference was facilitated by Mary Weisbord, one of the founders of Future Search, and was designed to cover all Future Search's five tasks (from reviewing the past to creating action plans, see above): i) describing the existing system; ii) documenting required changes; iii) proposing options for new systems; iv) agreeing a specification for a new design; and v) developing an implementation plan with buy-in from all key functions. Ikea's top executives were part of the process. Their role was to join in the discussions without stepping in and deciding what form the new system should take.

From the work, a range of changes to the product process were planned, including the involvement of customers and suppliers at the design stage, flattening the hierarchy, as well as changing the information system, so that coordination and control of the process could be improved.

After the conference, seven task forces, working across the world, developed the changes for the entire system, coordinating their efforts through conference calls and emails, demonstrating the capacity to self-organize across countries and hierarchies, with people who had no formal authority in the hierarchy taking charge of aspects of the change. Ikea and Mary Weisbord believed that the conference had been successful in both creating the change and achieving commitment to what needed to happen.[7-9]

Weisbord and Janoff (2000) consider their method to establish a 'learning laboratory' for creating a shared vision. There are a number of issues to address to create the conditions for this to occur. Firstly, there is a need to spend enough time planning the process in advance, checking out both the topic and consequently what constitutes the 'whole system'. Typically, organizations draw back from inviting difficult clients or stakeholders who have strongly divergent views, yet achieving the rich mix is crucial to the value of the intervention. In Change in Practice 10.4, a specific product was used to focus the discussion and Ikea was brave enough to involve a whole range of parties from across the world.

The process starts with a review of the past, and there is a danger that people get stuck in the problems of the past and find it difficult to move on; some suggest that starting in the present is more productive (Bunker and Alban, 1997). Certainly, there is the need to help the group to generate the quality of dialogue that prevents them getting stuck in advocacy—that is 'moving' and 'opposing'.

See Chapter 8 for more on dialogue: p. 175

The method is built on the belief that the process creates the energy to progress the work and that it is the responsibility of the participants not the facilitators to drive the actions forward. Given that such a conference typically lasts three days, after which the group disperses, there is a strong danger that the actions do not take off—that insufficient attention is given to planning the next steps. However, this was not the experience of the Ikea participants, who were well supported within the organization. In this case, clear actions were signed off before the close of the conference. Bunker and Alban (1997) report that review sessions, which bring the group back together at regular intervals, assist with maintaining momentum. The process clearly does not work where the group do not have enough interest in the issue, or where they are not used to managing themselves and find the responsibility difficult or at odds with the power dynamics within their organization. It is also a problem in organizations in which a small group of senior leaders hold control and are themselves not versed in working in this way, and find it difficult to adopt ideas that are not their own. These issues apply similarly to the further three interventions summarized below.

2. The Conference Model™: Work redesign—work design or structuring (when a strategic plan already exists)

The purpose of The Conference Model™ is to undertake a specific redesign of organization structure to meet new strategic needs. It aims to suppress design time and to increase commitment to design outcome by involving as many people as possible in the work as quickly as possible (Bunker and Alban, 1997, and see Figure 10.1). The method was developed by Dick and Emily Axlerod, based on the Future Search conference method and drawing on ideas from BPR. Customers and suppliers are invited to join the conferences. Its point of difference is that it typically comprises a series of five conferences (each lasting two or three days) over four to five months, with eighty or more attending each time and with work continuing between conferences. It concentrates on the technical work flow to develop a preferred design for the organization.

The five conferences each have a purpose, as follows.

i. Visioning—what people want

ii. Customer focus—customer requirements

iii. Technical focus—workflow, problems, and variance

iv. Design—new ways of working

v. Implementation—time frames for taking the work forward

A core group attends all five conferences. A 'simple commitment' process takes place at the end of each conference, whereby groups commit to actions that they can take forward in the next thirty days. 'Data assist' teams are trained to synthesize data from each conference and to facilitate a 'walk-through', a two-hour mini-conference, to describe outputs to those who did not attend and to solicit views and input, which then are fed into the next stage of the conference. Walk-throughs are intended to generate more interest in the change process and to get further people involved. A strong planning group is needed to sustain this structure (Holman and Devane, 1999).

When The Conference Model works well, it is known to increase the customer orientation of participants, who hear first-hand what the customer wants (Holman and Devanne, 1999). Because decisions directly affect the organization's design, it is important that senior managers are both prepared to let go of control, to enable the ideas to be freely generated, and committed to follow though the decisions to implementation (Bunker and Alban, 1997; Holman and Devane, 1999). The Conference Model does require commitment of time and resource to succeed; however, Bunker and Alban (1997) believe that the ultimate implementation happens more quickly because people have been part of the creation, unlike the issues highlighted in the implementation of BPR.

See Chapter 9 for more on BPR: p. 199

3. Open Space Technology: Work on current issues, problem identification, or process improvement

The purpose of Open Space Technology is to get representation of the whole system of the organization participating in dialogue as a means of surfacing important issues (see Figure 10.1). It is an approach for hosting conferences, which, whilst focused on a theme, unlike Future Search does not have a formal task, structure, or agenda that is planned in advance. It was created in the mid-1980s by an organizational consultant, Harrison Owen, in response to an expressed need for people to connect more effectively when attending conferences (Lewis et al., 2008). Owen realized that people attending his conferences enjoyed the coffee breaks more than the formal presentations and wanted to create the energy that was present in the breaks during the periods of conference activity. Hence the focus is on networking and community building to co-create new ideas or solutions.

The conference is built on the concept of a marketplace. When the conference convenes, the group starts by considering the predetermined theme and spends the first hour creating its own agenda, around that theme (Lewis et al., 2008), such that:

● anyone who wants to initiate a discussion or activity writes it down on a large sheet of paper, then stands up and announces it to the group, offering a time and meeting place for the discussions, then pins his or her paper to the wall;

● when everyone who wants to has announced and posted their initial offerings, participants have time to walk around the wall, putting together their individual schedules for the remainder of the conference. The first meetings begin immediately.

An Open Space Technology conference lasts from a half-day to three days: the longer the period, the greater depth is achieved through the process of people coming together to create ideas. The most basic principle is that everyone who comes to an Open Space conference must be willing to take some responsibility for creating ideas from being together, participating, and being interested in the topic. As part of this principle, the 'law of two feet' is adopted— that is, if someone is in a situation where he or she is not learning or contributing, that person must use his or her two feet to move on, to go somewhere else (Lewis et al., 2008). Sometimes, this may be to join another conversation, sometimes to be by themselves. From this, other random conversations may be born as others join them. All conversations are considered equally valid. Unlike AI and Future Search, disagreement is expected and seen to be part of the ingredients for creating fresh thinking. Drawing on complexity theory, it is expected that that ideas and order will emerge without planning and order being imposed.

See Chapter 3 for more on complexity theory: p. 55

Four key principles of Open Space Technology are as follows (Harrison, 1999).

i.   Whoever comes are the right people.

ii. Whatever happens is the only thing that could have happened.

iii. Whenever it starts is the right time.

iv. When it is over, it is over.

Norris (2000) notes that there has been little formal evaluation of its effectiveness, although the basic process is relatively straightforward, which makes it usable. He reports Bolton's findings that Open Space Technology encourages individuals and groups to develop their skills 'as lifelong learners and collaborative problem solvers', because they take responsibility for resolving differences amongst themselves and finding ways forward (ibid: 15). This, in turn, is likely to increase the organization's collective capability to adapt, to learn to cope with change on a continuous, incremental basis. It is more difficult to prove its direct impact on outcomes such as productivity.

4. Virtual conferencing using IT platforms: Maximizing involvement on day-to-day issues through application of IT

Virtual working has been practised for several years in a great number of organizations. Virtual conference sessions can be used for any purpose, from strategic planning to simply holding a team meeting. They can involve any number of people, working from wherever they are in the world. Typically, each of the participants works individually, in front of a computer with access to a shared IT platform and with a phone or headset for communicating. The web can be used for presentations. Break-out rooms can be created on the platforms to recreate the quality of small-group discussion used in other large-group methods.

Most organizations still use virtual events as add-ons to face-to-face conferences (Shimabukuro, 2000). This distracts from building effort into the virtual aspects. Whilst virtual conferences can be staged at any time, the level of concentration involved in being online and working with a headset means that they generally cannot be sustained for more than four hours. However, a virtual conference can be readily reconvened and we have often worked with organizations in which we have met virtually four hours per day for five consecutive days, in order to take forward key strategic planning, for example.

Virtual conferencing is still sometimes an unsatisfactory experience for those involved. The technology tends to drive people to brief exchanges, focused on task, rather than to build dialogue and generate ideas. Recent work has started to experiment with ways of building relationships and trust when working virtually, and it is expected that this will become an area of increased sophistication in the future (Caulat, 2010): it still holds more possibility for wide involvement than any of the methods we have considered.

As the selection in Table 10.2 demonstrates, many modern large-group methods for facilitated change aim to overcome the constraints of owning and planning change at the top of the organization, to allow diversity and involvement in decision-making. Those who wish to create the conditions for emergent change to occur are drawn to these methods. Increasingly, organizations are using IT platforms in more innovative ways to create virtual conferences, as well as using wikis and blogs to keep in touch and to maintain social networks by virtual means. These are creating new ways for ideas to form and for change to occur. They also are proving more difficult for leaders to control. Yet their capacity to change thinking, affect culture, and achieve learning is mentioned time and again. So perhaps the seeds of facilitated approaches are growing.

 ## Section 2 Summary

In this section, we have:

- examined a selection of facilitated change methods deployed to achieve both planned and emergent change;
- considered their relative strengths and weaknesses.

 ## Integrative Case Study

Culture change at O2

O2 is a leading provider of broadband and mobile phones, based in the UK. It is part of the Telefonica O2 Europe group, operating across the UK, Ireland, Germany, the Czech Republic, and Slovakia. It was launched in 2001 following separation of the business from British Telecom and was acquired by Telefonica at the end of 2005.

Part of the company relaunch in 2001–02 was the creation of a new name and a new brand image. Over the next two years, the brand became well recognized and its market share increased dramatically. To achieve this, a change programme was led from the top of the organization by the CEO for Europe, Peter Erskine, and the senior management team in the UK. There was some significant restructuring of the business to achieve a rapid organization transformation, to throw off the British Telecom history, to remove inefficiencies, and to make clear in the market that O2 was gripping issues—that it meant business. In the fast-moving competitive market, senior managers felt that speed was of the essence and a directive approach was adopted to effect the changes. By the summer of 2005, there were disputes over pay and job losses, and further redundancies. Strikes were just avoided after several months of negotiations between senior managers and unions.

At this point in 2005, the UK CEO, Matthew Key, decided that, alongside expansion, he wanted to focus on rewarding customer loyalty and increasing customer retention, by improving the service provided in shops and call centres, where behaviour was driven by sales targets and efficiency metrics; there was a need to re-establish the idea of relationship with the customer. A change programme of a different nature was instigated, adopting a facilitated approach, to get employees' input into how to change the customer experience. Key wanted also to unlock people's pride and passion in working for a big brand name, which is what O2 had become.

This change programme was based on experimentation and conversation. At local level, managers and staff were encouraged to experiment with different day-to-day ways of working to create a more empowered culture. There was 'permission' to break some of the rules that got in the way of serving the customer well. This became known as 'positive deviancy'. Different parties were brought together to develop relationships and to share practice across the business. The purpose was to adopt where possible the best of existing practice, rather than to force people to adopt one central model, or, conversely, to allow dozens of different initiatives without everyone getting the benefit.

The formal aspect of this change programme used the Appreciative Inquiry (AI) method, with a summit designed around the theme of a 'better place' attended by a cross-section of 300 employees. By the end of day three, some thirty employee-led projects had been launched, including: the creation of a 'shadow board' of employees, accepted by the board as part of its decision-making process, to ensure that 'the customer experience sat at the heart of all business decisions'; an environmental project to improve waste recycling rates; an inquiry process that offered some 1,000 employees the opportunity to input their view of the sort of place they wanted O2 to be. Matthew Key said: 'We (the O2 Board) were making a leap of faith, but this (was) real people engagement and we could see that' (Vanstone, 2007: 7).

As a result of the many suggestions, call centres handlers started to provide an end-to-end service, rather than hand over to others. Retail outlets were twinned with call centres to forge better relationships and understanding.

It is difficult to make direct connections between the initiative and profits. However, customer retention and customer satisfaction surveys improved between 2005 and 2006. Within the organization, every directorate recorded improvement in the employee engagement survey in 2006 and O2 was listed for the first time in the 'Best Place to Work' league tables.

Questions

1. Thinking back to Chapter 9, what part did a directed approach take in O2's change? Do you think this was an appropriate approach when it was adopted and, if so, why?

2. Against the backdrop of redundancies and threatened strikes, how might the change in approach in 2005 have been experienced?

3. To what extent do you think the changes that came about as a result of the summit were deep seated or cosmetic, and why?

4. Had you entered O2 as the organization development (OD) practitioner in 2005, how would you have gone about the diagnosis? What other interventions could assist the change?

5. What do your reflections tell you about working with a range of approaches to change?

Table 10.2 Summary of large-group methods

	Future Search	The Conference Model	Open Space	Virtual Conferencing
Attendees	Whole system representation	Whole system representation	Whole system representation	Whole system representation
Format	Set format: past, present, future, action-planning	Structured design process in five conferences: visioning; customer focus; technical; design; implementation	Least structured: large group creates agenda topics in market place format	Entirely flexible: structured to suit issue
Duration	Lasts three days	Two days + for each of the five conferences, three weeks between conferences	Lasts one–three days	Each conference limited to 4 hours as maximum online participation time
Process	Self-managed small groups within large group process	Structured groups working on each aspect of redesign; data assist teams work between meetings to increase range of those involved and maintain links	Interest groups form and self-regulate; adopt 'law of two feet'	Whole group or small groups as required; sub-groups work virtually between sessions
Approach	Minimizes differences, looks for common ground	Works with different opinions from wide range of stakeholders	Difference seen as part of the creativity	Opportunity for difference to be explored
Led by	Requires planning and facilitation, but not speakers or expert in put; senior manager part of process and not leading	Senior managers involved and needed to take forward implementation	No experts: one facilitator to lay out format and ground rules; senior managers part of process and not leading	Opportunities to be used for directive or facilitated approaches
Outcome	Specific strategic action plans	Growth in customer orientation; redesign of part of the organization/process	Growth in thinking and connectivity, which may also result in actions	According to purpose

Conclusion

In Chapters 9 and 10, we have explored the range of directed and facilitated change approaches that can be drawn on when implementing change, and considered a sample of different methods that support these approaches. Whilst Chapter 9 identifies directed methods that are regularly deployed in organizations, such as BPR, Lean, or Six Sigma, Chapter 10 suggests rather that recent methods have been designed to maximize input, with large-group processes gaining momentum; employee involvement has become the received wisdom, the 'must do' in order to achieve successful change (Burnes, 2009).

Yet is involvement really growing? Wilkinson et al. (2004) undertook eighteen case studies to examine the link between employees 'having a voice' and economic improvement. They found that employee **voice** had increased in its scope and impact over the past ten years, although the extent to which people had a say was still under managerial control. Employees were found to be highly articulate and to want engagement with a wide range of concerns, but, despite this, there was little solid evidence of collaborative approaches actually happening to any large extent in change programmes. It seems that sometimes managers go through the motions of involving staff in decisions that are already fixed and non-negotiable. Wilkinson et al. (2004: 306) note that despite managers talking about people having influence and say, managers are not 'seeking to convey the impression that this represents a situation in which changes are led by employees or that their voice is actually 'heard' by managers while making decisions'.

e Chapter 9 for ore on choice of proach: p. 195

As evidenced in Chapter 9, senior managers rarely work with just one approach; rather they make adjustments to meet changing circumstances. Bradford and Burke (2005) speak of the integration of hard-edged business decisions driven from the top, with facilitating people's input about what needs to happen in a seamless process. Dunphy and Stace (1993) note that each approach to change, whether directive or facilitated, has a key purpose that, over time, develops limitations, such that one approach will not serve forever. In our experience, senior managers often are not really sure what to do about involvement, sometimes lack the skills, and often simply cannot find the time to undertake such processes: involving people takes time and effort.

 Please visit the Online Resource Centre at **http://www.oxfordtextbooks.co.uk/orc/ myers** *to access further resources for students and lecturers.*

Change in Practice sources

1. Based on personal experience.
2. Based on personal consulting experience.
3. NS&I (undated) 'Who we are'. http://www.nsandi.com/about-nsi-who-we-are
4. Siemans (undated) 'IT solutions and services'. http://www.siemens.com/entry/cc/en/#189380
5. Nokia website: http://www.nokia.com/home

6. Vanstone, C. and Dalbiez, B. (2008) 'Revitalising corporate values in Nokia', in S. Lewis, J. Passmore, and S. Cantore (eds) *Appreciative Inquiry for Change Management: Using AI to Facilitate Organizational development*, London: Kogan Page, pp.183–95.

7. Future Search (undated) 'Future Search applications'. http://www.futuresearch.net/method/applications/

8. Ikea website: http://www.ikea.com

9. Weisbord, M. (for Future Search Network) (2004) 'A model for redesigning product lines at Ikea'. http://www.futuresearch.net/method/applications/uploads/business/ikea.pdf

Integrative Case Study sources

BBC News (2001) 'BT approves mobiles spin-off', 23 Oct. http://news.bbc.co.uk/1/hi/business/1615100.stm

O2 website: http://www.O2.co.uk

Ray, B. (2007) 'Peter Erskine calls it a day at O2', 29 Nov. http://www.theregister.co.uk/2007/11/29/erskine_steps_down/

Vanstone, C. (2007) 'Better place at O2', *Converse*, 5: 3–5.

Further reading

Bradford, D. and Burke, W. (2005) *The Future of OD in Reinventing Organization Development: New Approaches to Change in Organizations*, San Francisco, CA: Pfeiffer.
A series of essays critiquing the field of organization development.

Bunker, B. and Alban, B. (1997) *Large-group Interventions: Engaging the Whole System for Rapid Change*, San Francisco, CA: Jossey-Bass.
For detailed descriptions of a wide range of large-group interventions.

Watkins, J. and Mohr, B. (2001) *Appreciative Inquiry: Change at the Speed of Imagination*, San Francisco, CA: Jossey-Bass/Pfeiffer.
For a full description of the five stages of Appreciative Inquiry process.

11

Roles People Play in Change

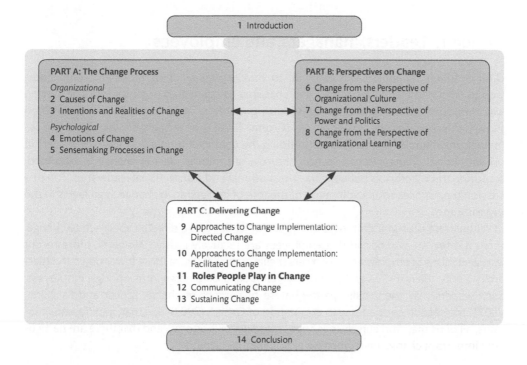

 ## Introduction

It is quite common to hear change talked about in quite abstract, even distant, terms, almost as if the organization itself were initiating or driving change. Yet, of course, it is the people within the organization who contribute to change and who play various roles to encourage, adapt, or slow it down. Directed and facilitated approaches to change have very different assumptions about the role to be played by leaders, as well as the role expected of employees. This chapter explores these and other ways of understanding the different roles that people may play in organizational change.

Section 1 examines the roles during organizational change of people internal to the organization. Leaders and employees may not view their jobs as being primarily about change, but they often find themselves being concerned with, or impacted by, change, which affects what they do in their jobs.

Section 2 explores the role of change agents, those for whom change is at the heart of their jobs. The skills required to be a change agent are examined, along with the different motivations for becoming involved in change. However, in the literature, there is also a growing emphasis on change agency as a distributed or shared role, suggesting that change happens only with the involvement of multiple players. People who see change management as central to their role include those in the HR function, internal consultants, and external consultants. The potential contributions and tensions around these different groups' involvement in organizational change conclude the chapter.

 Main topics to be covered in this chapter

- The role of leaders, managers, and employees
- The role of change agents

Section 1: Leaders, managers, and employees

Until relatively recently, it was common to view leaders as being those few senior individuals who had the power, vision, and charisma to change an organization. This notion was no doubt fuelled by the self-aggrandizing memoirs of so-called hero-leaders. Even though this 'belief in the power of one' (Gronn, 2000) is now being challenged, there remains considerable interest in understanding the contribution played by senior leaders in organizational change. In this section, the role of senior leaders in change is examined, exploring the differences between transformational and transactional leadership. The discussion then moves to an exploration of the role of leadership in change at all levels in the organization.

See Chapter 2 for more on hero-leaders: p. 26

When there is a significant focus on the senior leader, and a directed approach to change, there is often an assumption that employees are relatively passive. However, more recent interpretations of employees as followers (Kellerman, 2007) give those lower down the hierarchy a potentially more significant role. Leaders can also emerge from amongst employees. Such leaders may then challenge the nature or content of change (Zoller and Fairhurst, 2007). The section concludes with exploration of Oshry's (2007) idea that, in different situations, all of us may find ourselves as 'tops', 'middles', or 'bottoms', and that there are particularly important change roles when we are operating as 'middles'.

The role of leaders and leadership

The assumption that a **transformational leader** is required for radical, discontinuous change to occur is common amongst leaders and employees (Binney et al., 2005). Bass (1990) summarizes a transformational leader as someone who inspires employees to look beyond self-interest by giving them a vision, or sense of higher purpose about work, and communicates high expectations through: i) being charismatic and inspiring followers; ii) meeting their emotional needs; or iii) intellectually stimulating others by showing them new ways of looking at old problems. In contrast, a **transactional leader** responds to people's immediate self-interests and the relationship is one of exchange, with reward for performance and corrective action if something goes wrong.

See Chapter 12 for more on leader communication: p. 278.

The differences between leaders and managers have also traditionally been defined through lists of opposites (Grint, 1997). So, leaders focus on the long term, setting direction and challenging the status quo; managers focus on the short term, planning detail and accepting the status quo. Leaders have their eye on the horizon; managers have their eye on the bottom line. Leaders do the right things and have followers; managers do things right and have subordinates (Bennis and Goldsmith, 2003). This may imply that management is a lower level of activity that allows for continuous improvement, whilst only leadership can deliver discontinuous change. However, Kotter (1990: 103) argues that 'leadership and management are two distinctive and complementary systems of action' of equal value. He suggests people at the top of organizations need to provide both, because management is about coping with complexity, through planning and budgeting, whilst leadership is about coping with change and requires the actions of a transformational leader.

So let us look in Change in Practice 11.1 at three different leaders' involvement in changing one organization.

All three leaders at the BBC instigated change, supporting Romanelli and Tushman's (1994) findings that the installation of a new chief executive often increases significantly the likelihood of radical organizational change. This may in part be because new leaders have no vested interest in the past or in maintaining the status quo (Quinn, 1980). In addition, the arrival of a new leader often has symbolic impact (Pellegrin-Boucher, 2006), fuelling expectations of change in both insiders and outsiders, such as shareholders. Leaders themselves may also possess personal beliefs that, to be 'real' leaders, they need to instigate change (Grint, 2002). Which leader is going to stake his or her 'reputation by making an enthusiastic plea for the prevalence and value of inertia?' (Sorge and van Witteloostuijn, 2004: 1213).

See Chapter 2 for more on new leaders: p. 25

 Change in Practice 11.1

Three leaders at the BBC

In October 2010, the UK government announced that it had frozen the amount of money the BBC receives annually from the taxpayer, marking a 16 per cent decline in income in real terms. This continues a story of the BBC fighting for its independence and continued funding, which has played out over the last two decades under three different leaders.

The BBC, arguably one of the most prestigious media organizations globally, receives £3.5 billion of public money through the licence fee (a charge paid by UK residents for owning a television). In the BBC, the equivalent of the chief executive is called the Director General. John Birt was Director General in the period 1992–2000. Greg Dyke held the role in January 2000–January 2004. Mark Thompson has been the Director General since May 2004.

John Birt was an outsider, having run programming for a commercial television channel. As Director General, he was 'contemptuous of the entrenched culture, despised anyone who questioned his strategy' (*The Independent*, 21 August 2003), and believed that programme makers needed to be more aware of costs. Birt brought in strict financial controls with what many saw as puritanical zeal, and, using management consultants McKinsey as his advisers, introduced a centrally driven change programme called 'Producer Choice' that obliged programme makers to seek competitive quotes from outside companies, as well as internally, to reduce costs. Birt was deeply unpopular. Insiders likened him to Robespierre, Stalin, and Cromwell. Yet media commentators generally believe that the changes he introduced, and the licence fee that he renegotiated, actually saved the organization from being privatized or dismantled.

In his first week in the job, Dyke described his shock at seeing the pile of papers he was supposed to read over the weekend, a sign, he believed, of a risk-averse senior team who commissioned more and more analysis to postpone making controversial decisions. Dyke required papers to be one side of A4. In his first five months, Dyke visited all of the local radio and television stations, insisting that he wanted to meet real employees and drink tea from a mug in the canteen rather than the specially bought china teacups that had been required if Birt ever visited. Dyke claimed he found a climate of fear and thought that the BBC was 'hideously white', particularly at management level.

Dyke shocked many later that same year when the BBC moved the time of the flagship evening news from 9pm to 10pm, beating its main competitor, ITV, which was rumoured to be considering doing the same: 'The biggest impact of moving the news at two week's notice was the message it sent to the whole of the BBC . . . that we didn't have to be a large unwieldy organization that analyzed everything to death . . . we could move fast when we wanted to' (Dyke, 2004: 161). He also introduced targets for every part of the organization to increase their proportions of employees from ethnic backgrounds.

See Chapter 7 for more on coalitions: p. 144

See Chapter 10 for more on appreciative inquiry: p. 228

Two years into the job, Dyke sent three newly promoted BBC executives to the US to see what successful companies did there. They 'came back like converts, preaching the gospel of culture change' (ibid: 209) and became a powerful coalition for change: 'Making it Happen' was a culture change programme launched with seven different working groups looking at key areas such as creativity, audiences, and valuing people. To ensure that all employees who wanted to could be involved in the change, 'Just Imagine' was introduced, based on an Appreciative Inquiry method. Over half of employees participated and 25,000 ideas were generated, many of which were implemented locally. Dyke's assessment is that the 'Just Imagine' sessions 'changed the BBC profoundly . . . they reduced the "them and us" divide. People discovered that they didn't need permission to do things; they could do them for themselves. They also discovered management couldn't wave a wand and solve all their problems' (ibid: 219). Dyke resigned after a public inquiry criticized him for failing to investigate properly complaints about radio coverage of the British government's knowledge of Iraqi weapons of mass destruction. Thousands of staff cried and paid for a page advertisement in *The Telegraph* in support of their ex-leader.

During Dyke's tenure, headcount at the BBC had jumped from 23,000 to 27,000, and borrowing was at the £200 million limit and needed to be repaid promptly. Staff 'were on an absurd grief trip' (*The Independent*, 20 June 2005). Mark Thompson, who became the next Director General, was seen as a cerebral figure, happier writing his speech in the Bodleian Library in Oxford than in the staff canteen. Senior figures in the BBC spoke of him as being friendly in person, but operating in a self-contained way without a cadre of managers and communicators to put the positive case for change.

Thompson's vision for a 'stripped down, value-for-money, multi-media BBC' involved 6,000 redundancies, a review of hospitality and expenses, and relocating half of the staff outside London so that more money could be invested into programmes. However, few of his staff seemed to see or share the vision. He introduced a month-long staff consultation on his new vision, but, in a staff survey, only 13 per cent employees felt that Thompson and his top team listened to them—a significant decrease from the 53 per cent who saw Greg Dyke as a listening leader (*The Guardian*, 6 March 2006).

Commentators today tend to emphasize Thompson's political acumen and strategic thinking as a leader. A newspaper report early during his tenure quoted an industry insider, who said: 'Greg seemed to have little idea about the storm clouds that were gathering, but Mark knows all about storm clouds, because he was one of them when he was (leading) at Channel 4' (*The Guardian*, 13 December 2004). Thompson responded to the commercial sector's claims that the BBC was unfairly advantaged because of its sizeable government funding. By introducing what he called the Partnership Agenda, commercial media organizations could share BBC content. This silenced many critics when it came to the all-important task of renegotiating the licence fee, which was vital for the BBC's continued survival.

So, whilst all three leaders worked in the one organization, their approaches to change differed significantly.[1-7]

Leaders, through their early actions, may seek to amplify expectations of change and, at the same time, to challenge employees' current views of reality (Smirich and Morgan, 1982). In Dyke's case, there were two early signs that he wanted to change the culture of the BBC to be nimbler and less risk-averse: his insistence that written papers were a maximum of one side of A4 and the rapidity of the change to the time of the evening news programme. His promotion of the regional head from Northern Ireland to the executive team was a sign of his seriousness to make the BBC less dominated by those from London. Such moves can be seen as a mark of the new leader stamping his authority on the organization and as powerful symbols of his intent, a skill often associated with transformational leaders (Bass, 1990). However, employees may not always interpret symbolic actions in the way intended by the leader (Rickards and Clark, 2006). One of the authors remembers working in a consulting firm during a recession. The chief executive insisted that only discounted broken biscuits could be bought for staff. The gesture was intended to signal the need for cost control, but was interpreted as a lack of care for employees.

What does this case suggest about the importance of transformational leaders in change? Birt is now acknowledged for recognizing the potential impact of the digital revolution and his vision of a dominant BBC presence on the Internet is an example of how he fulfilled the requirement for a transformational leader to create a powerful vision for the future (Bass, 1990; Kotter, 1990). Yet he was far from charismatic in terms of his relationship with employees. Dyke was able to inspire and connect with employees, drinking tea from a mug with them in the canteen. However, he failed to engage well with the government or commercial media. Mark Thompson, Dyke's successor, was less charismatic and, despite trying to involve staff in consultation around his vision, his ratings in the employee survey demonstrate that he was far less successful at engaging them. However, his political acumen in offering BBC content to the commercial media did much to avoid a strategic threat. This suggests that change happens without leaders fulfilling all of the criteria of being a transformational leader. In addition, the fact that Dyke's change programme to increase workforce diversity was highly directed, whilst the culture change programme he initiated was very much facilitated, suggests that a single leader may adopt different approaches to change for different purposes. This supports the view of Bradford and Burke (2005) that leaders should have a range of styles rather than be either directive or facilitative. Similarly, recent research also suggests that the best leaders are both transformational and transactional in their behaviour (Rickards and Clark, 2006).

The approach to change adopted by a leader may also be determined in part by the type of strategy being pursued by the organization (Kakabadse and Kakabadse, 1999), rather than just the style and personal preferences of the leader. Strategies with a focus on cost, price, or

See Chapter 9 for more on directed and facilitated change: p. 194

numeric targets favour directive, controlling styles (for example Birt's 'Producer Choice'). Those concerned with issues around quality, creativity, responsiveness to market and consumer need, and high service orientation favour a more facilitated approach, with an emphasis on teamwork and open communication (for exmple Dyke's culture change).

However, it can be challenging for leaders to take a facilitated approach and to encourage employee participation. Shifting-problem solving to the people and tapping into resources at all levels can be personally challenging, requiring leaders to work in new ways—still in charge, but not in control. Such an approach can also be disturbing for employees who may want to continue to look to the leader to take the problems off their shoulders.

Even if leaders adopting a facilitated approach cannot control events, they can control to a greater extent how events are seen (Weick, 1979). The ability to 'provide meaningful interpretations for patterns of ambiguous information . . . has become the hallmark of the modern top manager' (Thomas et al., 1993: 240). This is sensegiving, or the management of meaning. It requires an ability to provide an 'intelligible formulation' of what for others may be a 'chaotic welter of impressions' (Shotter, 1993: 157). This allows others to make sense of situations collectively and can be what mobilizes employees into collective action.

See Chapter 5 for more on sensegiving: p.96

A more facilitated approach also requires humility in leadership (Morris et al., 2005). Whilst 'charismatics can charm the masses with their rhetoric and can draw the big picture . . . they deprive a community of its own power and utility' (Raelin, 2003: 46, quoted ibid: p. 1326), making the organization dependent on the decision-making and insights of the leader alone. Collins (2001) suggests that humble leaders, who are 'other-orientated' rather than 'self-orientated', allow more people to be involved in decision-making. Change initiated by such leaders tends be more long-lasting and sustainable because, by working in a facilitative manner, they develop others to lead beyond their own tenure. Such a view has much in common with Greenleaf's (1997) notion of **servant leaders**, who, rather than seeking glory for themselves, are keen to give credit to others.

Individual leaders at senior levels are often seen as disproportionately important and inextricably aligned with the fortunes of the companies they lead (Grint, 2007). A review by Khurana (2002) found that, over the last twenty years, chief executives were being increasingly viewed in the popular press as superheroes who single-handedly transformed their organizations' fortunes. Witness the rise and fall in the perceived stature of leaders such as Luc Vandervlede and Stuart Rose (Marks and Spencer), Kenneth Lay (Enron), and Tony Haywood (BP), all of whom found their personal standing rise and fall with that of their corporations. As Serge Tchuruk, the chief executive of Alcatel, the French telecommunications company, said: 'In times of crisis, executives are seen as imbeciles. In times of euphoria, they are seen as geniuses' (*Fortune*, 2002). However, 'by honing so relentlessly upon an individual, leadership tends to blind us to the complex, social nature of, particularly, large organizations' (Grey, 2002: 18). More facilitated approaches to change take the spotlight away from leaders to others in the organization so that leadership becomes less about the person in charge and more about how the collective are jointly engaged in action (Barker, 2002). This theme will be explored in more detail in the next part of this chapter.

In summary, leaders' roles in change are many and varied. Chief executives who are new to the organization tend to create expectations of change and bring in new perspectives.

Leaders may choose to adopt a directed approach at some times and a more facilitated approach at others; that choice may be influenced by personal preferences, but may also be constrained by the context. Successful change leaders exhibit transformational behaviours, with humility rather than charisma becoming seen as increasingly important for sustained change. This can be a significant relief to some leaders: 'As a leader trying to change performance of a charity or a business or a hospital, do you really need to pretend to be Nelson Mandela?' ask Binney et al. (2005: 10).

 Exercise 11.1

Think of a leader in an organization of which you are a member who has introduced some change.

● From what you have seen or heard, to what extent does the leader exhibit the traits of a transformational or transactional leader?

● Has he or she made any symbolic gestures in introducing change? If so, do you think you and others interpreted those symbolic gestures in the way in which the leader intended or were they interpreted differently?

● How would you describe the style of the changes that the leader has introduced—directed or facilitated or a mixture of both?

● How would you rate this leader for charisma, humility, and authenticity, and why?

● What do your observations tell you about the role that leaders play in change in practice?

The role of followers

Transformational leadership, as explored in the previous section, tends to lead to a particular view of employees, as well as of the leader. With:

> its emphasis on active leadership and unidirectional flow . . . (transformational leadership) may be likened to a hypodermic needle, with the active ingredient (vision) loaded into a syringe (words) which is injected into the patient (subordinate) to effect change.
>
> (Westley and Mintzberg, 1989: 18)

However, there is increasing interest in the notion of followership, which asserts that leadership can no longer be studied in isolation 'with only a small nod to followers', who are regarded as merely passive subordinates (Baker, 2007: 50). Flatter organizational structures and the creation of cross-functional teams can make it harder to know who is following and who is leading. Societal expectations of **Generation Y**, those who have entered the workforce between 2000 and 2010, influences what subordinates want and what role they are willing to play. 'One thing is clear,' writes Grint, 'leaders are in front of those they lead—but the enigma surrounds the issue of whether they are pulling or being pushed by those behind them' (Grint, 1997: 1).

Individuals may choose to play a role in change, regardless of what their bosses say or do. Indeed, at the micro level of individual jobs, recent research has identified the subtle ways in which individuals often modify what is written in their job descriptions, changing the task or performing the task differently, a phenomenon known as **job crafting**

See Chapter 9 for more on Lean: p 203.

(Wrzesniewski and Dutton, 2001). Job crafting can thus lead to incremental change as employees find better ways of performing tasks. When using methods such as Lean, such improvements are captured through process mapping by talking to, and watching, those working on a process rather than relying on what is written in manuals of policies and procedures.

Employees may also choose to personify change, identifying it with a particular leader because it meets their own psychological needs. It can simplify complex problems and make them apparently easier to tackle. Associating a change with a leader can be a means of simplifying it, dramatizing it and making sense of it. Identifying with famous figures can also make followers feel stronger and more powerful. However, it can also mean the abdication of responsibility, sitting back and passing the buck to the leader.

In choosing a directed approach to change, a leader may expect employees to do what they are told; if taking a facilitated approach, employees may be expected to be actively involved in change, sharing their ideas and knowledge to the common good. However, employees may not all respond in the same way as each other and they may not all behave as the leader desires. Conceptualizing employees as followers gives them a more independent role, and offers a richer way of understanding attitudes and behaviours towards leaders and change. As Kellerman (2007: 84) notes, 'followers who tag along mindlessly are altogether different from those who are deeply devoted'. She proposes a typology of followers based on their level of engagement, which is shown in Table 11.1.

This more textured approach to understanding followers is developed further in the idea that leadership is co-created between the leader and followers. Rather than being seen as passive, obedient people, followers play an active role in keeping the leader in control of a situation. Without their co-operation, the leader would have no authority, so leaders, as much as followers, are constrained to act in ways that are consistent with organizational goals, as understood by followers (Baker, 2007). Rost defines leadership as the 'influence

Table 11.1 A typology of followers

Isolates	Are completely detached; care little about what is going on around them, let alone what the leader says. 'By knowing and doing nothing, these types of followers passively support the status quo' (Kellerman, 2007: 87).
Bystanders	Observe, but do not participate; offer tacit support for the status quo, but can sometimes be persuaded to engage.
Participants	Engaged, but may be either for or against the leader. (This question does not even arise for isolates and bystanders.)
Activists	Feel strongly about their leaders and organizations, and act accordingly; can be highly supportive of leaders, but equally can undermine them if they believe that the leader is not acting in the interest of the organization.
Diehards	Rare amongst followers are those who are willing to endanger their own health and well-being in the service of their cause. Whistleblowers are examples of diehards.

Source: Based on Kellerman (2007)

relationship among leaders and followers who intend real changes that reflect their mutual purpose' (1993: 102). The relationship is based on influence that is multidirectional and non-coercive, and allows for there to be more than one leader, as well as multiple followers, and for followers to be active partners. The emphasis on 'real changes' suggests that leaders and followers work together to create substantive rather than superficial change, and have a mutual responsibility for the consequences that arise in the execution of their leadership relationship. Is this possible or purely aspirational? The perspective given in Chapter 6 would suggest such an approach to leadership and change will work only in cultures in which there is real dialogue between different groups, mutual trust and respect, and open communication. Some of the large-group method are expressly aimed at achieving this. From the perspective of power and politics, the question would be whether a sufficiently powerful and compelling mutual purpose can be identified that is able to supersede individual interests.

See Chapter 5 for more on trust and engagement: p. 97

See Chapter 10 for more on large group methods pp. 232–8

The notion of leadership as co-created by a leader and followers does not mean that they are equal. Although leaders and followers are so intertwined:

> the key distinctive role of leadership at the outset is that leaders take the initiative. They address their creative insights to potential followers, seize their attention, spark further interaction. The first act is decisive because it breaks up a static situation and establishes a relationship. (Burns, 2003: 172)

So although both are required, the leader's role is to initiate change. Goodwin (2005) uses the analogy of a conductor and musicians, who do not do the same thing in making music, but who are both essential to success. Such a view suggests that leaders and followers both have important roles to play in change.

However, leadership can also arise at any level, to initiate change or oppose it. Sometimes, formal leaders are those in denial of the need to change and it is individuals such as whistleblowers who seek to draw attention to the need for change. Zoller and Fairhurst (2007) introduce the term **resistance leadership** to describe the way in which leadership can emerge from amongst groups of employees who want to reject the changes being imposed by those in power. Resistant leaders schedule meetings with their fellow employees, and through conversation, create collective momentum to reject management's proposals and help others to imagine new, alternative possibilities. In doing this, they build resources for collective action. Resistance is often fuelled by perceptions of unfairness and injustice, accompanied by intense emotions such as disappointment, hurt, depression, ambivalence, and anger. 'Individuals may emerge as resistance leaders in the ways they are able to affirm individually felt emotions, labelling what is only vaguely felt or sensed' (Zoller and Fairhurst, 2007: 1350), so that they 'scaffold' or channel such emotion into collective action. In such cases, 'the "management of meaning" is as much the "management of feeling"' (ibid).

See Chapter 7 for more on resistance: pp. 150–9

In summary, employees may initiate changes to their jobs of their own accord or may choose to identify change with a particular leader. Reconceptualizing employees as followers suggests a number of potential roles in change and also allows leadership to be understood as co-created between leaders and followers. Resistance leadership may also arise from amongst employees.

The role of 'middles'

A further non-hierarchical perspective on the different roles that people play is offered by Oshry (2007). He draws attention to the way in which the same individual, in an organizational system, may at times be a 'top', a 'middle', or a 'bottom', in relation to others. These positions are therefore fluid, and vary according to the specific situations in which individuals find themselves. So a sales manager may be a 'top' in relation to her team, because she is their boss, but she may be a 'middle' in relation to the sales director. At the annual company conference, if her level is the most junior one present, the sales manager may feel like a 'bottom.' Alternatively she may feel like a 'bottom' when a new IT system is introduced with which some of her team are familiar with but she is not. Chief executives may be a 'top' to the majority of people in their organizations, but when change is imposed by new legislation or the industry regulator, they can feel like a 'bottom' player.

See Chapter 4 for more on the role of middle mangers: p. 80

'Middles', wherever they are in the formal hierarchy, often play significant change roles. Previously, we explored the important role that they play in helping 'bottoms' deal with the emotions associated with change because, unlike 'tops', they know personally the individuals in their teams. As they are also often far closer than 'tops' to the detail of work, they can be better placed to fine-tune or to adapt existing processes and procedures. 'Middles' also play a key sensemaking role for themselves and others around them. Yet 'middles' are only able to perform this role if they themselves are involved in the right meetings and therefore have information power. This can help to explain the strength of feeling aroused when someone's 'top' decides to exclude all but core members from team meetings. Not only do those excluded suffer a sense of demotion, but they also lose the source of information that enabled them to carry out their interpretive role for their own teams and themselves.

The impact of this interpretative role on 'middles' has been explored as part of a growing interest in understanding how individuals make sense of change and the implication that this has for their sense of who they are (their identity) and what they believe they are supposed to be doing at work (the job/role), and is often explored through the stories people tell about themselves and their context (Gabriel, 2000; Czarniawska, 1998). Exploration of the stories of 'middles', and particularly middle managers in a hierarchical sense (Sims, 2003; Thomas and Linstead, 2002), 'offers a narrative understanding of the peculiar loneliness, precariousness and vulnerability that characterize middle management' (Sims, 2003: 1195) as they seek to make sense of the changing organizational landscape.

'Middles' are under pressure to tell stories about their changing organization that make sense to three different audiences: i) their superiors or 'tops', who require a coherent account of what they are doing that is neater and tidier than the reality; ii) their subordinates or 'bottoms', who need to understand how what they are being asked to do fits in with the bigger picture to avoid a sense of meaninglessness; and iii) themselves, who are often fearful of losing the plot (Sims, 2003; Thomas and Linstead, 2002). This is a feature that Oshry (2007) graphically describes as 'tearing', as 'middles' are torn by demands and needs from those above them *and* below them. Juniors may view the stories told by 'middles' with suspicion or hostility, whilst 'tops' often publicly trample on and unwittingly destroy those carefully constructed stories (Sims, 2003). Amongst many sad stories, he offers that of a middle manager, Andy, who had been enthusing his team about their change project for two years, only to have it scrapped because of a political need to demonstrate to head office that costs were being got under control. What story can he tell now?

 Section 1 Summary

In this section, we have:

- explored the different behaviours of change leaders, examining the notion of transformational leaders;
- explored interpretations of employees as followers, which offers a view of them as co-creating leadership rather than being passive victims or mindless enthusiasts of change;
- examined the notion of 'tops', 'middles', and 'bottoms', and the critical role of 'middles' in change, working with emotional responses to change, implementing it, and interpreting it.

Section 2: Change agents

In section 2, we explore the skills and roles of different change agents, those for whom change is central to their work. It is becoming increasingly recognized that the label *change agent* 'is generic and ambiguous' (Buchanan, 2003: 646). The phrase can be used for leaders at the very top of the organization, although they are sometimes referred to as change champions (Peters and Waterman, 1983). A distinction is also sometimes made between the people who are responsible for the formulation and implementation of the change, whom Kanter, et al. (1992) call 'change strategists and implementers', and 'change recipients', who are those people responsible for implementing, adopting, or adapting to the change. Ford et al. (2008) define change agents in broader terms as 'those who are responsible for identifying the need for change, creating a vision and specifying a desired outcome, and then making it happen'. Our own experience of working in organizational change supports the view that rather than being defined as a single individual, change agents are more helpfully defined as a cast of characters involved in initiating, sponsoring, and managing change (Buchannan and Storey, 1997).

So, in this section, we explore some of the skills required of change agents, defined in this broader way, and look at the motivations for people wanting to be involved in change. We then turn our attention to different groups for whom change agency is central to their work: the HR function, and then internal and external consultants.

The skills required, and motivations of, change agents

Buchanan and Boddy (1992: 28) suggest that to implement change requires expertise in three parallel agendas:

1. the control agenda, requiring competence in a range of planning, budgeting, resourcing, and scheduling techniques;
2. the process agenda, in which the requirement is for interpersonal skills, and the ability to influence and work with power and politics behind the scenes;

3. the content agenda, which requires change agents to have some content knowledge about the change, for instance about IT systems or HR policies.

The control agenda involves change agents in key planning activities, identifying tasks, assigning responsibilities, agreeing the deliverables and deadlines, and initiating action. An elaborate project management structure is often put in place to ensure that the change programme is on track to deliver the change outcomes it has been designed to. This will generally include meeting and communication structures to ensure that the right individuals are aware of progress, and governance structures so that issues are resolved and decisions made with the appropriate information by the right people. Project management has became more widely developed and standardized, stimulated by the number and scale of large IT implementations. (Over one third of the global consulting market is in IT, according to Gross and Poor, 2008). Such approaches seek to align technology change with business change and are often referred to as 'total project management', or 'hard' change management (Paton and McCalman, 2004). Planning and monitoring can also be viewed as part of a public performance, which 'serves a symbolic, ritualistic and legitimating role for the change agent' (Buchanan and Boddy, 1992: 60).

See Chapter 7 for more on power and politics: p. 137

In contrast, the process agenda operates back stage in the territory of power, politics, and influence, where the change agent has a quiet word in the ear of someone senior, brokers a deal to ensure support from another key player, and pays attention to gossip and the word on the street. Knowledge of the content agenda, often because of job experience, can be critical to establishing change agents' credibility at the beginning of a change project (Maister, 2002). It is also often the reason for leaders choosing certain people to become change agents (Buchanan, 2003).

These three different agendas are all illustrated in Change in Practice 11.2. This example also illustrates some of the complexities that arise when a client organization works with external management consultants, which will be explored later in this chapter.

 Change in Practice 11.2

Unilever and Accenture in a US $1 billion outsourcing deal

In 2005, Unilever decided to outsource its transactional HR activities to contact centres run by Accenture. Outsourcing meant that instead of the personal service from HR to which employees were used they would access automated self-service-style HR. Many senior employees grumbled that the change meant they would have to do HR's work. North America and Europe were predicted to see significant savings in the cost of HR, but in lower wage parts of the world, such as Asia, the cost difference was often seen as insufficient to merit the hassle. A third of HR staff were predicted to lose their jobs.

Reg Bull, leading the Unilever team, was under intense pressure to adhere to the numbers and timelines in the original contract if the deal was to bring the savings that had been promised to the Unilever board. Accenture was under intense pressure to increase the value of the deal as it realized that it had underestimated the time required to implement the change.

Malcolm Howard, who headed the deal from Accenture, told a journalist, 'we worked really hard to put in place a governance structure that won't lead to us sinking under the weight of bureaucracy but where there's still a global hand on the tiller' (*People Management*, 2007). To govern the contract, there was an executive leadership committee at director level and a global management committee led by Howard and Bull. There were also country and regional bodies to escalate issues that they could not resolve themselves. The Excel spreadsheets required to coordinate a change of this scale were huge. Over forty different HR processes were included in the deal; there were many policy differences between countries, so these had to be aligned before the processes could be transferred to Accenture; each process had multiple steps; over ninety countries were involved, all on a different timescale; there were vastly more technical and cultural challenges than either Unilever or Accenture recognized before signing the deal, which had time and cost implications. A common complaint from the Unilever team was that as the plans were so complex that it could often feel that more time was spent on planning than doing. A common complaint from Accenture was that Unilever people did not take the plan sufficiently seriously and stick to it.[8-10]

The scale and scope of the change in Change in Practice 11.2 illustrate the need for the control agenda. The change simply could not be delivered without meticulous data and timescale tracking. Yet the process agenda was equally important, as initially there was significant resistance from employees at all levels within Unilever to a more self-service HR and there were limited financial benefits for lower-waged countries. This meant that Bull and his immediate change team within Unilever spent hours on the phone persuading and cajoling senior leaders across the globe to support the change, calling on the chief executive and the chief HR officer to use their influence on occasion. The business case became under increasing pressure as implementation uncovered unexpected complications leading to delays. This affected the potential savings from the deal for Unilever and the potential profit for Accenture, so both Howard and Bull needed to be active on the front stage and back stage of their respective organizations to keep their bosses informed and supportive. The content agenda was provided by change agents from Unilever's HR function, who were part of the team and brought their knowledge of Unilever HR policies and processes, and Accenture people, who brought knowledge of what was required to automate and outsource HR processes.

 Exercise 11.2

- How much importance does your organization or university give to issues of control? ?
- What does this tell you about what a change agent might need to do to bring about change in the organization?
- If you have been a change agent, how would you rate your expertise in the three different agendas?
- If you have experience of someone else being a change agent, how would you rate his or her expertise in the three different agendas?

So why do people want to become change agents and how do they experience the role? Buchanan (2003) interviewed change agents who were involved in a large hospital change programme in which there was a 'dispersed responsibility' model of change, and in which individuals from various functions and levels were seconded into full-time change roles for a number of months. At the beginning, most had knowledge of the content agenda, but little experience of change.

The themes that emerged from his study were as follows.

1. *Flexible drivers* This theme captures the flexibility that many respondents found they needed to adopt, particularly if they were acting variously as an agent for themselves, for their occupational group, for a senior manager, as well as for a project group or external stakeholders. 'Caught in this contradictory web of corporate and political agendas, they were agents ("double agents") for a plurality of interests' (Buchanan, 2003: 676). However, the flexibility contributed to the developmental nature of the experience.

2. *Determined contributors* This theme expresses the strong personal desire some had to be involved in change, sometimes because it was an opportunity to further what they believed was important, sometimes because involvement offered a change and a challenge from their normal routine.

3. *Pain absorbers* This label reflects the language respondents used to describe both their own personal stress and dealing with the stress of colleagues.

4. *Political manipulators* Most respondents used the term 'manipulation' to describe their approach to influencing colleagues. Much of the work to broker agreement and to gain support was carried out 'back stage'.

5. *Career enhancers* Nearly all respondents reported significant personal development as a result of being a change agent. Self-confidence, change management, interpersonal, political, and influencing skills all increased, and over half the respondents were promoted after their change agent role ceased, suggesting that involvement in change has positive career implications.

Such themes create a vivid picture of the lived experience of those playing the role of change agent. It also illustrates the different motivations for involvement in change programmes and the developmental gains incurred from being a change agent. However, the limitations of such an approach are that few insights are offered into how change agents should operate to be effective, as opposed to describing how they do operate. The approach also largely ignores the requirement of more concrete skills, such as the project management skills required for the control agenda that Change in Practice 11.2 showed can be critical.

The change agent role within HR

If being a change agent can enhance the career prospects of individuals, there are some commentators who hope that it is a role that can enhance the standing of the HR function. In the 1980s and 1990s, despite the opportunities and the rhetoric, few in the personnel/HR function were playing a change agent role (Guest, 1991; Hope Hailey et al., 1997). More often, HR people were experts in policy and process. However, Ulrich (1997: 31) offered a powerful vision of a reinvented HR function in which the competencies to manage change are 'the most important for success' as an HR professional and are critical to HR shedding some of the negative images from the past. 'Too often, HR functions are seen as lagging behind in innovation, flexibility and change, as the caretakers of tradition, embodied in policies and procedures, rather than as trailblazers', he writes (ibid: 218).

Ulrich's vision for HR has change agency at its heart. Does the rhetoric match the experience of those working in the function? A survey of personnel and HR managers by Caldwell (2001) found that 68 per cent saw themselves as change agents. Caldwell's analysis identifies four different change agent roles. He replicates the classical division of roles between leaders who initiate change and managers who implement it (Bass, 1990; Kotter, 1990), with his distinction between *change champions*, who are directors or senior executives who 'fulfill the ambitions of the HR professional to integrate business strategy with HR strategies of transformation and change at the highest level within the organization' (Caldwell, 2001: 45), who work within individual business units and translate the vision into practical actions. He makes a second distinction between the role of those who concentrate on one change project at a time, such as the redesign of a reward strategy, to whom he refers as *change consultants*, and *change synergists*, who strategically coordinate, integrate, and deliver complex, large-scale, and multiple change projects across the whole of the organization. The change consultant role combines the traditional process skills of HR interventions with the project management skills of planning, and adherence to time lines, deliverables, cost controls—that is, the control agenda—whilst, as Caldwell admits, the change synergist role often overlaps with the change champion.

His conclusion is that 'Personnel and HR managers in the real world will continue to live a variety of overlapping, conflicting and sometimes confusing roles, perhaps none more difficult to manage and sustain in the future than those of change agents' (Caldwell, 2001: 51). In addition, he found a fear at all levels that HR employees may be substituted for external consultants or interim managers with greater experience and expertise in change, a group to which we now turn our attention.

Internal and external consultants

There has been an exponential growth in the consulting market since the 1960s because the 'consultancy industry flourishes with this permanent drive for change in its client community' (Sorge and van Witteloostuijn, 2004: 1207). The worldwide consulting market was estimated to be worth US $210 billion in 2007, with 49 per cent in the US, 33 per cent in Europe, 10 per cent in Asia Pacific, and 8 per cent in the rest of the world (Gross and Poor, 2008). One survey revealed that 97 per cent of the top 200 companies in the UK and the US have used management consultants, and the ratio of consultants to managers has grown from 1:100 in 1965 to 1:13 in 1995 (McKenna, 2006: 249).

Key to most definitions of consulting is the distinction between those who have the power and authority to make decisions—line managers or senior leaders within the organization—and those who consult. So, Block (2000: 2) writes, 'a consultant is a person in a position to have some influence over an individual, a group or an organization, but who has no direct power to make changes or implement programs'. The notion of advice and help is also key to most definitions of consulting. Hagenmeyer (2007: 110) thus suggests that 'consulting is . . . a form of situation specific assistance provided by an independent expert that enables the person seeking advice to act in an "over complex" situation in which they did not feel competent to act in isolation'.

What role do consultants play in organizational change? There are numerous typologies that have been developed, but here we focus on those by two frequently cited writers: Block (2000) and Schein (1969; 1988; 2002). However, although management consultancy is being used more, questions remain about the value it brings. In CFO's recent survey of 400 finance executives, 55 per cent said they were only somewhat confident that their consulting spending was producing an acceptable return on investment, while 16 per cent said they were not confident or did not know (Banham, 2010). Doubts about the efficacy of consulting are apparent too in jokes about consultants, such as the one about them borrowing your watch to tell you what the time is, and then charging you a fortune for the privilege. They are also the focus of the critical literature:

> Consultants are 'love-hate' figures who occupy a highly marginalized position. Are they expert and essential helpers, or parasites whose skills are little better than those of the con man? Does the knowledge they disseminate—influential fashions in modern management—constitute a set of powerful organizational techniques, or is it snake oil? (Fincham and Clark, 2002–03: 10)

As Alvesson and Johansson (2002: 229) comment, 'few occupations trigger such strong reactions, both positive and negative'. So, in this last section of the chapter, we explore :

1. the benefits and limitations of using internal versus external consultants in organizational change;

2. the different roles consultants may play; and

3. a more critical approach to understanding the nature of consultancy.

1. Rationale for using internal and external consultants

External consultants work on a contractual basis with a range of different organizations and charge fees for their services, whereas internal consultants are full-time employees of one organization (McLean et al., 1982). Balgoun and Hailey (2004) view the use of external consultants as merely one choice in the change process and suggest that their use should be evaluated against other human resources within the organization itself. Whilst agreeing, Paton and McCalman (2004) suggest that the use of external consultants is driven either by internal skills deficit or the requirement of objectivity from an external person. In addition, as 'organizations have increasingly embarked on programmes of fundamental change . . . "change management" is now seen by many as a specialized skill that only outsiders possess' (Fincham and Clark, 2002: 9).

So what are the advantages of using internal consultants? For organizations, they may be a cheaper resource than external consultants, may be seen as more effective because they understand the culture and politics of the organization better, and, as employees, may be more committed to the long-term outcome of their work. Being an internal consultant gives an individual continuity and job security—unlike external consultants, who need to win clients to generate fees—and the satisfaction of seeing the longer-term impact of their work than is normally the case with external consultants.

However, there are a number of challenges to being an internal consultant. Arguably, those who are part of the organizational culture are less well placed to see the limitations of that culture because they are embedded in it. They may see fewer creative opportunities than external colleagues. It is also harder to be a prophet in your own land. As an insider, a consultant may be better placed to understand politics, yet his or her job grade and title may preclude him or her from gaining access to senior people. Indeed, a recent review suggests that the challenge for internal organization development (OD) consultants to get a 'seat at the table' is related to a number of interlinked issues. Internal OD consultants often lack competence in developing business plans (the control agenda), which means that senior executives fail to take them seriously. This, in turn, results in consultants' concomitant lack of confidence (Lacey and Tompkins, 2007). In addition, an internal consultant may also have a boss whose own interests need to be satisfied, but these interests may conflict with the internal client's request. Lastly, denial, defensiveness, and the need for challenge are part of the territory with change consultancy. Arguably, this is much easier to overcome as an external consultant, while the internal consultant has to be careful not to damage his or her reputation with senior people (Block, 2000) and longer-term career prospects.

Outsiders can fulfil a number of useful functions, introducing new ideas, providing external experience, and breaking resistance. The external consultant may also 'play the role of devil's advocate, exposing the client's weaknesses or articulating and sharpening her view of utopia. Moreover, whenever a change process turns into failure, the (un)skilful consultant may be targeted as the bogeyman' (Sorge and van Witteloostuijn, 2004: 1207).

External consultants, especially those working within the OD tradition, tend to see politics and the back stage activity of the process agenda as being outside their remit. This feature potentially differentiates their role from those internal to the organization. However, to claim no interest or role in politics may be disingenuous, because the ability to understand who has power and influence within the client organization, and to ensure that those people's views and expectations are sought out and managed, can be a critical to ensuring the long-term success of a consulting assignment (Keiser, 2002). 'When top management ceases to pay attention to a programme, no matter how much time, effort and money has been poured into it, the programme withers and dies' (Jackall, 1988: 140-1). One of the authors has experienced this when involved in a large culture change project for a European IT company. When the chief executive suddenly left, the whole programme—and our team of six consultants—were axed within a week then the new chief executive wanted nothing to do with his predecessor's regime.

2. Consultant roles in change

Within the literature, there is recognition that consultants may play different roles depending on the challenge facing the client organization, and the preferences of the contacts within the client organization, as well as the skills, expertise, and preferences of consultants themselves.

i) The expert

The consultant is in the role of expert when the buyer has already defined what needs to change, believes they know what needs to be done, and hires consultants for their requisite expert skills, knowledge, or information (Block, 2000). The assumption here is that consultants possess and use a toolkit of expertise. So, in Change in Practice 11.2, Accenture was hired for its expert knowledge of outsourcing HR, as well as its capabilities as a service provider, once the change had been implemented. In Change in Practice 11.1, McKinsey were hired for their expert knowledge in creating an internal market. Consultants' expertise may relate to specific aspects of an organization, such as IT or HR, or to particular approaches to change, such as Appreciative Inquiry, Lean, or Six Sigma. In addition, many consultants claim to have expertise around change management.

In their role as outside experts, management consultants can challenge the existing cognitive order. They can encourage double-loop learning by asking foolish or provocative questions, which can help organizational members to see their current reality differently. They may also encourage leaders to adopt more 'fashionable' approaches to change. The mere presence of management consultants in the strategy formulation process can also serve to signal symbolically that strategic reorientation and change is imminent and likely because expert knowledge is being applied to the challenges facing the organization (Pellegrin-Boucher, 2006).

However, for the expert role to work, there are a number of assumptions required, including that the client has correctly diagnosed the situation and correctly assessed the expertise of the consultant (Schein, 1988).

See Chapter 8 for more on double-loop learning: p. 166

See Chapter 2 for more on management fashions: p. 23

ii) The pair of hands

Consulting firms often have numerous levels. Individual consultants' fee rates are commensurate with level in the hierarchy, as is the role they are able to play within the client organization. So, even if senior partners in the consulting firm are working with senior leaders in the client organization providing new ideas and challenge, consultants lower down the pyramid may find that being hired as experts means actually carrying out tasks, because the client does not have the skills, time, or resources to do so. Block (2000) therefore distinguishes between the roles of 'expert' and 'pair of hands'. Junior consultants can be frustrated by this role and see it as not being a 'proper' consultant (Wiggins, 2005). Others regard doing menial, low-status activities as a way of building the relationship with the client, so that they can subsequently play other roles such as expert or process consultant. One consultant said:

> being a mistress is being the exciting consultant that really inspires the client to go and do something different . . . at the other end there's the wife that kind of does the ironing . . . and will deal with the little bits of dull stuff . . . and eventually they fall . . . in love with that consultant. (Ibid: 244)

iii) The doctor–patient model

When the consultant and client play the roles of doctor–patient, the client has generally not diagnosed the exact nature of the problem facing the organization, but is aware of some symptoms of 'sickness'. This may be poor performance in one division compared with another, high absenteeism or staff turnover, the results of the staff survey, or, as in Unilever's case, the fact that the cost of HR was far higher than for similar-sized organizations. In such scenarios, the consultant is invited in to find out what the problem is and to prescribe a programme of therapy or change to improve the situation. Consultants acting in such a role are likely to recommend directed approaches to change and therefore have a significant degree of power. However, this approach assumes that the 'patient' will reveal the nature of problem, which, given consultants are often seen as the hatchet men of senior management doing their dirty work, cannot be guaranteed (Schein, 1988).

iv) The process consultant

OD consultants focus on the process of change to help clients to diagnose the problem and to decide what kind of help they require, rather than to tell them what is needed. Process consulting is a facilitated approach to change as the consultant works collaboratively with the client in partnership to jointly explore the problem and co-create a solution. While the process consultant may make suggestions, decision-making about what to do remains with the client. A further feature of this role is the transfer of the skills to diagnose and fix organizational problems to the client. So organizational learning and capability building is often seen to be part of the change role of a process consultant (Schein, 1988).

See Chapter 10 for more on OD: p. 222

These different roles have different implications for consultants' power relationship with clients. In the 'pair of hands' role, consultants have little power or influence. When the consultant is in expert or doctor–patient mode, clients can be in a weak position because, in asking for help, clients are admitting to some kind of knowledge deficit and therefore vulnerability (Bloomfield and Vurdubakis, 2002). The process consulting role envisages a more equal distribution of power between client and consultant, yet here too Schein (2002: 24) suggests that the first task of a consultant is to build a helping relationship that redresses this power asymmetry. However, the literature often ignores the major source of power clients hold—reward power: they pay the consultants' fees. This can generate a feeling for consultants that they are only as good as their last meeting or email (Wiggins, 2005) and explains why Sturdy (1997b) refers to consultancy as an 'insecure business'.

 Exercise 11.3

Think about a situation that needs changing in an organization of which you are member. Imagine that you are the client and are hiring a consultant.

- What role would you want the consultant to play and why?
- What tasks and activities would you want the consultant to do?
- What possible advantages and disadvantages do you think might result from the consultant playing the role that you have chosen for him or her?
- What does this tell you about the different roles that consultants play in change?

In our experience, consulting roles can shift within a single meeting between a consultant and client, as well as over the lifetime of a change project. For instance, one of the authors was recently in a client meeting in which she: took the minutes because someone in the client organization was absent (pair of hands); talked about the key stages involved in Appreciative Inquiry (expert); was asked for an opinion on employee morale at the office that she had visited the previous week (doctor–patient); and then facilitated a discussion amongst the change team about some key issues for a paper that they needed to send to the executive team (process consultant).

3. A more critical view of consultants' role in change

Some journalists and academics are highly critical of consultancy in the sense of being both negative about, and concerned by, the potential for consultants to abuse their power. Critical inquiry has been prompted by the observation that 'consultant knowledge . . . appears mysterious and secretive, especially when managers remain addicted in the face of repeated and sometimes sensational failures' (Fincham, 1999c: 2). Consultants may talk about possessing professional knowledge (Maister, 1997; Alvesson, 1993), but unlike other professionals, such as doctors, lawyers, and accountants, no qualifications are required to be a consultant. Critical accounts therefore focus on consultants' role as sellers of change, exploring how consultants are able to convince clients of the worth of their ideas and advice (Clark and Fincham, 2002) and charge significant fees: 'consultants are drawn to money the way hornets are drawn to ripe cantaloupes at a late summer picnic,' write O'Shea and Madigan (1997: 11).

The critical approach views consultancy as 'the management of impressions . . . where each assignment provides an opportunity for a consultant to create or sustain his or her reputation' (Clark, 1995: 18). As management consultancy is a service, 'there is no complete physical form which can be perceived by the consumer at the pre-purchase stage, as an object or thing' (Oberoi and Hales, 1990: 70–1). Consultancy's intangibility leads to the emphasis on the interpersonal and social processes involved in impression management and the telling of persuasive stories of successful change (Clark 1995; Clark and Salaman, 2002).

It also leads to the view that consultancy is inherently a linguistic process, meaning that the words consultants use are essential to the process of consultancy and the way in which consultants sell and deliver change. Consultants use particular words to describe and re-frame the client's problem, and then to show that they have the experience and expertise to solve just such a problem. Their descriptions make the situation sound manageable and their help a logical consequence (Bloomfield and Vurdubakis, 1994). So, in the process of constructing, translating, or redefining problems, 'consultants do not so much target themselves at a particular niche, as seek to create a niche and then persuade clients that they are within it' (Bloomfield and Danieli, 1995: 28). Czarniawka-Joerges (1990) suggests that the words consultants use to reframe problems, and the ideas that they introduce allow the client to see and make sense of the situation in new ways, also help the client to see new possibilities for action. She describes these ideas and words as tools or 'linguistic artefacts', and the consultant as a 'travelling merchant, who sells tools for producing the meaning, and therefore the control, which is needed for collective action' (ibid: 142).

Commentators generally assume that consultants are motivated to construct the problem as a means of selling bigger, higher-revenue-earning jobs (Maister, 1997; Sturdy, 1997). In their advice to managers, O'Shea and Madigan therefore caution, 'it is the consulting company's interest to find trouble where you see calm waters. The consultant's goal will be to sell you much broader involvement than you might want or need' (1997: 301). Fincham too suggests that substantial levels of change have a powerful attraction for consultants because 'large scale projects mean large scale fees' (1999a: 11), but there is a delicate and complex balancing act required in trying to sell discontinuous, rather than incremental, change because the former can stoke manager's anxieties (Fincham, 1999b: 12). So consultants often have to scale down the original vision and provide 'quick wins' to 'manage' the client, reassuring them of their competence and winning trust.

Section 2 Summary

In this section, we have:

- looked at the expertise that change agents need to address the control, process, and content agendas, and at their motivations for involvement in change;

- explored the centrality of change agency to Ulrich's (1997) vision of a newly invigorated HR function;

- explored different ways of understanding the role of consultants in change, looking at the rationale for using internal versus external consultants, the various roles that consultants traditionally may play, and concluding with the challenges posed by a critical perspective on consulting that scrutinize the roles of selling, impression management, and the use of 'linguistic artefacts'.

 Integrative Case Study

The National Trust: A changing focus

The National Trust is a UK charity that looks after 350 historic properties, 700 miles of coastline, 600,000 acres of countryside, and has an annual turnover of £400 million. It employs 5,800 people. The original organizational purpose of conserving the past remains, but engaging visitors is now equally important. This means allowing visitors to handle certain objects, to experience playing billiards ,or to dress up in eighteenth-century costumes. It also means attracting a more diverse range of visitors. These changes are not being welcomed by all of the 55,000 volunteers who are essential to the functioning of the Trust and tend to be retired, middle-class people who work unpaid as tour guides and car park attendants.

'The Trust has come to be seen as something for the middle class. We want to embrace a wider sweep of society', said Simon Murray, a member of the senior management team (*Financial Times*, 2010). Another member of the senior management team said that the Trust is undergoing a cultural revolution and no longer wants to be seen as 'some sort of exclusive club for connoisseurs' (*The Guardian*, 2010). It is no longer just interested in stately homes, and recently bought Paul McCartney's house and Victorian workers cottages in the centre of Birmingham.

The role of the nine regional directors has become far more external facing, to attract new types of visitor, rather than just overseeing the properties in their region with the existing visitor profile. Following the redefining of their roles, all were asked to reapply for their jobs, but only a handful were successful, which sent shock waves through the organization. The forty most complex and high-priority properties are now run by newly titled 'general managers', many of whom were new to the Trust and had a business background. As part of the change to create a nimbler and more responsive organization, which meets the corporate goal of visitor enjoyment as much as conservation, general managers have been given more responsibility and accountability. This means that they have the authority to make decisions they believe to be in the best interest of their property. Before, decision-making, and therefore power, lay much more with the Trust's technical experts, whose areas of specialization range from archaeology and painting conservation, to landscape gardening, building maintenance, and land management. The technical experts have therefore needed to make a shift in their role, behaviour, and skill set, to become internal consultants who now need to regard the general managers as clients.

So the change in National Trust strategy has meant significant changes to the roles of many people within the organization.

Questions

1. What events serve to indicate to employees the scope and scale of the change being initiated by the leaders on the senior management team?

2. If you were the change agent, implementing this strategic change on behalf of the senior management team, what could you imagine yourself doing to fulfil the control agenda and the process agenda? What type of experience would be useful for managing the content agenda?

3. Using Kellerman's (2007) typology of followers, imagine how employees and the 55,000 volunteers may respond if asked to describe the change programme.

4. How might the descriptions of consulting roles help the technical experts to understand their new roles as internal consultants?

Conclusion

This chapter has explored the roles of multiple players involved in change in organizations. It demonstrates that change does not happen because one person, or even a number of leaders, want the change, but as the result of a powerful cocktail of context, the choices of leaders and followers, the behaviour and skills of change agents, and the dynamics of groups.

 Please visit the Online Resource Centre at **http://www.oxfordtextbooks.co.uk/orc/ myers** *to access further resources for students and lecturers.*

Change in Practice sources

1. BBC News (2006) 'Dyke: BBC is "hideously white"', 6 Jan. http://news.bbc.co.uk/1/hi/scotland/1104305.stm

2. Brown, M. (2006) 'Crisis management', *The Guardian*, 6 Mar: 1.

3. Dyke, G. (2004) *Inside Story*, London: Harper Collins.

4. Luckhurst, T. (2003) 'Can John Birt really hate Dyke's BBC this much?', *The Independent (Foreign edn)*, 21 Aug: 17.

5. Mulholland, J. (2009) 'At the heart of a cultural storm', *The Observer*, 17 May: 4.

6. Wells, M. (2004) 'The quiet revolutionary', *The Guardian*, 13 Dec: 2.

7. Wyatt, W. (2005) 'Shaken and stirred', *The Independent*, 20 June: 15.

8. Based on personal experience.

9. *HRO Today* (2009) 'Unilever finalizes contract terms in blockbuster HRO deal estimated to be worth over $1B'. http://www.hrotoday.com/news/3265/unilever-finalizes-contract-terms-blockbuster-hro-deal-estimated-be-worth-over-1b

10. *People Management* (2007) *Guide to HR Outsourcing*, London: CIPD.

Integrative Case Study sources

Desmond, B. (on behalf of Ashridge Consulting) (2010) *Developing Internal Consulting Capability with the National Trust: Submission Paper for the EFMD Excellence in Practice Award*, Berkhamsted: Ashridge Consulting.

Financial Times (2010) 'All eyes on how National Trust gets a helping hand', 9 July: 12.

Henley, J. (2010) 'How the National Trust is finding its *mojo*', *The Guardian*, 10 Feb. http://www.guardian.co.uk/culture/2010/feb/10/national-trust-opens-its-doors

Kellerman, B. (2007) 'What every leader needs to know about followers', Harvard Business Review, **85**(12): 84–91.

Further reading

Billsberry, J. (ed.) (2008) *Discovering Leadership*, Basingstoke: Palgrave Macmillan.
An excellent collection of important contributions to the field of leadership studies.

Buchanan, D. A. and Boddy, D. (1992) *The Expertise of the Change Agent: Public Performance and Backstage Activity*, Hemel Hempstead: Prentice Hall.
A classic exploration of the contrast between the public face of being a change agent and the hidden 'back stage' activity involved.

Communicating Change

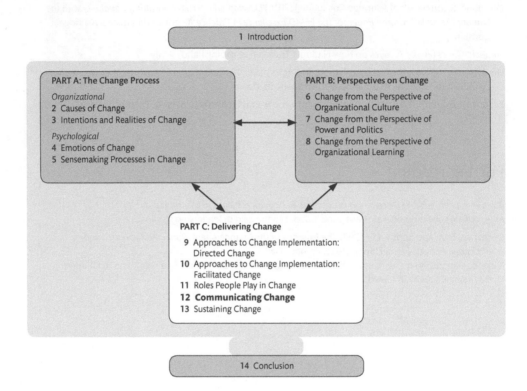

1 Introduction

PART A: The Change Process

Organizational
2 Causes of Change
3 Intentions and Realities of Change

Psychological
4 Emotions of Change
5 Sensemaking Processes in Change

PART B: Perspectives on Change

6 Change from the Perspective of Organizational Culture
7 Change from the Perspective of Power and Politics
8 Change from the Perspective of Organizational Learning

PART C: Delivering Change

9 Approaches to Change Implementation: Directed Change
10 Approaches to Change Implementation: Facilitated Change
11 Roles People Play in Change
12 **Communicating Change**
13 Sustaining Change

14 Conclusion

Introduction

At one level, communication is a very basic activity, involving the sending of a message and the receiving of that message by the listener. We are all practised communicators: we talk with others every day, debating, listening, inquiring, asserting, disagreeing, and encouraging. Communication is essential to building and maintaining relationships, but also to any kind of joint activity. So, for organizations, communication is not just an essential activity during change; it is essential to their very functioning. Without it, individuals cannot work together because communication is 'the central means by which individual activity is co-ordinated to devise, disseminate, and pursue organizational goals' (Gardner et al., 2001: 561).

However, although such an essentially human activity, there are many challenges with communication. As a message travels from communicator to listener, there are often various forms of 'noise' on the literal, or metaphorical, line, which means that the listener does not hear and make sense of the message in the way the speaker intended. Sometimes, that 'noise,' or interference, may be caused by the speaker using words that the listener does not really understand or because their tone of voice is alienating; sometimes, the listener cannot physically receive the message because the speaker is too quiet, or there is the equivalent of a crackle on the line; sometimes, the problems lie with the listener, who may not actually be paying attention, his or her mind elsewhere. We have probably all experienced the consequences of miscommunication in our personal life. In this chapter, we examine the challenges and consequences of communicating change for organizations.

 ## Main topics to be covered in this chapter

- Different approaches to communication strategy, including the links between approaches to organizational change and approaches to communication
- The tensions and practical choices in planning and delivering communication during change
- The communication challenges in particular change scenarios
- The limits of communication

Section 1: **Communication strategy**

In this opening section, we look at why communication is important to the successful implementation of change. In Chapters 9 and 10, different approaches to change were considered and, as will be explored here, those different approaches have a powerful influence on the communication strategy adopted.

The importance of communication in implementing change

Researchers are generally in agreement about the importance of communication during organizational change (Lewis and Siebold, 1998; Allen et al., 2007). Clear and consistent communication was seen as essential to successful change initiatives in a survey of over 400 leaders in large US firms (Smith, 1998). Communication was seen as the most important factor in achieving successful mergers, downsizing, and re-engineering, according to a KPMG survey of managers in Canada's top firms (Palmer et al., 2009). However, an in-depth study of twelve organizations involved in significant change found that ten had poor communication, leading to cynicism in employees (Beer and Eisenstadt, 2002). Lewis (2000), in a survey of those tasked with implementing change, found that they ranked communication one of the most problematic areas with which they needed to deal. However, 'although the centrality of communication during the change process is recognized, surprisingly little research has been undertaken' (Jones et al., 2004: 736).

For leaders, communication is often seen as a critical way of ensuring that employees understand change and are supportive of it. Leaders may also want to learn of potential flaws from listening to others. For employees, at all levels, communication, if done well, can be important means of reducing the anxieties that often accompany change. Communication can reduce their uncertainty about the strategy, as well as uncertainty about their own jobs and those of peers (Allen et al., 2007). Communication can also be seen as a means of re-assessing and renegotiating the psychological contract between employee and the organization (Hubbard and Purcell, 2001).

Communication strategies and their link with different approaches to change

In a world of finite resources and finite timescales, trade-offs need to be made, based on views as to what is most likely to be in the interests of the organization to ensure its ongoing survival and viability. Communication strategies involve making choices too because 'executives can communicate about anything, but they cannot communicate about everything,' (Clampitt et al., 2000: 41). This section explores two different approaches to understanding communication strategy:

1. programmatic versus participatory; and
2. a more differentiated approach to communication.

 Change in Practice 12.1

Commitment to communicate at Federal Express

When Federal Express acquired its rival in the air freight business, Flying Tiger Line, there were concerns from employees in both organizations about jobs, careers, issues of identity, and loyalty. Both organizations were in the same line of business, but employees in Flying Tiger were unionized and many had worked there for longer than Federal Express had been in existence.

Within two hours of the merger being announced on the Dow Jones Index, the Federal Express chairman and chief operating officer gave an unscripted and unrehearsed address over the company's satellite television network to 35,000 employees, who were based in 800 sites. The move was described as a merger, not an acquisition. Carol Presley, the senior vice president for marketing and corporate communications, said, the terminology 'didn't require a lot of debate or discussion . . . we wanted Flying Tiger people to feel we really did want them'.

In the months following the announcement, 'the FedEx management team would spend what some might view as an extravagant amount of time and money to communicate—talk *and* listen—with employees' (Young and Post, 1993: 32). Face-to-face meetings in all locations, company publications, videos, and television programmes were all used to explain and explore the consequences of the merger. In the words of the chief operating officer:

> Placing such an emphasis on internal communication has made us the company we are. We couldn't be anywhere near the size we are, and have the profitability or the relationship with our employees we have, if we weren't deeply into the business of communicating with people (ibid.)[1]

1. Programmatic versus participatory

A key influencer of an organization's communication strategy is the approach to change adopted. Those adopting a directed approach to change tend to have a *programmatic* communication strategy; a more facilitated approach to change tends to be accompanied by a more *participatory* communication strategy (Russ, 2008).

In **programmatic change communication**, the focus is on the top-down dissemination of information, telling employees about what will be happening, giving them facts and directives about how the change should be implemented, as in Change in Practice 12.1, in which senior leaders took immediate and early responsibility to tell employees what was happening and why. The purpose of such communication is to generate compliance, as well as to stimulate positive attitudes and beliefs about the planned change. It is not about seeking input. The underlying logic of this approach is that, with careful planning, the 'right' message will get to the 'right' people and this will minimize resistance and make implementation easier. A key success outcome of communication would be that employees understand the vision and see its relevance to them in their jobs. Power and control is held by a few decision-makers at the top of the hierarchy, so messages are sent down, but rarely upward (Russ, 2008). In this respect, the Federal Express example is a little different—it was reported that there was significant listening by senior leaders.

According to Lewis (2006), **participatory change communication** is used less frequently by organizations, but, ironically, has been the subject of greater research. The purpose of such communication is to gain employee input to shape the change programme, rather than to passively 'receive' it. The emphasis is, therefore, on two-way communication methods in which there is an opportunity for dialogue and listening, with communication seen as an ongoing activity, rather than a 'one-off event'. In the Federal Express example, there was significant two-way communication 'assuaging the concerns' (Young and Post, 1993) of staff, but this is not the same as actively seeking the input of employees to shape the change, which is the hallmark of true participatory change communication.

The benefits of programmatic communication strategies are that they can foster perceptions of organizational fairness—everyone is told the same information—and they are often highly efficient. The limitations are that leaders who use such approaches tend to assume that there is a perfect relationship between the message as sent and the message as received, a view that has been challenged from a theoretical point of view and a practical one (Shannon and Weaver, 1949, quoted in Truss, 2008). Programmatic approaches can also lead to an overabundance of unnecessary communication, which can increase employee uncertainty, anxiety, confusion, and disengagement.

Studies have shown that, with participatory approaches to communication, resistance tends to be minimized and motivation to implement planned change is enhanced; there is less employee uncertainty and increasing sense of control (Bordia et al., 2004); there is greater understanding of the rationale for change and overall satisfaction with the change initiative (Sagie and Kolowsky, 1994). Lewis (2006) also found a positive correlation between employees' perceptions that their input was valued and their evaluations that the implementation was 'successful'.

However, there are also some limitations inherent in participatory approaches. The original intent of the change can get lost in the desire to involve lots of employees and other stakeholders so that any sense of coherence, control, or direction is dissipated. This in itself can lead some to disengage. The approach can also be highly inefficient and can be perceived as such, particularly by leaders who are very task-focused. In addition, participatory approaches are sometimes perceived as insincere: a 'going through the motions' rather than a genuine desire to engage, listen, learn, and adapt the change programme. Participatory approaches can also put managers in the difficult position of being asked for something they are unable to provide, be that information, deeper understanding, resources, permissions, etc., which can perpetuate uncertainty.

Within organizations, the labels of communication and engagement can become political battlefields around which function 'owns' what is generally seen as the more important territory of employee engagement. Internal communication functions are now often renaming themselves the 'employee engagement function' but HR departments often claim this is 'their' area too. As the discipline of internal communication has evolved over the last twenty years, there has been a growing awareness that whilst leaders may have asked for products (communication plans, speeches, newsletters), what they actually wanted were outcomes, and the outcome required was initially termed 'employee satisfaction', while more recently 'employee engagement' has been emphasized. This is underpinned by a belief that engaged employees are more likely to be productive, innovative, and committed to the organization (Lewis, 1999), a belief that underpins facilitated approaches to change as well as participatory approaches to change communication.

See Chapters 5 and 10 for more on engagement: pp. 98, 200

2. A more differentiated approach to communication

Clampitt et al. (2000) offer a more nuanced and differentiated typology of communication strategies. Each strategy represents different beliefs and assumptions about the purpose of communication during change, as well as assumptions about the role of leaders and followers in change. Four out of the five approaches are, in essence, what we have described as programmatic communication, because leaders are directing and deciding what and how communication happens. Some of the benefits and limitations already enumerated will be in evidence here too.

- *Spray and pray*   This strategy is based on a belief that the more information there is, the better for employees. Leaders bombard staff with information and hope that they will make sense of it. Such an approach has the benefits of being seen to be open and transparent. However, it assumes that employees are able to sort out what is important from what is irrelevant and allows leaders to abdicate any meaning-making responsibilities. When working with leaders, one way in which we have demonstrated the limitations of this approach is by showering them with pieces of a jigsaw puzzle. When they cannot work out what the pieces mean, we shower them with more pieces to represent leaders' frequent response to employees' claims that they do not understand, which is simply to give them more communication. In fact, what is required is for people to be shown the picture on the box. Similarly, without leaders describing the context, the purpose of the change, or the key elements, information only confuses and over-whelms.

- *Tell and sell*   With this strategy, leaders do describe their organization's change equivalent of the picture on the jigsaw box: they tell employees what the key issues are and then sell the change solution that they, as leaders, have decided to pursue. Leaders often spend much time crafting their speeches or polishing their PowerPoint presentations. Such an approach is consistent with a directive approach to change. An underlying assumption is that leaders have the knowledge about what change is necessary, and that employees are passive recipients both of communication about change and indeed of change itself. Little time and energy is therefore spent on engaging in dialogue with staff or asking for feedback.

- *Underscore and explore*   The difference between 'underscore and explore' and 'tell and sell' is that, in this case, leaders are not only interested in disseminating their key messages; they are also interested in exploring those issues with employees, engaging in dialogue to foster understanding, and listening out for unrecognized obstacles and employee views and feedback. An assumption here is that employees need to have the opportunity to actively explore and make sense of the change. However, leaders still see themselves as having the licence and authority to author and drive the change. So although there is opportunity for some engagement, employees are not afforded the status of equal par-ticipants and co-creators in the change. Change in Practice 12.1 reflected this approach to a large extent.

- *Identify and reply*   This strategy focuses on employees' issues, so is not programmatic, but, without any commitment to alter the change programme as a result of the in-tervention, neither is it really participatory. Leaders focus on listening to identify what is preoccupying staff and then respond to those concerns. The assumption is that employees know what issues are of interest and concern to them better than senior management, and therefore they set the agenda. This approach assumes that employees know what questions to ask. Whilst logically feasible, the authors, in over twenty years of consulting, have never encountered an organization that adopted this approach with employees, although some do with other stakeholder groups or audiences, to use communication language, such as customers, clients, or patients.

- *Withhold and uphold*   With this approach, communication is on a 'need to know' basis. Leaders adopting this approach sometimes assume that employees are not so-phisticated enough to understand what is happening and, therefore, not worth com-municating with. Alternatively, they may see information as a source of power and therefore control communication tightly or, as Bridges (2003) suggests, they may withhold until they themselves know the answers.

See Chapter 7 for more on sources of power: p. 138

These five different strategies can be visualized in a crescent-shaped continuum, with strate-gies towards the middle offering employees most guidance in terms of prioritizing messages (see Figure 12.1). Those at the extreme provide either too much or too little or no communi-cation, making it hard for employees to make sense of organizational change.

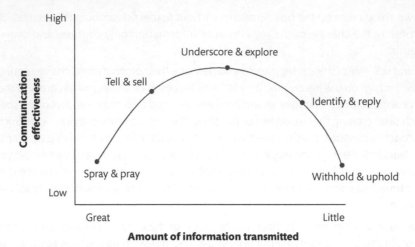

Figure 12.1 Communication strategy continuum

Source: From Clampitt et al. (2000)

 Exercise 12.1

Think of a change that you have experienced as an employee of an organization or as a student at your place of study.

- What type of communication strategy do you think was being employed, whether deliberately or not, when you learned about the change?
- What were the benefits and limitations of the communication you experienced?
- What alternative choices do you think those planning the communication could have made? And how would they have fared in terms of benefits and limitations?

 Section 1 Summary

In this section, we have:

- considered the reasons why communication is an essential element of implementing change;
- explored different ways of understanding communication strategies and how they are inextricably linked with the adopted approaches to change.

Section 2: **Tensions and choices in practice**

This section begins by asking: what are the practical choices facing those responsible for delivering communication during organizational change? The choices sound relatively simple, but mask some more complex dilemmas and tensions. We explore these choices in general and then as they relate to specific communication channels or media. These choices may relate to the strengths and limitations of different media, and the phases of the change programme.

Tensions and trade-offs

Whatever the communication strategy adopted, deliberately or by default, there are always a number of choices to be made at a tactical level by those responsible for communicating change.

- What should be communicate and what should be ignored or not mentioned? Communication professionals often refer to this as 'the message'.
- With whom should leaders communicate? The target of communication is often referred to as 'the audience'.
- How will leaders and employees communicate? Communication professionals refer to this as choosing which 'media' or 'channel' to use.
- Is the communication one-way or two-way?
- When and where will communication occur? Those charged with leading communication in organizations often refer to this as the 'communication plan'.

Efficiency or effectiveness?

At the heart of the choices that need to be made by those leading change or their communication advisers is the age-old tension between efficiency and effectiveness. For instance, if a merger between two divisions of a global organization is about to take place, it may be decided that the easiest way of communicating this change is to email news of the impending merger to all employees in the two divisions. This may be efficient and easy to execute, but is unlikely to foster much understanding or engagement to the change. Face-to-face communication is more costly in terms of time and effort, but, because it is two-way, it is a much more dynamic way of communicating than email and is therefore more likely to foster employee engagement, as demonstrated in Change in Practice 12.1.

Who gives the message?

Employee surveys routinely find that employees prefer to find out news from their line managers. Line managers, as they know their staff more intimately than senior leaders, are better able to contextualize and tailor communication to employees' specific needs and interests. They are also more likely to be trusted. However, often middle managers are themselves unaware of the full detail of a change and so do not have enough information to share with their people. Cascades, or team briefings, which are designed to flow down the hierarchy, with individuals hearing from their bosses before briefing their own teams, are intended to give line managers the information that they need. However, they are subject to significant variation and distortion in the way in which messages are given (think of an organization-wide game of Chinese whispers); the word 'cascade' suggests information pouring down the organization, but in reality it can take a long time for the information to reach the lower levels. As implementation is often patchy, with only some leaders taking their

See Chapter 11 for more on the communication challenges of middle managers: p. 252

communication role seriously, this can leave significant portions of employees without communication, especially if the blockage occurs high up the organization. So cascades, whilst giving a role to line managers, tend only to be used for routine change communication such as programme updates rather than for more significant announcements.

The alternative, especially for announcements about significant organizational change, such as mergers and acquisitions, or downsizing, is to use the chief executive or senior leaders to communicate to as many staff as possible. Because they are decision-makers and architects of the change, they are better placed to explain the rationale for, and broad parameters of, the change. However, not all organizations have their own television networks like Federal Express, which allow leaders to reach employees in multiple locations simultaneously. Other options include large-scale face-to-face events, including road shows travelling to key locations. The very fact that senior leaders are communicating about a change signals its importance. It can also make employees feel valued that their leader is taking the time to communicate with them. However, road shows can be costly in terms of the executives' time and the opportunity cost of large numbers of employees sitting in a room listening to their leaders. There can also be high environmental costs if executives are flying around the world. If senior executives visit only key sites, a communication imbalance is created, which may reinforce or exacerbate existing divisions of who is important and who are second-class citizens. In addition, by communicating to large employee groups, leaders can rarely tailor their message to specific groups or answer the all-important question of 'what's in it for me?' (WIIFM?). Communication professionals often differentiate between broadcast—talking to many—and narrowcast—communicating to more specific discrete groups. There can also be a danger of senior executives using words that mean little to those lower down the organization, either because they are couched in management jargon or because they relate to issues that are important for leaders, such as shareholder value, and return on investment (ROI), but which may lack direct relevance to the forklift driver or packer in the warehouse.

Leaders communicating through video links or teleconferencing with slides has the virtue of getting the message out quickly and potentially to all staff, but it is challenging to make them interactive (Larkin and Larkin, 1996). Also, without a live audience, it is hard to make such media motivating, even if they can be a good way of sharing information.

When to give the message?

Another tension revolves round the timing of communication. Is it preferable to wait until most of the details of a change programme are known, in the belief and hope that this will reduce employee uncertainty? Or is it better to communicate information as it emerges, even if the picture is incomplete, so that employees are not left in a vacuum, waiting and wondering?

Further tensions hover around the question of who should receive communication first? Should communication timing follow hierarchical lines, with more senior people being told before more junior ones, so as not to undermine the credibility (and status needs) of those further up the hierarchy? However, as explored earlier, this can slow down the dissemination of messages. Should those directly affected by the changes hear first? But can they easily be segmented? Many organizations uphold the principle that staff should always hear about changes internally before reading about them in the newspaper or hearing about them on the radio. However, if a change is share-price-sensitive, because it signals a major shift in an organization's strategy or prospects, there are legal constraints about the timing of communication. Many organizations opt to simultaneously release information to the stock market and employees through email or the intranet at 7am when the stock market opens.

Let us now look at how some of these tensions were addressed in one organization and how the communication approach is also sometimes a reflection of a leader's preferences.

 Change in Practice 12.2

Communication at Sun Microsystems

Sun Microsystems was a company selling computers. Founded in 1982, it was headquartered in California, with its main manufacturing sites in Oregon, US, and Linlithgow, Scotland. The company was badly affected by the dot.com crash. Shares dropped from a high of US $64 in 2000 to US $5 three years later. A series of sites were closed and employees laid off. In 2003, when Terry McKenzie joined as director of global employee communications, employee morale was low, and was worsened by the negative perceptions of the company in the market and the media. The company's new business strategy was to shift the focus from only hardware to solutions and systems. McKenzie's task was to build an informed, engaged, and aligned workforce who would deliver the new strategy.

The goal of the overall strategic communication campaign was to get employees to understand, accept, and act on difficult decisions aimed at turning the business around. McKenzie developed what she called the KAA model. For every piece of communication, the current and desired state of employees' knowledge, attitude, and action (KAA) was mapped to identify clear communication objectives. The KAA model incorporated four different phases of change: awareness; understanding; acceptance; and action. Each phase required a different communication approach, messages, and channels. 'Think of a shifting balance between one-way and two-way communication as you move through the stages. During the awareness phase, e-mails, audiocasts and webcasts are good methods to get basic messaging across. At the understanding phase, communication becomes all about the conversation and active listening', reported McKenzie (Melcrum, 2007a: 55).

By 2006, business performance had improved, when there was another significant change: the transition from the company's founder and chief executive, Scott McNealy, to a new chief executive, Jonathan Schwartz. Although the latter had been with the company for ten years, the transition evoked a great deal of emotion and also some uncertainty, as Schwartz's strong software background made many of the hardware engineers fear that he would move the company further towards software and away from their, and the company's, traditional core area of expertise, hardware.

The change of chief executive brought about a change in the openness and transparency of the communication culture, giving people more information, underpinned by a belief that they could handle the truth. Mckenzie described Schwartz as taking the company into adulthood and so the communication objectives then developed into: i) telling employees the unvarnished facts and letting them have the information that they need; ii) actively listening and genuinely changing plans to incorporate their suggestions; and iii) having the courage to communicate both successes and lessons learned.

Schwartz at the time was one of the most active chief executive bloggers, blogging at least twice a week. Blogging within Sun then became a key communication channel, with over 10 per cent of employees blogging. Together with message boards, blogs became a significant contributor to the flow of information and knowledge virally around the organization.

However, not everyone was positive about Schwartz blogging. There were issues with the company's lawyers and PR people at some of his comments, and, as one journalist wrote, 'as much as I'm impressed by Jonathan's blog, I wonder how he has the time to blog when he has a company that desperately needs management steered in the right direction' (Washington Post, 2006).[2-4]

Choice of media according to 'richness'

Lengel and Daft (1988) conceptualized different types of communication channel or media according to their 'richness'. **Media richness** refers to the level of cues and information available to a receiver of communication (see Figure 12.2). So, for instance, an announcement of the forthcoming merger between Federal Express and Flying Tiger Line, pinned on the notice board, would be described as a lean communication medium because, other than the words on the page, there are no additional cues or information to guide the receiver's understanding. The audiocasts used at Sun allow the receiver to hear tone of voice, so are a little richer. Face-to-face meetings would be described as a rich communication medium, because there are many other cues such as voice, who sits where, and how other people respond. These additional cues help employees to interpret and gauge the scope and scale of the change, to assess their confidence and trust in leaders, and to engage in dialogue.

Lengel and Daft recommend that routine, non-controversial communication should use lean media to avoid overloading people with information. In contrast, they see challenging or personal issues as requiring face-to-face communication. This is a contingency approach to communication. In Sun Microsystems, lean media, such as emails and audiocasts, were used at the beginning of the new strategy communication campaign, but later involved small-group face-to-face conversations. Certainly, in the 1990s, the general view was that, for communicating 'difficult' messages, face-to-face was best (Young and Post, 1993; Larkin and Larkin, 1996). However, advances in technology such as social networking and changing attitudes from younger people who have grown up using Facebook suggest that such assertions may not always be valid. New social media, which allow two-way communication without it being face-to-face, are considered later in this section.

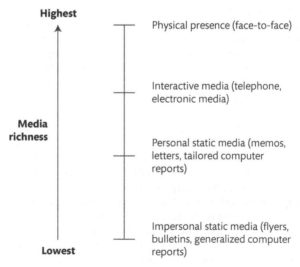

Figure 12.2 Media richness hierarchy
Source: Lengel and Daft (1988)

Choice of media according to the phases of change

Different stages are in evidence in Change in Practice 12.2, with Mckenzie differentiating between awareness, understanding, acceptance, and action, and using lean media for awareness, but richer, face-to-face meetings for understanding and acceptance. As she herself said, 'think of a shifting balance between one-way and two-way communication as you move through the stages'.

The different psychological stages associated with individuals' experience of change and transition have been used successfully to guide internal communicators' choices (Wiggins, 2008). As in Figure 12.3, the transition curve is, for practical purposes, divided into four quadrants. The horizontal line across the middle recognizes that, above the line, at the beginning and end of transitions, individuals are more willing to overtly talk about their emotions and attitudes towards the change. Below the line, when they are moving into the emotional territory of anger and depression, they are more likely to hide their feelings. This has consequences for the communication approach. The midpoint line dividing the curve into left and right halves suggests that when employees are psychologically occupying the left-hand side, they are focusing on the past, whilst on the right-hand side, they are more orientated towards the future. This too has communication implications.

See Chapter 4 for more on stage models: p. 69

The top-left quadrant is when employees first hear about the change. At this point, employees' greatest communication need is for information about the reasons for the change, the likely outcome, and the next steps. This is the K for 'knowedge' in Mckenzie's KAA model at Sun. Broadcast media with senior leaders, informing staff about what is happening, are appropriate at this stage. However, because employees may also be worrying about what may happen to them personally, some information is simply not heard. Repeating the message often

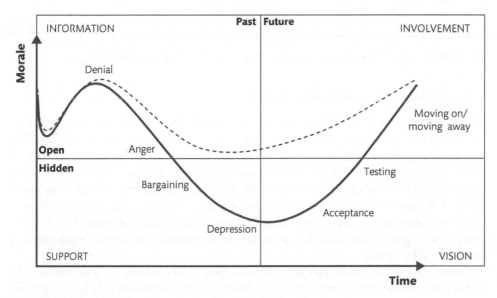

Figure 12.3 Communication choices depending on psychological stages

Source: Based on Wiggins (2008)

is therefore important at this stage, even though, in our experience, leaders may say: 'Well, I've already told them. Why do I have to tell them again?'

The bottom-left quadrant in Figure 12.3 is the point at which employees may be perceived as being resistant or ambivalent about change. Here, what is required is support. This is where middle-manager communication is critical, and involves listening to employees concerns and questions in small groups or one-on-one. This is perhaps where Clampitt et al.'s (2000) 'identify and reply' strategy may be most useful.

This is often one of the most challenging phases of change communication: many managers are uncomfortable dealing with the personal and emotional content of this type of face-to-face communication, and they themselves are rarely in possession of the facts to be able to reassure staff. They can resort to bland, patronizing statements such as: 'Oh, I'm sure you'll be fine.' In our experience, reminding people of what is staying the same, as well as what is changing, can be helpful in this quadrant.

A great temptation for leaders and managers is to want to talk about the future, the positives: Kotter's step four, the vision. Whilst this is hugely important, from personal experience, the timing of this is crucial. Only when employees are in, or moving towards, the bottom-right quadrant are they really able to hear and absorb such information. However, talk about the vision, and engagement in what it might mean for them and their teams, can help to 'pull' individuals through the curve. A critical role for communication, according to this model, is therefore to match the appropriate communication needs and media to the psychological state of the majority of employees. Change communication done well will not prevent employees experiencing the transition curve, but it can help them through the curve more quickly and can mean that their 'curve' may be less steep (see the dotted line in Figure 12.3).

Summarizing the strengths and limitations of different media

Some strengths and limitations of different media have already been mentioned in Change in Practice 12.1 and 12.2, and in relation to the tensions and choices that communicators face. This section concludes with additional exploration of specific channels.

1. Face-to-face, leader-led communication

'The reason why many organizations may encounter difficulties in reducing uncertainty during change is the often one-way nature of communication strategies' (Allen et al., 2007: 207). The real strength of face-to-face communication is that it is potentially two-way and rich, to use Lengel's and Daft (1988) terminology. However, the degree of two-way communication depends on the format face-to-face communication takes. It may involve large-scale meetings with hundreds of employees present, focus groups with cross-sections of employees, cascades or team briefings that flow down from the hierarchy with additional tailored content for each specific layer and location, or simple one-on-one communication between a boss and a subordinate.

There are those who advocate the absolute primacy of face-to-face communication: 'The best way to communicate a major change to the frontline workforce is face-to-face. Do not use videos. . . do not introduce the change in a company publication and do not hold large meetings with frontline employees', assert Larkin and Larkin (1996). However, as already

See Chapter 7 for more on resistance: p. 150

explored, face-to-face communication may not always be feasible. In addition, certain facilitative approaches to change such as Appeciative inquiry and Future Search have developed specific techniques for engaging large groups of people face-to-face.

See Chapter 10 for more on faciliated approaches: p. 219

Leaders often play a particularly important communication role in both announcing the change and communicating the vision. Referring to political, rather than business or organizational, leaders, Goodwin (1998) claims that a leader without communication skills will fail to have impact. Yet according to a communications consultant, the majority of senior business leaders 'don't make the strong audience connection—visceral, personal and emotional—needed to inspire trust and action' (Morgan, 2001). Implicit in this comment is an assumption that the role of the speech is not to give information, but to make an emotional connection that moves others to think, feel, and behave differently. The words of William Hazlitt (1807), quoted in Gill (2006), seem particularly apposite here: 'the business of the orator is . . . not to inform, but to rouse the mind . . . to add feeling to prejudice, and action to feeling.' As another writer says:

> A speech is part theatre and part political declaration; it is personal communication between a leader and his people . . . it is at once a thing of great power and great delicacy . . . A speech reminds us that words . . . have the power to make dance the dullest beanbag of a heart. (MacArthur, 1999: xxiv)

Two skills are essential to the use of inspirational language: *rhetorical crafting* and *framing* (Georgiades and Macdonnell, 1998). However, such skills do not belong only on the podium. When the purpose of a communication is to persuade or motivate, framing and rhetorical crafting apply equally to one-on-one and small-group conversations (Gill, 2006). **Rhetorical crafting** is the art of verbal expression, which can involve the use of repetition that aids recall, the use of different rhythms to keep the audience's interest, and the use of rhetorical questions and dramatic pauses, as well as the use of stories and metaphors.

Framing requires understanding your audience, and then connecting your message with their needs and interests (Conger, 1999). Effective leaders do this by listening to what matters to people from multiple conversations, asking questions of those they will later seek to persuade and experimenting with their argument/line of reasoning with trusted colleagues. Through such a process, framing develops a shared sense of destiny through dialogue (Kouznes and Posner, 1991), people feel that they have a stake in common problems (Goodwin, 1998), and leaders can create a sense of ownership for, and commitment to, organizational change and the creation of a new shared future.

Gill (2006) describes the following specific tactics for framing.

1. Catching attention, perhaps with a joke or a personal story with which the audience can identify (Morgan, 2001)
2. Timing: knowing when to introduce an initiative and when to pause
3. Appealing to common interests
4. Avoiding statistics where possible
5. Using vocabulary that matches the audience's own and limiting the use of multisyllabic words
6. Showing feelings through words, voice, posture, and gestures
7. Authenticity (which can be a particular challenge if someone else has written a speech)

8. Inclusivity, which involves framing your speech as 'we' and 'our', rather than 'I' (such inclusive language unifies rather than divides followers)

9. Presenting a solution as well as a challenge and then 'reading' an audience's response through non-verbal signals to generate agreement and commitment to the message, adjusting it if necessary

10. Ideally, the audience should be involved in some form of physical activity related to your message (Morgan, 2001). In large-group settings, we have seen the audience encouraged to shout a slogan, to sing, to sign up on a large wall, to write commitment cards, and to use electronic voting devices to show their commitment to a particular change. This introduces an element of two-way communication into what is otherwise one-way.

 Exercise 12.2

Find an opportunity to hear a leader talking about change—either someone in your own organization or at your university, or from listening to some famous speeches on the Internet.

- Evaluate the success of the speech as a communication event.
- What did it make you think and feel?
- Were you part of the target audience? If so, do you think you responded in the way the speaker intended?
- What reframing and rhetorical devices did you notice? Were they effective or not? If so, why?

A risk with paying too much attention to leader communication is that is gives undue prominence to large events. Communication does not stop only because the formal set piece has come to an end. As will be explored at the end of the chapter, alignment between different communication channels and employees' general experience in the organization critically influences whether or not formal communication and the big set pieces are believed. A client recently told of us of a large meeting to tell staff that the organization was being wound down. Whilst one of the leaders was giving a speech, the other leaders sat working on their Blackberries in full view of staff. When later challenged, one of them sheepishly said, 'Sorry. I was only trying to keep up with my emails', seemingly oblivious to the unintended message of lack of care that he and his colleagues were sending. However skilled at rhetoric and framing the leader making the speech, the behaviour of his co-leaders will have tarnished any positive impact that he may have hoped to make.

Line managers' endorsement or rejection of leaders' communication also significantly impact the effectiveness of the latter's communication (Bass, 1990: 25).

2. Print, publications, and intranets

Print and publications, such as company newsletters and magazines, are generally good for sharing stories and photos of life and people within the organization, including demonstrating progress with change programmes. Because they have physical form, they create a sense of substance and permanence, and can be perused on the way home or by employees' families. However, they are not suitable for communicating fast-changing news or for making announcements. These are better handled by emails or news sites on the company intranet. Some organizations provide a weekly news round-up of changes and news to try to avoid overloading employees with information. Large organizations such as Unilever and BT often have sophisticated teams of journalists to keep employees updated daily with changes to products, advertising campaigns, media reactions, share price changes, and departures and arrivals in the senior ranks. Such news sites are often also used to support major announcements or leaders' speeches by carrying reports or summaries of what was said. Many such sites can now also include video clips or podcasts of news or leaders' speeches, so that those who were not there or who are not based in offices, such as salespeople, can still be kept up to date. These also tend to be divided to provide content relevant for specific audiences or employee groups.

During a merger or immediately after the announcement of significant changes, weekly or fortnightly branded newsletters can be a means of keeping people informed of the latest decisions that have been made. The branding is important to create 'stand out' from all of the general communication and emails that people receive. Print can also be used as part of a change campaign on a particular issue targeted at a particular audience. For instance, several years ago one of BP's UK refineries wanted to improve its safety record. Rather than send out more safety bulletins and pin them on notice boards, a fortnightly newspaper was produced in the visual and easy-to-read style of British tabloid newspaper *The Sun*, which was what most refinery workers read. The campaign was a huge success as people wanted to read it and, within eighteen months, the refinery had one of the best safety records in the company (Melcrum, 2007a).

3. Social media

Social media is the name given to a range of online technologies and practices such as blogs, message boards, podcasts, and wikis. People use these media to share opinions, experiences, and perspectives with each other. New applications are continually emerging. The burgeoning use and availability of new technologies have led some commentators to question whether face-to-face communication is still the ideal communication channel (Lievrouw et al., 2001, quoted in Jones et al., 2004).

Whilst there is no doubt that social media form an important evolution of the Internet and provide new ways of people connecting with each other, questions remain as to the role of social media within organizations and the possibilities that such new forms of connecting pose for communicating change. According to a global survey of internal communicators (Melcrum, 2007c), the perceived benefits of social media were as follows: 71 per cent believed it leads to improved employee engagement, followed by improved internal collaboration (59 per cent), the development of internal communities (51 per cent), and the ability to create two-way dialogue with senior executives (47 per cent). Interestingly, only 28 per cent of internal communicators who responded to the survey said they knew how to use social media as part of an integrated communication strategy.

One of the challenges perhaps lies in the inherently democratic nature of social media, which can be at odds with the culture of organizations that are more top-down and have a directed approach to change. By definition, social media are 'pull' rather than 'push' technologies—that is, users decide how and when they want to use the media. So, whilst they may be very effective during emergent change, they are not a channel that leaders can force on employees as part of directed change or indeed control.

In some organizations, such as IBM, BT, Sun Microsystems, and Microsoft, the culture and the employee profile means that there has been significant proactive experimentation with social media. As mentioned in Change in Practice 12.2, Jonathan Schwartz of Sun Microsystems has been one of the most high-profile chief executive bloggers. An authentic voice is essential for blogging, so this only works if senior executives are willing to invest time in their blog and write it themselves. Nevertheless, executive bloggers can attract criticism: 'Why are leaders blogging when they have an organization to run?' (*Washington Post*, 2006). However, senior leaders who blog can suddenly seem less remote and more human; it allows them to share their views with anyone who wants to connect rather than only the upper echelons. A comment on the blog of Unilever's Senior Vice President HR, from an HR manager in Nigeria, was: 'Suddenly you are only two clicks of a button away rather than 1000 miles.'

The use of social media to foster employee engagement, improved collaboration, and the growth of internal communities suggest that they are often used to increase participation and connection rather than to get messages out about a particular change. In this sense, social media are being used to make the culture of an organization more participative rather than being communication channels for talking about the change. For instance, companies such as IBM, Sun Microsystems, American Electric Power, and Nortel are using social media, such as blogging and message boards, to facilitate 'side-to-side' conversation between employees (Melcrum, 2007c). The most extreme form of using technology to involve large numbers of employees has been IBM's **Jams**. The first, held in 2001, involved 50,000 employees participating in a real-time, online idea-sharing session about the company's future direction. Subsequently, they invited all 300,000 employees to a ValuesJam, giving the workforce the opportunity to redefine the core IBM values for the first time in nearly a hundred years. Here, technology is being used to involve employees in change, which could be labelled communication, engagement, or a participatory approach to change.

See Chapter 9 for more on the Alfa Laval example: p. 198

IBM now sells its jamming capability to other organizations, but it is not a cheap option. Other virtual technologies such as using web-based conferencing can be effective, less costly ways of involving groups globally in change.

4. External communication

See Chapter 7 for more on stakeholders: p. 147

Some of the stakeholders that may be affected directly, or have a view on, an organization's plans to change are external to the organization and may include investors, regulators, customers, and local or national government. Communicating regularly with such interest groups about the plans and progress of a change programme can be vital to ensuring their continued support or, at a minimum, ensuring that they do not intervene to jeopardize proceedings.

The metaphor of front stage and back stage activity (Buchanan and Boddy, 1992) applies here too. In terms of communication, the latter may take the form of an informal conversation over dinner or on the golf course to reassure an important stakeholder that the change programme is on track and that there are no dangers to quality control or supply. It may also take the form of lobbying to influence regulatory or government decision-makers. External communication may also involve more front stage activities, such as specifically targeted messages, or events for particular audiences, such as briefings for investors on a company's quarterly results, or customer events to launch new products or services. It may also include PR activities, such as press releases and newspaper interviews with senior leaders for the specialist or general press. From a communication point of view, the most important requirement is to ensure alignment between internal and external messages, as otherwise neither version is believed and the leader's credibility seriously diminished.

See Chapter 7 for more on this metaphor

 Section 2 Summary

In this section, we have:

- examined some of the practical tensions and trade-offs facing those tasked with communicating change;
- looked at communication choices in relation to the richness of different media and the various stages of the change process;
- reviewed the benefits and limitations of different media.

Section 3: **Communication in specific change scenarios**

This section draws on much of the preceding sections, but highlights the communication challenges and requirements as they relate to two specific change situations: crises, and mergers and acquisitions (M&As).

Crisis

A crisis 'represents an unusual situation outside the normal operating frameworks of the affected organization; if standard operating procedures can handle the event, it is not a crisis' (Reilly, 2008: 331). Crises may be caused by: natural disasters, such as Hurricane Katrina, which devastated New Orleans in 2005, and the earthquake and tsunami in Japan in 2010; industrial accidents; wrongdoing of top management, such as the collapse of Enron in 2001, or individual wrongdoing, such as fraud or excessive risk taking by individual bankers, for example Julian Tzolv at Credit Suisse in 2009 or Nick Leeson at Barings Bank in 1995. Crisis communication is included here because there is often significant organizational change in the aftermath of a crisis. In addition, the way in which communication is handled during a crisis often shapes the possibilities for change available afterwards.

See Chapter 6 for more on Enron: p. 115

Change in Practice 12.3

Communicating a crisis at BP

The Deepwater Horizon oil well in the Gulf of Mexico, operated by BP, exploded on 20 April 2010, killing eleven people. It became one of the world's worst environmental disasters. It was also a corporate disaster: the value of BP's shares fell by half from their pre-crisis levels but this did not just affect institutional investors—70 per cent of British pensioners have BP shares in their portfolios.

The chief executive, Tony Haywood, was visible from early on, basing himself in Houston, rather than staying in London headquarters. At the beginning, he was over-reassuring, talking of 'a relatively tiny' amount of oil spilling into 'a very big ocean' (*The Guardian*, 14 May, 2010). The shocking visual imagery of dead turtles and sea birds soaked in oil, seen on the Internet and in the media, suggested a different story. The Coast Guard Admiral, Thad Allen, initially came to be seen as better informed and the more credible spokesperson for the disaster than the company itself. BP had no response on the Internet for a week and no company content on Google, YouTube, twitter, or Facebook.

Days after the explosion, BP announced that it would not try to hide behind the US $75 million statutory liability limit for marine oil spills, but would pay all legitimate claims. Instead of praising this decision, commentators complained that the word 'legitimate' was a loophole that could let BP out of paying some claims.

Haywood did make an apology in his 18 June testimony before the US government Energy and Commerce Committee. However, he would not admit responsibility or accept that BP had done anything wrong, maintaining that the facts of the accident were not yet known. This may have been an appropriate stance from a litigation perspective; it was poor from the perspective of crisis communication and stakeholder management. When interviewed on NBC's *Today* show, Haywood said, 'there's no-one who wants this over more than I do. I'd like my life back'. This remark was widely criticized for being uncaring and arrogant, and made corporate expressions of compassion for the real victims sound hollow. When the embattled chief executive attended a yacht race round the Isle of Wight while the oil was still pumping out in the Gulf, further vilification followed, with Obama's Chief of Staff publicly referring to this as yet another in a 'long line of PR gaffes' (*New York Times*, 19 June, 2010: A20).

> The lesson for other CEOs and crisis spokespeople is that you have to be on the ball the whole time. Mr Hayward's 'gaffes' probably account for 0.001% of the words he has communicated to the media over the last month, but they are the ones for which he will be remembered. In a crisis, you must be word perfect every minute of every day. Indeed, this applies to body language as well as what you actually say. (Hemus, 2010)

Three other factors made this crisis particularly difficult for BP. One was its poor accident record. With an explosion at its Texas City oil refinery in 2005 and an oil spill in Alaska in 2006, BP looked like an organization that was not learning from its mistakes. Secondly, the spill reopened questions about the company's culture and preference for profit over safety. Thirdly, BP's inability to stop the oil flow for so long further diminished perceptions of it as an organization well prepared to deal with a crisis. 'As the oil continues to seep away, so does BP's credibility' and reputation (ibid). [5-10]

As we have already seen, change communication is far from simple at the best of times. In a crisis, the need for speed exacerbates the challenges and possibility of miscommunication: 'At no time in an organization's life is it more critical to communicate openly, sensitively and quickly . . . than during a major crisis' (Pincus and Acharya, 1988: 182). Reilly talks of the importance of 'the rapid transmission of the firm's damage control message' (2008: 333). BP did not respond quickly or openly enough, with dire consequences.

In a crisis, the tendency is often for senior leaders to seek to impose control, developing a consistent message and telling managers and their subordinates what to do and say, but this can be at the cost of speed. With the complexity, magnitude, and sheer pace of some crises, there is often a need for effective upward communication from those on the ground, dealing with the crisis. Yet employees dealing with the crisis may be too busy to send reports up the hierarchy; if they do send information, it may be sanitized to be more palatable to senior management, or if it is expressed with too much technical data, it may not be appropriately understood and interpreted by those more senior.

Other challenges to good communication during a crisis include the tendency or desire amongst leaders to restrict the free flow of information until details and the severity of the situation become clearer or to minimize them, as Haywood did. At the other end of the spectrum, there can be information overload as everyone helpfully tries to communicate with everyone: with no filtering mechanisms in place, or official version or single spokesperson, confusion can reign. During crises, emotions also tend to be heightened, which can impact on the way in which communications are understood. This was certainly the case in terms of US media coverage of the BP oil spill.

For organizations, key to effective crisis management communication is having an outline plan in advance with the purpose of maintaining reputation (Lockwood, 2005, cited in Reilly, 2008: 337) and which ensures the consistency between external communication and internal communication. Plans tend to specify who will be the key spokesperson, the roles and responsibilities of internal and external communicators, HR, and senior leaders, who will update the Internet, and may include logistical details such as phone numbers and email addresses.

Leaders staying highly visible is seen to be essential to good crisis communication—positive examples would include New York Mayor Rudy Giuliani, who was on the scene of the attacks in the World Trade Centre in 2001 within minutes, and Sir Michael Bishop, chairman of British Midland, who was a very public presence when one of its planes crashed onto a motorway, killing thirty-nine people. Haywood, in Change in Practice 12.3, was visible, but, unfortunately for him, some of his comments and his failure to admit responsibility early on severely tarnished his ability to be a credible spokesperson for the company.

Organizational crises evoke strong emotional reactions because of their unexpectedness, and the uncertainties about the scale and scope of what is happening, and unknown consequences for the organization. So, as well as the need for information sharing up and down the organization, people in stressful situations such as crises need the opportunity to voice their worries (Reilly, 2008). Listening is therefore an essential part of a crisis communication plan to provide 'emotional first aid' to employees (Jick, 1990). Crises can have a long-term impact, often changing an organization's culture, identity, and the stories told about it by those inside and outside the firm. An important element of recovery from a crisis can, therefore, be to reinforce, through communication, changes to policies and procedures.

See Chapter 4 for more on emotions: p. 62

Mergers and acquisitions

See Chapter 3 for more on mergers and acquisitions: p. 46

Research on acquisitions has consistently found that about half are deemed to have failed (Hubbard and Purcell, 2001; KPMG 1997, 1999) and that communication is a particular issue. Most commentators would argue that the notion of a merger, which suggests a 50:50 partnership, is extremely rare and more of a rhetorical device about how leaders would like both sides to feel rather than anything more substantive.

One of the authors experienced a particularly graphic example of this when working with the heads of communication from two banks, one of which had acquired the other. We were sitting together in a room, planning a two-page weekly newsletter to be emailed to all staff in both banks to keep them updated as decisions were made. The newsletter had a logo made from each bank's corporate colour. 'The logo should have twice as much blue as green,' said the communications director of one of the banks, 'because we are twice as big as the other bank.'

One of the most significant communication issues in acquisition announcements is that of false reassurances that nothing will change, or that any changes will be minor and insignificant. A manager in one such case reported:

> Business as usual was the message that went out to all the clients and my staff, and it was a lie as it transpired ... Business as usual ... is a coded message for within six to eight weeks we will have a radical rethink of the whole business and structurally change things. (Hubbard and Purcell, 2001: 24)

 Change in Practice 12.4

Kraft's acquisition of Cadbury's

After a six-month battle, the American food giant Kraft won control of British confectionery maker Cadbury, in January 2010. As the hostile takeover battle had intensified in September the previous year, shareholders were told that Kraft 'would be in a position to continue to operate the factory' near Bristol which Cadbury themselves had earmarked for closure (*The Times*, 9 February 2010). Irene Rosenfeld, chair and chief executive of Kraft, was reported as saying 'We have a great respect for Cadbury's brands, heritage and people ... We believe they will thrive as part of Kraft Foods' (*BBC News*, 19 January 2010). She met the British Trade and Industry Secretary, Lord Mandelson, on 2 February and indicated that there would be no formal statement about job cuts for six months. Six days later, Kraft announced the closure of Cadbury's Somerdale factory near Bristol, which made Crunchie bars and Curly Wurlys. It was reported that production would move to Poland.

MPs described Kraft's change of mind 'as either incompetent or a cynical ploy' (*The Times*, 27 May 2010). Jennie Formby, national officer of the Unite Union, said: 'Some of the workers have had their hopes raised by Kraft management, and if they are going to lose their jobs then that is shameful' (*The Times*, 9 February 2010). Two days later, when the closure was confirmed, she said: 'This sends the worst possible message to the 6,000 other Cadbury workers in the UK and Ireland. It tells them that Kraft cares little for their workers and has contempt for the trade union that represents them' (*The Times*, 11 February 2010). Kraft executives were summoned to a group of MPs to explain their actions and to give reassurances on future plans, although Irene Rosenfeld chose not to attend in person. Media reports all emphasized the significant time and effort that the US food group will have to invest to restore its public reputation.[11-14]

Change in Practice 12.4 demonstrates the impact of what are perceived to be broken promises on multiple stakeholder groups—government, unions, and employees. Kraft spokespeople said that, because it had been a hostile takeover bid, it had not been able to inspect Cadbury's accounts prior to making its commitments, so it was not fully appraised of the situation. However, in communication terms, the moral battle, the corporate reputation, and the credibility of Kraft's leaders and spokespeople had already been lost, and such comments were merely excuses: 'Failure to manage expectations in the early period can cast a long shadow over subsequent attitudes towards the company management' (Hubbard and Purcell, 2001: 30).

In such circumstances, whatever channels or individual leaders are used to communicate the message, they are, or rapidly become, tarnished as sources of information and will no longer be deemed credible. In addition, such communication contributes to the creation of a culture of mistrust between the two companies, and/or between leaders and other employees. Employees' understanding of, and attitudes to, change are not shaped only by what they hear about through formal communication; they are also shaped to an even greater extent by what they experience of management action.

See Chapter 5 for more on trust: p. 97

 Section 3 Summary

In this section, we have:

- examined the communication challenges during a crisis;
- explored some of the communication issues in relation to mergers and acquisitions.

Section 4: **The limits of formal communication**

This chapter started by emphasizing how important communication is to the successful implementation of change. It ends with some reflections on the limits of formal change communication, drawing on some of the themes that have emerged throughout the chapter.

Informal communication

Communication about change does not happen only through formal channels; it also happens through gossip, rumour, and informal chat around the edges of meetings and over lunch or a coffee. Depending on the nature of the change and the culture of the organization, such informal communication, particularly with co-workers, can provide support and opportunity for sensemaking and learning. An employee whose boss had been removed as part of a restructure, said:

> we didn't have anyone, but then the service managers supported each other as a group, and you sort of form your own little network and lines of communication and support. (Allen et al., 2007: 197)

In consulting work facilitating action learning sets, we have also often experienced employees using the space and peer support to communicate and share their own change stories. Similarly, executive coaching, whilst not a communication channel per se, is often used by leaders and managers to process and come to terms with their own roles in organizational change.

Management action

There is an old and familiar saying that 'actions speak louder than words'. This is particularly true when it comes to change communication. However impressive the communication strategy, or creative the way in which different channels are used, employees and other stakeholders will not believe the message if their own experience is contrary to it. This was demonstrated in Change in Practice 12.4, when Kraft announced the decision to close the Bristol factory despite earlier communication that there were to be no job cuts for six months. Similarly, BP's communication that it was in control of the situation was manifestly undermined by the fact that it took the company five months to stop the oil spill. The alignment between communication and management action is thus critical to the credibility of communication, both in terms of specific pieces of communication as well as ongoing communication more generally.

Trust and company culture

It sounds obvious to say that change communication does not take place in a vacuum. The very choice of communication strategy will be shaped by the norms and values of the organization, or, at the very least, by those of the leaders and by their approach to change. However, the effectiveness of the communication strategy, and tactics adopted, depend as much on the culture of the organization as on any executional brilliance. Organizational subcultures, structures, silo behaviours, and other intergroup factors can frequently inhibit internal communication, but perhaps one of the most significant factors is the level of trust that exists in the organization: 'The lesson for managers is to learn how to navigate . . . changes in a way that preserves employees' sense of trust' (Robinson, 1996: 597).

Employees' perceptions of trust are mainly influenced by prior experiences and the relationships they have developed with other members of the organization. Rousseau and Tijoriwala (1999) were interested in how employees in a large hospital undergoing significant restructuring evaluated information presented to them by senior leaders to explain the reasons for the change. They found that employees were more likely to perceive the rationale for the change as legitimate in conditions of high trust, rather than low trust.

Company performance

Effective communication, such as that during the Federal Express merger, can make a significant contribution to the success and sustainability of an organizational change. Effective crisis communication can also ensure the ongoing viability of the organization. Very astute communication can also subtly shift the meaning that employees give to events. When the

Royal Bank of Scotland won the hostile takeover bid of ABN Amro, the Barclays communication team was busily finalizing the copy of the external and internal communication, having lost the deal. The story goes that the corporate communications director suddenly entered the room and changed the press release headline to 'Barclays walks away from the deal', subtly reframing events (Gill, 2009) to appear that Barclays actively chose to walk away from the deal rather than lost it.

However, in other cases, the effectiveness of communication, whilst necessary, is not sufficient to ensure the ongoing viability of an organization. No communication strategy could have averted the collapse of Enron or Barings Bank. Mckenzie's communication strategy at Sun Microsystems, with its chief executive blogger, was not enough to ensure the independence of the company—Oracle bought the company in January 2010. So, whilst communication can play an extremely important role in organizational change, it is also important to keep that role in perspective.

 Section 4 Summary

In this section, we have:

- considered some of the limitations of formal change communication—namely the role of informal communication and the impact of management action, trust, culture, and company performance.

 Integrative Case Study

Pfizer: Communicating with field staff during major change

In one of Pfizer's UK business units employing 1,000 people, 70 per cent were in sales and worked from home. What communication strategy and tactics would work for them after the organization announced a global transformation programme in October 2006?

Between October 2006 and July 2007, staff experienced significant uncertainty. High-level changes to the structure, headcount reductions, and the closure of one of the regional offices were announced in February. Previously, communication had been through regional leaders, but this was no longer possible as these roles were abolished. The new situation placed much greater communication responsibility on two senior directors: one in sales and one in customer marketing. They held regular formal consultation meetings with employee representatives, which were always followed within 24 hours by an audio broadcast to which all employees were invited to dial up and listen in. Each manager was encouraged to keep close to their homeworkers through the telephone and face-to-face meetings.

In July 2007, to mark the birth of the new organizational structure, the two senior directors held twenty-one face-to-face meetings to symbolize 'Day One' in which people were introduced to their new managers. A conference that brought everyone together to hear about the vision for the new organization happened in September. In the run-up to the conference, ten volunteer salespeople were asked to take a camcorder to create a video diary recording their reflections on the new organization and meetings with customers and colleagues. These were shown at the conference, interspersed with talking to the volunteers in daytime TV style. The video diaries were a complete change from the consultation process, which, of legal necessity, had been very formal and top-down.

'As part of the transformation, we want people to take more accountability, be more innovative and take more risks. This communication process demonstrated those corporate aspirations' said Edwards, the internal communications manager. The video diaries from employees were then put on the intranet.

With the new structure, a new leadership team of ten was created. To keep employees updated on the change programme, the ten leaders themselves began producing video summaries to explain progress with different workstream initiatives after their monthly meeting. This was published on the intranet, along with key messages, supporting documents, and a feedback tool. The video diary summaries improved the ten leaders' visibility and encouraged them to use a more non-corporate style of communication. In addition, members of the leadership team held road shows for groups of ten to twelve sales managers, with chairs, but no tables, and no formal agenda or presentations.

Questions

1. What types of communication strategy do you think were being used and why?

2. What do you imagine are the strengths and weakness of the media used in this case?

Conclusion

In this chapter, we have looked at different ways of conceptualizing communication strategies and seen the close link between approaches to change and approaches to communication. The practical tensions and choices that require managing when responsible for change communication demonstrated why getting communication right can be difficult, despite the plethora of different channels and media available. The specific challenges for communication during crises and mergers and acquisitions were explored. The chapter ended with reflections on the limits of change communication.

 Please visit the Online Resource Centre at **http://www.oxfordtextbooks.co.uk/orc/ myers** *to access further resources for students and lecturers.*

Change in Practice sources

1. Young, M. and Post, J.E. (1993) 'Managing to communicate, communicating to manage: How leading companies communicate with employees', *Organizational Dynamics*, **22**(1): 31–43.

2. Melcrum (2007a) *Delivering Successful Change Communication: Proven Strategies to Guide Major Change Programs*, London: Melcrum Publishing.

3. Vance, A. (2008) 'Crisis hits tech sector with layoffs as sales slump', *New York Times*, 15 Nov. http://www.nytimes.com/2008/11/15/technology/companies/15sun.html

4. *Washington Post* (2006) 'Sun CEO among the few chiefs who blog', 16 Sep.

5. Hanson, A. (2010) 'Digital PR perspectives: The BP oil spill', *Arikhanson.com*, 14 May. http://www.arikhanson.com/2010/05/14/digital-pr-perspectives-the-bp-oil-spill/

6. Hemus, J. (2010) 'Why BP's oil spill is the mother of all crises', *The Drum*, 10 June. http://www.thedrum.co.uk/opinion/2010/06/10/why-bp%C3%A2%E2%82%AC%E2%84%A2s-oil-spill-mother-all-crises

7. *New York Times* (2010) 'BP chief draws outrage for attending yacht race', 19 June: A20. http://www.nytimes.com/2010/06/20/us/20spill.html

8. Sandman, P.M. (2010) 'Risk communication: Lessons from the BP spill', *The Synergist: Journal of the American Industrial Hygiene Association*, Sep: 29–31.

9. Webb, T. (2010) 'Gulf oil spill? It's just a drop in the ocean, says BP chief', *The Guardian*, 14 May: 1.

10. BBC News (2010) 'Cadbury agrees Kraft takeover bid', 19 Jan. http://news.bbc.co.uk/1/hi/8467007.stm

11. Boyle, C. (2010) '400 Cadbury workers to lose jobs despite promise', *The Times*, 9 Feb.

12. Boyle, C. (2010) 'Kraft censured for breaching the takeover code on Cadbury', *The Times*, 27 May.

13. Jagger, S. (2010) 'Mandelson attacks Kraft over closing Cadbury plant', *The Times*, 11 Feb.

14. Wearden, G. (2010) 'Kraft executives grilled by MPs over Cadbury takeover', *The Guardian*, 16 Mar. http://www.guardian.co.uk/business/2010/mar/16/cadbury-takeover-kraft-executives-grilled

Integrative Case Study sources

Melcrum (2008) *Melcrum's Top 50 Internal Communication Case Studies*, London: Melcrum Publishing.

Further reading

Ford, J. D. (1999) 'Organizational change as shifting conversations', *Journal of Organizational Change Management*, **12**(6): 480–500.
An article that takes an alternative view of change communication, regarding organizations themselves as networks of conversations, so that achieving change and new communications are, in a sense, the same thing.

Fox, S. and Amichai-Hamburger, Y. (2001) 'The power of emotional appeals in promoting organizational change programs', *Academy of Management Executive*, **15**(4): 84–94.
A discussion of the emotional aspects of change communication.

Sustaining Change

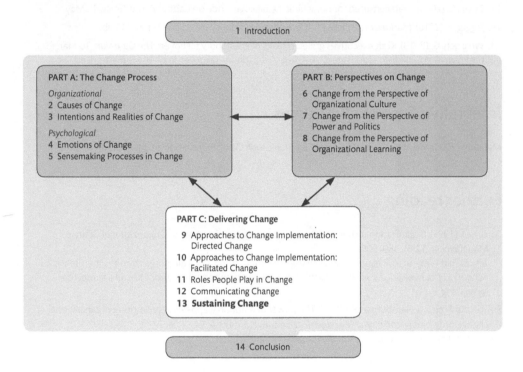

```
                          ┌─────────────────────┐
                          │   1  Introduction   │
                          └─────────────────────┘

PART A: The Change Process          PART B: Perspectives on Change

Organizational                      6  Change from the Perspective of
2  Causes of Change                    Organizational Culture
3  Intentions and Realities of Change 7  Change from the Perspective of
                                       Power and Politics
Psychological                       8  Change from the Perspective of
4  Emotions of Change                  Organizational Learning
5  Sensemaking Processes in Change

                    PART C: Delivering Change

                     9  Approaches to Change Implementation:
                        Directed Change
                    10  Approaches to Change Implementation:
                        Facilitated Change
                    11  Roles People Play in Change
                    12  Communicating Change
                    13  Sustaining Change

                          ┌─────────────────────┐
                          │   14  Conclusion     │
                          └─────────────────────┘
```

 ## Introduction

Sustaining change has been described as 'the process through which new working methods, performance enhancements and continuous improvements are maintained for a period appropriate to a given context' (Buchanan et al., 2007: xxii). This sounds straightforward enough. But what does it really mean? How can we be sure what is expected of the change? When can change be considered to have happened, in order for it to be 'maintained', and how can we judge the 'appropriate' amount of time for it to continue before things need to change again? In organizational life, change initiatives may come and go, one after another, some sticking, others making a temporary difference to how things are done, others creating 'changes' to be worked around, in the knowledge that they will probably quickly fade away. Senge et al. (1999: 6) claim that 'sustaining significant change is so elusive' that, in fact, it 'rarely happens'. Yet huge investment is put into organizational change, sometimes incurring high costs, such that leaders feel under pressure to demonstrate the return on investment. Because of this, and for the very reason of its apparently elusive nature, the ability to sustain new practices and reap the benefits of performance improvement has become a strategic imperative for many organizations (Buchanan et al., 2007).

This chapter will consider what is meant by sustainable change and the issues associated with defining it. It will then examine, in a practical way, what organizations can do to improve the likelihood of changes sticking, by reviewing: the conditions that encourage the change process to be maintained (**momentum of change**); the times when the change then becomes embedded into the normal ways of working (**institutionalized change**); and the times when the change happening in one place is adopted in other parts of the industry or organization (**spread of change**).

In doing so, the chapter will review the broad landscape of change that we have examined in the previous chapters of this book to consider the following topics.

◉ Main topics covered in this chapter

- Whether sustainable organizational change can be defined in relation to planned change, emergent change, and the unintended consequences of change
- The enablers and inhibitors identified in sustaining momentum and institutionalizing planned change
- The nature of measurement and evaluation of change, both planned and emergent
- The implications for managing sustainable organizational change

Section 1: Perspectives on sustaining change

Is sustaining change important?

Before turning to the practicalities of sustaining change, we want to draw your attention to why we see change sustainability as crucially important, why without paying due regard to this issue there seems little point in writing about change management. We said earlier that change is now seen to be a strategic imperative for leaders (Buchanan et al., 2007). Invariably, organizational strategies carry the implication of change and, as such, 'change management is the very mechanism by which contemporary organizations deliver their strategy and remain competitive' (Leppitt, 2006). Yet, despite the time and money spent on change, there is little evidence to suggest that organizations get what they hope for as a result of change programmes. A study conducted for KPMG as far back as 1999, which took an international sample of over a hundred cross-border mergers and acquisitions, found that only 17 per cent of deals added value to the combined company, that 30 percent produced no discernable difference, and some 53 per cent 'destroyed value' (KPMG, 1999a). By 2010, Accenture was suggesting that boards had got better at successfully executing mergers and acquisitions, because some half of corporate mergers created 'at least marginal returns' (Herd, 2010). In 2006, Hughes reviewed a range of sources examining change initiatives in general and noted the persistently high failure rate of all such initiatives. So, not much to boast about in any of these and, as Hughes (2006) adds, not many signs of hope. Yet without the hope that change can bring positive results, for shareholders, for employees, and for the future sustainability of the organization, why would organizations embark on change at all? We certainly think it important to understand the key considerations in establishing the nature of sustainable change and to identify approaches that may maximize the chances of achieving this.

Sustainable change: What does this mean?

What, then, do we mean by 'sustaining change'? At its simplest, it is when new practices or ways of thinking have a positive impact on performance and stop being considered new or different—that is, become part of the place. But here is the first stumbling block: this definition involves taking a view about how things were before the change, what was intended by the change, what actually happened, and whether we can show that genuinely new ways of working are now embedded in such a way that performance is improved. That is a long list of causal links, most of which are difficult to establish with certainty. As we have explored throughout this book, there are many ways of considering change, each bringing different expectations and, therefore, different thinking to how we might view such causal linkages. We shall recall some of these differences now, to illustrate the areas for debate in understanding change sustainability.

See Chapter 3 for more on planned and emergent change: p. 48

One of the most significant issues is that of defining an end state, knowing when change has been 'delivered'. In Chapter 3, we noted that the change literature is dominated by two very different views of change: the planned view and the emergent view. A planned view focuses on deliberate decisions within the change process, with the expectation that organizations will move through different stages in order to progress from an unsatisfactory state to an identified desired state. This lends itself well to evaluation of the 'before and after', so that you might imagine being able to establish the extent to which change has been achieved and subsequently sustained. The emergent view, on the other hand, emphasizes that change does not happen through a series of linear, planned events; it highlights the importance of being flexible, being able to respond to a whole range of complex factors, identifying options for change, which are continuously reviewed and adjusted (By, 2005). Emergence actually covers a range of ideas rather than offers one unified alternative approach. The whole topic of emergent change sustainability needs to be approached in a different way from planned change, perhaps focusing on the quality of the ongoing process, the extent to which fresh thinking and new learning is enabled. Clearly, standard evaluation processes are unlikely to establish this. We will consider this further in a review of evaluation in section 2 of this chapter.

Our examination in Chapter 3 of the different scales of change, from incremental to discontinuous, similarly raises issues of when or what constitutes the 'end state'. Typically, incremental changes happen gently, steadily, are focused, and bounded. Some also understand incremental change to be continuous, the means by which ongoing improvement is achieved, with no fixed end (By, 2005). Whilst discontinuous change, in contrast, is executed swiftly, sometimes dramatically, even this does not always happen in one hit or indeed lead to one specified outcome. Weick and Quinn (1999: 382) describe the trajectory of change as 'more often spiral or open-ended than linear'. Pettigrew et al. (2001) note that it used to be common for change to be viewed as an event, with a clear beginning, middle, and end, which meant that assessment could be made about the drivers and inhibitors of change at particular snapshots in time, but that is now an out-of-date view of organizational change. Assessments of change sustainability need to be able to be applied to change as it really happens, not as theories suggest it should.

Even within the planned change paradigm, a particular paradox of trying to institutionalize change is that the very act of sustaining an approach may prevent the implementation of other new ideas. Fitzgerald and Buchanan (2007) point out that the survival of new practices may only be achieved by adapting them to meet new challenges. Within the learning perspective, we looked specifically at the claim that an organization's capacity to learn may be its only source of competitive advantage (Senge et al., 1999). Being able to swiftly reallocate people to new priorities without worrying about job descriptions, or hierarchies, or having flexible IT platforms that can be adjusted to deliver new processes may help to ensure that organizations do not get stuck and are not afraid of constant change and renewal. As such, it may be unhelpful for organizations to aim for a fixed end state; institutionalizing a set of practices so firmly may, in itself, lead to inertia (Buchanan et al., 2007).

See Chapter 8 for more on the learning perspective

A further consideration is the focus of the change. In Part A of the book, we explored change that occurs at industry, at organization, and at group or individual levels. Taking first industry-wide change, we noted that change at this level is often instigated in response to changes in the external environment, such as depletion of raw materials or price rises in commodities such as oil, or changes in political or economic conditions or legal and regulatory changes, etc. Change becomes characterized as a trend when sufficient new patterns or behaviour emerge. This encourages change to spread further and to be sustained at industry level. We also considered the influence of management fashions, whereby stories of well-known companies successfully embracing new ideas or ways of working legitimize others to follow suit. Here, change typically starts at an organizational level adopted by a few organizations; it then spreads to others and across the industry, such that it becomes standard within the industry. For example, in Chapter 3, we looked at the growth of outsourcing, which started as an experiment for a small number of organizations, yet soon began to offer a consistent financial business case for achieving costs savings. These positive reports created an increase in take-up, which in turn resulted in outsource providers becoming more sophisticated, and improving the quality and reliability of their service, thereby making the case for implementation even more compelling. Now, outsourcing is simply seen as an established service provision option. Yet, sometimes industry-wide change turns out to be no more than a passing fad, which, through the passing of time, withers rather than takes root. This may suggest that there are ways of understanding change sustainability at the industry level if one takes a sufficiently long-term view, tracking influences, trends, and outcomes of the adoption of new practices, rather than trying to assess each new change as it occurs.

See Chapter 2 for more on the external environment: p. 15

We looked also at change within an organization and the span of such change—that is, whether it focuses on a few individuals, one business unit, or the whole organization: change may mean a small project taking a few months or a major programme lasting several years. The examples we studied led to the conclusion that changing structures and processes, even across a whole organization, is, in itself, more straightforward and measurable than changing the attitudes or beliefs of individuals or teams, but less likely on its own to result in automatic performance improvement. Deep-seated attitudinal change, known as second-order change, is difficult to achieve, unlikely to happen swiftly, and even more difficult to measure. This leads us to the question of short-term versus long-term sustainability. As noted, shareholder pressure in the private sector, or government pressure in the public sector, can create a push for short-term results; indeed the demonstration of such results may be essential to secure the long-term viability of the organization. Equally, long-term sustainable improvements are also expected of organizations, often proposing changes to their culture and capabilities to achieve sustainable growth (Leppitt, 2006). Assessment of sustainability needs to take account of these issues.

See Chapter 3 for more on the span of change: p. 37

See Chapter 4 for more on emotions

A further question is that of whose view counts when deciding whether change has been institutionalized, whether it has achieved a positive outcome. In Chapter 4, we explored the part played by employee emotions in change. When changes are made, everybody involved undergoes a transition. Workplaces develop their own norms or 'display rules' about which emotions can be expressed. Certain 'displays' of emotion may also be required of employees in the workplace as part of what they are paid for, such as airline stewards being required to keep smiling in the face of passenger abuse (Hochschild, 1983). This can make it difficult to know what is really going on. Responses to what is happening at that moment may also get mixed up with toxic emotions—that is, negative emotions that have become ingrained as a result of previous negative experiences (Frost and Robinson, 1999). It can be difficult even for individuals themselves to know why they are responding to change as they are, or how they really feel. Perhaps you can remember a time when change impacted your plans, for example when a course you were due to attend was cancelled at short notice. Perhaps you felt both irritated because you had specifically chosen the course and yet relieved because you had not finished the pre-reading and were very busy in any case. What did you say or not say in protest and to what extent did your actions actually reflect your feelings? Such examples illustrate the complexities of knowing what is really going on.

In exploring the political perspective, we noted the importance of stakeholders in managing change, acknowledging that when change is a good outcome for some, for others it may be deemed less successful or less impactful. As Pettigrew (2000) points out, judgements about the success of change are dependent on who is doing the assessing and most change processes are not universally popular. We noted the example of employees at lower levels in the organization experiencing the change as low-key and incremental—that is, not of great importance to their lives—when senior managers, who had planned and led the change, described it as discontinuous and revolutionary. In the Integrative Case Study on the National Trust, the general managers who found themselves with more autonomy and authority as a result of the change were likely to assess the impact of the programme more positively than the technical experts, who can no longer take the decisions that they used to and can now only input their expert knowledge to influence decisions. Inevitably, where change occurs, people have different interests and, therefore, sustainability means different things to them.

See Chapter 11 for more on the National Trust: p. 263

 Exercise 13.1

Consider a change with which you have been involved in your organization or university (changed work practices or policies, an office move, etc.).

- Do you know what the aim of the change was—what it was expected to achieve?

- In your opinion, did it achieve its aim?

- Would you therefore consider the change to have been successfully implemented? If not, why not? What assumptions do you hold in making your assessment?

- Consider the view that your chief executive, head of school, or someone in a very different role from you might take of the change. In what ways might his or her assessment differ from your own and why?

A final consideration, which has grown in strength in the past decade, is the pressure to adopt business strategies at the industry or organizational level that embrace sustainability in its broadest sense—having a sustainable business model that in turn aims to sustain human and natural resources. An issue that started out primarily as a compliance reporting matter for large organizations is becoming an integral part of performance improvement (KPMG and Economic Intelligence Unit, 2011). KPMG undertook a global survey of some 350 organizations in Europe, the US, and Asia Pacific, and found the majority had a strategy for corporate sustainability, with regulatory requirements and brand enhancement increasing the importance of doing so. As such, sustainability is becoming an inherent part of strategic change management planning. Risk management issues following environmental disasters such as BP's Macondo well in the Gulf of Mexico in 2010 have also increased the pressure to take a long-term view, counterbalancing and sometimes outweighing cost implications (although cost remains an issue). For example, large retailers have influenced suppliers in how they present and package food, use plastic bags, etc. Such actions create changes across whole ranges of different industries and organizations, thereby increasing the momentum and spreading the practice of sustainability as integral to change management.

For all of these reasons, it is not straightforward to establish whether change has been institutionalized and, if so, whether this has resulted in increased performance, or whether change momentum is sustained such that the change is of ongoing positive effect (Buchanan and Huczynski, 2010; Pettigrew, 2000; Palmer et al., 2005). Yet we would suggest that this in itself is not a reason to disregard the issue; rather that acknowledging the complexity helps to surface the decisions that organizations face in managing change. Buchanan et al. (2005) suggest that the only way in which to tackle this complexity is to consider the definition of sustainable change as *whatever matters* in a given industry or organization context. In our view, determining whether or not change has been sustained to positive effect is contingent upon the profile of the change in question such that sustainability can mean:

- consolidating the change so that it becomes institutionalized, part of the normal business operations;
- sustaining the change process, so that momentum is maintained, changes are built upon, and the industry or organization continues to improve its operation and is dynamic and responsive;
- change being sustainable in terms of contributing to the viability of the industry or organization in the long term;
- change being sustainable in terms of its effect on the environmental impact of the industry or organization.

 Section 1 Summary

In this section, we have:

- explored the complexities of defining and measuring the sustainability of change;
- considered the nature of sustainability in relation to different change contexts and perspectives;
- recommended a contingency approach to the definition and assessment of change sustainability.

Section 2: **Sustaining momentum and institutionalizing change**

In this section, we will focus specifically on a range of factors and processes that are seen to impact the sustaining of momentum and institutionalizing of change. We will look back on Part C of the book, approaches to delivering change, to assess the extent to which implementation choices increase the likelihood of achieving sustainable change. As such, this review lends itself particularly to a planned view of change, but we will return to the issue of emergent change at the end of the section.

Change in Practice 13.1 describes an encouraging story of sustaining change, to which we will refer throughout this section.

 Change in Practice 13.1

Farmers, innovation, and sustainable change

In 2001, a change programme began in a small number of farms in the Welsh valleys. It took a year for momentum to gather. Ten years later, the change was not only sustained, but had spread to 'become a force for regeneration and innovation, embracing over 1,000 Welsh farmers' (Campbell, 2010).

At the turn of the decade, many farms in Wales were struggling and searching for ways in which to renew their business model and hold their farming communities together. There was a lack of community leaders, problems with inspiring young people to stay and work on the farms, and general social and cultural decline in rural areas. Both the government—the Welsh Assembly—and the European Union were keen to support initiatives to reverse these trends and to ensure that farming in Wales had a viable future.

Although there was a desire to experiment with new ways of working and to achieve sustainable change, the farming community was not used to working on issues collectively: farming life is tough, traditional, and independent by nature; it does not lend itself to sharing, conversation, or experimentation. Despite this, the Welsh Assembly government chose to deliver the farmers' change programme using a process of peer-based learning. Using two rural development agencies with strong expertise in the farming world and, therefore, credibility to work with farming families, they set up farmers' action learning sets, facilitated by the development agencies.

The agencies themselves had to learn new skills to undertake this role well. They were accustomed to working in an advisory capacity, as expert agricultural consultants, so needed to learn to hold back from offering expert views and to undertake a truly facilitative role, demonstrating an understanding of the difficult decisions that the farmers faced, whilst enabling the groups to explore the issues and reach their own ways forward. In fact, one of the biggest challenges for the programme was the choosing and training of facilitators. Not everybody recruited found himself or herself suited to a position that required him or her to play such a non-directive role.

Developing and implementing a programme of this size across dispersed communities was highly dependent on the groups finding the discipline and desire to want to stay together. The initiative started with a small number of groups meeting to support and challenge each other's thinking and to make informed choices about future options. As news of the initiative spread, interest grew and further groups were formed. In all, there have been more than 120 action learning sets established in this way throughout Wales.

See Chapter 10 for more on action learning: p. 226

Many farming innovations have been implemented as a result of this change programme, including contracts to sell meat to large supermarkets, turning a farmhouse homebrew into a commercial product, setting up a micro-brewery in a redundant granary, and bringing together eight businesses, which together had 135, 000 hens to develop their own brand of eggs, 'The Bluebell Egg' group, sharing production and management ideas.

There is no sign of the change programme reaching an 'end'; instead it continues to evolve to meet the participants' needs.[1-2]

Enabling sustainable change

A number of parties have undertaken studies to try to capture the factors most likely to create sustainable change. Buchanan et al. (2005) completed a literature review, covering fifty years of research and examining the work of many theorists on sustaining change. Cummings and Worley (2005) created a change framework to illustrate the interplay of a range of factors and processes that contribute to the institutionalization of change interventions. From all of the studies, it is clear that a contingent approach is recommended, that matching the change to the circumstances, culture, and people capabilities of the organization determines the acceptable level of change for an organization—that is, a level at which the change is likely to be absorbed and sustained.

Figure 13.1 illustrates a combination of the key aspects established by these studies that were found to impact the momentum and institutionalization of the change process.

The diagram shows that the nature of the organization's context, plus its culture and infrastructure, affect the likely success of the change—even before the change is embarked upon. This background combined with the content of the change—that is, its structure, scale and pace—set the backdrop for the choices to be made in delivering the change. Change is executed through the organization's people and process: gaining leaders' commitment; adopting an appropriate style of leadership to achieve engagement with the change from those affected; and working successfully with the power and politics of that particular organizational context. The indicators of institutionalization that the organization chooses to recognize reflect its own understanding of the change it is trying to achieve. The measurement and reward of institutionalization in turn serve to reinforce the institutionalization process (Cummings and Worley, 2005; Buchanan et al., 2005; Greenhalgh et al., 2004).

We will now consider these aspects of change in more detail to identify their impact on choices for delivering planned change.

1. External context and organizational context

External environment

The external context plays a significant role in creating the momentum for change. External trends can be catalysts for change at industry or organization level, as can an organization's desire to survive, to compete, or to grow in the external market. For example, throughout the book, we have tracked the fortunes of companies such as Sony and Nokia, which pursue technological advances to continue to compete in the field of best-known electronic providers, as demands from customers for constant product upgrades get ever greater. Here, the

See Chapter 2 for more on external trends: p. 16

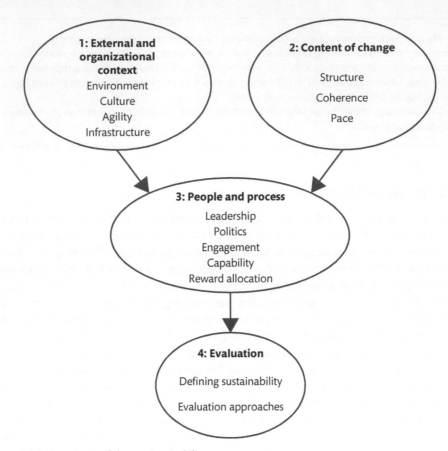

Figure 13.1 Key aspects of change sustainability

environment is one of the drivers of momentum and the subsequent spread of change across the industry; it is then incumbent on each organization to find ways of sustaining the change needed within its own ways of working to keep up and compete. Applying the PES-TLE analysis tool, Chapter 2 examined a range of other external drivers, including economic conditions, such as those experienced in 2010 that drove change in European organizations, when pay freezes and restructurings were implemented, which may not have been accepted in less austere times. In Change in Practice 13.1, the farmers were responding to intense economic pressure, plus encouragement and grants from the European Union, to find new ways forward—and were placed into the change programme by the Welsh government. Typically, where the change agenda is seen as an appropriate response to the environment, so the likelihood of change being accepted increases (Buchanan et al., 2005).

Organizational culture

The internal congruence of change is equally important. In taking a cultural perspective on change in Chapter 6, we explored the informal patterns in organizational life that can obstruct or encourage formal change strategies. The importance of paying attention to these patterns is highlighted in studies of sustaining change. Where change programmes do not work with the shared values of the organization, there is less likelihood of the changes being accepted or sustained (Greenhalgh et al., 2004). Svyantek and DeShon (1993) found that where changes violated beliefs held at a deep level, they were strongly and generally successfully resisted, or 'culture eats strategy for breakfast' (*Wall Street Journal*, 23 January 2006). They suggest that to alter the system 'requires more resources, commitment and time on the part of all parties in the change effort than may be psychologically or economically possible' (Svyantek and DeShon, 1993: 349).

See Chapter 6 for more on values: p. 118

However, small alterations to the system can cause rapid change, if careful leverage points are identified, as described in Change in Practice 6.2 on Thames Reach, where the socialization of new ways of thinking about homelessness was enabled through increasing the number of employees with a personal history of homelessness. This served to counterbalance the deeply entrenched views held by the majority of employees. In Change in Practice 13.1, the application of facilitated action learning sets contravened many of the expected ways of working in farmers' communities. Nevertheless the process enabled a group of fiercely independent farmers, whose collective expertise could not be surpassed, to take their own decisions and find new ways forward in which they believed: it offered an important fit with their values.

See Chapter 6 for more on Thames Reach: p. 129

Agility

We have noted the attention that is now given to creating agility in organizations. The capacity to learn and ability to respond quickly and flexibly to new demands is now seen as important. It is also apparent that when organizations are accustomed to creating continuous improvement, they are better able to work with change. For example, in our examination of disruptive process changes such as business process re-engineering, we noted that organizations that had previously undertaken some form of process review reported less anxiety and resistance from their people, as well as lower training costs. In the case of the Welsh farmers in Change in Practice 13.1, their first experiment to secure a contract with a large supermarket was cautious. As they became accustomed to making changes and as their confidence increased through success, so their innovations became bolder, such that they were increasingly able to adapt to new market conditions and opportunities. Being agile in responding to change impacts both maintaining momentum and institutionalizing the change.

See Chapter 9 for more on BPR: p. 199

Infrastructure

Change sometimes fails to be sustained simply because systems such as the budget approval process do not move at the pace needed to maintain change momentum (Reisner, 2002). Often, the IT systems cannot support the change. This can be a particular hazard, for example, in mergers and acquisitions, in which there is a need to bring two IT platforms together in order to streamline two organizations' systems into one, and to make the necessary changes to accounting and business processes. This has been known to take years rather than months to achieve and can seriously damage change momentum.

2. Content of the change

Structure and coherence of the programme

The structure of the change and the coherence of the programme are important to people's understanding of the change. Sustaining change begins in the planning stages (Kotter, 1996; Greenhalgh et al., 2004). Having clear and specific goals helps to direct energy and impacts the organization's ability to appropriately reward and reinforce the most helpful changes that are achieved in order to institutionalize the change (Buchanan et al., 2007; Pettigrew, 2000).

The level of the change target is important. Where the change is a small group or a team, it may be easier to focus the effort and influence thinking. Equally, where the rest of the organization remains uninvolved with the change, the affected group may find itself trying to run against the prevailing organizational norms and susceptible to countervailing influence from others in the organization (Cummings and Worley, 2005). The scale of the change is similarly important in this. Where the changes are small and gradual, they are less likely to create resistance and be rejected, such that sustainability should be increased. Equally, incremental change may lack impact and importance. Discontinuous changes, on the other hand, are episodic and deliberate, expected to result in fundamentally new ways of working within a planned timescale. They may serve to consolidate opposition if not positioned appropriately. Change leaders need to be alert to these issues, constantly adjusting the approach to address them, to prevent momentum being blocked.

Pace

The pace and sequence of changes need to be carefully phased, pushing ahead to maintain momentum, but noticing when to allow time for change to become part of the way of operating (Buchanan et al., 2007). Many of our examples illustrate just how long it can take to create change that sticks. In Change in Practice 10.2, we looked at the case of NS&I, a programme of culture change that lasted some four years. After the first year, good progress had been made and this could have been considered sufficient. Instead, the organization chose to continue its change interventions, involving a greater range of stakeholders, including their outsourced provider. In Change in Practice 13.1, the Welsh farmers worked together over some ten years, through which they have, in effect, institutionalized the value of continuous improvement in the farming community. In our experience, the time and persistence involved to sustain change are generally greatly underestimated.

See Chapter 10 for more on NS&I: p. 224

3. People and processes

Leadership

A persistent theme in both maintaining momentum and institutionalizing change is that of the quality and commitment of the leadership of the change. At the outset of the change, top management commitment is crucial to getting started and maintaining momentum (Buchanan et al., 2007; Kotter, 1996). This includes leaders being explicit about their commitment, owning the change not just at a superficial level, but also in how they behave on a day-to-day basis (Pettigrew, 2000; Senge et al., 1999). In our examination of change leaders, we found that those who were successful do not need to be heroic and charismatic; to sustain change it is more important to be authentic and highly attuned to others. It is helpful that new leaders hired as the change progresses represent new approaches and thinking, and continue to champion the change (Kotter, 1996). As practitioners, we have found that this is often the point at which sustainability is sacrificed to enable new leaders to 'make their own mark', such that another set of initiatives are set in train and the original purpose of the programme becomes confused or lost completely.

Kotter (1996) speaks of the danger of leaders declaring victory too soon, moving attention to new goals that are not compatible with the original intention or vision—at the point at which change has yet to be truly adopted. He argues (step seven) that, to maintain momentum, further changes need to be instigated as the first are implemented, but only in ways that continue to build, not contradict, what has been achieved. Jerald (2005: 3) describes the need to adopt a 'very intentional kind of opportunism'—that is, enacting new improvement as work carries on—to maintain the growth and hold of the change, but ensuring that there is a connection between the changes, which is clearly communicated, so that one builds on the other, with a core set of values or a central vision that serve to create constancy and make sense of the changes. A strong message is that unless organizations keep trying and keep communicating the picture of the future and success stories along the way, they jeopardize their improvements and start sliding backwards.

Over the long term, maintaining and extending change initiatives is not enough. There is a need for the change initiative to 'evolve or die' (Jerald, 2005: 4). Jerald (2005) refers to studies of change programmes in US schools, which show that, after the fifth year of implementation, the effects begin to increase substantially. The study found schools that made sustained improvements made deeper and more consistent changes, kept pushing, and did not become complacent. In Change in Practice 13.1, the Bluebell Egg Group, formed of eight businesses coming together to brand and share the production of their 135,000 eggs, came some significant way into the change programme. It was one of the boldest moves in terms of financial sharing and marketing initiatives. In terms of sustainability, this means being continually alert to the opportunities that the change programme continues to present as it evolves, whilst ensuring that the goals and process continue to be communicated and make sense.

Senge et al. (1999) report the need for leaders to really buy into the change, to get past the superficial issues, implement the 'low-hanging fruit', and tackle the 'undiscussable issues'. Informed by Argyris' (1990) work, they consider the problems created when unspoken, deep-seated differences in leadership teams go unresolved; such differences, sometimes over mundane issues, can stand in the way of change being sustained. Reisner (2002), reporting on the modernization of the US postal service, found that managers promoted and supported the change for the first years of reform, but did not understand the need to change further. Their ambivalence and indifference was not surfaced until the programme was faltering and close to failure. In exploring facilitated approaches to change, we considered a range of methods designed to explore differences and to derive new ways forward. For example, we considered the process of dialogue in change, which can enable senior teams to work together to come to new ways of thinking. Part of the skill in achieving sustainable change is in selecting the appropriate method for that moment to overcome the issues that may get in the way of progress.

See Chapter 10 for more on facilitated approaches

We noted the crucial role played by middle managers in implementing change, where they are much closer to the detail of the work and can manage the programme within their own unit. It often falls to middle managers to interpret the change on behalf of the employees and to work with the emotions generated by the change. Having also a good spread of sponsors, champions, and change agents who can diffuse the impact of powerful opposers impacts directly on change momentum (Kotter, 2007).

Politics

See Chapter 7 for more on power and politics

In reviewing the issues of power and politics in change, we examined the metaphor of front and back stage activity, whereby campaigning, lobbying and withholding of information go on behind the scenes (Pettigrew, 2000). In Change in Practice 7.1, we explored the introduction of new technology in a hospital, in which the alternate revealing and withholding of information to meet the needs of different stakeholders was integral to the change being accepted and the adoption of the new system being sustained. Often, employees will watch and wait to see whether proposals have enough senior support before engaging in any way. Political factors are generally most at play during the introduction of change, when leaders are fighting to retain and/or increase their power, and resisting changes that might diminish their authority. This is particularly likely to impede change momentum; once change has reached a certain point, lobbying has diminished impact.

Engagement

In all studies of change sustainability, the issue of engaging people early and throughout the change is seen as one of the most crucial aspects of change management. We have explored the relative success of changes pursued by directive or facilitated approaches. Whilst both are seen to have their place, with different approaches being effective at different times (Dunphy and Stace, 1993), higher levels of understanding of the change, and engagement with the change, are achieved through the facilitated approaches that enable the maximum involvement of people in actually creating the changes. For example, we found that change introduced through business process re-engineering can be difficult to sustain because it is often implemented at speed, which does not always allow people the time to understand and adapt to the new processes. They therefore resist during implementation and regress as soon as the programme is complete. Whilst facilitated approaches may take more time and effort, once the change has been fully accepted and adopted, it is no longer dependent on any one person, but starts to exist as part of the culture of the organization, such that back sliding is less likely (Buchanan et al., 2007; Cummings and Worley, 2005).

See Chapter 10 for more on Lewin: p. 224

In exploring organization development (OD) we reviewed the early research of Lewin, who described change as a process of unfreezing, moving, and refreezing behaviour. This is perhaps the first description of creating momentum (moving) and institutionalizing change (refreezing). The focus of Lewin's work was the group: he researched the outcomes of group discussions, in which people's views changed through exposure to, and exploration of, new ideas; the change was consolidated by people's desire to adhere to the (new) group norms. This approach to group process sits at the heart of Change in Practice 13.1, in which the farmers' action learning sets offered the individuals access to challenge to their thinking and exposure to new thinking. In reviewing facilitated approaches in Chapter 10, we noted a range of large group processes, such as Open Space Technology and Future Search, which are designed to offer groups a high level of participation in the change process.

A study of sustainability in the health services found strong evidence that any relative advantage or opportunity that the change brings (such as its cost-effectiveness) must be recognized and acknowledged by all key players (Greenhalgh et al., 2004). The study reports on the creation of the change's 'relative advantage' (ibid: 13) as a socially constructed phenomenon, which means that lengthy periods of negotiation are needed with potential adopters, in which the meaning is 'discussed, contested and reframed' (ibid). The study notes also the power of individuals to influence colleagues, whereby 'negative' opinion leaders only need to show some level of indifference to the change to inhibit its spread. Thus, leaders need to be able both to engage people in the change process and to be alert to the potential blockers at the same time. This is crucial at the stage of momentum maintenance.

People need also some organizational continuity in order to cope well with change. Having a coherent direction for the business and holding key executives in place long enough to see major change initiatives through increases the likelihood of momentum being maintained during implementation (Pettigrew, 2000). In Change in Practice 13.1, facilitators from the development agencies remained involved with the farmers' process for some ten years. The stability of the internal social context includes constructive management of relationships with the trade unions (Jacobs, 2002). Reisner (2002) describes the failure to achieve union cooperation in the turnaround of the US postal service as a 'momentum buster': change, which had been in train for some three years, faltered and then collapsed in the face of union opposition, alongside some degree of management indifference and budget processes that inhibited progress. He counsels against treating trade unions lightly, but rather sees their cooperation as critical to the engagement of employees at large.

Capability

Often, training in the new skills needed to undertake the change is neglected (Jacobs, 2002; Buchanan et al., 2007). Being unsure that you have the capability to try something new and different can drive resistance and anxiety. Greenhalgh et al. (2004) found a strong relationship between successful implementation and offering trials and experiments to intended users of changes, which makes them more readily adopted. Jacobs (2002: 2) notes that there is an implicit developmental order in managing change, such that 'employees having the competence related to the intervention is prerequisite to employees having the level of commitment to carry out the change'. This may mean undertaking straightforward skills training to take on the requirements of a new role, or offering training to help people to understand and cope with the emotions that they are experiencing as a result of the change.

 See Chapter 4 for more on emotions

Reward allocation

Reward and recognition systems can be powerful in institutionalizing change—and are often used too little too late (Pettigrew, 2000). People need to understand new behaviours or change before they can perform them effectively. Then being rewarded for adopting new behaviours starts to affect people's preferences. Through this, the change becomes normalized as the way of doing things, which may ultimately result in a shift in the organization's values (Cummings and Worley, 2005). Palmer et al. (2005) suggest that rewards should include public recognition of behaviours consistent with the desired change. Similarly, ignoring or even continuing to reward those who fail to adopt new standards or behaviours instantly dilutes the chances of change sticking or spreading. For example, KPMG, the consultancy and accountancy firm, wanted to change the focus of consultants' behaviour so that *how* they delivered work (in terms of client care, team working, etc.) became as important as *how much* revenue they earned. They introduced new behavioural objectives as part of the performance appraisal process and reinforced the change by applying the new criteria to decide on the allocation of performance bonuses. Within two years, people understood that behaviour was as important as the revenue billed; over time, this became an accepted organizational value. Linking such change in attitude to the organization's performance improvements is also important, and difficult for people to do for themselves: leaders need to make these connections explicit for employees (Buchanan et al., 2005; Kotter, 1996).

 Exercise 13.2

Look back on a change that you have experienced at work or university.

- Which aspects of how the change was managed would help the change to be sustained and which militated against this?
- Did you experience any unintended outcomes from the change?
- What in the organization's handling enabled or prevented the institutionalization of this change?

4. Evaluation

Defining sustainable change: Reinforcement through definition

The final set of factors (Figure 13.1) are those that relate to the definition, measurement, and reinforcement of the change. Here, we return to the debate that we surfaced in section 1: how to agree the indicators of change momentum and institutionalized change in order to undertake evaluation. As we noted, traditional evaluation processes lend themselves to planned change approaches, under which assessment can be made of the 'starting state' and the 'end state'. Yet, as we have demonstrated, other perspectives on change are very much part of the change agenda in modern organizations. We support the view that organizations need to make choices about the expectation of the change and be ready to find ways in which to assess and acknowledge the organizational learning that occurs throughout the process of change (Buchanan et al., 2007). The act of defining these issues in itself focuses attention on priorities for encouragement and reinforcement as changes occur.

Evaluation approaches

Evaluation is concerned with collecting data about the progress of the change. As such, it encompasses both the success of the immediate implementation and the long–term results produced by the change. To do this, traditionally, data are collected to assess the new state against the starting position and/or against the anticipated future state. Assessment can involve a combination of hard data collection (such as financial performance measures) or observation (in the workplace), objective calculation (based on questionnaire feedback), or subjective judgement (drawing on interviews and focus group feedback).

Cummings and Worley (2005) recommend that decisions about the measurement of variables and the design of the evaluation process should be made early and integrated with the change interventions. The process of reinforcement begins as soon as such measures are promulgated. We have already seen that some approaches to change, such as OD, do typically build in feedback mechanisms to their process, so that, following a change intervention, feedback from those involved and other stakeholders impacted by the change may lead to further diagnosis and subsequent adjustment of the change programme. This is known as **implementation feedback** (Cummings and Worley, 2005). The very act of making such assessments surfaces issues, and offers the opportunity to afford them attention, which in turn serves to increase the likelihood of the organization remaining focused on the programme and persevering to ensure the sustainability of the changes. Longer-term assessment to establish the outcome of the change programme and the extent to which the change has been institutionalized is known as **evaluation feedback** (Cummings and Worley, 2005).

Kaplan and Norton (1992) devised one of the earliest and most enduring organizational frameworks for agreeing, setting, and monitoring organizational performance, known as the **balanced scorecard**. Its purpose is to help organizations to agree their key strategic tasks and the activities that will best deliver these tasks, in order to get to an agreed future state. In the belief that 'what you measure is what you get' (Kaplan and Norton, 1992: 71), the scorecard is used to monitor each of the dimensions deemed crucial for success and, as such, is a good source of both implementation feedback and reporting progress against key measures, as well as evaluation feedback at the end of the programme. Traditionally, it encompasses four key aspects: financial measures (which report the results of actions already taken); operational measures, such as customer satisfaction; internal processes; and the organizations' innovation and improvement activities (which are the drivers of future financial performance) (Kaplan and Norton, 1992).

Generally, organizations adapt the balanced scorecard to their own language and needs, evolving their own measures relating to the four key aspects. When used well, it can involve the management team in important conversations about where they are going and how they want to get there, thereby assisting the definition and communication of the strategy (Marr, 2010). In general, monitoring draws attention to the need to renew efforts in a particular area, to revise objectives or to revisit assumptions, or indeed to decide whether the change plan itself is still valid. In 2008, research suggested that evaluation systems based on the scorecard were in use in some 50 per cent of organizations across the US, the UK, Northern Europe, and Asia (Marr, 2010).

Yet, even where versions of the scorecard are deemed to have been useful, it is difficult to know what the organization might have achieved had the programme of measures not been introduced. Senge et al. (1999) talk of harnessing soft measures, such as assessments of morale and motivation, as indicators of how the change is working, which, whilst they cannot be measured in any precise way, do offer a sense of the impact of some of the changes. They suggest creating local 'dashboards' of measures that are meaningful to people in that group, using internal websites to share the data and using it as a discussion vehicle:

> As you talk about these issues, you will hopefully bring to the surface your mental models about the business, your team and the external environment. Rather than merely providing data, a performance dashboard sparks conversation that builds managers' own capacity to learn. (ibid: 138)

See Chapter 5 for more on escalation of commitment: p. 95

A danger of the scorecard is that data measurement takes over from focus on change outcomes; hitting targets becomes an end in itself, more important than deciding whether the change has improved customer care, for example. Reviewing measurement data can take up significant amounts of leaders' time. As such, politics may intervene and get in the way of what Staw and Ross (1987) refer to as 'candid reporting'. They explore how managers get locked into driving change programmes, even when they are not going well. As we noted when exploring sensemaking, the escalation of commitment to a project is particularly the case when managers are personally responsible for the negative consequences. Staw and Ross (1987) suggest that managers should be rewarded for the quality of the evaluation analysis and the decision-making that they take during the change, as much the results of any change. This would serve to guard against people inflating the prospects of their own projects and ignoring the cost of persistence.

 Exercise 13.3

Consider an organization for which you have worked or your current university.

- Which aspects of the organization's performance are measured and reported (for example, finance, budgets, risk registers, staff survey data, etc.)?

- How important are these measures? What happens if a unit is deemed to underperform against these measures?

- Are there other factors that are deemed important or influential, which do not form part of the measurement process?

- What does that tell you about the connection between measurement, performance, and influence in the organization?

Change in Practice 13.2 is an example of a longitudinal evaluation study, built into the change process.

Change in Practice 13.2

Evaluating change at the Ministry of Justice

The UK Ministry of Justice has responsibility for different parts of the justice system, including the courts, prisons, and probation services. It employs 95,000 people in the UK and holds a budget of £9.2 billion.

Background

In 2009, the Ministry of Justice embarked on a major change programme, known as the 'Transforming Justice' initiative, with implementation planned over a five-year period. The changes impacted all aspects of the approach to justice, as well as methods of delivery across the wider justice system. An independent body, the Institute for Government, which undertakes research with the aim of improving government bodies, was invited to gather evaluation information in 'real-time' on how the transformation was progressing.

Evaluation methodology

In evaluating the change, the Institute for Government drew on John Kotter's eight-step model, as the guiding framework by which the Ministry intended to implement the change, see figure 9.3, reproduced below. The intention was to pay attention to the momentum of the process and the sustainability of the changes as they were implemented over this five-year period. The ministry added some further dimensions aimed at assessing the interdependencies between different aspects of Kotter's challenges.

See Chapter 9 for more on Kotter: p. 212

So, for example, in terms of Kotter's step one, establishing a sense of urgency, the evaluation aimed to assess:

- the extent to which the Ministry of Justice had people with the capabilities to assess the context and draw conclusions;
- the authority of managers to make changes in staff to gather the appropriate resources around them;
- whether the organization strategy fitted with the plan for change;
- the extent to which the organization's culture, values, and structure were enabling or inhibiting leaders in creating a sense of urgency.

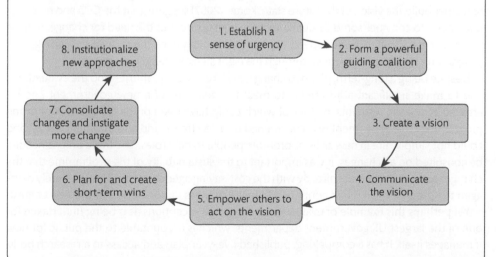

The process of evaluation included surveys, semi-structured interviews, observation at key meetings, and analysis of programme documentation.

The first two research exercises undertaken in the organization were in:

- July 2009, when a baseline assessment identified the initial areas for evaluation focus; and
- February 2010, to gauge progress six months later against the first three dimensions of Kotter's model.

Outcomes

The findings of the first two exercises suggested that:

- the case for change was widely recognized within the department;
- a leadership coalition had been formed that cut across the different business groups;
- financial savings had been identified.

As a result of the evaluation, it became clear that:

- the leadership coalition needed to be further expanded;
- work on developing the vision needed to be built on;
- different change programmes happening in different parts of the business needed to be brought together under one overarching strategy.[3-4]

In Change in Practice 13.2, leaders got regular, objective feedback on progress from an independent source, with the aim of inputting that feedback to their change management decision-making. The evaluation was built around the implementation framework: in this case, Kotter's eight-step framework. We find that many organizations use Kotter's or other similar frameworks to guide their implementation. It is interesting that the evaluation recommends putting further effort into developing the early steps within the framework, indicating the time and effort involved in building and sustaining the momentum of a change programme of this scale. For example, the report draws attention to the need to strengthen their coalition, so that the leadership across the Ministry has the strength to pursue the programme consistently and to further build the vision of the future state. Kotter (2007) suggests that the CEO and his or her team need to convince some 75 per cent of the management of the need for change in order to be successful. Often, these aspects are hurried through once the change gets going, with programme leaders keen to move through the eight steps as speedily as possible.

Despite being a long-term, planned change, in 2010, the programme—and the evaluation—had to make significant adjustments to meet the demands of a new government and increased economic restraints, neither of which could have been predicted at the start of the programme. The department was constrained by a pay freeze and a recruitment freeze, and could not simply hire in new skills or promote people to new roles. The trade unions needed be consulted on all changes. It was important to the sustainability of the programme that the change was seen to connect directly with the cost-saving agenda; it could have severely damaged the programme if it had continued to make changes in isolation from the new context.

Yet perhaps this example of evaluation is one of the exceptions. It is being undertaken for one of the largest UK government departments, which is accountable to the public for how it manages itself. It has a compelling, published five-year plan and access to a research body, funded by benefactors, to undertake services that improve government. It therefore has a strong imperative to undertake the study, as well as access to resources that do not ordinarily exist. The evaluation itself serves to 'showcase' the change, and, through doing so, the department achieved positive publicity and attention. This combination of factors is untypical. Buchanan et al. (2005) suggest that studying change sustainability is seen as dull, for it is in effect the search for evidence of stability. In many organizations, moving things on is deemed more important than assessing what is and, in our work as consultants, we find it rare for clients to want to invest in evaluation.

Learning and emergent change

The choices identified in Figure 13.1 and the structures of the evaluation processes described above lend themselves less well to emergent change processes, in which there is no formal plan, no defined outcome, but rather people create new ways of operating through a process of experimentation and continuous learning (Pascale et al., 2000). Whilst emergent change theorists draw attention to the need to work with the context, to create agility in the organization, they describe this as a process of fluid responsiveness, in which people try things out, experiments fail, and people try again. Senge et al. (1999) point to the application of inappropriate measurement of people's performance, and comment that prevalent attitudes such as 'managers should never present problems, only solutions' all get in the way of learning in order to sustain change. They also note that eliminating all judgements and evaluations simply makes organizations more vulnerable, both to the loss of their own judgement and to outside criticism. They suggest rather that the gathering of data about results and the open discussion of the meaning of those results should be used to inform the next moves.

In summary, evaluating the sustainability of change is unusual, and doing it well and objectively is difficult—but the benefits of the exercise are immediate and can inform the change process as it evolves.

Enabling factors and processes: The implications

Spread of change

In this review, we have concentrated primarily on the issues of momentum and institutionalization. A connected question is how change spreads. In their research, Buchanan et al. (2007) note that, in some instances, change or innovation need to spread across more than one area within an organization, so that they may then become institutionalized. In others, there may be a need to demonstrate that the changes can be sustained in one area before others will attempt to adopt the approach. The same principle applies at industry level, with momentum coming either from the industry itself to bring about change within organizations, or by a sufficient number of organizations sustaining the change such that adoption spreads across the industry. They suggest that the process can run in either direction depending on the context. In terms of the nature of the change, sometimes it may be replicated exactly, for example adopting the same performance appraisal system, with the same measures, process, and paperwork in all units of a global organization; at other times, broad principles of the original change are adopted elsewhere, for example applying consistent performance measures globally whilst retaining different processes and paperwork.

Sustaining momentum and institutionalizing change

The first three key factors in Figure 13.1—namely the context, content, and process of change—have been seen to collectively impact change sustainability. However, research evidence suggests that they cannot be weighted or prioritized (Fitzgerald and Buchanan, 2007). Pettigrew et al. (2001) take a **processual** perspective, paying attention to the flow of events, such that some factors may be more important than others in certain settings at particular times. The interactions of the factors may be important, such that neglecting one may not be fatal, but failing to pay attention to several may result in failure. Fitzgerald and Buchanan (2007) conclude that it is too difficult to isolate one factor and to relate it to one specific outcome. Similarly, there is no guarantee that the mix of contextual and leadership issues that enable momentum will automatically ensure institutionalization of the change and there is a need to continually readjust the approach, taking a long-term time frame. The fourth factor, evaluation, also impacts importantly on the change outcome: the choice of dimensions to be measured and the way in which the evaluation process is applied can serve to distract from or reinforce the achievement of the desired change.

 Section 2 Summary

In this section, we have:

- identified key enablers and inhibitors of sustaining momentum and institutionalizing change, and considered their impact on choices for implementing change;
- considered approaches to change evaluation, including issues of experimentation, learning, and failure in relation to evaluation;
- noted the collective rather than individual impact of all of the factors, taking a processual perspective of the change process.

 Integrative Case Study

Telemedicine: A case of poor spread and low sustainability

The term 'telemedicine' refers to the use of IT as an integral part of clinical healthcare provision. It ranges from simple dial-up telephone services, to using satellite technology and video-conferencing to conduct real-time consultations between clinical experts in different countries, or indeed clinicians and their patients in different locations, undertaking remote medical procedures or examinations.

The introduction of telemedicine is an advance that has the capacity to transform organizations and the healthcare industry, improving the quality of provision for individuals. Economically, the case has been made for the opportunity to deliver enhanced services to a wider audience in an affordable way. Greenhalgh et al. (2004: 306) assert that 'the widespread adoption and assimilation of telemedicine could potentially have significant impacts on healthcare delivery systems as well as intra-and inter-organization structures of healthcare organizations'. If it were to achieve full saturation, it would affect all existing structures and cultures.

There are a number of factors that have made this challenging. Information technology, which has proved to be a key enabler of change in other contexts, faces problems in the health sector because of scale and range of different IT systems within different parts of the health economy. The need for a range of interrelated services and organizations to adopt change simultaneously adds to the complexity. Health care in Europe is a highly emotive issue, with citizens having strong views, which means that changes take place in the media spotlight; clinical experts, whose involvement is critical, are wary of any threats to their entrenched power base. As a result, it has suffered from 'relatively poor spread and low sustainability' (Greenhalgh et al., 2004).

Telemedicine was originally instigated to help remote or underserved areas to get better access to services. More recently, one of the most used and straightforward applications of telemedicine in the UK was the introduction of a 24-hour helpline, using web and telephone services, called NHS Direct. In 2010, it received 14,000 calls per day and employed more than 3,000 staff, 40 per cent of whom were trained nurses. The benefits of the service included the rapidity of response that could be achieved—for example, getting speedy telephone access to an expert whilst still keeping the continuity of face-to-face care with the local physician and staying close to home for treatment. Yet not all doctors supported the service, and it was seen by the government and other key stakeholders as expensive to run, so that, although patient demand continued to grow, funding was reduced.

Also of potentially great impact on the system at large is the use of telemedicine for file transfers, such as interactive still images or video images for diagnostic services. For example, a London teaching hospital formed a partnership with an Australian healthcare company to read and interpret X-rays in real time—that is, the service was provided for London's nightshift workers by Australian radiologists during their dayshift. This created significant savings: there was no need to have an expensive consultant radiologist on call during the night in London and the results were of high quality because the clinicians dealing with the diagnosis in Australia were not tired. The practitioners themselves had greater access to knowledge transfer and professional networks through such working practices. The patient received expert care whilst being treated locally. Yet, by 2011, such innovative approaches had not been widely adopted.

Despite the strength of the cases made for telemedicine, implementation has taken many years of false starts. The introduction of telemedicine has rarely been conducted except by experiment with short-term funding. Typically, the work has been driven by small teams of enthusiasts giving their own time and resources. Early attempts to use technology were in Arctic regions and other areas with remote populations. Whilst each of these attempts was planned to create a change in service delivery, the evaluation tended to focus on implementation problems rather than progress or benefits. In early experiments, the costs tended to be high and the technology proved unreliable, so that attempts rarely survived beyond the trial period. By 2011, some key services had been established, but not linked up to one coherent service in any country, never mind across countries. Despite a period of investment in technology, operating across different systems was still unpredictable. Where telemedicine was introduced, its use was not always aligned to the strategic plans or the needs of clinicians and patients. The case for clinical advantage had yet to be proven in reality. Reported barriers to building sustainable programmes tended to reflect the concerns of large hospitals and healthcare systems, rather than the smaller groups of members or rural participants in programmes.

Even so, proponents remained optimistic. Technology was becoming increasingly user-friendly; the price/performance ratio continued to improve. Technology companies were starting to understand the need for involvement with the client during the initial development of the software, as well as during implementation, allowing better tailoring to the users' needs. There was hope that telemedicine would yet be a change initiative that transformed health care on a long-term, sustainable basis.

Questions

1. What do you think are the cultural and political enablers and inhibitors of these changes in the healthcare industry?

2. The case describes programmes created through small teams of enthusiasts. What are the opportunities for these teams to act as change agents? What other types of leadership are needed to make this change sustainable?

3. Which theories and perspectives do you find most helpful in exploring this case?

Conclusion

We have considered three key issues in this chapter: what constitutes sustainable change; choices in change implementation that enable the maintenance of momentum and the institutionalization of change; and the nature of the evaluation of change.

In the introduction to this chapter, we reported the perceived wisdom that change is difficult, and that sustaining momentum and institutionalizing change is more so, such that change programmes often fail. This may be true. Yet consistent data to support such claims is difficult to find. Jacobs (2002) notes that interest in organizational failure and the persistence of change first emerged in research literature in the early 1980s. Typically, reports tended to describe what was happening during the initial stages of the project, before momentum declined and the programme collapsed. This suggests that being sure about the outcomes of change programmes requires longitudinal study. Such studies are undertaken rarely and tend to happen in the public sector more than the private sector. For these reasons, it remains uncertain that change programmes are as likely to be as doomed as some of the rhetoric suggests.

Due to the number of factors involved in the change process and the interaction between contributing factors, there is no simple way of offering a definitive list of those that, with certainty, will enable success in sustaining change. Paying attention to the organization's context, leading in ways that engage staff, as well as constantly reinforcing and rewarding the nature of the change that is desired, are seen to improve the likelihood of success. As Buchanan et al. (2007: 23) point out: 'There are no simple prescriptions for managing sustainability. It requires a vigilant diagnostic approach to monitoring the factors which either support or threaten sustainability and monitoring the timescale over which sustainability should be encouraged.' In our experience, when time and attention is given to the issues that we have highlighted, change programmes do produce at least some of the hoped-for improvements, and indeed can impact the long-term health and viability of the organization.

Please visit the Online Resource Centre at **http://www.oxfordtextbooks.co.uk/orc/ myers** *to access further resources for students and lecturers.*

Change in Practice sources

1. Campbell, K. (2010) 'Change in the valleys', *Converse*, 7: 28–9.

2. Pearce, D. and Williams, E. (2010) *Seeds for Change: Action Learning for Innovation*, Aberystwyth: Menter a Busnes.

3. Gash, T. and McCrae, J. (for the Institute for Government) (2010) *Transformation in the Ministry of Justice: 2010 Interim Evaluation Report.* http://www.instituteforgovernment.org.uk/pdfs/ transformation_in_the_ministry_of_justice.pdf

4. Institute for Government (undated) 'About us'. http://www.instituteforgovernment.org.uk/content/1/ about-us

Integrative Case Study sources

BBC News (2010) 'Government confirms plan to scrap NHS direct helpline', 29 Aug. http://www.bbc.co. uk/news/uk-11120853

Greenhalgh, T., Robert, G. Bate, P., Kyriakidou, O., McFarlane, F., and Peacock, R. (2004) *How to Spread Good Ideas: A Systematic Review of the Literature on Diffusion, Dissemination and Sustainability of Innovations in Health Service Delivery and Organisation—Report for the National Co-ordinating Centre for NHS Service Delivery and Organisation R&D (NCCSDO).* http://www.sdo.nihr.ac.uk/files/project/ SDO_FR_08-1201-038_V01.pdf

Grigsby, W. (2002) 'Telehealth: An assessment of growth and distribution', *The Journal of Rural Health*, **18**(2): 348–58.

NHS Direct (2010) *NHS Direct Business Plan 2010/11.* http://www.nhsdirect.nhs.uk/About/~/media/Files/ AboutUsPDFs/BusinessPlan2010-11.ashx

NHS Direct website: http://www.nhsdirect.nhs.uk/

Further reading

Buchanan, D., Fitzgerald, L., and Ketley, D. (2007) *The Sustainability and Spread of Organizational Change*, London: Routledge.
For a detailed illustration of the nature of change sustainability in the health service.

Leppitt, N. (2006) 'Challenging the code of change part 1: Praxis does not make perfect', *Journal of Change Management*, **6**(2): 121–42.
For research and comment on critical success factors for organizational change and the importance of a contingency paradigm.

Marr, B. (2010) *Balanced Scorecards for the Public Sector*, London: Ark Group.
For a range of case studies of the application of balanced scorecards in organizations in 2010.

14 Conclusion

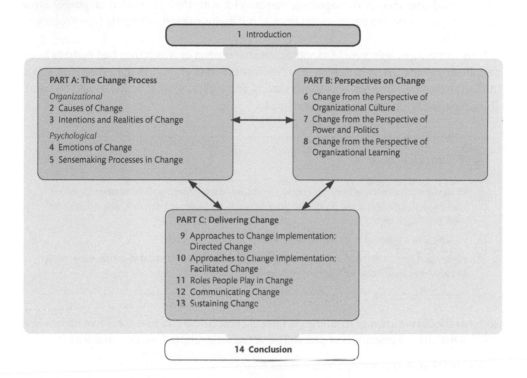

This book was designed to provide a picture of the landscape of change, a sense of the territory, navigating through various perspectives and the different languages and concepts used in describing change. Familiarity with this landscape matters because beliefs and actions regarding change vary according to the perspective taken and the ideas employed; organizational change looks very different depending on whether one focuses on its planned or emergent aspects, and whether one looks at it through the lens of culture, power and politics, or organizational learning; directed and facilitated methods of implementing organizational change involve very different techniques.

Many academics and writers of best-selling management books subscribe to the view that the pressures on managers mean that they are mainly interested in simple, punchy, and plausible solutions to their problems. In our work, both teaching organizational change and consulting to clients, we have indeed encountered people who want a cookbook with simple-to-follow recipes. And, when we seek to explain that change is complex and messy and cannot be reduced to a linear programme with guaranteed outcomes, there are some who cannot accept this. However, we also have found others who want theories and frameworks that have practical application and relevance, but who do not naively assume that they will offer a universal panacea. They value being introduced to new frameworks that provide a language and conceptual map for making sense of their experience in their work, whether initiating change themselves or feeling themselves 'on the receiving end'. There is evidence from linguistics that language influences our thinking. For instance, in the Native American language, Zuni, the words for the colours yellow and orange are the same. Zuni speakers perform far worse on memory tasks that require yellow and orange items to be distinguished than do English speakers, who have separate words for each colour. In a similar way, it has been argued that change management frameworks, with *their* associated language, allow those in organizations to perceive and think about their situation differently (von Krogh and Roos, 1995).

New frameworks help people to appreciate phenomena of which they had perhaps been peripherally aware. These can create 'aha!' moments of recognition. In our experience, this is the first step to new insights, new conversations, and exploring what action should be taken. This is how we hope the book has been helpful.

 Exercise 14.1

- What were you expecting from this textbook when you started reading it? To what extent have your expectations been met? If some of those expectations have not been met, why do you now think that might be?

- Which frameworks and ideas from this book have resonated for you?

- What was it about them that attracted you? Did they help you to understand your own experiences? Did they make a practical difference to your work?

So, what should we attempt to address in this conclusion? We aim to explore two issues—one about *what* change practitioners deal with, and the other about *how* they deal with it.

1. Is more change happening and is it all necessary?
2. Getting change 'right'.

Is more change happening and is it all necessary?

We shall start by seeking to explore whether there really is more organizational change than ever before, or whether in fact such talk is part of a broader phenomenon, which has been referred to as an addiction to change (Grey, 2003). Firstly, we ask you to reflect on this yourself.

 Exercise 14.2

- Do *you* think there is more change now, or less, or the same amount as there used to be?
  - To which era are you comparing the present day?
  - What experiences or information are influencing your view?
- Talk to someone who is from a different generation and explore his or her answers to the same questions.

If you open a book on change, or look at the introduction to a company's annual accounts, or talk to a senior manager in a large organization, public or private, the chances are that there will be some words to the effect that there has never been so much change. Many writers argue that the world is changing in unprecedented ways, with increasing turbulence and uncertainty. 'There is a clear consensus that the pace of change has never been greater than in the current continuously evolving business environment' claims By (2005: 378). Such sentiments are heard so often that they begin to become the norm, socially accepted givens, not open to challenge or question. Just as hardly anyone questions that the earth is round, it is widely assumed that there is more change now than ever before. However, a few writers do question such assumptions. 'Change seems, just now, to have precisely the character of a solid social construction, a thing plainly in the domain of truth rather than falsity. It is its very taken-for-grantedness that seems to . . . be of interest' suggests Grey (2002: 3) in what he describes as his 'polemical critique of the current orthodoxy' (ibid.: 1). So, what evidence is there to support the claim that we are living in times of unprecedented change? We would agree with Grey (2002: 5), who argues that 'there is no basis upon which it would be possible to sustain or evaluate such claims'.

We now turn to whether the present extent of organizational change is *necessary*. Grint (1997: 35) refers to a fetish for change that has become an overarching implicit or explicit rationale and justification for specific change programmes. Sorge and van Witteloostuijn (2004: 1205) use the metaphor of a virus, suggesting that 'the global business world is infected by a virus that induces a permanent need for organizational change'. Just like a flu virus, the change virus mutates, resulting in different fads and fashions (Abrahamson, 1996), as explored in Chapters 2 and 11.

See Chapters 2 and 11 for more on management fashions: pp. 24, 258

What explanations are offered for how this obsession with change has come about? Sorge and van Witteloostuijn (2004) suggest that it is because organizational change has become the raison d'être of two powerful groups—top managers and management consultants. One of the features that supposedly differentiates leaders from managers is the former's capacity to initiate change (Kotter, 1990). Therefore, addiction to change is a way in which leaders can sustain a particular sort of identity for themselves, so that they consider 'absence of change is a deficiency' (Sorge and van Witteloostuijn, 2004: 1207). Leadership and management roles tend to be characterized by action and doing, with little time for thinking and reflection (Binney et al., 2009). But help is at hand, from the second group whose raison d'être and identity is inextricably bound up with change—the management consultants. Some commentators see the relationship as a very negative one, with consultants selling hype for profit (Clark, 1995); others claim that consulting firms help organizations to deal with change (Armbrüster and Glückler, 2007); a third view suggests that the relationship is one of mutually self-reinforcing dependency and insecurity (Sturdy,1997). Whatever view is adopted of the relationship between the buyers and sellers of management knowledge, the outcome is the same: an increased demand for change, change management, and consultancy.

See Chapter 11 for more on the leadership of change: p. 244

See Chapter 11 for more on consultants and change: p. 257

Why then are there not more people extolling the virtues of stability? Perhaps the reason is that change is an idea that favours the interests of those who already have power and that, therefore, their voices dominate. 'Who is willing to sacrifice her or his career and reputation by making an enthusiastic plea for the prevalence and value of inertia and rigidity?'

See Chapter 4 for more on the emotional impact of change: pp. 69–77

See Chapter 7 for more on resistance: p. 150

ask Sorge and van Witteloostuijn (2004: 1213). Yet organizational inertia can be seen as a benefit because stable structures and processes can guarantee the reliability of, for instance, goods or services (Hannan and Freeman, 1984), and organizational change can damage the lives of individuals and communities. Much of the change literature closes off the possibility that change might be undesirable. As discussed in Chapter 7, those who resist change are often stigmatized as afraid or obstructive, yet, whatever the relevance of psychological explanations for resistance, there can also be plain economic ones: 'most change management initiatives entail, at least for some, more work, less pay, or no job. If they did not, it would probably not be resisted' (Grey, 2002: 15). So who is giving voice to the interests of those on the receiving end of change? Instead of seeing resistance as a problem, there is growing interest in resistance as a potential form of leadership that mobilizes energy and challenges management's views about the need for, and approaches to, change (Zoller and Fairhurst, 2007).

Getting change 'right'

Getting change 'right' could refer both to accomplishing change effectively and to accomplishing change ethically. Whether or not there is more change in organizations today than there once was, these are two vital challenges. Focusing first on accomplishing change *effectively*, a major challenge for research into change is the extent to which evidence from studies on organizational change 'rarely penetrates into the organization's decision-making headquarters and . . . never leaves academia's inner circle' (Sorge and van Witteloostuijn, 2004: 1224). So one route forward is to try to build closer links between the world of practice and the world of research (Austin and Bartunek, 2003).

As discussed in Chapter 1, it might be comforting if change management theory could offer predictions rather than possibilities, and templates rather than tentative suggestions. However, as explored in Chapter 13, the statistics on the outcomes of change programmes rarely demonstrate clear cause-and-effect links between change interventions and desired outcomes. Should we read from this that change management does not work or that is there something else going on? Sorge and van Witteloostuijn (2004: 1223) suggest that 'the challenge is to deal with the paradox that much scholarly knowledge is framed in universal terms, whereas practical problem-solving requires specific solutions'. Certainly much change management literature is based on the assumption that what has worked (supposedly) in one situation can be applied to another—that is, that the findings can be generalized.

See Chapter 5 for more on the escalation of commitment: p. 95

There are challenges, too, in considering the *ethics* of organizational change processes. In Chapter 5, we explained how escalation of commitment may lead people to adjust their ethical principles rather than adjust their behaviour. Ethical conflicts in an organizational transition may arise for people at any level in organizations in terms, for example, of honesty, respect, responsibility, fairness, or kindness (including for people opposing change as well as those supporting it). When they have put a lot of overt effort into their part in the change process, they may make sense of their situation by altering their principles rather than reconsidering their conduct (Bazerman and Tenbrunsel, 2011). If people's ethical principles are moulded by their behaviour, rather than the other way around, assessing the ethics of organizational change is problematic. For example, people may unconsciously lower the weight they give to environmental sustainability *because* organizational changes are damaging the environment.

Another phenomenon that undermines the idea that ethical judgements about change are dispassionate is 'moral luck' (Ciulla, 2004). We tend to assess whether conduct has been morally good or bad based on its outcomes, as well as the behaviour itself. Leaders, in particular, get judged on outcomes.

- Ken Lay was seen as a good leader of change at Enron, applauded for his commitment to 'innovation', until the company collapsed (see Change in Practice 6.1). If his risk-taking had continued to pay off, ethical judgements of his leadership might have continued to be positive.

- Fred Goodwin, the former chief executive of RBS, was lauded and knighted before becoming widely seen as a 'bad' banker only after the decline and part-nationalization of the bank in 2008.

See Chapter 6 for more on Enron: p. 115

What is needed, in our view, is a practical understanding of what helps people to establish, maintain, and apply their principles as they engage with organizational transitions (Gentile, 2010). This is still a field of knowledge in its infancy.

We agree with Beer (2000) that action research is perhaps a promising direction for future investigation into both accomplishing change effectively and accomplishing change ethically. The primary aim of action research is to create knowledge that is useful to those involved in the research, rather than to try to find generalizable laws. It explicitly adopts a participatory approach, advocating that research should be *with*, *for*, and *by* people, rather than *on* them (Reason and Bradbury, 2001); so all participants, whether researchers or practitioners, work collaboratively in the action research enterprise. Cycles of action aimed at increasing understanding or at stimulating change are interspersed with periods of reflection (Marshall, 2001).

In summary, there is certainly evidence that change and the imperative for change is a significant feature of how leaders, consultants, and, indeed, many other employees see their roles. Some writers suggest that we have become obsessed with change and ignore the virtues of stability. Some practitioners want prescriptions and predictions from the change management literature, even though it may be impossible to make law-like generalizations. Others find that knowing about different ways of thinking about change improves their own understanding of change situations, enabling them to consider a wider range of choices about what to do next. However, in any event, it should be acknowledged that the effective and the ethical accomplishment of organizational change remain fields that are not fully understood. In the future, it would be beneficial to see closer links between the world of research and the world of practice, and, perhaps, action research offers one of the most promising ways in which to achieve this.

Please visit the Online Resource Centre at **http://www.oxfordtextbooks.co.uk/orc/ myers** *to access further resources for students and lecturers.*

Glossary

360° feedback process feedback is provided by subordinates, peers, and supervisors/bosses. It also includes a self-assessment and, in some cases, feedback from external sources such as customers and suppliers or other interested stakeholders.

4I model Mary Crossan's model according to which organizational learning involves four learning processes: *intuiting*, coming up with initial ideas; *interpreting*, understanding their implications; *integrating*, developing cohesive action at the group level; and *institutionalizing*, incorporating learning across the organization.

action learning Small group work aimed at exploring problems, where the learning comes from the exploration of the issues with others. The action may be a shift in someone's thinking or the decision to do something differently.

action research Derived from Lewin's planned approach to change, it puts action at the heart of research. It recognizes that successful action comes from analysing the situation accurately and choosing the most appropriate solution. The cycle of data collection, diagnosis, feedback, intervention, and evaluation may be repeated: the action research cycle.

acquisition The takeover of one organization by another.

Aftermath The final stage in Isabella's model of how managers understand events as their organizations change, in which they take time to evaluate changes that have taken place in terms of their consequences, their strengths and weaknesses, the winners and losers, and so on.

anticipation The first stage in Isabella's model of how managers understand events as their organizations change, in which they gather scattered information as they realize something is going on, without a clear understanding of events.

anticipatory change Change made in expectation of the need to do so.

apparent culture change A change in which the culture accommodates change and does not genuinely alter, despite appearances.

appraisal theory perspective on emotions The view that prior cognitive interpretations of situations trigger emotions.

Appreciative Inquiry An inquiry process based on exploring existing strengths and developing greater capacity in those strengths.

artefacts Observable features—the objects, structures, and patterns of behaviour that typify an organization.

assumptions Beliefs and values—about work, organizations, relationships, people, etc.—that have become so ingrained they are often unrecognized.

back stage Activity that is covert and behind the scenes.

balanced scorecard An approach to defining organizational effectiveness in which a combination of quantitative and qualitative measures are used to assess performance.

behavioural commitment Retrospectively discovering beliefs that explain or justify actions.

BRIC An acronym comprising the first letters of the four fastest-growing, major economies in the world: Brazil, India, China and Russia.

business process re-engineering The radical redesign of business processes to achieve performance improvements.

bystanding In conversation, when someone stands back from the issue and provides perspective on what is happening.

calculative psychological contract A psychological contract based on the exchange of work for the satisfaction of needs, such as money, social and career opportunities, promotion, training, and a sense of achievement.

change curve A visual representation of a stage model of individual adaptation to organizational change in the form of a graph, which dips during the initial stages of transition before rising in later stages (see Figure 4.1).

chaos theory Unpredictable outcomes are produced over the long term, with patterns within that unpredictability.

charismatic transformations In which corporate transformation is required and management adopts a charismatic style to gain emotional commitment to the future vision of the organization.

coalition The coming together into groups of those who share particular interests, or who want to advance specific approaches to change.

coercive psychological contract A psychological contract established when individuals are working completely against their wishes.

coercive style Change is imposed in staff without attempts to persuade them: compliance is required.

collaborative merger A merger or acquisition involving integration of cultures.

collaborative style Involves widespread participation by employees in important decisions about the organization's future.

complexity theory The theory that physical and social reality is composed of a wide range of interacting orderly, complex, and disorderly phenomena.

complex responsive processes perspective (of organizations) Organizations are viewed as patterns of interaction between people, which produces further interaction.

confirmation The second stage in Isabella's model of how managers understand events as their organizations change, in which they begin to develop explanations of what is happening based on their past experience.

consultative style Offers limited involvement in decision-making. Employees are asked for their views, which management will consider.

content (of a change) The actual change that takes place.

context (of a change) The causes, constraints, and opportunities that influence a change.

contextual environment The general environment in which an organization operates.

contingency approach The choice of approach is dependent on the circumstances.

continuous process improvement A process aimed at simultaneously increasing quality and reducing costs through seeing the process as a whole system and involving staff in the process of review.

cooperative psychological contract A psychological contract based on employees identifying with the perceived goals of the organization, and having a voice in the selection of those goals and how they are achieved.

core competencies An interdependent system of collective skills within an organization, including employee skills and explicit knowledge, technical and communication processes, and managerial systems and values, which provides a unique competitive advantage—not in any one particular situation, but in a sustainable way over time.

core processes Processes that are at the heart of the organization's activities, crucial to the delivery of the product to the customer, for example.

corporate transformation Organization-wide change: changes in structures, processes, and ways of thinking.

culmination The third stage in Isabella's model of how managers understand events as their organizations change, in which understandings are amended as they compare past and present, and new explanations and mental models are constructed.

cultural acquirer (In a redesign merger) the organization with the culture that prevails in the merged group.

cultural dynamics model The model of how values, artefacts, symbols, and assumptions relate in a cycle, developed by Mary Jo Hatch.

culture The name given to the collection of accepted ways of doing things and values that are shared by and influence people's behaviour in an organization.

deep acting A form of emotional labour in which an employee attempts genuinely to feel, or not feel, an emotion.

defects (Lean) Faults in the product or dips in the quality of the finished product or instances in which they do not meet the customer requirements.

defects (Six Sigma) Instances in which the product of a process does not meet the customer requirement.

defects per million opportunities (DPMO) (Six Sigma) The number of defects that occur in a million attempts to deliver a specific product or process.

delayering The removal of a layer of the organization's hierarchy.

developmental transitions Change made by constant adjustment to environmental conditions, with management adopting a consultative approach.

DFSS (Six Sigma) Design for Six Sigma: the systematizing of product development.

dialogue Conversation that begins by really listening and understanding each other's points of view with a commitment to understanding one another's underlying assumptions and decision-making frameworks, so that double-loop learning can take place.

differentiation viewpoint A viewpoint on organizational culture that focuses on consistency *within subcultures*.

directed approach Change that is driven from the top of the organization, employing firm persuasion to engage those affected.

directive style Leaders take the decisions about the change and create a vision of the future that they want staff to buy into.

discontinuous change Major organizational change, conducted rapidly.

discretionary effort Employees taking on work that is not strictly part of their job role.

display rules Implicit or explicit guidelines as to what emotions should be shown and how they should be expressed.

DMAIC (Six Sigma) An approach to problem-solving: define the issue; measure the problem; analyse the data; improve the process; and control the outcome.

double-loop learning Learning that involves reassessing the value of intended outcomes or the assumptions and values behind current practices.

downsizing A reduction in headcount, typically by redundancies.

dynamic capabilities A system within an organization—based on a set of processes to integrate, reconfigure, gain, and release resources—to adapt the organization's core competencies and how they are applied in rapidly changing environments.

ecosystem A way in which complex natural systems evolve.

edge of chaos Systems are poised between order and disorder.

emergent change Change based on the assumption that it is a continuous unpredictable process of aligning and realigning in response to environmental changes.

emotional balancing The development of a balance between middle managers who are emotionally committed to change and those who attend to emotional support for subordinates during change.

emotional contagion The direct spread of emotions from one person to others.

emotional intelligence The ability to perceive and understand one's own and others' emotions, and to use this information to guide one's thinking and behaviour.

emotional labour The suppression or apparent expression of emotions that is required as part of a person's work.

employee engagement People expressing themselves in their work physically, cognitively and emotionally.

enculturation People tending to adopt the patterns of behaviours, values, symbolic meanings, and assumptions of the culture while they work in an organization.

entrepreneurial intuiting Intuiting that involves finding a new way in which to view the organizational environment.

environment The forces external to the organization, for example markets, customers, the economy, and government policy.

evaluation feedback Data collected to undertake long-term assessment of the impact of change.

evaluation (of change) Data that is collected to review the progress and impact of a change programme.

escalation of commitment The phenomenon whereby the more people go through for a course of action, the more convincing they make their reasons for pursuing it.

espoused values Values that are stated in speeches, internal documents, posters, advertisements, corporate websites, etc.

expert intuiting Intuiting that involves identifying patterns, for example in the internal or external business environment.

explicit knowledge Knowledge that can be formally expressed and easily articulated.

explicit knowledge at a collective level Stories, jargon, and metaphors that circulate in the informal organization and provide capabilities that support effective working and organizational achievement.

extension merger A merger or acquisition in which the two former organizations continue to operate independently, and have separate cultures.

external environment The world outside the organization. The term assumes that there is a boundary, at least metaphorically, between an organization's external and internal environment.

facilitated approach An approach involving the wider membership of the organization in the shaping of change.

facilitated change Change in which the wider membership of the organization is involved in shaping the change.

fine-tuning Gentle change at departmental or unit level, for example changing policies or procedures.

first-order change Doing more of the same more efficiently or effectively.

following In conversation, when someone supports and develops an idea.

force field analysis A planning tool that examines the forces (positive and negative) that may influence a change process.

formal organization The officially defined aspects of an organization—hierarchy, structure, production processes, etc.

fragmentation viewpoint A viewpoint on organizational culture that recognizes that the same event might be interpreted in contradictory ways even within a single subculture, or even by a single person.

framing The art of moderating your message to connect with your audience's needs and interests.

front stage An activity that is overt and complies with formal, logical norms of how things should happen within an organization.

Future Search A large group method to undertake strategic action planning.

Generation Y A term for the demographic cohort following Generation X, which is those born between the mid-1970s and 2000.

geographic trend Patterns of activity that are specific to an area of the world.

GRIN technologies An acronym formed from the first letters of four technologies that some scientists believe are most likely to transform society in the twenty-first century: genetics; robotics; information technology; and nanotechnology.

group process Working with the dynamics within a group, noticing what gives rise to patterns of behaviour within the group.

implementation feedback Data collected to assess whether a change intervention is having the intended impact.

incremental adjustment Adjustments made in response to the changing environment. Such modifications are distinct, but not radical, for example adapting structures or strategies at unit or departmental level.

incremental change Small-scale changes that are relatively minor or conducted step by step.

incremental cultural change The incorporation of new values and assumptions (and usually corresponding symbols and artefacts) into an existing organizational culture.

industry trends Patterns in activity that are specific to an industry or sector of the economy.

informal organization Those aspects of an organization that are not officially defined, are often less visible, and are characteristically human.

inner context The context of change inside the organization.

institutionalized (change) Change that has become an accepted part of an organization's ways of doing things.

institutionalizing (4I model) The organization-level process of incorporating what has been learned in one setting into other groups or work units, or across the organization, by embedding it in systems, structures, routines, and practices.

integrating (4I model) The process of putting new understandings into action at the group and organizational level by doing things differently.

integration viewpoint A viewpoint on organizational culture that ignores subcultural differences and other inconsistencies, or treats them simply as irregularities to be eliminated.

interpreting (4I model) The process of understanding an idea in more detail, as an individual or through conversation.

intervention Everything that a change practitioner does to disturb or intervene in the organizational system.

intuiting (4I model) The initial, individual-level process of coming up with new ideas or insights.

issue selling A process by which individuals draw others' attention to what they believe matters in order to influence decision-making and change.

Jams Events with online threaded discussions on set issues, which can involve thousands of people, initiated and popularized by IBM.

job crafting The subtle ways in which individuals often modify what is written in their job descriptions, changing the task or performing the task differently.

Lean A process management philosophy that aims to review processes to identify waste.

learning organization An organization in which organizational learning is especially effective so that it 'is continually expanding its capacity to create its future' (Senge, 2006:14).

life cycle A biological metaphor that suggests that organizations, like organisms, are born, grow through different phases, and then die, or are reborn or renewed.

logical incrementalism The development of change in small stages, through continual low-scale change, with the opportunity to adapt as the situation moves on.

long-run agility The capacity to change technology or products in order to respond to requirements.

management fashions Beliefs, widely held by managers at a particular times, that certain management techniques are able to solve organizational problems.

media richness The level of cues and information available to a receiver of communication.

mental models Habitual ways of thinking about, and responding to, familiar situations.

merger When two organizations join together to become one single new entity.

metaphor A description or a way of looking at a thing (or a situation) as if it were something else.

Model 1 theories of action Implicit rules by which people often interact: to be in unilateral control over situations; to maximize winning and minimize losing; to avoid anxiety and embarrassment; and to be seen to be rational.

modular transformation A major realignment of one or more departments (not the whole organization).

momentum (change) Sustaining the energy and focus of the change process.

move In conversation, when someone proposes an idea or advocates a way forward.

movement The second step in Lewin's model of change. The chosen approach to change is implemented and it is expected to see people doing things differently.

normative knowledge Individuals' understanding of the norms of expected or appropriate behaviour.

offshoring Moving the outsourced service to another part of the world.

Open Space Technology A large group method undertaken in marketplace format to enable networking and the creation of new ideas to solve organizational issues.

opposing In conversation, when someone challenges what has been said.

organizational citizenship behaviour Employees going out of their way to help colleagues in the workplace.

organizational culture Organizational processes that enable people to understand events, situations, objects, and actions in a shared and distinctive way.

organizational learning Learning that *is affected by* the systems, structures, routines, and practices of the organization and which *changes* these systems, structures, routines, and practices.

organization development A planned approach to organizational change, which is managed from the top, through interventions in the organization's processes to improve the well-being and/or the effectiveness of the organization.

outer context The context of change outside the organization.

overproduction Making too much (of a product) or making it too early, or making it 'just in case'.

participatory change communication Communication to gain employee input to shape a change programme.

PESTLE A framework for analysing six categories of external trends. The acronym comprises the first letter of each the categories: political; economic; social; technological; legal; and environmental.

planned change Having a deliberate intention to change, with clearly defined start and end points.

pluralist A perspective on organizations that acknowledges the existence of different interest groups, and therefore the likelihood of political behaviour.

positive psychology A recent branch of psychology that believes in helping individuals and organizations to identify their strengths and to use them to increase and sustain their respective levels of well-being. This includes creating effective interventions to build thriving individuals, families, and communities.

procedural justice Justice in which there is due notice and explanation.

process (of change or transition) How the people involved, in practice, accomplish a change—psychologically and practically.

process re-engineering The redesign of business processes to achieve performance improvements.

processual approach (change) Approach that sees change as a complex and dynamic process. It focuses on the interrelatedness of individuals, groups, organizations, and society, rejecting the idea that there is a single cause or simple explanation for events.

programmatic change communication The top-down dissemination of information, telling employees about what will be happening and how a change should be implemented.

psychological availability The belief that you possess the physical, emotional, and psychological resources to personally engage at work despite challenges and distractions.

psychological contract A subjective, implicit agreement between an individual and his or her employer, including both what can be expected from the employee and what can be expected from the employer.

psychological contract violation A situation in which the implicit promises of the psychological contract (as understood by the individual) are broken.

psychological meaningfulness The belief that you are making a difference by expressing yourself at work.

psychological safety The belief that you can reveal and be yourself without fear of negative consequences.

pull (Lean) The flow of the process towards the customer.

punctuated equilibrium A model of change that sees organizations evolving through long periods of stability, which are broken (punctuated) by bursts of discontinuous change.

quality circle A group that meets to solve work related problems together, the circle of people remaining intact from project to project.

rapid improvement event A workshop used in the Lean process to make small, quickly introduced changes.

reactive change Change made in response to circumstances, because the industry or wider business environment conditions have changed.

realization The role of the leadership team in organizations of weaving strategic achievements (and failures) into a coherent storyline.

realized strategy Strategy as it turned out in pratice, recognized retrospectively in patterns of actual organizational behaviour.

recreation Fundamental changes to the organization in response to crisis.

redesign merger A merger or acquisition involving the orginal culture of one organization prevailing in the whole group.

refreeze The third step in Lewin's model of change, which seeks to embed and normalize the changes.

relational knowledge Individuals' understanding of the intentions, concerns, and interests of other individuals and social relationships.

relational processes Processes focusing on the relationship between two or more people, intervening in the patterns and dynamics to effect change.

resistance Acts deliberately done, or not done, in opposition to others' desires.

resistance leadership A leader who galvanizes fellow resistors into collective action

resource-based view of strategy A perspective on strategy that focuses on the internal resources of the organization.

resources The assets available to an organization. These can be physical (inventory, plant, factories, buildings), monetary (credit, cash), and human (skills, knowledge, client relationships).

revolutionary cultural change A change in which the organization is forced into *abandonment* of values by adoption of new, antagonistic ones. In effect, it becomes a new organization.

rhetorical crafting The art of verbal expression, which can involve the use of repetition, which aids recall, the use of different rhythms to keep the audience's interest, the use of rhetorical questions and dramatic pauses, as well as the use of stories and metaphors.

scale of change How rapid and substantial the change is.

scenario planning A strategic planning exercise through which different possible versions of an organization's future are imagined.

scope of a metaphor The aspects of something, or some situation, to which a metaphor is relevant.

second-order change Thinking completely differently about something—operating from a completely different perspective or frame of reference.

self-directed groups Groups in which there is no one leader automatically assigned as a result of seniority.

self-organization and emergence The interaction between people that creates population-wide patterns, for which there is no blueprint or plan.

self-organize How order emerges and is maintained in complex systems.

sensegiving Active efforts to influence the way in which events are interpreted in organizations.

sensemaking The way in which people establish interpretations and link them with their own actions.

shared beliefs Views regarded as true by many employees.

shared meanings or understandings Ways of understanding a situation (or event or action or communication) that are shared among many employees or across the whole organization.

shared values Goals and standards to which many employees aspire.

short-run responsiveness The capacity to flex the costs and resources quickly to respond to new needs.

single-loop learning Learning based on planning, implementation of plans, monitoring the impact, and analysing how to improve performance to meet a pre-existing goal, and based on pre-existing values and assumptions.

situated perspective on emotions The view that emotions are distinctive ways in which to engage with, and alter, social situations.

Six Sigma A change method that aims to minimize variation in outputs.

social constructionism The view that 'reality' as we perceive it—including the reality of organizations—derives from, and is maintained by, interactions between people.

social constructionist perspective on emotions The view that emotions, and the ways in which they are expressed, are formed and shaped by societal culture.

socialization activities Following a merger or acquisition, activities that enable employees from the two former organizations to meet and work together.

span The extent of the organization that is affected by the change, from one team or unit, to the whole organization and its partners.

spread (change) New practices adopted in one part of the organization or industry spread more widely.

standard deviation The square root of the variance. This is the most commonly applied measure of variation and takes into account all data points and their distances from the mean.

strategic alliance A formal relationship, between two or more parties, to pursue agreed goals jointly.

strategic knowledge Individuals' awareness of the organization's goals, competitors, and broader environmental context.

strategy The mix of deliberate plans and emergent patterns that integrate an organization's major goals, policies, and action sequences.

strategy core value A value that is likely to be central to the successful implementation of an intended strategy.

strategy peripheral value A value that is likely to be helpful for the successful implementation of an intended strategy, but which is of only minor importance to this.

strong organizational culture An organizational culture in which there is a deeply held consensus on values, symbols, beliefs, and assumptions among the employees.

subculture A distinct group of employees with values, beliefs, symbols, and assumptions that differ from those of other employees.

surface acting A form of emotional labour in which an employee feigns emotion that he or she does not feel, or hides what is really felt.

survivors People who remain working for an organization after redundancies have been made.

survivor syndrome The characteristic emotions and attitudes found among survivors of redundancy programmes.

sustaining change The process through which new working methods, performance enhancements, and continuous improvements are maintained for a period appropriate to a given context.

symbols Particular established shared meanings associated with certain artefacts.

systems thinking Mapping out interrelationships between different factors or issues inside and outside the confines of an organization, and viewing their interaction as a system.

tacit knowledge Knowledge that cannot easily be articulated, and which is rooted in action rather than theory or information; can include both skills and mental models.

tacit knowledge at a collective level The routines, work practices, communication styles, and patterns of decision-making and social interaction in the informal organization that provide capability which supports effective working and organizational achievement.

task environment The immediate environment with which an organization interacts directly, such as customers, competitors, suppliers, and trade unions.

task-focused transitions Constant adjustments made to specific areas of the organization, with management adopting a directive style.

The Conference Model™ The large group method applied to redesign the organization or its processes. Undertaken as a series of five conferences.

tipping point The point at which a relatively slow pattern or trend suddenly grows exponentially, as is the case with epidemics.

toxic emotions Negative emotions that have become ingrained and rigidified among employees.

toxin handlers Employees who support and protect colleagues who are suffering emotionally.

transactional leader Someone who responds to employees' immediate self-interests. The relationship is one of exchange, with reward for performance and corrective action if something goes wrong.

transformational leader Someone who inspires employees to look beyond self-interest by giving them a vision, or sense of higher purpose, and communicates high expectations.

transition (or process of change) The way in which the people involved, in practice, accomplish a change—psychologically and practically.

transporting (waste, Lean) Moving goods from one place to another.

trend A pattern of behaviour or activity that emerges in the external environment.

trust A form of sensemaking in which people willingly accept vulnerability based on positive expectations of someone else.

turnarounds Fast discontinuous change transformations, in which management adopt a coercive style.

unfreeze The first step in Lewin's model of change in which any restraining forces preventing the change are destabilized.

unitarist A perspective on organizations that emphasizes cooperation and collaboration towards shared organizational goals, and therefore does not countenance the legitimacy of different interest groups.

unlearning The abandonment of previous knowledge.

values-in-use Values that can be recognized by the way in which employees behave.

value stream mapping Mapping a process: when, where, what, why, and how things happen within that process, and identifying which parts of the process add value.

variation (Six Sigma) Differences in quality or standard from one production or instance to the next.

virtual conferencing A large group method to enable any number of people to work together via IT-enabled platforms to address organizational issues.

vision An image of the future of an organization.

waiting (waste, Lean) Any time during which goods are not moving—waiting to be worked on, waiting for parts, waiting to be delivered, etc.

wastage (Lean) Activities that create no value, but which are currently necessary to be maintain operations, in which elimination is a priority.

whole system All of the stakeholders of the organization, issue, or community.

References

Chapter 1

Balogun, J. and Johnson, G. (2005) 'From intended strategies to unintended outcomes: The impact of change recipient sensemaking', *Organization Studies*, **26**(11): 1573-601.

Bridges, W. (2003) *Managing Transitions: Making the Most of Change*, 2nd edn, London: Nicholas Brealey Publishing.

Brief, A. P. and Dukerich, J. M. (1991) 'Theory in organizational behavior: Can it be useful?', in B. M. Staw and L. L. Cummings (eds) *Research in Organizational Behaviour*, Greenwich, CT: JAI Press, pp. 327-52.

Harris, L. C. and Ogbonna, E. (2002) 'The unintended consequences of culture interventions: A study of unexpected outcomes', *British Journal of Management*, **13**(1): 31-49.

Pettigrew, A. M. (1999) 'Is corporate culture manageable?', In D. Wilson and R. Rosenfeld (eds) *Managing Organizations: Text, Readings and Cases*, 2nd edn, London: McGraw-Hill, pp. 313-19.

Chapter 2

Abrahamson, E. (1996) 'Management fashion', *Academy of Management Review*, **21**(1): 254-85.

Aldrich, H. (1999) *Organizations Evolving*, London: Sage.

Barney, J. B. (1991) 'Firm resources and sustained advantage', *Journal of Management*, **17**(1): 99-120.

Boxall, P. and Purcell, J. (2008) *Strategy and Human Resource Management*, Basingstoke: Palgrave Macmillan.

Brinkley, I., Fauth, M., and Theodoropoulou, S. (2009) *Knowledge Workers and Knowledge Work*, London: The Work Foundation.

Bryne, J. A. (1986) 'Business fads: What's in—and out', *Business Week*, Jan: 40-7.

Burt, T. and McIvor, G. (1998) 'Land of midnight mobiles', *Financial Times*, 30 Oct: 18.

Carlson, N. (2011) 'Facebook has 600 million users, Goldman tells clients', *Business Insider*, 5 Jan. http://articles.businessinsider.com/2011-01-05/tech/30100720_1_user-facebook-pr-goldman-sachs

Carnall, C. (1999) *Managing Change in Organizations*, Harlow: Financial Times/Prentice Hall.

Clark, T. (1995) *Managing Consultants; Consultancy as the Management of Impressions*, Buckingham: Open University Press.

Datamonitor (2004) 'Ben & Jerry's case study: Developing premium food brands through innovative marketing', Aug: 1-13.

Dawson, S. (1992) *Analysing Organizations*, Basingstoke: Macmillan Press.

EABIS/Ashridge (2010) *Adapting to a Changing Context: The Role of Management Education*. http://www.ashridge.org.uk/Website/IC.nsf/wFARATT/Adapting%20to%20a%20changing%20context%3A%20the%20role%20of%20management%20education/$File/AdaptingToAChangingContext.pdf

Fincham, R. and Clark, T. (2002) 'Management consultancy: Issues, perspectives and agendas', *International Studies of Management and Organization*, **32**(4): 3-18.

Francis, C.-B. (2001) 'Quasi-public, quasi-private trends in emerging market economies: The case of China', *Comparative Politics*, **33**(3): 275-94.

Futures Company (2008) *Global Monitor*. http://blog.thefuturescompany.com/

Futures Company (2009) *Global Monitor*. http://blog.thefuturescompany.com/

Ghoshal, S. and Bartlett, C. A. (1998) *The Individualized Corporation*, London: William Heinemann.

Ginsberg, A. and Abrahamson, E. (1991) 'Champions of change and strategic shifts: The role of internal and external change advocates', *Journal of Management Studies*, **28**(2): 173-90.

Gladwell, M. (2000) *The Tipping Point: How Little Things Can Make a Big Difference*, London: Little Brown.

Goldman Sachs (2010) 'Is this the "BRICs decade"?'. http://www2.goldmansachs.com/our-thinking/brics/brics-decade.html

Greiner, L. E. (1998) 'Evolution and revolution as organizations grow, *Harvard Business Review*, **76**(3): 55-68.

Grey, C. (2003) 'The fetish of change', *Tamara: Journal of Critical Postmodern Organization Science*, **2**(2): 1-19.

Guest, D. (1992) 'Right enough to be dangerously wrong: An analysis of the In Search of Excellence phenomenon', in G. Salaman (ed.) *Human Resource Strategies*, London: Sage, pp. 192–236.

Hirschmann, A. O. (1970) *Exit, Voice and Loyalty: Responses to Decline in Firms, Organisations and States*, Cambridge, MA: Harvard University Press.

Huczynski, A. A. (1993) *Management Gurus: What Makes Them and How to Become One*, London: Routledge.

Kotter, J. and Cohen, D. (2002) *The Heart of Change*, Boston, MA: Harvard Business School Press.

Lawrence, P. (2002) *The Change Game: How Today's Global Trends are Shaping Tomorrow's Companies*, London: Kogan Page.

Leonard, D. (1998) *Wellsprings of Knowledge: Building and Sustaining the Sources of Innovation*, Boston, MA: Harvard Business School Press.

Mobelitor.com (2008) 'Nokia Remade concept phone goes green', 9 Apr. http://www.mobiletor. com/2008/04/09/nokia-remade-concept-phone-goes-green/

Morgan, G. (1986*) Images of Organization*, London : Sage.

Paavola, J. and Adger, W. N. (2005) 'Institutional ecological economics', *Ecological Economics*, **53**(3): 353–68.

Palmer, I., Dunford, R., and Akin, G. (2006) *Managing Organizational Change: A Multiple Perspectives Approach*, New York: McGraw Hill-Irwin.

Pearson, J. P. (2000) (ed.) *International Directory of Company Histories, Vol. 38*. Chicago, IL: St James Press.

Peng, M. W. and Shrekshina, S. V. (2001) 'How entrepreneurs create wealth in transition economies', *The Academy of Management Executive*, **15**(1): 95–110.

Phelps, R., Adams, R., and Bessant, J. (2007) 'Life cycles of growing organizations: A review with implications for knowledge and learning', *International Journal of Management Reviews*, **9**(1): 1–30.

Porter, M. and Kramer, M. (2006) 'Strategy and society: The link between competitive advantage and corporate social responsibility', *Harvard Business Review*, Dec: 78–92.

Prahalad, C. K. and Hamel, G. (1990) 'The core competence of the corporation', *Harvard Business Review*, **68**(3): 79–91.

PriceWaterhouseCoopers (2007) 'The Millenials are coming: Companies must keep up with the workforce of the future', Press release, 22 Mar. http://www. ukmediacentre.pwc.com/content/detail.aspx?releasei d=2290&newsareaid=2

Quinn, J. B. (1980) *Strategy for Change: Logical Incrementalism*, Homewood, Ill: Irwin.

Rawsthorn, A., (2008). New tools to help with information overload *International Herald Tribune*,

[internet]5 December. Available at: http: // www.int. com/articles/2008/12/08/arts/design 8 php

Romanelli, E. and Tushman, M. L. (1994) 'Organizational transformation as punctuated equilibrium: An empirical test' *Academy of Management Journal*, **36**(5): 1141–66.

Serwer, A. (1999) 'Ben & Jerry's is back: Ice cream and a hot stock', *Fortune*, **140**(3): 267–8.

Shapiro, E. (1998) *Fad Surfing in the Boardroom*, Oxford: Capstone Publishing.

Shim, S., Eastlick, M. A., and Lotz, S. (2000) 'Examination of US Hispanic-owned, small retail and service businesses: An organizational life cycle approach', *Journal of Retailing and Consumer Services*, 7(1): 19–32.

Smircich, L. and Stubbart, C. (1985) 'Strategic management in an enacted world', *Academy of Management Review*, **10**(4): 724–36.

Sorge, A. and van Witteloostuijn, A. (2004) 'The (non) sense of organizational change: An essai about universal management hypes, sick consultancy metaphors, and healthy organization theories', *Organization Studies*, **25**(7): 1205–31.

Starbuck, W. H. (1976) 'Organizations and their environments', in M. D. Dunnette (ed.) *Handbook of Organizations*, Chicago, IL: Rand McNally, pp. 1067–123.

Steinbock, D. (2001) *The Nokia Revolution: The Story of an Extraordinary Company that Transformed an Industry*, New York: AMACOM.

Stubbart, C. I. and Smalley, R. D. (1999) 'The deceptive allure of stage models of strategic processes', *Journal of Management Inquiry*, **8**(3): 273–87.

Sturdy, A. (1997) 'The consultancy process: An insecure business', *Journal of Management Studies*, **34**(3): 389–413.

Thompson, S. (2001) 'Player profile: Ben & Jerry's puts Freese on global warming, sales', *Advertising Age*, 27 Aug. http://adage.com/article/people-players/ player-profile-ben-jerry-s-puts-freese-global-warming-sales/53985/

Transparency International (2009) *Global Corruption Report 2009*. http://www.transparency.org/ publications/gcr/gcr_2009

Vian, K. (2005) *Ten-year Forecast Perspectives*, Institute for The Future. http://www.iftf.org

Welch, J. (2001) *Jack: What I've Learned Leading a Great Company and Great People*, London. Warner Books.

Wiggins, E. A. (2005) 'Making sense of consultancy: A qualitative analysis of the challenge of constructing a positive work identity for management consultants', Unpublished PhD, Birkbeck College, University of London.

Wills, A. (2008) 'Behind Ben & Jerry's "cool" brand values we find fresh environmental initiatives that work', *Travel Trade Gazette UK & Ireland*, 9 Dec: 22–3.

Chapter 3

BBC (2000) *Panorama: Gap and Nike: No Sweat?*, 15 Oct. http://cdnedge.bbc.co.uk/1/hi/programmes/panorama/970385.stm

BBC News (2000) 'NatWest merger's mixed fortunes', 11 Feb. http://news.bbc.co.uk/1/hi/business/639201.stm

BBC News (2009) 'Q&A: Royal Mail disputes', 5 Nov. http://news.bbc.co.uk/1/hi/business/8260701.stm

Beer, M. and Nohria, N. (2000) (eds) *Breaking the Code of Change*, Boston, MA: Harvard Business School Press.

Beugelsdijk, S. and Slangen, A. (2001) 'Shapes of organizational change: The case of Heineken Inc.', *Journal of Organizational Change Management*, **15**(3): 311–26.

Boxall, P. and Purcell, J. (2008) *Strategy and Human Resource Management*, 2nd edn, Basingstoke: Palgrave Macmillan.

Buchanan, D. and Boddy, D. (1992) *The Expertise of the Change Agent*, London: Prentice Hall International.

Burke, W. (2008) *Organization Change: Theory and Practice*, 2nd edn, Thousand Oaks, CA: Sage.

Burnes, B. (2009) *Managing Change: A Strategic Approach to Organizational Dynamics*, 5th edn, Harlow: FT Prentice Hall.

By, T. R. (2005) 'Organisational change management: A critical review', *Journal of Change Management*, **5**(4): 369–80.

Conger, J. (2000) 'Effective change begins at the top', in M. Beer and N. Nohria (eds) *Breaking the Code of Change*, Boston, MA: Harvard Business School Press, pp. 97–113.

Dawson, S. (2003) *Organizational Change: A Processual Approach*, London: Paul Chapman Publishing.

Dunphy, D. and Stace, S. (1993) 'The strategic management of corporate change', *Human Relations*, **46**(8): 905–20.

Frohman, A. (1997) 'Igniting organizational change from below: The power of personal initiative', *Organizational Dynamics*, **25**(3): 39–53.

Griffin, D. (2002) *The Emergence of Leadership: Linking Self-organization and Ethics*, London/New York: Routledge.

Griffin, D. and Stacey, R. (2005) *Complexity and the Experience of Leading Organizations*, London/New York: Routledge.

Hamel, G. (2000) *Leading the Revolution*, Boston, MA: Harvard Business School Press.

Handy, C. (1994) *The Empty Raincoat*, London: Hutchinson.

Hatch, M. J. and Cunliffe, A. L. (2006) *Organization Theory: Modern, Symbolic and Postmodern Perspectives*, 2nd edn, Oxford: Oxford University Press.

Hirschhorn, L. and Gilmore, I. (1992) 'The new boundaries of the "boundaryless" company', *Harvard Business Review*, May–June: 104–15.

Holbeche, L. (2006) *Understanding Change: Theory, Implementation and Success*, Oxford: Butterworth-Heinemann.

Hurst, D. (2002) *Crisis and Renewal: Meeting the Challenge of Organizational Change*, Boston, MA: Harvard Business School Press.

Johnson, G. (1993) 'Processes of managing strategic change', in C. Mabey and B. Mayon-White (eds) *Managing Change*, 2nd edn, London: Paul Chapman Publishing, pp. 59–64.

IFPI (2009) *Digital Music Report 2009: New Business Models for a Changing Environment*. http://www.ifpi.org/content/library/DMR2009-real.pdf

Lawrence, P. (2002) *The Change Game: How Today's Global Trends are Shaping Tomorrow's Companies*, London: Kogan Page.

Locke, R. (2002) *The Promise and Perils of Globalization: The Case of Nike*, IPC Working Paper 02 007, Cambridge, MA: Massachusetts Institute of Technology Industrial Performance Centre. http://web.mit.edu/ipc/publications/pdf/02-007.pdf

Mintzberg, H. (1991) *The Strategy Process: Concepts, Contexts, Cases*, 2nd edn, London: Prentice-Hall.

Nadler, D. and Tushman, M. (1995) 'Types of organizational change, from incremental improvement to discontinuous transformation', in D. Nadler, R. Shaw, and E. Walton (eds) *Discontinuous Change: Leading Organizational Transformation*, San Francisco, CA: Jossey-Bass, pp. 15–34.

Nike Inc. (undated) 'Responsibility at Nike Inc.'. http://www.nikebiz.com/responsibility/cr_governance.html

Pascale, R., Milleman, M., and Gioja, L. (2000) *Surfing the Edge of Chaos: The Laws of Nature and New Laws of Business*, London: Texere Publishing Ltd.

Pritchard, J. (2009) 'Virgin Money overview', *About.com*. http://banking.about.com/od/loans/p/circlelending.htm

Quinn, J. (1980) *Strategies for Change*, Homewood, IL: Irwin.

Romanelli, E. and Tushman, M. (1994) 'Organizational transformation as punctuated equilibrium: An empirical test', *Academy of Management Journal*, **37**(5): 1141–66.

Schumpeter (2009) 'The pedagogy of the privileged', *The Economist*, 24 Sep. http://www.economist.com/node/14493183

Senge, P. (2005) *Presence: Exploring Profound Change in People, Organizations and Society*, London: Nicholas Brealey.

Shaw, P. (2002) *Changing Conversations in Organizations: A Complexity Approach to Change*, London/New York: Routledge.

Stacey, R. (2002–03) 'Organizations as complex responsive processes of relating', *Journal of Innovative Management*, **8**(2): 27–39.

Stacey, R. (2011) *Strategic Management and Organisational Dynamics*, 6th edn, Harlow: FT Prentice Hall.

Sutherland, R. (2007) 'Barclays box: RBS overpaid for ABN Amro', *The Observer*, 7 Oct: 1.

TNT Group (2010) *Annual Report*. http://group.tnt.com/annualreports/annualreport10/

Tushman, M. and Nadler, D. (1986) 'Organizing for innovation', *California Management Review*, **28**(3): 74–92.

Tushman, M., Newman, W., and Romanelli, E. (1986) 'Convergence and upheaval: Managing the unsteady pace of organizational evolution', *California Management Review*, **29**(1): 29–44.

Wearden, G. (2010) 'Royal mail to be privatized or sold', *The Guardian*, 10 Sep. http://www.guardian.co.uk/uk/2010/sep/10/government-privatise-sell-royal-mail

Weick, K. (2000) 'Emergent change as universal in organizations', in M. Beer and N. Nohria (eds) *Breaking the Code of Change*, Boston, MA: Harvard Business School Press, pp. 223–43.

Wilson, A. (2008) 'RBS now 58% owned by UK government', *The Telegraph*, 28 Nov. http://www.telegraph.co.uk/finance/newsbysector/banksandfinance/3532604/RBS-now-58pc-owned-by-UKgovernment.html

Chapter 4

Archer, J. and Rhodes, V. (1987) 'Bereavement and reactions to job loss: A comparative review', *British Journal of Social Psychology*, **26**(3): 211–24.

Ashforth, B. E. and Humphrey, R. H. (1993) 'Emotional labor in service roles: The influence of identity', *Academy of Management Review*, **18**(1): 88–115.

Averill, J. R. and Nunley, E. P. (1992) *Voyages of the Heart: Living an Emotionally Creative Life*, New York: The Free Press.

Barsade, S. G. (2002) 'The ripple effect: Emotional contagion and its influence on group behaviour', *Administrative Science Quarterly*, **47**(4): 644–75.

Bridges, W. (2003) *Managing Transitions: Making the Most of Change*, 2nd edn, London: Nicholas Brealey Publishing.

Brockner, J., Grover, S., Reed, T., DeWitt, R., and O'Malley, M. (1987) 'Survivors' reactions to layoffs: We get by with a little help for our friends', *Administrative Science Quarterly*, **32**(4): 526–41.

Brockner, J., Wiesenfeld, B. M., and Martin, C. L. (1995) 'Decision frame, procedural justice, and survivors reactions to job layoffs', *Organizational Behavior and Human Decision Processes*, **63**(1): 59–68.

Bryant, M. and Wolfram Cox, J. (2004) 'Conversion stories as shifting narratives of organizational change', *Journal of Organizational Change Management*, **17**(6): 578–92.

Bryant, M. and Wolfram Cox, J. (2006) 'The expression of suppression: Loss and emotional labour in narratives of organizational change', *Journal of Management and Organization*, **12**(2): 116–30.

Buchanan, D. A. and Boddy, D. (1992) *The Expertise of the Change Agent: Public Performance and Backstage Activity*, Hemel Hempstead: Prentice Hall.

Clair, J. A. and Dufresne, R. L. (2004) 'Playing the grim reaper: How employees experience carrying out a downsizing', *Human Relations*, **57**(12): 1597–625.

de Rivera, J. (1977) *A Structural Theory of the Emotions*, New York: International Universities Press.

Eliot, G. (2006; 1866) *Felix Holt: The Radical*, London: Penguin Classics.

Eriksson, C. B. (2004) 'The effects of change programs on employees' emotions', *Personnel Review*, **33**(1): 110–26.

Fineman, S. (2003) *Understanding Emotion at Work*, London: Sage.

Freeman, S. F. (1999) 'Identity maintenance and adaptation: A multilevel analysis of response to loss', in B. M. Staw and R. M. Sutton (eds) *Research in Organizational Behaviour, Vol. 21*, Greenwich, CT: JAI Press, pp. 247–94.

Frost, P. J. (2003) *Toxic Emotions at Work: How Compassionate Managers Handle Pain and Conflict*, Boston, MA: Harvard Business School Press.

Frost, P. J. and Robinson, S. (1999) 'The toxic handler: Organizational hero—and casualty', *Harvard Business Review*, **77**(4): 96–106.

Fryer, D. (1985) 'Stages in the psychological response to unemployment: A (dis)integrative review', *Current Psychological Research and Reviews*, **4**(3): 257–73.

Goleman, D. (1995) *Emotional Intelligence: Why It Can Matter More Than IQ*, New York: Bantam.

Griffiths, P. E. and Scarantino, A. (2009) 'Emotions in the wild: The situated perspective on emotion', in P. Robbins and M. Aydede (eds) *The Cambridge Handbook of Situated Cognition*, Cambridge: Cambridge University Press, pp. 437–53.

Härtel, C. E. J. and Zerbe, W. J. (2002) 'Myths about emotions during change', in N. M. Ashkanasy, W. J. Zerbe, and C. E. J. Härtel (eds) *Managing Emotions in the Workplace*, Armonk, NY: M. E. Sharpe, pp. 70–4.

Heelas, P. (1996) 'Emotion talk across cultures', in R. Harré and W. G. Parrott (eds) *The Emotions: Social, Cultural and Biological Dimensions*, London: Sage, pp. 171–99.

Hochschild, A. R. (1983) *The Managed Heart: Commercialization of Human Feeling*, Berkeley, CA: University of California Press.

Hopson, B. (1981) 'Response to the papers by Schlossberg, Brammer and Abrego', *Counseling Psychologist*, **9**(2): 36–9.

Hopson, B. and Adams, J. (1976) 'Towards an understanding of transition: Defining some boundaries of transition dynamics', in J. Adams, J. Hayes, and B. Hopson (eds) *Transition: Understanding and Managing Personal Change*, London: Martin Robertson, pp. 3–25.

Huy, Q. N. (1999) 'Emotional capability, emotional intelligence, and radical change', *Academy of Management Review*, **24**(2): 325–45.

Huy, Q. N. (2002) 'Emotional balancing of organizational continuity and radical change: The contribution of middle managers', *Administrative Science Quarterly*, **47**(1): 31–69.

Kübler-Ross, E. (1969) *On Death and Dying*, New York: Scribner.

Lazarus, R. S. (1982) 'Thoughts on the relations between emotion and cognition', *American Psychologist*, **37**(9): 1019–24.

Lutz, C. A. (1988) *Unnatural Emotions: Everyday Sentiments on a Micronesian Atoll and Their Challenge to Western Theory*, Chicago, IL: University of Chicago Press.

Matthews, G., Roberts, R. D., and Zeidner, M. (2004) 'Seven myths about emotional intelligence', *Psychological Inquiry*, **15**(3): 179–96.

Mayer, J. D., Roberts, R. D., and Barsade, S. G. (2008) 'Human abilities: Emotional intelligence', *Annual Review of Psychology*, 59: 507–36.

Mayer, J. D., Salovey, P., and Caruso, D. R. (2004) 'Emotional intelligence: Theory, findings, and implications', *Psychological Inquiry*, **15**(3): 197–215.

Meyerson, D. E. (2000) 'If emotions were honoured: A cultural analysis', in S. Fineman (ed.) *Emotion in Organizations*, 2nd edn, London: Sage, pp. 167–83.

Myers, P. (2007) 'Sexed up intelligence or irresponsible reporting? The interplay of virtual communication and emotion in dispute sensemaking', *Human Relations*, **60**(4): 609–36.

Opengart, R. (2005) 'Emotional intelligence and emotion work: Examining constructs from an interdisciplinary framework', *Human Resource Development Review*, **4**(1): 49–62.

Parkinson, B. (1995) *Ideas and Realities of Emotion*, London: Routledge.

Parkinson, B. (1997) 'Untangling the appraisal-emotion connection', *Personality and Social Psychology Review*, **1**(1): 62–79.

Parkinson, B., Fischer, A. H., and Manstead, A. S. R. (2005) *Emotion in Social Relations: Cultural, Group, and Interpersonal Processes*, Hove: Psychology Press.

Roseman, I. J. and Smith, C. A. (2001) 'Appraisal theory: Overview, assumptions, varieties, controversies', in K. R. Scherer, A. Schorr, and T. Johnstone (eds) *Appraisal Processes in Emotion: Theory, Methods, Research*, New York: Oxford University Press, pp. 3–19.

Salovey, P. and Mayer, J. D. (1990) 'Emotional intelligence', *Imagination, Cognition, and Personality*, **9**(3): 185–211.

Schlossberg, N. K. (1981) 'A model for analyzing human adaptation to transition', *The Counseling Psychologist*, **9**(2): 2–18.

Solomon, R. C. (1976) *The Passions*, Garden City, NY: Anchor Press/ Doubleday.

Stearns, P. N. and Knapp, M. (1996) 'Historical perspectives on grief', in R. Harré and W. G. Parrott (eds) *The Emotions: Social, Cultural and Biological Dimensions*, London: Sage, pp. 132–50.

Stuart, R. (1995) 'Experiencing organizational change: Triggers, processes and outcomes of change journeys', *Personnel Review*, **24**(2): 3–87.

Sugarman, L. (2001) *Life-span Development: Frameworks, Accounts and Strategies*, 2nd edn, Hove: Psychology Press.

Wolfram Cox, J. R. (1997) 'Manufacturing the past: Loss and absence in organizational change', *Organization Studies*, **18**(4): 623–54.

Wright, B. and Barling, J. (1998) '"The executioners' song": Listening to downsizers reflect on their experiences', *Canadian Journal of Administrative Sciences*, **15**(4): 339–54.

Zell, D. (2003) 'Organizational change as a process of death, dying, and rebirth', *The Journal of Applied Behavioral Science*, **39**(1): 73–96.

Chapter 5

Badaracco, J. L. (1997) *Defining Moments: When Managers Must Choose between Right and Right*, Boston, MA: Harvard Business School Press.

Balogun, J. (2006) 'Managing change: Steering a course between intended strategies and unanticipated outcomes', *Long Range Planning*, **39**(1): 29–49.

Balogun, J. and Johnson, G. (2005) 'From intended strategies to unintended outcomes: The impact of change recipient sensemaking', *Organization Studies*, **26**(11): 1573–601.

BBC News (2010) 'China condemns decision by Google to lift censorship', 23 Mar. http://news.bbc.co.uk/1/hi/8582233.stm

BBC News (2010) 'Timeline: China and net censorship', 23 Mar. http://news.bbc.co.uk/1/hi/world/asia-pacific/8460129.stm

Bridges, W. (2003) *Managing Transitions: Making the Most of Change*, 2nd edn, London: Nicholas Brealey Publishing.

Currie, G. and Brown, A. D. (2003) 'A narratological approach to understanding processes of organizing in a UK hospital', *Human Relations*, **56**(5): 563–86.

Dose, J. (1997) 'Work values: An integrative framework and illustrative application to organizational socialization', *Journal of Occupational and Organizational Psychology*, **70**(3): 219–40.

Dunford, R. and Palmer, I. (1996) 'Metaphors in popular management discourse: The case of corporate restructuring', in D. Grant and C. Oswick (eds) *Metaphor and Organizations*, London: Sage, pp. 95–109.

Fineman, S. (2003) *Understanding Emotion at Work*. London: Sage.

Gentile, M. C. (2010) *Giving Voice to Values: How to Speak Your Mind When You Know What's Right*, New Haven, CT: Yale University Press.

Gioia, D. A. and Chittipeddi, K. (1991) 'Sensemaking and sensegiving in strategic change initiation', *Strategic Management Journal*, **12**(6): 433–48.

Google (2004) '2004 Founders' IPO letter'. http://investor.google.com/corporate/2004/ipo-founders-letter.html

Google (2006) 'Google's "20 percent time" in action', *The Google Official Blog*, 18 May.

http://googleblog.blogspot.com/2006/05/googles-20-percent-time-in-action.html

Google (2010) 'A new approach to China', *The Google Official Blog*, 12 Jan. http://googleblog.blogspot.com/2010/01/new-approach-to-china.html

Greenberg, D. N. (1995) 'Blue versus gray: A metaphor constraining sensemaking around a restructuring', *Group & Organization Management*, **20**(2): 183–209.

Handy, C. (1993) *Understanding Organizations*, 4th edn, London: Penguin Books.

Harris, S. G. (1994) 'Organizational culture and individual sensemaking: A schema-based perspective', *Organization Science*, **5**(3): 309–21.

Harter, J. K., Schmidt, F. L., Killham, E. A., and Agrawal, S. (2009) *Q12® Meta-Analysis: The Relationship Between Engagement at Work and Organizational Outcomes*. http://www.gallup.com/consulting/File/126806/MetaAnalysis_Q12_WhitePaper_2009.pdf

Helms Mills, J. (2003) *Making Sense of Organizational Change*, London: Routledge.

Hurst, D. K. (1986) 'Why strategic management is bankrupt', *Organizational Dynamics*, **15**(2): 5–27.

Hurst, D. K., Rush, J. C., and White, R. E. (1989) 'Top management teams and organizational renewal', *Strategic Management Journal*, **10**(S1): 87–105.

IBM (2008) *2008 Corporate Responsibility Report*. http://www.ibm.com/ibm/responsibility/ibm_crr_downloads/pdf/2008_IBMCRR_FullReport.pdf

IBM (2009) *2009 Corporate Responsibility Report*. http://www.ibm.com/ibm/responsibility/IBM_CorpResp_2009.pdf

IBM (undated) 'Diversity 3.0: A new charter'. http://www.ibm.com/ibm/responsibility/diversity.shtml

IBM (undated) 'Diversity 3.0: Leveraging our differences for innovation, collaboration and client success'. http://www-03.ibm.com/employment/us/diverse

IBM (undated) 'Heritage'. http://www-03.ibm.com/employment/us/diverse/heritage_ibm_1990.shtml

IBM4diversity (2010) 'Why IBM works', Short film. http://www.youtube.com/watch?v=au8OIXXHnyk&feature=player_embedded

Isabella, L. A. (1990) 'Evolving interpretations as a change unfolds: How managers construe key organizational events', *Academy of Management Journal*, **33**(1): 7–41.

Kahn, W. A. (1990) 'Psychological conditions of personal engagement and disengagement at work', *Academy of Management Journal*, **33**(4): 692–724.

Kahn, W. A. (1992) 'To be fully there: Psychological presence at work', *Human Relations*, **45**(4): 321–49.

Kärreman, D. and Alvesson, M. (2001) 'Making newsmakers: Conversational identity at work', *Organization Studies*, **22**(1): 59–89.

Kotter, J. P. (2007; 1995) 'Leading change: Why transformation efforts fail', *Harvard Business Review*, **85**(1): 96–103.

Lawrence, A. T. (2009) 'Google, Inc.: Figuring out how to deal with China', in E. Raufflet and A. J. Mills (eds) *The Dark Side: Critical Cases on the Downside of Business*, Sheffield: Greenleaf Publishing, pp. 250–67.

Lewicki, R. J., McAllister, D. J., and Bies, R. J. (1998) 'Trust and distrust: New relationships and realities', *Academy of Management Review*, **23**(3): 438–58.

Macey, W. H. and Schneider, B. (2008) 'The meaning of employee engagement', *Industrial and Organizational Psychology*, **1**(1): 3–30.

Maitlis, S. (2005) 'The social processes of organizational sensemaking', *Academy of Management Journal*, **48**(1): 21–49.

Maitlis, S. and Lawrence, T. B. (2007) 'Triggers and enablers of sensegiving in organizations', *Academy of Management Journal*, **50**(1): 57–84.

May, D. R., Gilson, R. L., and Harter, L. M. (2004) 'The psychological conditions of meaningfulness, safety and availability and the engagement of the human spirit at work', *Journal of Occupational and Organizational Psychology*, 77: 11–37.

McKnight, D. H. and Chervany, N. L. (2001) 'Trust and distrust definitions: One bite at a time', in R. Falcone, M. Singh and Y.-H. Tan (eds) *Trust in Cyber-societies: Integrating the Human and Artificial Perspectives*, Berlin: Springer-Verlag, pp. 27–54.

Mintzberg, H. (1987) 'The strategy concept I: Five Ps for strategy', *California Management Review*, **30**(1): 11–24.

Mintzberg, H. (1989) *Mintzberg on Management: Inside our Strange World of Organizations*, New York: Free Press.

Mintzberg, H. (1994) *The Rise and Fall of Strategic Planning*, New York: Prentice Hall.

Mintzberg, H., Ahlstrand, B., and Lampel, J. B. (2009) *Strategy Safari: The Complete Guide through the Wilds of Strategic Management*, 2nd edn, Harlow: FT/Prentice Hall.

Morgan, G. (2006) *Images of Organization*, Updated edn, London: Sage.

Morrison, E. W. and Phelps, C. C. (1999) 'Taking charge at work: Extrarole efforts to initiate workplace change', *Academy of Management Journal*, **42**(4): 403–19.

Myers, P. (2005) 'Knowledge: Distributed and impassioned', Paper presented at the Sixth International Conference on Organizational Learning and Knowledge: The Passion for Learning and Knowing, 9–11 June, Trento, Italy.

Myers, P. (2007) 'Sexed up intelligence or irresponsible reporting? The interplay of virtual communication and emotion in dispute sensemaking', *Human Relations*, **60**(4): 609–36.

Nonaka, I. (1991) 'The knowledge-creating company', *Harvard Business Review*, **69**(6): 96–104.

Pink, D. H. (2009) *Drive: The Surprising Truth about What Motivates Us*, New York: Riverhead Books.

Porter, M. E. (1996) 'What is strategy?', *Harvard Business Review*, **74**(6): 61–78.

Quinn, J. B. (1998) 'Strategies for change', in H. Mintzberg, J. B. Quinn and S. Ghosal (eds) *The Strategy Process*, Rev'd European edn, Hemel Hempstead: Prentice Hall Europe, pp. 5–13.

Radia, R. (2010) 'China renews Google's license', *The Technology Liberation Front*, 9 July. http://techliberation.com/2010/07/09/china-renews-googles-license/

Raelin, J. (2006) 'Finding meaning in the organization', *Sloan Management Review*, **47**(3): 64–68.

Robinson, D., Perryman, S., and Hayday, S. (2004) *The Drivers of Employee Engagement*, Eastbourne: Institute for Employment Studies.

Robinson, S. L., Dirks, K. T., and Ozcelik, H. (2004) 'Untangling the knot of trust and betrayal', in K. S. Cook and R. M. Kramer (eds) *Trust and Distrust in Organizations: Dilemmas and Approaches*, New York: Russell Sage Foundation, pp. 327–41.

Rousseau, D. M. (1995) *Psychological Contracts in Organizations: Understanding Written and Unwritten Agreements*, Thousand Oaks, CA: Sage.

Rousseau, D. M. (2001) 'Schema, promise and mutuality: The building blocks of the psychological contract', *Journal of Occupational and Organizational Psychology*, **74**(4): 511–41.

Rousseau, D. M. (2004) 'Psychological contracts in the workplace: Understanding the ties that motivate', *Academy of Management Executive*, **18**(1): 120–7.

Rousseau, D. M., Sitkin, S. B., Burt, R. S., and Camerer, C. (1998) 'Not so different after all: A cross-discipline view of trust', *Academy of Management Review*, **23**(3): 393–404.

Salancik, G. R. and Pfeffer, J. (1978) 'A social information-processing approach to job attitudes and task design', *Administrative Science Quarterly*, **23**(2): 224–53.

Senge, P. M. (2006) *The Fifth Discipline: The Art and Practice of the Learning Organization*, 2nd edn, New York: Random House Books.

Seurat, R. (1999) 'Sustained and profitable growth', *Business Strategy Review*, **10**(1): 53–57.

Shotter, J. (1989) 'Social accountability and the social construction of "you"', in J. Shotter and K. J. Gergen (eds) *Texts of Identity*, London: Sage, pp. 133–51.

Sims, D. (2003) 'Between the millstones: A narrative account of the vulnerability of middle managers' storying', *Human Relations*, **56**(10): 1195–211.

Staw, B. M. and Fox, F. V. (1977) 'Escalation: Determinants of commitment to a chosen course of action', *Human Relations*, **30**(5): 431–50.

Staw, B. M. and Ross, J. (1987) 'Knowing when to pull the plug', *Harvard Business Review*, **65**(2): 68–74.

Steare, R. (2009) *Ethicability®: How to Decide What's Right and Find the Courage to Do It*, 3rd edn, Kemsing: Roger Steare Consulting Ltd.

Stensaker, I. and Falkenberg, J. (2007) 'Making sense of different responses to corporate change', *Human Relations*, **60**(1): 137–77.

Stensaker, I., Falkenberg, J., and Grønhaug, K. (2008) 'Implementation activities and organizational sensemaking', *Journal of Applied Behavioral Science*, **44**(2): 162–85.

Stevens, M. (2010) 'IBM wins Stonewall equality list top spot: Technology company is first in diversity index for second time since 2007', *People Management*, 13 Jan.

Stone, B. and Barboza, D. (2010) 'Google to stop redirecting China users', New York Times, 29 June. http://www.nytimes.com/2010/06/30/technology/30google.html

Stonewall (2010a) 'Diversity champions Scotland: The journey towards LGB equality', PowerPoint presentation. http://www.stonewall.org.uk/other/startdownload.asp?openType=forced&documentID=2311

Stonewall (2010b) 'Stonewall Top 100 Employers 2010: The Workplace Equality Index'. http://www.stonewall.org.uk/at_work/stonewall_top_100_employers/default.asp

Thomas, D. A. (2004) 'Diversity as strategy', *Harvard Business Review*, **82**(9): 98–108.

Turnley, W. H. and Feldman, D. C. (1999) 'The impact of psychological contract violations on exit, voice, loyalty, and neglect', *Human Relations*, **52**(7): 895–922.

Vise, D. A. and Malseed, M. (2008) *The Google Story*, Updated edn, London: Pan.

Walsh, J. P. (1995) 'Managerial and organizational cognition: Notes from a trip down memory lane', *Organization Science*, **6**(3): 280–321.

Weick, K. E. (1987) 'Substitutes for strategy', in D. Teece (ed.) *The Competitive Challenge*, Cambridge, MA: Ballinger, pp. 221–33.

Weick, K. E. (1995) *Sensemaking in Organizations*, Thousand Oaks, CA: Sage.

Weick, K. E. (2000) 'Emergent change as a universal in organizations', in M. Beer and N. Nohria (eds) *Breaking the Code of Change*, Boston, MA: Harvard Business School Press, pp. 223–41.

Weick, K. E. and Roberts, K. H. (1993) 'Collective mind in organizations: Heedful interrelating on flight decks', *Administrative Science Quarterly*, **38**(3): 357–81.

Weick, K. E., Sutcliffe, K. M., and Obstfeld, D. (2005) 'Organizing and the process of sensemaking', *Organization Science*, **16**(4): 409–21.

Chapter 6

Brown, A. D. (1995) *Organisational Culture*, London: Pitman Publishing.

Buono, A. F., Bowditch, J. L., and Lewis, J. W. (1985) 'When cultures collide: The anatomy of a merger', *Human Relations*, **38**(5): 477–500.

Cameron, K. S. and Quinn, R. E. (2006) *Diagnosing and Changing Organizational Culture: Based on the Competing Values Framework*, Rev'd edn, San Francisco, CA: Jossey-Bass.

Cartwright, S. and Cooper, C. L. (1993) 'The psychological impact of merger and acquisition on the individual: A study of building society managers', *Human Relations*, **46**(3): 327–47.

Chatman, J. A. and Cha, S. E. (2003) 'Leading by leveraging culture', *California Management Review*, **45**(4): 20–34.

Churchard, C. (2010) 'In the top set', *People Management*, **16**(7): 18–21.

Cruver, B. (2002) *Anatomy of Greed: The Unshredded Truth from an Enron Insider*, New York: Carroll & Graf.

Cummings, T. G. and Worley, C. G. (2008) *Organization Development and Change, International Edition*, 9th edn, Mason, OH: Cengage.

Daymon, C. (2000) 'Culture formation in a new television station: A multi-perspective analysis', *British Journal of Management*, **11**(2): 121–35.

Dyer, L. D. and Shafer, R. A. (1999) 'From human resource strategy to organizational effectiveness: Lessons from research on organizational agility', in P. M. Wright, L. D. Dyer, J. W. Boudreau, and G. T. Milkovich (eds) *Research in Personnel and Human Resource Management, Supplement 4: Strategic Human Resources Management in the Twenty-First Century*, Stamford, CT: JAI Press, pp. 145–74.

Enron (2001) 'Enron values', 2 Dec. http://www.enron.com

Feldman, M. S. (1991) 'The meanings of ambiguity: Learning from stories and metaphors', in P. J. Frost, L. F. Moore, M. R. Louis, C. C. Lundberg, and J. Martin (eds) *Reframing Organizational Culture*, Newbury Park, CA: Sage, pp. 145–56.

Fox, L. (2003) *Enron: The Rise and Fall*, Hoboken, NJ: John Wiley & Sons.

Fusaro, P. C. and Miller, R. M. (2002) *What Went Wrong at Enron: Everyone's Guide to the Largest Bankruptcy in US History*, Hoboken, NJ: John Wiley & Sons.

Gagliardi, P. (1986) 'The creation and change of organizational cultures: A conceptual framework', *Organization Studies*, **7**(2): 117–34.

Gaydon, N., Hall, S., and Ezard, J. (2008) 'Pace analyst briefing'. http://www.pace.com/media/corporate/PDF/080619_pace_analyst_briefing.pdf

Ginsburg, L. and Miller, N. (1992) 'Value-driven management', *Business Horizons*, **35**(3): 23–7.

Greiner, L. (1998) 'Evolution and revolution as organizations grow', *Harvard Business Review*, **76**(3): 55–68.

Harding, D. and Rouse, T. (2007) 'Human due diligence', *Harvard Business Review*, **85**(4): 124–31.

Harris, S. G. (1994) 'Organizational culture and individual sensemaking: A schema-based perspective', *Organization Science*, **5**(3): 309–21.

Hatch, M. J. (1993) 'The dynamics of organizational culture', *Academy of Management Review*, **18**(4): 657–93.

Hatch, M. J. and Cunliffe, A. L. (2006) *Organization Theory: Modern, Symbolic and Postmodern Perspectives*, 2nd edn, Oxford: Oxford University Press.

Hope Hailey, V. (1999) 'Managing culture', in L. Gratton, V. Hope Hailey, P. Stiles, and C. Truss (eds) *Strategic Human Resource Management: Corporate Rhetoric and Human Reality*, Oxford: Oxford University Press, pp. 101–16.

Johnson, G., Scholes, K., and Whittington, R. (2008) *Exploring Corporate Strategy*, 8th edn, Harlow: Pearson Education.

Kotter, J. P. and Heskett, J. L. (1992) *Corporate Culture and Performance*, New York: Free Press.

Larsson, R. and Lubatkin, M. (2001) 'Achieving acculturation in mergers and acquisitions: An international case survey', *Human Relations*, **54**(12): 1573–607.

Lorsch, J. W. (1985) 'Strategic myopia: Culture as an invisible barrier to change', in R. H. Kilmann, M. J. Saxton, and R. Serpa (eds) *Gaining Control of the Corporate Culture*, San Fransisco, CA: Jossey-Bass, pp. 84–102.

Martin, J. (1992) *Cultures in Organizations: Three Perspectives*, New York: Oxford University Press.

Meyerson, D. E. (1991) '"Normal" ambiguity? A glimpse of an organizational culture', in P. J. Frost, L. F. Moore, M. R. Louis, C. C. Lundberg, and J. Martin (eds) *Reframing Organizational Culture*, Newbury Park, CA: Sage, pp. 131–44.

Meyerson, D. E. and Martin, J. (1987) 'Cultural change: An integration of three different views', *Journal of Management Studies*, **24**(6): 623–47.

Mintzberg, H., Ahlstrand, B., and Lampel, J. B. (2009) *Strategy Safari: The Complete Guide through the Wilds of Strategic Management*, 2nd edn, Harlow: FT/Prentice Hall.

Morgan, G. (1997) *Images of Organization*, 2nd edn, Thousand Oaks, CA: Sage.

Murphy, M. G. and Mackenzie Davey, K. (2002) 'Ambiguity, ambivalence and indifference in organisational values', *Human Resource Management Journal*, **12**(1): 17–32.

Myers, P. (2008) 'Idleness and corporate scandal: Examining computer mediated gossip', Paper presented at the 24th European Group for Organizational Studies Colloquium, 10–12 July, Vrije Universiteit, Amsterdam.

Pace Executive Committee (2010) 'Code of Business Ethics'. http://www.pace.com/media/corporate/PDF/bus_ethics_apr10.pdf

Pace plc (2008) 'Transaction overview'. http://www.pace.com/media/corporate/pdf/080331_transaction_overview.pdf

Palmer, M. (2010) 'Pace to take second set-top box slot', *Financial Times*, 1 Mar: 22.

Pant, P. N. and Lachman, R. A. N. (1998) 'Value incongruity and strategic choice', *Journal of Management Studies*, **35**(2): 195–212.

Peters, T. J. (1992) *Liberation Management*, New York: Alfred A. Knopf.

Peters, T. J. and Waterman, R. H. (1982) *In Search of Excellence: Lessons from America's Best-Run Companies*, New York: Harper & Row.

Pettigrew, A. M. (1999) 'Is corporate culture manageable?', in D. Wilson and R. Rosenfeld (eds) *Managing Organizations: Text, Readings and Cases*, 2nd edn, London: McGraw-Hill, pp. 313–19.

Phelps, R., Adams, R., and Bessant, J. (2007) 'Life cycles of growing organizations: A review with implications for knowledge and learning', *International Journal of Management Reviews*, **9**(1): 1–30.

Powers Jr, W. C., Troubh, R. S., and Winokur Jr, H. S. (2002) *Report of Investigation by the Special Investigative Committee of the Board of Directors of Enron Corp*. http://fl1.findlaw.com/news.findlaw.com/wp/docs/enron/specinv020102rpt1.pdf

Schein, E. H. (1985) *Organizational Culture and Leadership: A Dynamic View*, San Francisco, CA: Jossey-Bass.

Schein, E. H. (2004) *Organizational Culture and Leadership*, 3rd edn, San Francisco, CA: Jossey-Bass.

Schein, E. H. (2009) *The Corporate Culture Survival Guide*, 2nd edn, San Francisco, CA: Jossey-Bass.

Schneider, B. (1987) 'The people make the place', *Personnel Psychology*, **40**(3): 437–53.

Schwartz, H. and Davis, S. M. (1981) 'Matching corporate culture and business strategy', *Organizational Dynamics*, **10**(1): 30–48.

Skilling, J. (1998) 'Competitive corporate cultures: Why innovators are leading their industries', *World Energy Magazine*. http://www.worldenergysource.com/articles/text/skilling_EH_v1n1.cfm

Smith, M. E. (2003) 'Changing an organisation's culture: Correlates of success and failure', *Leadership and Organization Development Journal*, **24**(5): 249–61.

Stafford, P. (2008) 'Change of channel for TV set-top boxmaker', *Financial Times*, 16 Apr: 24.

Chapter 7

Ashforth, B. E. and Mael, F. A. (1998) 'The power of resistance: Sustaining valued identities', in R. M. Kramer and M. A. Neale (eds) *Power and Influence in Organizations*, Thousand Oaks, CA: Sage, pp. 89–120.

Bacharach, S. B. and Lawler, E. J. (1998) 'Political alignments in organizations: Contextualization, mobilization and co-ordination', in R. M. Kramer and M. A. Neale (eds) *Power and Influence in Organizations*, Thousand Oaks, CA: Sage, pp. 67–88.

Baddeley, S. and James, K. (1987) 'Owl, fox, donkey or sheep: Political skills for managers', *Management Education and Development*, **18**(1): 3–19.

Beckhard, R. and Harris, R. T. (1987) *Organizational Transitions: Managing Complex Change*, 2nd edn, Reading, MA: Addison-Wesley.

Benafari, R. C., Wilkinson, H. E., and Orth, C. D. (1986) 'The effective use of power', *Business Horizons*, **29**(3): 12–16.

Bingham, J. and Porter, A. (2009) 'HBOS whistleblower Paul Moore breaks silence to condemn Crosby', *The Telegraph*, 11 Feb. http://www.telegraph.co.uk/finance/newsbysector/banksandfinance/4592025/HBOS-whistleblower-Paul-Moore-breaks-silence-to-condemn-Crosby.html

Bridges, W. (2003) *Managing Transitions: Making the Most of Change*, 2nd edn, London: Nicholas Brealey Publishing.

Brown, A. D. (1995) 'Managing understandings: Politics, symbolism, niche marketing and the quest for legitimacy in IT implementation', *Organization Studies*, **16**(6): 951–69.

Buchanan, D. and Badham, R. (1999) *Power, Politics and Organizational Change: Winning the Turf War*, London: Sage.

Buchanan, D. and Badham, R. (2008) *Power, Politics and Organizational Change: Winning the Turf War*, 2nd edn, London: Sage.

Buchanan, D. and Boddy, D. (1992) *The Expertise of the Change Agent: Public Performance and Backstage Activity*, London: Prentice Hall.

Clegg, S. R. and Hardy, C. (1996) 'Conclusion: Representations', in S. R. Clegg, C. Hardy, and W. R. Nord (eds) *Handbook of Organizational Studies*, London: Sage, pp. 676–708.

Conner, D. S. (2006) 'Human resource professionals' perceptions of organizational politics as a function of experience, organizational size and perceived independence', *The Journal of Social Psychology*. **146**(96): 717–32.

Czarniawska, C. Z. (1997) *Narrating the Organization: Dramas of Institutional Identity*, Chicago, IL: University of Chicago Press.

Davey, K. (2008) 'Women's accounts of organizational politics as a gendering process', *Gender, Work and Organization*, **15**(6): 650–71.

Dutton, J. E., Ashford, S. J., O'Neil, R. M., and Lawrence, K. A. (2001) 'Moves that matter: Issue selling and organizational change', *Academy of Management Journal*, **44**(4): 716–36.

Ferris, G. R. and Kacmar, K. M. (1992) 'Perceptions of organizational politics', *Journal of Management*, **18**(1): 93–116.

Ferris, G. R., Frink, D. D., Bhawk, D. P., Zhou, J., and Gilmore, D. C. (1996) 'Reactions of diverse groups to politics in the workplace', *Journal of Management*, **22**(2): 23–44.

Ferris, G. R., Perrewe, P. L., Anthony, W. P., and Gilmore, D. C. (2000) 'Political skill at work', *Organizational Dynamics*, **28**(94): 25–37.

Fincham, R. (1999) 'The consultant–client relationship: Critical perspectives on the management of organizational change', *Journal of Management Studies*, **36**(3): 335–51.

Floyd, S. W. and Wooldridge, B. J. (2000) *Building Strategy from the Middle: Reconceptualising the Strategy Process*, Thousand Oaks, CA: Sage.

Ford, J. D., Ford, L. W., and D'Amelio, A. (2008) 'Resistance to change: The rest of the story', *Academy of Management Review*, **33**(2): 362–77.

French Jr, J. R. P. and Raven, B. (1958) 'The bases of social power', in D. Cartwright and A. Zander (eds) *Group Dynamics*, 3rd edn, New York: Harper & Row, pp. 259–69.

Gandz, J. and Murray, V. V. (1980) 'The experience of workplace politics', *Academy of Management Journal*, **23**(2): 237–51.

Grey, C. (2003) 'The fetish of change', *Tamara: Journal of Critical Postmodern Organization Science*, **2**(2): 1–19.

The Guardian (2009) 'Daggers drawn: Conflict at HBOS' 12 Feb. http://www.guardian.co.uk/business/2009/feb/12/pau-moore-james-crosby-hbos

Huczynski, A. (1996) *Influencing within Organizations*, London: Prentice Hall.

Kanter, R. M., Stein, B. A., and Jick, T. D. (1992) *The Challenge of Organizational Change: How Companies Experience It and Leaders Guide It*, New York: Free Press.

Knights, D. and Vurdubakis, T. (1994) 'Foucault, power, resistance and all that', in J. M. Jarmier, D. Knights, and W. R. Nord (eds) *Resistance and Power in Organizations*, London: Routledge, pp. 167–198.

Kotter, J. P. (1977) 'Power, dependence and effective management', *Harvard Business Review*, **55**(4): 125–36.

Kotter, J. P. and Cohen, D. S. (2002) *The Heart of Change*, Boston, MA: Harvard Business School Press.

Kotter, J. P. and Schlesinger, L. A. (1979) 'Choosing strategies for change', *Harvard Business Review*, **57**(2): 106–14.

Kramer, R. M. and Neale, M. A. (1998) *Power and Influence in Organizations*, Thousand Oaks, CA: Sage.

Lukes, S. (1990; 1974) *Power: A Radical View*, Basingstoke: Palgrave Macmillan.

Meston, C. and King, N. (1996) 'Making sense of "resistance"; Responses to organizational change in a private nursing home for the elderly', *European Journal of Work and Organizational Psychology*, **5**(1): 91–102.

Mintzberg, H. (1985) 'The organization as a political arena', *Journal of Management Studies*, **22**(2): 133–54.

Morgan, G. (1986) *Images of Organization*, London: Sage.

Ocasio, W. (1997) 'Toward an attention-based view of the firm', *Strategic Management Journal*, 18: 187–20.

Pettigrew, A. (1974) 'The influence process between specialists and executives', *Personnel Review*, **3**(1): 24–30.

Pfeffer, J. (1992) *Managing with Power: Politics and Influence in Organizations*, Boston, MA: Harvard Business School Press.

Pfeffer, J. (2010) 'Power play', *Harvard Business Review*, **88**(7/8): 85–92.

Piderit, S. K. (2000) 'Rethinking resistance and recognizing ambivalence: A multidimensional view of attitudes toward an organizational change', *Academy of Management Review*, **25**(4): 783–94.

Poon, J. (2003) 'Situational antecedents and outcomes of organizational politics and perceptions', *Journal of Managerial Psychology*, **18**(2): 138–55.

Scholes, K. (1998) 'Stakeholder mapping: A practical tool for managers', in V. Ambrosini, G. Johnson, and K. Scholes (eds) *Exploring Techniques of Analysis and Evaluation in Strategic Management*, Harlow: Prentice Hall Europe, pp. 152–68.

The Telegraph (2009) 'HBOS whistleblower Paul Moore: Evidence to House of Commons' 'Banking Crisis' hearing', 11 Feb. http://www.telegraph.co.uk/finance/newsbysector/banksandfinance/4590996/HBOS-whistleblower-Paul-Moore-Evidence-to-House-of-Commons-Banking-Crisis-hearing.html

The Telegraph (2009) 'Gordon Brown must go says HBOS whistleblower Paul Moore', 15 Feb. http://www.telegraph.co.uk/finance/financialcrisis/4629670/Gordon-Brown-must-go-says-HBOS-whistleblower-Paul-Moore.html

Tucker, J. (1993) 'Everyday forms of employee resistance', *Sociological Forum*, **8**(1): 25–45.

Watzlawick, P., Weakland, J., and Fisch R. (1974) *Problem Formation, Change*, New York: W. W. Norton & Co, pp. 31–73.

Zanzi, A. and O'Neill, R. M. (2001) 'Sanctioned versus non-sanctioned political tactics', *Journal of Managerial Issues*, **13**(2): 245–62.

Zoller, H. M. and Fairhurst, G. T. (2007) 'Resistance leadership: The overlooked potential in critical organization and leadership studies', *Human Relations*, **60**(90): 1331–60.

Chapter 8

Akbar, H. (2003) 'Knowledge levels and their transformation: Towards the integration of knowledge creation and individual learning', *Journal of Management Studies*, **40**(8): 1997–2021.

Argyris, C. (1990) *Overcoming Organizational Defenses: Facilitating Organizational Learning*, Needham Heights, MA: Allyn and Bacon.

Argyris, C. (1994) 'Good communication that blocks learning', *Harvard Business Review*, **72**(4): 77–85.

Argyris, C. and Schön, D. A. (1996) *Organizational Learning II: Theory, Method, and Practice*, Reading, MA: Addison-Wesley.

Baker, A. C., Jensen, P. J., and Kolb, D. A. (2005) 'Conversation as experiential learning', *Management Learning*, **36**(4): 411–27.

Balogun, J. and Jenkins, M. (2003) 'Re-conceiving change management: A knowledge-based perspective', *European Management Journal*, **21**(2): 247–57.

Barney, J. B. and Clark, D. N. (2007) *Resource-based Theory: Creating and Sustaining Competitive Advantage*, Oxford: Oxford University Press.

Baumard, P. and Starbuck, W. H. (2005) 'Learning from failures: Why it may not happen', *Long Range Planning*, **38**(3): 281–98.

BBC News (1999) 'Bolsin: The Bristol whistleblower'. http://news.bbc.co.uk/1/hi/health/532006.stm

BBC News (2002) 'Dyson plant shuts up shop', 26 Sep. http://news.bbc.co.uk/1/hi/england/2282809.stm

BBC News (2010) 'Q&A: Toyota recalls', 18 Feb. http://news.bbc.co.uk/1/hi/business/8496902.stm

BBC News (2010) 'Toyota boss Akio Toyoda apologises for faults', 24 Feb. http://news.bbc.co.uk/1/hi/business/8533352.stm

BBC News (2010) 'Toyota faces record $16m fine from US over pedal recall', 5 Apr. http://news.bbc.co.uk/1/hi/business/8604150.stm

BBC News (2010) 'Toyota agrees to pay $16.4m fine', 20 Apr. http://news.bbc.co.uk/1/hi/business/8630447.stm

Beard, A. (2010) 'Life's work', *Harvard Business Review*, **88**(7/8): 172.

Boxall, P. and Purcell, J. (2011) *Strategy and Human Resource Management*, 3rd edn, Basingstoke: Palgrave Macmillan.

Carlson, N. (2011) 'The real history of Twitter', *Business Insider*, 13 Apr. http://www.businessinsider.com/how-twitter-was-founded-2011-4?op=1

Carroll, J. S., Rudolph, J. W., and Hatakenaka, S. (2004) 'Learning from organizational experience', in M. Easterby-Smith and M. A. Lyles (eds) *The Blackwell Handbook of Organizational Learning and Knowledge Management*, Oxford: Blackwell Publishing, pp. 575–600.

Collins, N. (2005) 'Dyson is making pots of money for Britain by going to Malaysia', *The Telegraph*, 28 Feb. http://www.telegraph.co.uk/comment/personal-view/3615244/Dyson-is-making-pots-of-money-for-Britainby-going-to-Malaysia.html

Cook, S. D. N. and Brown, J. S. (1999) 'Bridging epistemologies: The generative dance between organizational knowledge and organizational knowing', *Organization Science*, **10**(4): 381–400.

Cornelius, P., Van de Putte, A., and Romani, M. (2005) 'Three decades of scenario planning in Shell', *California Management Review*, **48**(1): 92–109.

Crossan, M. M., Lane, H. W., and White, R. E. (1999) 'An organizational learning framework: From intuition to institution', *Academy of Management Review*, **24**(3): 522–37.

de Geus, A. (1999) *The Living Company: Habits for Survival in a Turbulent Business Environment*, Boston, MA: Harvard Business School Press.

de Holan, P. M. and Phillips, N. (2003) 'Organizational forgetting', in M. Easterby-Smith and M. A. Lyles (eds) *The Blackwell Handbook of Organizational Learning and Knowledge Management*, Oxford: Blackwell, pp. 393–409.

Dyson, J. (2004) 'The Richard Dimbleby lecture: Engineering the difference'. http://news.bbc.co.uk/1/shared/bsp/hi/pdfs/dyson_10_12_04.pdf

Dyson, J. (2005) 'James Dyson on innovation', *Ingenia*, 24: 31–4.

Dyson Ltd (undated) 'Inside Dyson'. http://www.dyson.co.uk/insidedyson/default.asp

The Economist (2007) 'Suck it and see: The hazards of being an entrepreneur', 1 Feb. http://www.economist.com/node/8582349

Eden, C. and Ackermann, F. (2010) 'Competences, distinctive competences, and core competences', *Research in Competence-Based Management*, **5**(1): 3–33.

Eisenhardt, K. M. and Martin, J. A. (2000) 'Dynamic capabilities: What are they?', *Strategic Management Journal*, **21**(10/11): 1105.

Frommer, D. (2011) 'Chart of the day: The iPhone is now half of Apple's business', *Business Insider*, 21 Apr. http://www.businessinsider.com/chart-of-the-day-apple-revenue-by-segment-2011-4

Garvin, D. A. (2000) *Learning in Action: A Guide to Putting the Learning Organization to Work*, Boston, MA: Harvard Business School Press.

Garvin, D. A., Edmondson, A. C., and Gino, F. (2008) 'Is yours a learning organization?', *Harvard Business Review*, **86**(3): 109–16.

Gribben, R. (2003) 'Dyson production moves to Malaysia', *The Telegraph*, 21 Aug. http://www.telegraph.co.uk/finance/2860995/Dyson-production-moves-to-Malaysia.html

The Guardian (2010) 'Toyota president Akio Toyoda's statement to Congress', 24 Feb. http://www.guardian.co.uk/business/2010/feb/24/akio-toyoda-statement-to-congress

Hamel, G. (1997) 'Killer strategies that make shareholders rich', *Fortune*, **135**(12): 70–84.

Hirst, C. (2005) 'James Dyson: Dyson cleans up in America, but has he brushed a few things under the carpet?', *The Independent*, 27 Feb. http://www.independent.co.uk/news/business/analysis-and-features/james-dyson-dyson-cleans-up-in-america-but-has-he-brushed-a-few-things-under-the-carpet-484994.html

Hoe, S. L. (2007) 'Is interpersonal trust a necessary condition for organisational learning?', *Journal of Organisational Transformation and Social Change*, **4**(2): 149–56.

Isaacs, W. (1999a) 'Dialogical leadership', *The Systems Thinker*, **10**(1): 1–5.

Isaacs, W. (1999b) *Dialogue and the Art of Thinking Together: A Pioneering Approach to Communicating in Business and in Life*, New York: Doubleday.

Kennedy, I. (2001) *Learning from Bristol: The Report of the Public Inquiry into Children's Heart Surgery at the Bristol Royal Infirmary 1984–1995*. http://www.bristol-inquiry.org.uk/final_report/the_report.pdf

Kleiner, A. and Roth, G. (1997) 'How to make experience your company's best teacher', *Harvard Business Review*, **75**(5): 172–7.

Kleysen, R. F. and Dyck, B. (2001) 'Cumulating knowledge: An elaboration and extension of Crossan, Lane and White's framework for organizational learning', Paper presented at the Fourth International Conference for Organizational Learning and Knowledge Management, 1–4 June, London, ON, Canada.

Lawler, E. E. and Worley, C. G. (2006) *Built to Change: How to Achieve Sustained Organizational Effectiveness*, San Francisco, CA: Jossey-Bass.

Leonard-Barton, D. (1995) *Wellsprings of Knowledge: Building and Sustaining the Sources of Innovation*, Boston, MA: Harvard Business School Press.

Liker, J. (2004) *The Toyota Way: 14 Management Principles from the World's Greatest Manufacturer*, New York: McGraw-Hill Professional.

Madsen, P. M. and Desai, V. (2010) 'Failing to learn? The effects of failure and success on organizational learning in the global orbital launch vehicle industry', *Academy of Management Journal*, **53**(3): 451–76.

Mazutis, D. and Slawinski, N. (2008) 'Leading organizational learning through authentic dialogue', *Management Learning*, **39**(4): 437–56.

Mesure, S. and Beard, M. (2002) 'The appliance of science sucks Dyson eastwards', *The Independent*, 6 Feb. http://www.independent.co.uk/news/business/news/last-month-james-dyson-said-the-decline-of-british-manufacturing-was-a-tragedy-659618.html

Nonaka, I. and Takeuchi, H. (1995) *The Knowledge-creating Company: How Japanese Companies Create the Dynamics of Innovation*, New York: Oxford University Press.

Pedler, M., Aspinwall, K., and Aspinall, K. (1998) *A Concise Guide to the Learning Organization*, London: Lemos & Crane.

Pedler, M., Burgoyne, J., and Boydell, T. (1996) *The Learning Company: A Strategy for Sustainable Development*, London: McGraw-Hill Professional.

Polanyi, M. (1966) *The Tacit Dimension*, London: Routledge/Kegan Paul.

Prahalad, C. K. and Hamel, G. (1990) 'The core competence of the corporation', *Harvard Business Review*, **68**(3): 79–91.

Quinn, R. W. and Dutton, J. E. (2005) 'Coordination as energy in conversation', *Academy of Management Review*, **30**(1): 36–57.

Sanchez, R. (2005) *Knowledge Management and Organizational Learning: Fundamental Concepts for Theory and Practice*, Working Paper Series, Lund: Lund Institute of Economic Research.

Scharmer, C. O. (2009) *Theory U: Learning from the Future as It Emerges—The Social Technology of Presencing*, San Francisco, CA: Berrett-Koehler.

Senge, P. M. (2006) *The Fifth Discipline: The Art and Practice of the Learning Organization*, 2nd edn, New York: Random House Books.

Senge, P. M., Kleiner, A., Roberts, C., Ross, R. B., and Smith, B. J. (1994) *The Fifth Discipline Fieldbook: Strategies and Tools for Building a Learning Organization*, London: Nicholas Brealey Publishing.

Senge, P. M., Scharmer, C. O., Jaworski, J., and Flowers, B. S. (2005) *Presence: Exploring Profound Change in People, Organizations, and Society*, London: Nicholas Brealey Publishing.

Shaw, P. (2002) *Changing Conversations in Organizations: A Complexity Approach to Change*, London: Routledge.

Spear, S. and Bowen, H. K. (1999) 'Decoding the DNA of the Toyota production system', *Harvard Business Review*, **77**(5): 96–106.

Stewart, T. A. and Raman, A. P. (2007) 'Lessons from Toyota's long drive', *Harvard Business Review*, **85**(7/8): 74–83.

Szulanski, G. and Winter, S. (2002) 'Getting it right the second time', *Harvard Business Review*, 80(1): 62–9.

Takeuchi, H., Osono, E., and Shimizu, N. (2008) 'The contradictions that drive Toyota's success', *Harvard Business Review*, **86**(6): 96–104.

This is Money (2004) 'Survival, Dyson style', 21 Mar. http://www.thisismoney.co.uk/news/article.html?in_article_id=322783&in_page_id=2

Tsang, E. W. K. and Zahra, S. A. (2008) 'Organizational unlearning', *Human Relations*, **61**(10): 1435–62.

Tucker, A. L. and Edmondson, A. C. (2003) 'Why hospitals don't learn from failures: Organizational and psychological dynamics that inhibit system change', *California Management Review*, **45**(2): 55–72.

Tucker, A. L., Edmondson, A. C., and Spear, S. (2002) 'When problem solving prevents organizational learning', *Journal of Organizational Change Management*, **15**(2): 122–37.

Uhlig, R. and Litterick, D. (2002) '800 jobs to go as Dyson goes to the Far East', *The Telegraph*, 6 Feb. http://www.

telegraph.co.uk/news/uknews/1383870/800-jobs-to-go-as-Dyson-goes-to-the-Far-East.html

Vera, D. and Crossan, M. (2004) 'Strategic leadership and organizational learning', *Academy of Management Review*, **29**(2): 222–40.

Webb, T. (2010) 'Toyota recalls 1.66m cars worldwide amid fears over brakes and engines', *The Guardian*, 21 Oct. http://www.guardian.co.uk/business/2010/oct/21/toyota-recalls-166m-cars-faulty-brakes-engines

Webb, T., Booth, R., McCurry, J., and Harris, P. (2010) 'How did Toyota veer so far off course?', *The Guardian*, 7 Feb. http://www.guardian.co.uk/business/2010/feb/07/toyota-veer-off-course

Weick, K. E. and Sutcliffe, K. M. (2003) 'Hospitals as cultures of entrapment: A reanalysis of the Bristol Royal Infirmary', *California Management Review*, **45**(2): 73–84.

Zollo, M. and Winter, S. G. (2002) 'Deliberate learning and the evolution of dynamic capabilities', *Organization Science*, **13**(3): 339–51.

Chapter 9

Alfa Laval (undated) 'Our company'. http://www.alfalaval.com/about-us/our-company/pages/our-company.aspx

Ashridge Business School and Alfa Laval (2008) 'Submission paper for the EFMD Excellence in Practice Award 2009 "Partnership in Learning & Development"'. http://www.ashridge.org.uk/Website/IC.nsf/wFARATT/Partnership%20in%20Learning%20%26%20Development/$File/PartnershipInLearning&Development.pdf

Beer, M. and Nohria, N. (2000) 'Resolving the tension between theories E and O of change', in M. Beer and N. Nohria (eds) *Breaking the Code of Change*, Boston, MA: Harvard Business School Press, pp. 1–33.

Beer, M. and Nohria, N. (2003) 'Cracking the code of change', in T. Jick and M. Peiperl (eds) *Managing Change: Cases and Concepts—Module 6*, New York: McGraw-Hill Higher Education, pp. 483–515.

Bicheno, J. (2004) *The New Lean Toolbox: Towards Fast, Flexible Flow*, Buckingham: Picsie Books.

Bicheno, J. and Catherwood, P. (2005) *Six Sigma and the Quality Toolbox*, Buckingham: Picsie Books.

Bradford, D. and Burke, W. (2005) 'The future of OD?', in D. Bradford and W. Burke (eds) *Reinventing Organization Development: New Approaches to Change in Organizations*, San Francisco, CA: Pfeiffer/Wiley, pp. 195–214.

Caron, J., Jarvenpa, S., and Stoddard, D. (1994) 'Business reengineering at Cigna Corporation: Experiences and lessons learned from the first five years', *Management Information Systems Quarterly*, **18**(3): 233–50.

Davenport, T. (1996) 'The fad that forgot people', *Fast Company*, 1 Nov: 70–4.

Dunphy, D. (2000) 'Embracing paradox: Top-down versus participative management of organizational change—A commentary on Conger and Bennis', in M. Beer and N. Nohria (eds) *Breaking the Code of Change*, Boston, MA: Harvard Business School Press, pp. 123–38.

Dunphy, D. and Stace, D. (1993) 'The strategic management of corporate change', *Human Relations*, **46**(8): 905–18.

Financial Times (2004) 'The joys of crossing a terrier with a retriever', 9 July.

Floyd, S. and Wooldridge, B. (2000) *Building Strategy from the Middle: Reconceptualising Strategy Process*, Thousand Oaks, CA: Sage.

Frahm, S. (2003) 'Six Sigma: Where is it now? SCRC', *Supply Chain Management*, 24 June. http://scm.ncsu.edu/scm-articles/article/six-sigma-where-is-it-now

Grover, V. Jeong, S., Kettinger, W., and Teng, J. (1995) 'The implementation of business process reengineering', *Journal of Management Information Systems*, **12**(1): 109–44.

Hall, G., Rosenthal, J., and Wade, J. (1993) 'How to make reengineering really work', *Harvard Business Review*, **71**(6): 97–108.

Hammer, M. (1990) 'Re-engineering work: Don't automate, obliterate', *Harvard Business Review*, **68**(4): 104–13.

Hammer, M. and Champy, J. (1993) *Reengineering the Corporation: A Manifesto for Business Revolution*, London: Nicholas Brealey.

Hammer, M. and Champy, J. (2001) *Reengineering the Corporation: A Manifesto for Business Revolution*, 3rd rev'd edn, London: Nicholas Brealey.

Hanna, J. (2007) *Bringing Lean Principles to Service Industries Software Services*, Working Paper No. 08-001, Boston, MA: Harvard Business School.

Harry, M. and Schroeder, R. (2000) *Six Sigma*, New York: Random House.

Hayes, J. (2010) *The Theory and Practice of Change Management*, 3rd edn, Basingstoke: Palgrave Macmillan.

Hindo, B. (2007) 'At 3M, a struggle between efficiency and creativity', *Business Week*, 6 June. http://www.businessweek.com/magazine/content/07_24/b4038406.htm

Hindo, B. and Grow, B. (2007) 'Six Sigma: So yesterday?', *Business Week*, 11 June. http://www.businessweek.com/magazine/content/07_24/b4038409.htm

Jarrar, Y. and Aspinwall, E. (1999) 'Business process re-engineering: Learning from organizational experience', *Total Quality Management*, **10**(2): 173–86.

Jones, D. and Mitchell, A. (for the Lean Enterprise Academy) (2006) *Lean Thinking for the NHS. Report Commissioned by the NHS Confederation*. http://www.nhsconfed.org/Publications/reports/Pages/Leanthinking.aspx

Kotter, J. (1996) *Leading Change*, Boston, MA: Harvard Business School Press.

Kotter, J. (2007) 'Leading change: Why transformation efforts fail', *Harvard Business Review*, **85**(1): 96–103.

Kotter, J. and Cohen, D. (2002) *The Heart of Change: Real-life Stories of How People Change Their Organizations*, Boston, MA: Harvard Business School Press.

Leppitt, N. (2006) 'Challenging the code of change: Part 1—Praxis does not make perfect', *Journal of Change Management*, **6**(2): 121–42.

Marston, R. (2009) 'Sir Stuart Rose's legacy at M&S', BBC News, 18 Nov. http://news.bbc.co.uk/1/hi/business/8366635.stm

McNulty, T. and Ferlie, E. (2002) *Reengineering Health care: The Complexities of Organizational Transformation*, Oxford: Oxford University Press.

Neveling, N. (2007) 'Tax bosses look to boost staff morale', *Accountancy Age*, 24 May. http://www.accountancyage.com/accountancyage/news/2190607/tax-bosses-look-boost-staff

Pande, P., Neuman, R., and Cavenagh, R. (2000) *The Six Sigma Way: How GE, Motorola and Other Top Companies are Honing Their Performance*, New York: McGraw-Hill.

Radnor, Z. and Bucci, G. (2007) *Evaluation of Pacesetter: Lean, Senior Leadership and Operational Management within HMRC Processing—Final Report September 2007*. http://www.hmrc.gov.uk/about/pacesetter-final-report.pdf

Radnor, Z., Walley, P., Stephens, A., and Bucci, G. (for the Warwick Business School) (2006) *Evaluation of the Lean Approach to Business Management and its Use in the Public Sector*. http://www.scotland.gov.uk/Publications/2006/06/13162106/15

Randall, J. (2004) *Managing Change/Change Managers*, London: Routledge.

Shah, R., Chandrasekaran, A., and Linderman, K. (2008) 'In pursuit of implementation patterns: The context of Lean and Six Sigma', *International Journal of Production Research*, **46**(23): 6679–99.

Stace, D. (1996) 'Transitions and transformations', in Storey, J. (eds) *Blackwell Cases in Human Resources and Change Management*, Oxford: Blackwell Publishers Ltd, pp. 43–73.

Stace, D. and Dunphy, D. (1991) 'Beyond traditional paternalistic and developmental approaches to organizational change and human resource strategies', *The International Journal of Human Resource Management*, **2**(3): 263–83.

Stoddard, D. and Jarvenpaa, S. (1995) 'Business process redesign: Tactics of managing radical change', *Journal of Management Information System*, **12**(1): 81–107.

Tax Advantage (2010) 'HMRC tax code fiasco', 15 Sep. http://www.tax-advantage.co.uk/news/hmrc-tax-code-fiasco.html

The Telegraph (2006) 'How M&S was turned around', 10 Jan. http://www.telegraph.co.uk/finance/2929807/How-MandS-was-turned-around.html

Womack, J. and Jones, T. (1994) 'From Lean production to the Lean enterprise', *Harvard Business Review*, **72**(2): 93–103.

Womack, J. and Jones, T. (2005) 'Lean consumption', *Harvard Business Review*, **83**(3): 58–69.

Chapter 10

Austin, J. and Bartunek, J. (2006) 'Theories and practices of organizational development', in J. Gallos (ed.) *Organization Development*, San Francisco, CA: Jossey-Bass, pp. 89–128.

BBC News (2001) 'BT approves mobiles spin-off', 23 Oct. http://news.bbc.co.uk/1/hi/business/1615100.stm

Beckhard, R. (2006) 'What is organization development?', in J. Gallos (ed.) *Organization Development*, San Francisco, CA: Jossey-Bass, pp. 3–12.

Bradford, D. and Burke, W. (2005) *The Future of OD in Reinventing Organization Development: New Approaches to Change in Organizations*, San Francisco, CA: Pfeiffer.

Bunker, B. and Alban, B. (1997) *Large-group Interventions: Engaging the Whole System for Rapid Change*, San Francisco, CA: Jossey-Bass.

Bunker, B., Alban, B., and Lewicki, R. (2005) 'Ideas in currency and OD practice: Has the well gone dry?', in D. Bradford and W. Burke (eds) *The Future of OD in Reinventing Organization Development: New Approaches to Change in Organizations*, San Francisco, CA: Pfeiffer, pp. 163–95.

Burke, W. (2008) *Organization Change, Theory and Practice*, Thousand Oaks, CA: Sage.

Burnes, B. (2009) *Managing Change*, 5th edn, Harlow: Prentice-Hall.

Caulat, G. (2010) 'Virtual leadership: Rethinking virtual teams', *Danish Leadership Review* (English version), Sep–Oct. http://black-gazelle.com/_resources/pdf/Article%20Ledelse%20i%20Dag%20English%20Version.pdf

Cooperrider, D. and Srivastva, S. (2008) 'Appreciative Inquiry in organizational life', in D. Cooperrider, D. Whitney, and J. Stavros (eds) *Appreciative Inquiry Handbook*, 2nd edn, San Francisco, CA: Berrett-Koehler, pp. 350–60.

Cooperrider, D., Whitney, D., and Stavros, J. (2008) *Appreciative Inquiry Handbook for Leaders of Change*, 2nd edn, San Francisco, CA: Berrett-Koehler.

Dunphy, D. and Stace, D. (1993) 'The strategic management of corporate change', *Human Relations*, **46**(8): 905–18.

Freedman, A. (2006) 'Action research: Origins and applications for ODC practitioners', in B. Jones and M. Brazzel (eds) *The NTL Handbook of Organization Development and Change: Principles, Practices and Perspectives*, San Francisco, CA: Pfeiffer/Wiley. pp. 83–104.

French, W. and Bell, C. (1999) *Organization Development: Behavioural Science Interventions for Organization Improvement*, 6th edn, Upper Saddle River, NJ: Prentice Hall.

Future Search (undated) 'Future Search applications'. http://www.futuresearch.net/method/applications/

Greiner, L. and Cummings, T. (2005) 'OD: Wanted more alive than dead', in D. Bradford and W. Burke (eds) *Reinventing Organizational Development*, San Francisco, CA: Pfeiffer, pp. 87–112.

Harrison, O. (1999) 'Open space technology', in P. Holman and T. Devane (eds) *The Change Handbook: Group Methods for Shaping the Future*, San Francisco, CA: Berrett-Koehler, pp. 233–45.

Holbeche, L. (2006) *Understanding Change: Theory, Implementation and Success*, Oxford: Butterworth-Heinemann.

Holbeche, L. (2009) 'Organisational development: What's in a name?', *Impact: Quarterly Update on CIPD Policy and Research*, 26: 6–9.

Holman, P. and Devane, T. (1999) (eds) *The Change Handbook: Group Methods for Shaping the Future*, San Francisco, CA: Berrett-Koehler.

Isaacs, W. (1999a) *Dialogue: The Art of Thinking Together*, New York: Doubleday.

Isaacs, W. (1999b) 'Dialogical leadership', *The Systems Thinker*, **10**(1): 1–5.

Kotter, J. (1996) *Leading Change*, Boston, MA: Harvard Business School Press.

Kotter, J. and Cohen, D. (2002) *The Heart of Change: Real-life Stories of How People Change their Organizations*, Boston, MA: Harvard Business School Press.

Lewin, K. (1997; 1951) *Resolving Social Conflicts and Field Theory in Social Science*, Washington, DC: American Psychological Association.

Lewis, S., Passmore, J., and Cantore, S. (2008) *Appreciative Inquiry for Change Management: Using AI to Facilitate Organizational Development*, London: Kogan Page.

Marshak, R. (2005) 'Contemporary challenges to the philosophy and practice of organization development', in D. Bradford and W. Burke (eds) *The Future of OD in Reinventing Organization Development: New Approaches to Change in Organizations*, San Francisco, CA: Pfeiffer, pp. 19–42.

Mirvis, P. (2006) 'Revolutions in OD', in J. Gallos (ed.) *Organization Development*, San Francisco, CA: Jossey-Bass, pp. 39–88.

Norris, R. (2000) *Abstract of the HRDV 6000 Report: A Grounded Theory Study on the Value Associated with Using Open Space Technology*. http://www.openspaceworld.org/tmnfiles/OSTResearch2000.htm

NS&I (undated) 'Who we are'. http://www.nsandi.com/about-nsi-who-we-are

O'Reilly, C. (1996) 'Corporations, culture and commitment: Motivation and social control in organizations', in R. Steers, L. Porter, and G. Bigley (eds) *Motivation and Leadership at Work*, 6th edn, New York: McGraw-Hill International Editions, pp. 370–82.

Palmer, I., Dunford, R., and Akin, G. (2006) *Managing Organizational Change*, Boston, MA: McGraw-Hill/Irwin.

Pedler, M. (1997) *Action Learning in Practice*, 3rd edn, Aldershot: Gower.

Ray, B. (2007) 'Peter Erskine calls it a day at O2', 29 Nov. http://www.theregister.co.uk/2007/11/29/erskine_steps_down/

Revans, R. (1997) 'Action learning: Its origins and nature', in M. Pedler (ed.) *Action Learning in Practice*, 3rd edn, Aldershot: Gower, pp. 3–14.

Schein, E. H. (1999) *Process Consultation Revisited: Building the Helping Relationship*, Harlow: Addison Wesley.

Schein, E. H. (2006) 'Foreword', in J. Gallos (ed.) *Organization Development*, San Francisco, CA: Jossey-Bass, pp. xv–xix.

Shimabukuro, J. (2000) 'The evolving virtual conference: Implications for professional networking', *The Technology Source*, Sep–Oct. http://technologysource.org/article/evolving_virtual_conference/

Siemans (undated) 'IT solutions and services'. http://www.siemens.com/entry/cc/en/#189380

Stace, D. (1996) 'Transitions and transformations', in J. Storey (ed.) *Blackwell Cases in Human Resources and Change Management*, Oxford: Blackwell, pp. 43–73.

Stacey, R. D. (2002–03) 'Organizations as complex responsive processes of relating', *Journal of Innovative Management*, **8**(2): 27–39.

Tolbert, M. and Hanafin, J. (2006) 'Use of self in OD consulting: What matters is presence', in B. Jones and M. Brazzel (eds) *The NTL Handbook of Organization Development and Change: Principles, Practices and Perspectives*, Chichester: Wiley. pp. 69–82.

van der Haar, D. and Hosking, D. (2004) 'Evaluating appreciative inquiry: A relational, constructionist perspective', *Human Relations*, **57**(8): 1017–36.

Vanstone, C. (2007) 'Better place at O2', *Converse*, 5: 3–5.

Vanstone, C. (2010) *An Introduction to Appreciative Inquiry: Change, Performance and Engagement*, Berkhamsted: Ashridge Consulting.

Vanstone, C. and Dalbiez, B. (2008) 'Revitalising corporate values in Nokia', in S. Lewis, J. Passmore, and S. Cantore (eds) *Appreciative Inquiry for Change Management: Using AI to Facilitate Organizational Development*, London: Kogan Page, pp. 183–95.

Watkins, J. and Mohr, B. (2001) *Appreciative Inquiry: Change at the Speed of Imagination*, San Francisco, CA: Jossey-Bass/Pfeiffer.

Weisbord, M. and Janoff, S. (2000) *Future Search: An Action Guide to Finding Common Ground in Organizations and Communities*, San Francisco, CA: Berrett-Koehler.

Weisbord, M. (for Future Search Network) (2004) 'A model for redesigning product lines at Ikea'. http://www.futuresearch.net/method/applications/uploads/business/ikea.pdf

Whitney, D. (1998) 'Let's change the subject and change our organization: An Appreciative Inquiry approach to organization change', *Career Development International*, **3**(7): 314–19.

Wilkinson, A., Dundon, T., Marchington, M., and Ackers, P. (2004) 'Changing patterns of employee voice: Case studies from the UK and Republic of Ireland', *Journal of Industrial Relations*, **46**(3): 298–322.

Chapter 11

Alvesson, M. and Johansson, A. W. (2002) 'Professionalism and politics in management consultancy work', in T. Clark and R. Fincham (eds) *Critical Consulting: New Perspectives on the Management Advice Industry*, Oxford: Blackwell Publishers Ltd, pp. 228–46.

Baker, S. D. (2007) 'Followership: The theoretical foundation of a contemporary construct', *Journal of Leadership and Organizational Studies*, **14**(1): 50–60.

Balgoun, J. and Hailey, V. H. (2004) *Exploring Strategic Change*, 2nd edn, London: Prentice Hall.

Banham, R. (2010) , *CFO*, June: 56–9.

Bass, B. M. (1990) 'From transactional to transformational leadership: Learning to share the vision', *Organizational Dynamics*, **18**(3): 19–31.

BBC News (2006) 'Dyke: BBC is "hideously white"', 6 Jan. http://news.bbc.co.uk/1/hi/scotland/1104305.stm

Beer, M. and Nohria, N. (2000) 'Resolving the tension between Theories E and O of change', in M. Beer and N. Nohria (eds) *Breaking the Code of Change*, Boston, MA: Harvard Business School Press, pp. 1–33.

Bennis, W. G. and Goldsmith, J. (2003) *Learning to Lead: A Workbook on Becoming a Leader*, New York: Basic Books.

Billsberry, J. (2009) (ed.) *Discovering Leadership*, Buckingham: Open University Press.

Binney, G., Wilkes, G., and Williams, C. (2005) *Living Leadership: A Practical Guide for Ordinary Heroes*, Harlow: FT/Prentice Hall.

Block, P. (2000) *Flawless Consulting: A Guide to Getting your Expertise Used*, 2nd edn, Austin, TX: Learning Concepts.

Bloomfield, B. P. and Danieli, A. (1995) 'The role of management consultants in the development of information technology: The indissoluble nature of socio-political and technical skills', *Journal of Management Studies*, **32**(1): 23–46.

Bloomfield, B. P. and Vurdubakis, T. (2002) 'The vision thing: Constructing technology and the future in management advice', in T. Clark and R. Fincham (eds) *Critical Consulting: New Perspectives on the Management Advice Industry*, Oxford: Blackwell, pp. 115–29.

Bradford, D. and Burke, W. (2005) 'The future of OD', in *Reinventing Organization Development: New Approaches to Change in Organizations*, San Fransisco, CA: Pfeiffer/Wiley, pp. 195–214.

Brown, M. (2006) 'Crisis management', *The Guardian*, 6 Mar: 1.

Buchanan, D. A. (2003) 'Demands, instabilities, manipulations, careers: The lived experience of driving change', *Human Relations*, **56**(6): 663–84.

Buchanan, D. A. and Boddy, D. (1992) *The Expertise of the Change Agent: Public Performance and Backstage Activity*, London: Prentice Hall.

Buchanan, D. A. and Storey, J. (1997) 'Role taking and role switching in organizational change: The four pluralities', in I. McLoughlin and M. Harris (eds) *Innovation, Organizational Change and Technology*, London: International Thomson, pp. 127–45.

Burns, J. M. (2003) *Transforming Leadership: A New Pursuit of Happiness*, New York: Atlantic Monthly Press.

Caldwell, R. (2001) 'Champions, adaptors, consultants and synergists: The new change agents in HRM', *Human Resource Management Journal*, **11**(3): 39–52.

Clark, T. (1995) *Managing Consultants: Consultancy as the Management of Impressions*, Buckingham: Open University Press.

Clark, T. and Fincham, R. (2002) (eds) *Critical Consulting: New Perspectives on the Management Advice Industry*, Oxford: Blackwell.

Clark, T. and Salaman, J. (1996b) 'The management guru as organizational witchdoctor', *Organization*, **3**(10): 85–107.

Clark, T. and Salaman, J. (1998a) 'Management gurus' narratives and the construction of managerial identity', *Journal of Management Studies*, **35**(2): 137–61.

Clark, T. and Salaman, J. (1998b) 'Creating the right impression: Towards a dramaturgy of management consultancy', *Service Industries Journal*, **18**(1): 18–38.

Collins, J. (2001) *Good to Great: Why Some Companies Make the Leap and Others Don't*, New York: Harper Business.

Czarniawska, B. (1998) *A Narrative Approach to Organization Studies*, London: Sage.

Czarniawska-Joerges, B. (1990) 'Merchants of meaning: Management consulting in the Swedish public sector', in B. Turner (ed.) *Organizational Symbolism*, New York: du Gruyter, pp. 139–50.

Desmond, W. (on behalf of Ashridge Consulting) (2010) *Developing Internal Consulting Capability with the National Trust: Submission Paper for the EFMD Excellence in Practice Award*, Berkhamsted: Ashridge Consulting.

Dutton, J. E., Ashford, S. J., O'Neil, R. M., and Lawrence, K. A. (2001) 'Moves that matter: Issue selling and organizational change', *Academy of Management Journal*, **44**(4): 716–36.

Dyke, G. (2004) *Inside Story*, London: Harper Collins.

Financial Times (2010) 'All eyes on how National Trust gets a helping hand', 9 July: 12.

Fincham, R. (1999a) 'The consultant-client relationship: Critical perspectives on the management of organizational change', *Journal of Management Studies*, **36**(3): 335–51.

Fincham, R. (1999b) 'Extruded management: Contradiction and ambivalence in the consultancy process', Paper presented at the Critical Management Studies Conference, 14–16 July, Manchester.

Fincham, R. (1999c) 'Rhetorical narratives and the consultancy process', Paper presented at the British Academy of Management Conference, 1–3 September, Manchester Metropolitan University, Manchester.

Fincham, R. (2002) 'Charisma versus technique: Differentiating the expertise of management gurus and management consultants', in T. Clark and R. Fincham (eds) *Critical Consulting: New Perspectives on the Management Advice Industry*, Oxford: Blackwell, pp. 191–205.

Fincham, R. and Clark, T. (2002–03) 'Management consultancy: Issues, perspectives and agendas', *International Studies of Management and Organization*, **32**(4): 3–18.

Floyd, B. and Wooldridge, B. (1997) 'Middle management's strategic influence and organizational performance', *Journal of Management Studies*, **34**(3): 465–85.

Ford, J. D., Ford, L. W., and D'Amelio, A. (2008) 'Resistance to change: The rest of the story', *Academy of Management Review*, **33**(2): 362–77.

French, J. R. P. and Raven, B. (1959) 'The bases of social power', in D. Cartwright (ed.) *Studies in Social Power*, Ann Arbour, MI: Institute for Social Research, pp. 150–67.

Fullerton, J. and West, M. A. (1996) 'Consultant and client: Working together?', *Journal of Managerial Psychology*, **11**(6): 40–9.

Gabriel, Y. (2000) *Storytelling in Organizations: Facts, Fictions, Fantasies*, Oxford: Oxford University Press.

Ginsberg, A. and Abrahmson, E. (1991) 'Champions of change and strategic shifts: The role of internal and external change advocates', *Journal of Management Studies*, **28**(2): 173–90.

Goffee, R. and Jones, G. (2005) 'Managing authenticity: The paradox of great leadership', *Harvard Business Review*, **83**(12): 1–8.

Goodwin, N. (2006) *Leadership in Health Care: A European Perspective*, Oxford: Routledge.

Greenleaf, R. K. (1997) *Servant Leadership: A Journey into the Nature of Legitimate Greatness*, Mahwah, NJ: Paulist Press.

Grey, C. (2002) 'The fetish of change', *Tamara: Journal of Critical Postmodern Organization Science*, **2**(2): 1–19.

Grint, K. (2007) 'Reading Tolstoy's Wave', in K. Grint (ed.) *Leadership: Classical, Contemporary, and Critical Approaches*, Oxford: Oxford University Press, pp. 1–26.

Gronn, P. (2002) 'Distributed leadership as a unit of analysis', *Leadership Quarterly*, **13**(4): 423–5.

Gross, A. C. and Poor, J. (2008) 'The global management consulting sector', *Business Economics*, **43**(4): 59–68.

Guest, D. (1991) 'Personnel management: The end of orthodoxy?', *British Journal of Industrial Relations*, **29**(2): 149–76.

Hagenmeyer, U. (2007) 'Integrity in management consulting: A contradiction in terms?', *Business Ethics: A European Review*, **16**(2): 107–13.

Heifetz, R. A. and Laurie, D. L. (1997) 'The work of leadership', *Harvard Business Review*, **75**(1): 124–34.

Henley, J. (2010) 'How the National Trust is finding its mojo', *The Guardian*, 10 Feb. http://www.guardian.co.uk/culture/2010/feb/10/national-trust-opens-its-doors

Hope-Hailey, V., Styles, P., and Truss, C. (1997) 'A chameleon function: HRM in the 1990s', *Human Resource Management Journal*, **7**(3): 5–18.

HRO Today (2009) 'Unilever finalizes contract terms in blockbuster HRO deal estimated to be worth over $1B'. http://www.hrotoday.com/news/3265/unilever-finalizes-contract-terms-blockbuster-hro-deal-estimated-be-worth-over-1b

Huczynski, A. A. (1993) *Management Gurus: What Makes Them and How to Become One*, London: Routledge.

Huy, Q. N. (2002) 'Emotional balancing of organizational continuity and radical change: The contribution of middle managers', *Administrative Science Quarterly*, **47**(1): 31–69.

The Independent (1993) 7 Mar.

The Independent (2003) 21 Aug.

The Independent (2005) 20 June.

Jackall, R. (1988) *Moral Mazes: The World of Corporate Managers*, New York: Oxford University Press.

Jackson, B. and Parry, K. (2008) *A Very Short, Fairly Interesting and Reasonably Cheap Book about Studying Leadership*, London: Sage.

Kakabadse, A. and Kakabadse, N. (1999) *Essence of Leadership*, London: International Thomson Business Press.

Kellerman, B. (2007) 'What every leader needs to know about followers', *Harvard Business Review*, **85**(12): 84–91.

Khurana, R. (2002) *Searching for a Corporate Saviour: The Irrational Quest for Charismatic CEOs*, Princeton, NJ: Princeton University Press.

Kieser, A. (2002) 'On communication barriers between management science, consultancies and business organizations', in T. Clark and R. Fincham (eds) *Critical Consulting: New Perspectives on the Management Advice Industry*, Oxford: Blackwell, pp. 206–27.

Kotter, J. (1990) 'What leaders really do', *Harvard Business Review*, **68**(3): 103–11.

Lacey, M. Y. and Tompkins, T. C. (2007) 'Analysis of best practices of internal consulting', *Organization Development Journal*, **25**(3): 123–31.

Luckhurst, T. (2003) 'Can John Birt really hate Dyke's BBC this much?', *The Independent (Foreign edn)*, 21 Aug: 17.

Maister, D. H. (1997) *True Professionalism: The Courage to Care about Your People, Your Clients and Your Career*, New York: The Free Press.

Maister, D. H. (2002) *The Trusted Advisor*, London: Simon and Schuster.

McKenna, C. D. (2006) *The World's Newest Profession: Management Consulting in the Twentieth Century*, New York: Cambridge University Press.

McLean, A. D., Simms, I., Mangham, I., and Tuffiled, D. (1982) *Organization Development in Transition: Evidence for an Evolving Profession*, Chichester: John Wiley & Sons.

Morris, J. A., Brotheridge, C. M., and Urbanksi, J. C. (2005) 'Bringing humility to leadership', *Human Relations*, **58**(10): 1323–50,.

Mulholland, J. (**2009**) 'At the heart of a cultural storm', *The Observer*, 17 May: 4.

O'Shea, J. and Madigan, C. (1997) *Dangerous Company: The Consulting Powerhouses and the Businesses They Save and Ruin*, London: Nicholas Brealey.

Oberoi, U. and Hales, C. (1990) 'Assessing the quality of the conference hotel service product: Towards an empirically based model', *Service Industries Journal*, **10**(4): 700–21.

The Observer (2009) 17 May.

Oshry, B. (2007) *Seeing Systems: Unlocking the Mysteries of Organizational Life*, 2nd edn, San Francisco, CA: Berrett-Koehler.

Paton, R. A. and McCalman, J. (2004) *Change Management: A Guide to Effective Implementation*, London: Sage.

Pellegrin-Boucher, E. (2006) 'Symbolic functions of consultants', *Journal of General Management*, **32**(2): 1–16.

People Management (2007) *Guide to HR Outsourcing*, London: CIPD.

Peters, T. J. and Waterman Jr, R. H. (1982) *In Search of Excellence: Lessons from America's Best-run Companies*, New York: Harper Row.

Quinn, J. B. (1980) *Strategy for Change: Logical Incrementalism*, Homewood, IL: Irwin.

Rickards, T. and Clark, M. (2006) *Dilemmas of Leadership*, London: Routledge.

Romanelli, E. and Tushman, M. L. (1994) 'Organizational transformation as punctuated equilibrium: An empirical test', *Academy of Management Journal*, **36**(5): 1141-66.

Rost, J. C. (1993) *Leadership for the Twenty-First Century*, Westport, CT: Praeger.

Schein, E. H. (1969) *Process Consultation: Its Role in Organization Development*, Reading, MA: Addison Wesley.

Schein, E. H. (1988) *Process Consultation: Volume 2—Lessons for Managers and Consultants*, Reading, MA: Addison-Wesley.

Schein, E. H. (2002) 'Consulting: What should it mean?', in T. Clark and R. Fincham (eds) *Critical Consulting: New Perspectives on the Management Advice Industry*, Oxford: Blackwell, pp. 21-7.

Shotter, J. (1993) *Conversational Realities: Constructing Life through Language*, London: Sage.

Sims, D. (2003) 'Between the millstones: A narrative account of the vulnerability of middle managers' storying', *Human Relations*, **56**(10): 1195-211.

Smirich, L. and Morgan, G. (1982) 'Leadership: The management of meaning', *Journal of Applied Behavioural Science*, **18**(3): 257-73.

Sorge, A. and van Witteloostuijn, A. (2004) 'The (non) sense of organizational change: An essai about universal management hypes, sick consultancy metaphors, and healthy organization theories', *Organization Studies*, **25**(7): 1205-231.

Sturdy, A. (1997a) 'The dialectics of consultancy', *Critical Perspectives on Accounting*, **8**(5): 511-35.

Sturdy, A. (1997b) 'The consultancy process: An insecure business', *Journal of Management Studies*, **34**(3): 389-413.

Thomas, J. B., Clark, S. M., and Gioia, D. A. (1993) 'Strategic sensemaking and organizational performance: Linkages among scanning, interpretation, action and outcomes', *Academy of Management Journal*, **36**(2): 239-70.

Thomas, R. and Linstead, A. (2002) 'Losing the plot? Middle managers and identity', *Organization*, **9**(1): 71-93.

Ulrich, D. (1997) *Human Resource Champions*, Boston, MA: Harvard Business School Press.

Weick, K. (1979) *The Social Psychology of Organizing*, 2nd edn, Reading, MA: Addison Wesley.

Wells, M. (2004) 'The quiet revolutionary', *The Guardian*, 13 Dec: 2.

Westley, F. and Mintzberg, H. (1989) 'Visionary leadership and strategic management', *Strategic Management Journal*, 10 (special issue), 17-32.

Wiggins, L. (2005) 'Making sense of consultancy: A qualitative analysis of the challenge of constructing a positive work identity for management consultants', Unpublished PhD thesis, Birkbeck College, University of London.

Williams, A. and Woodward, S. (1994) *The Competitive Consultant: A Client-orientated Approach for Achieving Superior Performance*, Basingstoke: MacMillan Press.

Wrzeniewski, A. and Dutton, J. E. (2001) 'Crafting a job: Revisioning employees as active crafters of their work', *Academy of Management Review*, **26**(2): 179-201.

Wyatt, W. (2005) 'Shaken and stirred', *The Independent*, 20 June: 15.

Zoller, H. M. and Fairhurst, G. T. (2007) 'Resistance leadership: The overlooked potential in critical organization and leadership studies', *Human Relations*, **60**(90): 1331-60.

Chapter 12

Allen, J., Jimmieson, N. L., Bordia, P., and Irmer, B. E. (2007) 'Uncertainty during organizational change: Managing perceptions through communication', *Journal of Change Management*, **7**(2): 187-210.

Bass, B. M. (1990) 'From transactional to transformational leadership: Learning to share the vision', *Organizational Dynamics*, **18**(3): 19-31.

BBC News (2010) 'Cadbury agrees Kraft takeover bid', 19 Jan. http://news.bbc.co.uk/1/hi/8467007.stm

Beckhard, R. and Harris, R. T. (1987) *Organizational Transitions: Managing Complex Change*, 2nd edn, Reading, MA: Addison-Wesley.

Beer, M. and Eisenstadt, R. A. (2002) 'The silent killers of strategy implementation and learning', *Sloan Management Review*, **41**(4): 29-40.

Boje, D. M. (1991) 'The storytelling organization: A study of story performance in an office-supply firm', *Administrative Science Quarterly*, **36**(1): 106-126.

Bordia, P., Hobman, E., Jones, E., Gallois, C., and Callan, V. J. (2004) 'Uncertainty during organizational change: Types, consequences and management strategies', *Journal of Business and Psychology*, **18**(4): 507-32.

Boyle, C. (2010) '400 Cadbury workers to lose jobs despite promise', *The Times*, 9 Feb.

Boyle, C. (2010) 'Kraft censured for breaching the takeover code on Cadbury', *The Times*, 27 May.

Bridges, W. (2003) *Managing Transitions: Making the Most of Change*, 2nd edn, London: Nicholas Brealey Publishing.

Buchanan, D. and Boddy, D. (1992) *The Expertise of the Change Agent: Public Performance and Backstage Activity*, Hemel Hempstead: Prentice Hall Europe.

Clampitt, P. G., DeKoch, R. J., and Cashman, T. (2000) 'A strategy for communicating about uncertainty', *Academy of Management Executive*, **14**(4): 41–57.

Conger, J. (1999) 'The new age of persuasion', *Leader to Leader*, 12: 37–44.

Daft, R. and Lengel, R. (1986) 'Organizational information requirements: Media richness and structural design', *Management Science*, **32**(5): 554–71.

Ford, J. D. (1999) 'Organizational change as shifting conversations', *Journal of Organizational Change Management*, **12**(6): 480–500.

Fox, S. and Amichai-Hamburger, Y. (2001) 'The power of emotional appeals in promoting organizational change programs', *Academy of Management Executive*, **15**(4): 84–94.

Gardener, J. Paulsen, N. Gallois, C., Callan, V., and Monaghan, R. (2001) 'An intergroup perspective on communication in organizations', in H. Giles and W. P. Robinson (eds) *The New Handbook of Language and Social Psychology*, Chichester: John Wiley & Sons, pp. 561–84.

Georgiades, N. and Macdonnell, R. (1998) *Leadership for Competitive Advantage*, Chichester: John Wiley & Sons.

Gill, R. (2006) *Theory and Practice of Leadership*, London: Sage.

Goodwin, D. K. (1998) 'Lessons of presidential leadership', *Leader to Leader*, 9: 23–30.

Hanson, A. (2010) 'Digital PR perspectives: The BP oil spill', *Arikhanson.com*, 14 May. http://www.arikhanson.com/2010/05/14/digital-pr-perspectives-the-bp-oil-spill/

Hemus, J. (2010) 'Why BP's oil spill is the mother of all crises', *The Drum*, 10 June. http://www.thedrum.co.uk/opinion/2010/06/10/why-bp%C3%A2%E2%82%AC%E2%84%A2s-oil-spill-mother-all-crises

Hubbard, N. and Purcell, J. (2001) 'Managing employee expectations during acquisitions', *Human Resource Management Journal*, **11**(2): 17–33.

Jagger, S. (2010) 'Mandelson attacks Kraft over closing Cadbury plant', *The Times*, 11 Feb.

Jick, T. D. (1990) *The Recipients of Change*, Harvard Business School Case Study No. 9-491-039, Boston, MA: Harvard Business School Press.

Jones, E., Watson, B., Gardner, J., and Gallois, C. (2004) 'Organizational communication: Challenges for the new century', *Journal of Communication*, **54**(4): 722–50.

Kiefer, T. (2002) 'Understanding the emotional experience of organizational change: Evidence from a merger', *Advances in Developing Human Resources*, **4**(1): 39– 61.

Kotter, J. (1996) *Leading Change*, Boston, MA: Harvard Business School Press.

Kouznes, J. M. and Posner, B. Z. (1991) *The Leadership Challenge*, San Francisco, CA: Jossey-Bass.

KPMG (1997) *Consulting the Map: Mergers and Acquisitions in Europe*, London: KPMG.

KPMG (1999) *Mergers and Acquisitions: Global Research Report 1999—Unlocking Shareholder Value: The Key to Success*, London: KPMG.

Larkin, T. J. and Larkin, S. (1996) 'Reaching and changing frontline employees', *Harvard Business Review*, **74**(3): 95–104.

Lengel, R. H. and Daft, R. L. (1988) 'The selection of communication media as an executive skill', *Academy of Management Executive*, **2**(3): 225–32.

Lewin, K. (1951) *Field Theory in Social Science: Selected Theoretical Papers*, ed. D. Cartwright, New York: Harper & Row.

Lewis, L. K. (1999) 'Disseminating information and soliciting input during planned organizational change: Implementers' targets, sources and channels for communicating', *Management Communication Quarterly*, **13**(1): 43–75.

Lewis, L. K. (2000) '"Blindsided by that one" and "I saw that one coming": The relative anticipation and occurrence of communication problems in implementers' hindsight', *Journal of Applied Communication Research*, **28**(1): 44–67.

Lewis, L. K. (2006) 'Employee perspectives on implementation communication as predictors of perceptions of success and resistance', *Western Journal of Communication*, **70**(1): 23–46.

Lewis, L. K. and Siebold, D. R. (1998) 'Reconceptualising organizational change implementation as a communication problem: A review of literature and a research agenda', in M. E. Roloff (ed.) *Communication Yearbook 21*, Thousand Oaks, CA: Sage, pp. 93–151.

MacArthur, B. (1999) (ed.) *The Penguin Book of Twentieth Century Speeches*, 2nd rev'd edn, London: Penguin.

McKee, R. (2003) 'Storytelling that moves people', *Harvard Business Review*, **81**(6): 51–5.

Melcrum (2007a) *Delivering Successful Change Communication: Proven Strategies to Guide Major Change Programs*, London: Melcrum Publishing.

Melcrum (2007b) *Essential Techniques for Employee Engagement*, London: Melcrum Publishing.

Melcrum (2007c) *How to Use Social Media to Engage Employees*, London: Melcrum Publishing.

Melcrum (2008) *Melcrum's Top 50 Internal Communication Case Studies*, London: Melcrum Publishing.

New York Times (2008) 'Crisis hits tech sector with layoffs as sales slump', 15 Nov.

New York Times (2010) 'BP chief draws outrage for attending yacht race', 19 June: A20. http://www.nytimes.com/2010/06/20/us/20spill.html

Palmer, I., Dunford, R., and Akin, G. (2009) *Managing Organizational Change: A Multiple Perspectives Approach*, 2nd edn, New York: McGraw-Hill.

Pincus, J. D. and Acharya, L. (1988) 'Employee communication strategies for organizational crises', *Employee Responsibilities and Rights Journal*, **1**(3): 181–99.

Reilly, A. H. (2008) 'The role of human resource development competencies in facilitating effective crisis communication', *Advances in Developing Human Resources*, **10**(3): 331–51.

Robinson, S. L. (1996) 'Trust and the breach of the psychological contract', *Administrative Science Quarterly*, **41**(4): 574–99.

Rousseau, D. M. and Tijoriwala, S. A. (1999) 'What's a good reason to change? Motivated reasoning and social accounts in promoting organizational change', *Journal of Applied Psychology*, **84**(4): 514–28.

Russ, T. L. (2008) 'Communicating change: A review and critical analysis of programmatic and participatory implementation approaches', *Journal of Change Management*, **8**(3/4): 199–211.

Sagie, A. and Kolowsky, M. (1994) 'Organizational attitudes and behaviours as a function of participation in strategic and tactical change decisions: An application of path: Goal theory', *Journal of Organizational Behaviour*, **15**(1): 37–47.

Sandman, P. M. (2010) 'Risk communication: Lessons from the BP spill', *The Synergist: Journal of the American Industrial Hygiene Association*, Sep: 29–31.

Saulny, S. (2006) 'A legacy of the storm: Depression and suicide', *New York Times*, 21 June.

Smith, D. (1998) 'Invigorating change initiatives', *Management Review*, **87**(5): 43–8.

Stone, D., Patton, B., and Heen, S. (2000) *Difficult Conversations*, London: Penguin.

The Times (2010a) '400 Cadbury workers to lose jobs despite promise', 9 Feb.

The Times (2010b) 'Mandelson attacks Kraft over closing Cadbury plant', 11 Feb.

The Times (2010c) 'Kraft censured for breaching the takeover code on Cadbury', 27 May.

Vance, A. (2008) 'Crisis hits tech sector with layoffs as sales slump', *New York Times*, 15 Nov. http://www.nytimes.com/2008/11/15/technology/companies/15sun.html

Young, M. and Post, J. E. (1993) 'Managing to communicate, communicating to manage: How leading companies communicate with employees', *Organizational Dynamics*, **22**(1): 31–43.

Washington Post (2006) 'Sun CEO among the few chiefs who blog', 16 Sep.

Wearden, G. (2010) 'Kraft executives grilled by MPs over Cadbury takeover', *The Guardian*, 16 Mar. http://www.guardian.co.uk/business/2010/mar/16/cadbury-takeover-kraft-executives-grilled

Webb, T. (2010) 'Gulf oil spill? It's just a drop in the ocean, says BP chief', *The Guardian*, 14 May: 1.

Wiggins, L. (2008) 'Managing the ups and downs of change communication', *Strategic Communication Management*, London: Melcrum Publishing.

Chapter 13

Argyris, C. (1990) *Overcoming Organizational Defences: Facilitating Organizational Learning*, Needham Heights, MA: Allyn and Bacon.

BBC News (2010) 'Government confirms plan to scrap NHS direct helpline', 29 Aug. http://www.bbc.co.uk/news/uk-11120853

Beer, M. and Nohria, N. (2000) (eds) *Breaking the Code of Change*, Boston, MA: Harvard Business School Press.

Buchanan, D. and Huczynski, A. (2010) *Organizational Behaviour*, Harlow: Pearson/FT/Prentice Hall.

Buchanan, D., Fitzgerald, L., and Ketley, D. (2005) 'No going back: A review of the literature on sustaining organizational change', *International Journal of Management Reviews*, **7**(3): 189–205.

Buchanan, D., Fitzgerald, L., and Ketley, D. (2007) *The Sustainability and Spread of Organizational Change*, London: Routledge.

By, R. T. (2005) 'Organisational change management: A critical review', *Journal of Change Management*, **5**(4): 369–80.

Campbell, K. (2010) 'Change in the valleys', *Converse*, 7: 28–9.

Cummings, T. and Worley, C. (2005) *Organization Development and Change*, 8th edn, Mason, OH: Thomson South Western.

Dunphy, D. and Stace, D. (1993) 'The strategic management of corporate change, *Human Relations*, **46**(8): 905–18.

Fitzgerald, L. and Buchanan, D. (2007) 'The sustainability and spread story: Theoretical developments', in

D. Buchanan, L. Fitzgerald, and D. Ketley (2007) *The Sustainability and Spread of Organizational Change*, London: Routledge, pp. 227–48.

Frost, P. J. and Robinson, S. (1999) 'The toxic handler: Organizational hero—and casualty', *Harvard Business Review*, **77**(4): 96–106.

Gash, T. and McCrae, J. (for the Institute for Government) (2010) *Transformation in the Ministry of Justice: 2010 Interim Evaluation Report*. http://www.instituteforgovernment.org.uk/pdfs/transformation_in_the_ministry_of_justice.pdf

Greenhalgh, T., Robert, G. Bate, P., Kyriakidou, O., McFarlane, F., and Peacock, R. (2004) *How to Spread Good Ideas: A Systematic Review of the Literature on Diffusion, Dissemination and Sustainability of Innovations in Health Service Delivery and Organisation—Report for the National Co-ordinating Centre for NHS Service Delivery and Organisation R&D (NCCSDO)*. http://www.sdo.nihr.ac.uk/files/project/SDO_FR_08-1201-038_V01.pdf

Grigsby, W. (2002) 'Telehealth: An assessment of growth and distribution', *The Journal of Rural Health*, **18**(2): 348–58.

Hayes, J. (2002) *The Theory and Practice of Change Management*, 2nd edn, Basingstoke: Palgrave Macmillan.

Herd, T. (2010) 'M&A success: Beating the odds', *Business Week*, 22 June. http://www.businessweek.com/managing/content/jun2010/ca20100622_394659.htm

Hochschild, A. R. (1983) *The Managed Heart: Commercialization of Human Feeling*, Berkeley, CA: University of California Press.

Hughes, M. (2006) *Change Management: A Critical Perspective*, London: CIPD.

Institute for Government (undated) 'About us'. http://www.instituteforgovernment.org.uk/content/1/about-us

Jacobs, R. (2002) 'Institutionalizing organizational change through cascade training', *Journal of European Industrial Training*, **26**(2–4): 177–82.

Jerald, C. (2005) *More than Maintenance: Sustaining Improvement Efforts over the Long Run*, The Center for Comprehensive School Reform and Improvement (Center for CSRI) Policy Brief. http://www.centerforcsri.org/files/Center_PB_Sept_fnl.pdf

Kaplan, R. and Norton, D. (1992) 'The balanced scorecard: Measures that drive performance', *Harvard Business Review*, **70**(1): 71–9.

Kotter, J. (1996) *Leading Change*, Boston, MA: Harvard Business School Press.

Kotter, J. (2007) 'Leading change: Why transformation efforts fail', *Harvard Business Review*, **85**(1): 96–103.

KPMG (1999) *Mergers and Acquisitions: Global Research Report 1999—Unlocking Shareholder Value: The Key to Success*, London: KPMG.

KPMG and the Economic Intelligence Unit (2011) *Corporate Sustainability: A Progress Report*. http://www.kpmg.com/global/en/issuesandinsights/articlespublications/pages/corporate-sustainability.aspx

Leppitt, N. (2006) 'Challenging the code of change: Part 1—Praxis does not make perfect', *Journal of Change Management*, **6**(2): 121–42.

Malina, M. and Selto, F. (2001) 'Communicating and controlling strategy: An empirical study of the effectiveness of the balanced scorecard', *Journal of Management Accounting Research*, 13: 47–90.

Marr, B. (2010) *Balanced Scorecards for the Public Sector*, London: Ark Group.

NHS Direct (2010) *NHS Direct Business Plan 2010/11*. http://www.nhsdirect.nhs.uk/About/~/media/Files/AboutUsPDFs/BusinessPlan2010-11.ashx

Palmer I., Dunford, R., and Akin, G. (2005) *Managing Organizational Change*, Boston, MA: McGraw-Hill.

Pascale, R., Millemann, M., and Gioja, L. (2000) *Surfing the Edge of Chaos: The Laws of Nature and New Laws of Business*, London: Texere.

Pearce, D. and Williams, E. (2010) *Seeds for Change: Action Learning for Innovation*, Aberystwyth: Menter a Busnes.

Pettigrew, A. (2000) 'Linking change processes to outcomes', in M. Beer and N. Nohria (eds) *Breaking the Code of Change*, Boston, MA: Harvard Business School Press, pp. 243–67.

Pettigrew, A., Woodman, R., and Cameron, K. (2001) 'Studying organizational change and development: Challenges for future research', *Academy of Management Journal*, **44**(4): 697–713.

Reisner, R. (2002) 'When a turnaround stalls', *Harvard Business Review*, **80**(2): 45–52.

Senge, P., Kleiner, A., Roberts, C., Ross, R., Roth, G., and Smith, B. (1999) *The Dance of Change: The Challenges of Sustaining Momentum in Learning Organizations*, London: Nicolas Brealey Publishing.

Staw, B. and Ross, J. (1987) 'Knowing when to pull the plug', *Harvard Business Review*, **65**(2): 68–74.

Svyantek, D. and DeShon, R. (1993) 'Organizational attractors: A chaos theory explanation of why cultural change efforts often fail', *Public Administration Quarterly*, **17**(3): 339–55.

Weick, K. and Quinn, R. (1999) 'Organization change and development', *Annual Review Psychology*, 50: 361–86.

Chapter 14

Abrahamson, E. (1996) 'Management fashion', *Academy of Management Review*, **21**(1); 254–85.

Armbrüster, T. and Glückler, J. (2007) 'Organizational change and the economics of management consulting: A response to Sorge and van Witteloostuijn', *Organization Studies*, **28**(12); 1873–85.

Austin, J. R. and Bartunek, J. M. (2003) Theories and practice of organizational development, in W. Borman, D. Ilgen, R. Klimoski, and I. Weiner (eds) *Handbook of Psychology*, vol.12, New York: Wiley. Reprinted in Gallos, J. V. (ed.) (2006) *Organization Development: A Jossey-Bass Reader*, San Francisco: Jossey-Bass.

Bazerman, M. H. and Tenbrunsel, A. E. (2011) *Blind Spots: Why We Fail to Do What's Right and What to Do about It*, Princeton, NJ,: Princeton University Press.

Beer, M. (2000) 'Research that will break the code of change: The role of useful normal science and usable action science: a commentary on Van de Ven and Argyris', in M. Beer and N. Nohria (eds) *Breaking the Code of Change*, Boston, MA: Harvard Business School Press , pp. 429–46.

Binney, G., Wilke, G., and Williams, C. (2009) *Living Leadership: A Practical Guide for Ordinary Heroes:*, 2nd edn, Harlow: FT Prentice Hall.

By, T. R. (2005) 'Organisational change management: A critical review', *Journal of Change Management*, **5**(4); 369–80.

Ciulla, J. B. (2004) 'Ethics and leadership effectiveness', in J. Antonakis, A. T. Cianciolo, and R. J. Sternberg (eds) *The Nature of Leadership*, Newbury Park, CA: Sage Publications, pp. 302-27.

Clark, T. (1995) *Managing Consultants: Consultancy as the Management of Impressions*, Buckingham: Open University Press.

Gentile, M. C. (2010) *Giving Voice to Values: How to Speak Your Mind When You Know What's Right*, New Haven, CT: Yale University Press.

Grey, C. (2002) 'The fetish of change', *Tamara: Journal of Critical Postmodern Organization Science*, **2**(2): 1–19.

Grint, K. (1997) *Fuzzy Management*, Oxford: Oxford University Press.

Hannan, M. T. and Freeman, J. (1984) 'Structural inertia and organizational change', *American Sociological Review*, **49**: 149-64.

Kotter, J.P. (1990) *A Force for Change: How Leadership Differs from Management*, New York: Free Press.

Marshall, J. (2001) 'Self-reflective inquiry practices', in P. W. Reason and H. Bradbury (eds) *Handbook of Action Research*, London: Sage, pp. 433–9.

Reason, P. W. and Bradbury, H. (2001) (eds) *Handbook of Action Research*, London: Sage.

Sorge, A. and van Witteloostuijn, A. (2004) 'The (non) sense of organizational change: An essai about universal management hypes, sick consultancy metaphors, and healthy organization theories', *Organization Studies*, **25**(7): 1205–31.

Sturdy, A. (1997) 'The consultancy process- An insecure business', *Journal of Management Studies*, **34**(3): 389–413.

von Krogh, G. and Roos, J. (1995) *Organizational Epistemology*, London: Macmillan Press.

Zoller, H. M. and Fairhurst, G. T. (2007) 'Resistance leadership: The overlooked potential in critical organization and leadership studies', *Human Relations*, **60**(9): 1331–60.

Index

Glossary terms are highlighted in purple.